W9-DDI-424

CAREER

OPPORTUNITIES

in

CASINOS AND
CASINO HOTELS

SECOND EDITION

CAREER OPPORTUNITIES in

CASINOS AND CASINO HOTELS

SECOND EDITION

SHELLY FIELD

Ferguson

An imprint of Infobase Publishing

...edicated with love to my parents, Ed and Selma;
Jessica and Debbie; brother-in-law, Norman;
Geoffrey; Susan; Sawyer; Iselle;
Honey; Quincy; Samantha; Tiny; Chesea;
and all the aunts, uncles, and cousins.
I hit the jackpot . . .
I could not pick a better family!

Career Opportunities in Casinos and Casino Hotels, Second Edition

Ferguson
An imprint of Infobase Publishing
132 West 31st Street
New York NY 10001

Library of Congress Cataloging-in-Publication Data

Field, Shelly.
    Career opportunities in casinos and casino hotels / Shelly Field. —2nd ed.
        p. cm.
    Includes bibliographical references and index.
    ISBN-13: 978-0-8160-7803-5 (hardcover : alk. paper)
    ISBN-10: 0-8160-7803-3 (hardcover : alk. paper) 1. Casinos—Employees—Vocational guidance—
    United States. 2. Gambling—Employees—Vocational guidance—United States. I. Title.
    HV6711.F54 2009
    795.023'73—dc22   2008045340

Ferguson books are available at special discounts when purchased in bulk quantities for businesses, associations, institutions, or sales promotions. Please call our Special Sales Department in New York at (212) 967-8800 or (800) 322-8755.

You can find Ferguson on the World Wide Web at http://www.fergpubco.com

Series design by Kerry Casey
Cover design by Takeshi Takahashi

Printed in the United States of America

VB Hermitage 10   9   8   7   6   5   4   3   2   1

This book is printed on acid-free paper.

CONTENTS

HOW TO USE THIS BOOK

When the last edition of this book was published in 2000, the gaming industry had just begun to explode. Today, legalized gaming is bigger than ever, reaching throughout the United States and the world.

Legalized gaming is a booming business. It includes casino gaming, state lotteries, pari-mutuel wagering (including horse and dog racing), and charitable gaming. According to the U.S. Bureau of Labor Statistics, gaming is a multibillion-dollar industry responsible for the creation of a number of unique service occupations, with the majority of all gaming services workers being employed in casinos.

Gaming is big business, and many job seekers want a piece of that action. While many other industries are downsizing, the gaming industry is expanding. There are hundreds of thousands of jobs in casinos and casino hotels. One of them can be yours. If your dream is a career in an interesting, exciting, fun, and glamourous industry, this book is for you.

The U.S. Bureau of Labor Statistics indicates that employment of gaming service workers is expected to grow much faster than the average for all other occupations. Gaming is also one of the few industries in which dedicated, hardworking employees can quickly move up the career ladder—especially if they have strong customer-service skills.

Thousands of people are currently employed in the gaming industry in a variety of jobs. Many more are eager to enter the sector but have no idea how to obtain a postion in this exciting field. They have no concept of what opportunities are available or where to find them. They are uncertain about the qualifications needed or the training required.

Career Opportunities in Casinos and Casino Hotels is the single most comprehensive source for learning about job opportunities in gaming. This updated edition is chock-full of even more jobs, information, and helpful resources.

This book was written for everyone who aspires to work in the industry but does not know how to enter it. The 101 jobs discussed in this book include careers not only on the gaming floor but in the business, administration, and management areas; security and surveillance; entertainment, hotel management, and service; food and beverage service; health clubs and spas; Web services, retail; and more.

The gaming industry offers an array of opportunities and requires people with a variety of different skills and talents. It needs dealers, floorpeople, cashiers, hosts, slot-repair technicians, publicists, marketing people, servers, desk clerks, health and fitness personnel, salespeople, secretaries, receptionists, administrative assistants, managers, human resources people, trainers, cooks, bakers, servers, nurses, IT professionals, security and surveillance officers, webmasters, content producers, executives, and more. The key to getting the job you want is to develop your skills. Once you have your foot in the door, you can climb the career ladder.

What's New in the Second Edition

The second edition of *Career Opportunities in Casinos and Casino Hotels* provides completely updated information. All salaries, employment and advancement prospects, special licensing and certifications, training and educational requirements, and unions and associations for each job profile were reviewed and amended where necessary. The information in every appendix has been updated as well, giving you the most recent names, addresses, phone numbers, and Web sites of gaming academies and dealer schools; colleges and universities; trade associations, unions, and other organizations; American casinos; Canadian casinos; cruise lines; gaming conferences and expos; seminars and workshops; and gaming industry Web sites. New books and periodicals have been included in the bibliography.

Two new appendixes have been added to make it easier for you to locate more job opportunities. These include an appendix with career and employment Web sites and one with casinos, casino hotel and hospitality search firms, and recruiters and headhunters.

While the first edition of *Career Opportunities in Casinos and Casino Hotels* was comprehensive in its coverage of careers and key jobs, nine new job profiles have been added to this new edition, bringing the total number of careers profiled to more than 100. A section highlighting special requirements, such as necessary licenses or certification, has also been added.

Sources of Information

Information for this book was obtained through interviews; questionnaires; seminars; conferences; a variety of books, magazines, newsletters, and other literature; television and radio programs; and more. Some information was gained through personal experience working in the industry. Other data was obtained from business associates in various areas of the gaming industry.

Among the people interviewed were men and women engaged in all aspects of the gaming and hospitality industries in both the gaming and non-gaming areas, including individuals working in the business, administration, and management end of the industry, as well as frontline employees and support personnel. Also interviewed were human resources directors and staff, training managers, publicists, marketing managers, bellpersons, serv-

ers, housekeepers, security and surveillance people, PBX operators, valets, concierges, marketing coordinators, public relations directors, hosts, tour and travel coordinators, desk personnel, convention managers, entertainers, slot managers, cashiers, dealers, floorpersons, pit managers, webmasters, Web content producers, technicians, cooks, pastry chefs, bartenders, benefit coordinators, sales associates, secretaries, administrative assistants, and more. Interviewees included personnel from large luxury casinos as well as smaller land-based casinos, docked and floating riverboat casinos, Indian gaming facilities, cruise line casinos, racinos, schools, colleges, unions, and trade associations.

Organization of Material

Career Opportunities in Casinos and Casino Hotels is divided into 11 general employment sections: Casino Operations and the Gaming Area; Casino and Casino Hotel Marketing, Public Relations, and Sales; Casino and Casino Hotel Security and Surveillance; Casino Hotels; Casino and Casino Hotel Entertainment; Casino and Casino Hotel Food and Beverage Service; Casino and Casino Hotel Human Resources Departments; Casino Hotel Health Clubs and Spas; Casino and Casino Hotel Retail Shops; Casino and Casino Hotel Support Personnel; and Casino and Casino Hotel Web Sites. Within each of these sections are descriptions of individual careers.

There are two parts to each job classification. The first part offers job information in chart form. The second part presents information in a narrative text. In addition to the basic career description, you will find additional information on unions and associations and special requirements as well as tips for entry.

Eleven appendixes are offered to help locate information you might want or need to get started looking for a job in the field. These appendixes include gaming academies and dealer schools; college and university degree programs in hospitality administration and management, and hotel and restaurant management and administration; trade associations, unions, and other organizations; American casinos; Canadian casinos; cruise lines; gaming conferences; seminars; gaming Web sites, career and job Web sites and recruiters; search firms, and head hunters. A bibliography of gaming and hospitality related books and periodicals is also included.

This book will help you take the first step toward preparing for a great career. Job opportunities exist throughout the country and the world and are increasing as more areas legalize commercial gambling and Indian gaming. Opportunities may be located in luxury casinos, smaller casinos, poker rooms, casino hotels, docked and floating riverboat casinos, racinos, Indian gaming facilities, bingo halls, and cruise ships.

No matter what facet of the casino and casino hotel job market you choose to explore, you can find a career that is rewarding and fun. The jobs are out there waiting for you; you just have to go after them. Persevere and you will hit the jackpot in the job market.

—Shelly Field
www.shellyfield.com

ACKNOWLEDGMENTS

I thank every individual, casino, hotel, company, corporation, agency, association, and union that provided information, assistance, and encouragement for this book and its previous edition.

First and foremost, I acknowledge with appreciation James Chambers for helping to bring this book to fruition as well as for his assistance, advice, insight, and patience over the years. I would also like to express my sincere thanks to Sarah Fogarty. This book could not have been completed without her assistance and patience. I must additionally thank Ed Field for his ongoing support and encouragement in this and all of my projects.

Others whose help was invaluable include: Academy of Casino Training, Inc.; Ellen Ackerman; Terry Alexander, Ameristar Casino, Vicksburg; Julie Allen; American Federation of Musicians; Ameristar Casinos; Argosy Casinos; Barbara Ashworth; Beth Ayjian; Lloyd Barriger; Allan Barrish; Beauty School of Middletown; Linda Bernbach; Phil Berman, Catskill Development; Steve Blackman; BNP Media; Robert Boone; Sam Boyd's California Hotel and Casino; Katrina Bull; Theresa Bull; Kim Butler, Trump Casino Resorts; Caryn Cammeyer, Advertising Research Foundation; Eileen Casey; Casino Career Center; Casino Career Institute, Atlantic City, N.J.; Casino Employment Opportunities; Casino Management Association; Catskill Regional Medical Center, Harris, N.Y.; Connecticut Expos; Anthony Cellini, Town of Thompson Supervisor; Brandi Cesario; Patricia Claghorn; Andy Cohen; Bernard Cohen, Horizon Advertising; Dr. Jessica L. Cohen; Lorraine Cohen; Norman Cohen; ConJel Company; Jan Cornelius; Crawford Memorial Library Staff; Margaret Crossley, Nevada Society of Certified Public Accountants; Meike Cryan; Peter Curan; Gina Damato; Daniel Dayton; W. Lynne Dayton, Direct Mail/Marketing Association, Inc.; Carrie Dean; Direct Marketing Educational Foundation, Inc.; Donna Dossey-Aust, American Airline Advantage Sales Reservationist; Scott Edwards; Dan England, University of Nevada, Las Vegas; Cliff Ehrlich, Catskill Development; Ernest Evans; Deborah K. Field, Esq.; Greg Field; Lillian (Cookie) Field; Mike Field; Robert Field; Field Associates, Ltd.; Rob Fier; Finkelstein Memorial Library Staff; David Garthe, CEO, Graveyware.com; John Gatto; Sheila Gatto; Gem Communications; George Glantzis; Kaytee Glantzis; Sam Goldych; Lillian Henrickson; David Hernandez, Community College of Southern Nevada; Hermann Memorial Library staff; Joan Howard; International Alliance of Theatrical Stage Employees (IATSE); Isle of Capri Casinos; Jimmy "Handyman" Jones; Howard Kaiser, *Las Vegas Review Journal*; Liberty Public Library staff; Michael Madzy; Ginger Maher; Ernie Martinelli; Robert Masters, Esq.; Pat Matthews; Richard Mayfield; Patricia M. McQueen, events editor, *Gaming*, BNP Media; MGM Grand, Las Vegas, Nev.; Phillip Mestman; Rima Mestman; Beverly Michaels, Esq.; Martin Michaels, Esq.; Monticello Central High School Guidance Department; Monticello Central High School Library staff; Monticello Gaming and Raceway; Jennifer Morganti; Navegante Group; Earl Nesmith; Nevada Society of Certified Public Accountants; Janet Newberg; Marvin Newman; New York State Employment Service; New York State Nurses Association; Ellis Norman, University of Nevada, Las Vegas; Peter Notarstefano; Christine Pearon, Casino Employment; Herb Perry; Barbara Pezzella; Public Relations Society of America; Doug Puppel; Harry Rachlin; Ramapo Catskill Library System; Doug Richards; Martin Richman; John Riegler; Michele Roberts, Travel Planners; Genice Ruiz;

Diane Ruud, Nevada Society of Certified Public Accountants; Bob Saludares, Community Employment Training Center, Las Vegas, Nev.; Bob Sertell; Matt Sjoquist; Stuart Slakoff, Professional Programs, Inc.; M. D. Smith, Slot Office Secretary, California Hotel and Casino; Raun Smith, Casino Career Center; John Sohigian; Eve Steinberg; Matthew E. Strong; Sullivan County Community College; Thrall Library Staff; Trump Casinos and Resorts; Turning Stone Casino; United States Department of Labor; Brian Vargas; Brian Anthony Vargas; Sarah Ann Vargas; Amy Vasquez; Pat Vasquez; Kaytee Warren; Marc Weiswasser, Navegante Group; Bill Wilder, Academy of Casino Training; Carol Williams; John Williams; John Wolfe; Johnny World; World Gaming Congress; WSUL Radio; WVOS Radio; and Ken Zeszutko, Turning Stone Casino.

In addition, because there is such mystique surrounding a great deal of the gaming industry, much of the material was provided by sources who wish to remain anonymous. My thanks to them, all the same.

FOREWORD

The gaming industry is an exciting and rewarding field. It is where the action is! What other workplace offers such a unique mix of high rollers, celebrities, entertainers, and just plain interesting people? It includes retail shops, restaurants and other dining facilities, a variety of hotels and resorts, table games, slot machines, and a whole lot more! The industry is continually expanding, with new properties being developed within the United States and around the world. Once you enter the industry, you are linked to colleagues across the globe.

Whether you have earned a high school diploma or an M.B.A., the gaming industry will welcome you. One essential quality required is an altruistic spirit. If you like helping others to have fun, this is the industry for you. We call it "the tail wagging the dog," that is, the casino is a lucrative appendage of the hospitality function.

Shelly Field has captured the essential elements to guide you through the many choices available to you in the casino industry. She provides the career profiles, career ladders, salaries, job requirements, and employment prospects for all of the possible career opportunities in the field. Not sure of the difference between poker, bingo, blackjack, and baccarat? She discusses opportunities in the field related to these card games. Want to move up from a floor supervisor to pit manager to director of table games? Shelly can tell you what is needed to get under way. This hospitality industry also has additional opportunities, such as convention sales and service roles, front desk operations, housekeeping, retailing, restaurant managers, pastry chefs, and health club managers. In addition, it has support functions such as information technology, purchasing, accounting, finance, and my field of human resources.

Field also provides details about gaming schools and choosing degree programs. Her directories of trade associations, casinos, conferences, expos, seminars, and workshops are second to none. Then, too, her gaming industry Web sites are where most may begin to discover a casino resort—directly online. Whether you want a land-based or cruise-based operation, this book details it all for you.

There is no question that casinos and casino hotels offer a variety of jobs. The gaming industry has grown tremendously, and it is an important factor in an area's economic growth as a provider of employment. A skilled workforce is imperative to the success of each facility, whether at a resort such as Foxwoods, or in any of the thousands of other casinos throughout the country. Foxwoods Resort Casino is North America's largest casino. Located in southeastern Connecticut and owned by the Mashantucket Pequot Tribal Nation, Foxwoods features six casinos with more than 7,200 slots, 380 table games, and a 100-table WPT World Poker Room. The property features more than 1,416 guest rooms and suites in three hotels, more than 30 restaurants, a salon and spa, 24 retail shops, and five entertainment venues.

In May 2008, the MGM Grand at Foxwoods debuted, adding 824 guest rooms and suites; restaurants featuring some of the nation's most celebrated chefs; a new 4,000-seat MGM Grand Theater; a new nightlife venue, Shrine; new retail outlets; and a new casino floor.

Most casinos offer training in a variety of skills to help prepare you for a job and, even more important, assist you in moving up the career ladder.

Today, many colleges and schools are developing credit and noncredit programs, seminars, workshops, and classes that may be useful to those interested in pursuing careers in gaming. These programs are also of tremendous value to the casinos and casino hotels, which need to fill jobs with qualified individuals.

Whether programs or courses are devoted specifically to the casino and gaming industries, some aspect of the hospitality industry, or a peripheral area, each may provide valuable knowledge to help you to position yourself for a job or promotion.

In addition to creating jobs, casinos can significantly affect the economics of the geographic areas in which they are located. Depending on the specific location, casinos, casino hotels, their restaurants, retail establishments, and entertainment venues can potentially generate millions of dollars in tax revenue for state and local governments. These monies offer areas with gaming the opportunity to provide a variety of services and other benefits to the community that they might not otherwise have been able to afford.

I have worked both in Atlantic City gaming at Tropicana Casino and Resort and in Native American gaming at Foxwoods Resort Casino. At the Tropicana Casino and Resort, there were four hotel towers with more than 2,000 rooms. It was an older property, where many staff members had been employed since gaming was legalized in 1978. A new food, retail, and entertainment area called "The Quarter" was added, which made the resort appealing to people of all ages.

Foxwoods Resort Casino began with bingo and later grew into a full-gaming establishment. Table games and slot machines were added, in addition to many restaurants, retail outlets, and entertainment venues. Guests come from more than five surrounding states; the resort is two hours from Boston and from New York City. Foxwood's staff comes from more than 35 countries and speaks many different languages. We communicate with our staff in multiple languages, and memorandums are translated so that employees better understand the message. But giving eye contact, smiling, and providing a warm greeting to guests is understood universally. And it is fun to celebrate New Year's Eve on December 31st and then again later at the Chinese lunar new year. We teach our English-speaking staff to say *gong hay fat choy* to our Chinese guests to wish them a Happy New Year! Gaming is very much a part of Chinese culture, and Chinese patrons make up a big part of the gaming market. We also teach an Asian cultural awareness class to help staff understand the cultural differences between our Chinese, Korean, and Vietnamese guests.

I began my hospitality career at the Disney Resorts in Florida as a recruiter and then moved into the compensation area and then training. My last role at Disney was running the Disney Institute professional development programs for business professionals who wanted to benchmark with Disney and learn how they got the staff to be so friendly in spite of the Florida heat. I specialized in the different functional areas of human resources and then left Disney to take on a more general role in human resources.

I worked from Dallas, Texas, as a regional vice president of human resources at the Wyndham Hotels and Resorts. As such, I traveled to the many Wyndham properties and shared the best practices and guidelines to improve their functions and processes. The properties in the Caribbean had casinos associated with the resorts.

It is easy to go to work each day when you know that interesting people, opportunities, and challenges await. Finding ways to bring moments of magic to our guests provides a unique challenge that keeps me and the staff motivated to give our very best. The camaraderie between our fellow team members and our guests is what keeps us coming back each day. This industry has a high repeat guest visitation factor, which means you get to know the guests well from their multiple visits to the property. They become friends and part of your life experience. That is why so many choose to stay in this industry. It has been fun to share my career stories with new students at gaming and hospitality colleges to entice more to enter this growing profession. There will be a lot of career opportunities both in the United States as well as worldwide. So join in and have some fun at work!

Stephen Heise
Vice President of Human Resources
Foxwoods Resort Casino and the
MGM Grand at Foxwoods
sheise@foxwoods.com
www.foxwoods.jobs
www.YourDream.jobs

INTRODUCTION

Throughout history gambling has existed in some form. In some cases it was legal; in others it was not. Legal or not, over the years gambling had its supporters and detractors.

In the early part of the 20th century gambling was outlawed by many U.S. states. In 1910 Nevada became the last U.S. state to make gambling illegal. In 1931, nevertheless, it also became the first state to legalize gambling again. And while casinos were prevalent throughout Nevada, Las Vegas soon became the premier gaming destination for both individuals who wanted to gamble and those looking for interesting and unique vacations. To date, Nevada is still the only state that allows gaming throughout its borders.

For many years Nevada remained the only option for those interested in legalized casino gaming and gaming tourist destinations. In 1976, however, that changed. That year, in an effort to revitalize its economy, Atlantic City passed a referendum legalizing casino gaming as well.

At the time, no one knew just how large the gaming industry would become. No one knew the opportunities it would create. Today, more than 30 years later, the casino gaming industry has virtually exploded and is larger than ever before.

Whether to increase state revenues, invigorate a depressed economy, or create jobs, more states have now legalized commercial gaming. As of this writing, commercial casinos are located in various areas of Colorado, Illinois, Indiana, Iowa, Louisiana, Michigan, Mississippi, Missouri, Nevada, New Jersey, Pennsylvania, and South Dakota.

Additionally, in 1987 the United States Supreme Court removed restrictions on gambling on Indian reservations. In 1988 Congress passed the Indian Gaming Regulatory Act (IGRA). The act authorized casino gaming on Indian reservations and created the National Indian Gaming Commission (NIGC), a regulatory body to oversee the industry. The door was now open for Native American gaming in the United States, creating even more casinos. Today Indian gaming facilities can be found in Alabama, Alaska, Arizona, California, Colorado, Connecticut, Florida, Idaho, Iowa, Kansas, Louisiana, Michigan, Minnesota, Mississippi, Missouri, Montana, Nebraska, New Mexico, New York, North Carolina, North Dakota, Oklahoma, Oregon, South Dakota, Texas, Washington, Wisconsin, and Wyoming.

Racetrack casinos, also known as racinos, are currently located in Delaware, Florida, Indiana, Iowa, Louisiana, Maine, New Mexico, New York, Oklahoma, Pennsylvania, Rhode Island, and West Virginia. And that does not include pari-mutuel wagering and lotteries.

More and more casinos are jumping on the bandwagon, evolving into large entertainment and resort gaming establishments and destinations unto themselves. Many feature world-class entertainment, restaurants, and accommodations, in addition to gaming. This, too, has created a variety of new job opportunities. There are now literally thousands of job opportunities in traditional casinos and casino hotels as well as racinos, riverboat casinos, card rooms, Indian gaming facilities, bingo halls, and on cruise ships, making this industry full of very viable career options.

While the gaming industry continues to expand globally, there are currently more casinos in the United States than any other country in the world. Whether it is the glitter, the glamour, or the gold associated with the casino industry, or the ability to parlay almost any skill and educational background an individual has into a job, more and more people want to find a way to build a career in this very exciting world of gaming.

The gaming industry is a multibillion-dollar business. There are thousands and thousands of people working in the industry and room for many more. One of them can be you!

It is interesting to note that even one casino can generate thousands of job opportunities. Foxwoods in Ledyard, Connecticut, for example, is the largest casino in the country, employing more than 11,000 people.

Casinos and casino hotels often resemble miniature cities and require the services of people with many diverse skills. In addition to jobs in casino operations and on the gaming floor, there is a vast array of employment possibilities available for people with every skill imaginable.

People are needed to handle marketing, public relations, and sales; provide security and surveillance; manage hotels; move luggage; open doors; greet people; provide guest services; clean rooms; answer phones; handle accounting services; develop special events; coordinate and implement activities; repair air-conditioning; entertain guests; prepare and serve food and beverages; hire, train, and pay employees; style guests' hair; teach guests how to use health club equipment; pamper guests in spas; handle retail sales; provide clerical and secretarial support; develop, run, and maintain Web sites; provide medical services; and entertain guests.

In a world in which many industries are downsizing, the gaming industry is growing dramatically. New casinos and casino hotels are under construction every year, and many in existence are expanding.

Casinos and casino hotels offer many high-paying jobs without requiring a great deal of prior education or training. For many jobs you need only a high school diploma or GED and a great attitude.

Most facilities offer flexible hours and liberal fringe-benefit packages. These benefits may include health, dental, and life insurance; pension plans; profit-sharing programs; educational reimbursement; child care; sick and vacation pay; and more.

Casinos and casino hotels offer opportunities for those just entering the workforce, job changers, and retirees and senior citizens.

Whichever area you choose to work in, your gaming industry job can be a satisfying and rewarding career experience. Within each section of this book, you'll find information to acquaint you with job possibilities in casinos and casino hotels. A key to the organization of each entry follows:

Alternate Title(s)

Many jobs in the gaming industry have alternate titles. Job titles often vary from casino to casino. The duties these jobs consist of are similar; only the names are different.

Career Ladder

The career ladder illustrates a possible career path. Remember that in the gaming industry, there are no set rules. Advancement may occur in almost any manner. In some situations, advancement may be achieved by entering completely different career area than the one in which you were working.

Position Description

Every effort has been made to give well-rounded job descriptions. Be aware that no two casinos are identically structured, so no two jobs will be precisely the same. For example, casinos might have various supervisors doing the same type of job or might eliminate certain positions entirely.

Salary Range

Salary ranges for the jobs profiled in this book are as accurate as possible. Earnings for a job will depend on the size, location, and prestige of the casino and casino hotel, as well as on the experience, education, training, and responsibilities of the individual.

In jobs where employees receive tips (which may also be referred to as *tokes* or *tokens*), earnings will depend heavily on the customer-service skills and personality of the individual. Annual salary ranges given for jobs that are normally paid on an hourly or other basis are estimates based on full-time employment.

Employment Prospects

If you choose a job that has an excellent, good, or fair rating, you are lucky. You will have an easier time finding employment. If, however, you would like to work at a job that has a poor rating, do not despair. The rating means only that it may be difficult to obtain a job, not that finding one is totally impossible.

This section also discusses possible locations and settings for jobs in each area. It should be noted that casino opportunities are available in many different locations throughout the country and the world. Because many states now host legalized commercial gambling as well as Native American Indian gaming, riverboats, floating casinos, and racinos, the gambling capitals are just the beginning.

Since casinos are often open 24 hours a day, seven days a week, this section may also discuss available shift possibilities. Generally, the three main shifts are the day shift, from 8 A.M. to 4 P.M.; swing shift or evening shift, from 4 P.M. to midnight; and graveyard shift or overnight shift, from midnight to 8 A.M. Keep in mind that every casino may not have the same shift hours, and some may overlap shifts for effective employee coverage.

Advancement Prospects

Try to be as cooperative and helpful as possible in the workplace. Do not attempt to see how little work you can do. Be enthusiastic, energetic, and outgoing. Go that extra step that no one expects you to go. Learn as much as you can. When there is a possibility of advancement, make sure that you are prepared to take advantage of it.

A variety of options for career advancement are included. However, as noted previously, there are no hard and fast rules for climbing the career ladder in the gaming industry. While work performance is important, advancement in many jobs is based on experience, education, training, employee attitude, customer service, and, of course, individual career aspirations.

Many casinos promote from within. The best way to advance your career is to get your foot in the door and then climb the career ladder.

Education and Training

This section presents the minimum educational and training requirements for each job area. This does not mean that you should obtain only the minimum requirements. Try to get the best training and education possible. It will often give you the edge over applicants with standard qualifications.

As noted previously, there are many high-paying jobs in casinos and casino hotels that do not require any formal education beyond a high school diploma. Depending on the job, training requirements may also include attendance at dealers' and gaming schools and academies, technical and vocational schools, colleges and universities, or on-the-job training. Many casinos offer their own in-house training programs. Additionally, some casinos offer programs to assist those not holding a high school diploma to obtain a GED.

Special Requirements

This section covers any licensing or credentials necessary for specific jobs. Each state, locality, and casino has its own set of rules that must be followed. Most states require those working in casinos to be licensed by the gaming authority in the specific state in which they work. Each area has its own licensing rules and regulations. These may include background checks, minimum age requirements, possession of sheriff's cards and/or attendance or certification from alcohol-awareness programs.

Experience, Skills, and Personality Traits

This section indicates experience requirements as well as specific skills and personality traits necessary for each job.

Best Geographic Location

While jobs in the gaming industry may be located throughout the country or the world, certain areas have more opportunities. As many states now host various forms of legalized gaming, the gambling capitals are just the beginning.

Unions and Associations

This section offers other sources for career information and assistance. Unions and trade associations offer valuable help in obtaining career guidance, support, and personal contacts. They may also offer training, continuing education, scholarships, fellowships, seminars, and other beneficial programs.

Tips for Entry

Use this section to gather ideas on how to get a job, gain entry into the area in which you are interested, or excel in a current position.

When applying for any job, always be as professional as possible. Dress neatly and conservatively. Do not wear sneakers. Do not chew gum. Do not smoke. Do not wear heavy perfume or men's cologne.

Always have a few copies of your résumé with you. These, too, should look neat and professional. Have them typed and presented well, checked and rechecked for grammar, spelling, and content.

If asked to fill out an application, complete it entirely, even if you brought a résumé with you. Print your information neatly.

Whether you are applying for jobs or filling in applications, be prepared. Make sure you know your Social Security number. Know the name and address of your former employers. Ask people in advance whether you can use them as references. Make sure you know their full names, addresses, and phone numbers. Secure at least three personal references and three professional references.

No matter the aspect of the gaming industry that piques your interest, you need to be computer literate. The ability to go online, whether from a home computer or one in a school or public library, puts you at a great advantage in locating jobs, reading about industry information, and keeping up with trends.

Many casinos, newspapers, and magazines feature Web sites that may be helpful in your quest for that perfect job. You can go online to obtain information about casinos and their current job opportunities, gaming news, or even classified sections of publications from areas hosting gaming.

Be on time for everything. This includes job interviews, phone calls, meetings, work, and so forth. Habitual lateness will have a negative effect on your prospects for obtaining a job, keeping a job, and career advancement.

The gaming industry blends aspects of the entertainment and hospitality industries. Customer service is essential to success in every job, no matter what area it is in the industry. Consider taking a seminar or workshop on customer-service skills. It may help your career tremendously.

Many people spend their lives wishing for a job they enjoy going to every day; one that is interesting, exciting, and never routine. If a job like this is your dream too, you do not have to wish anymore. You have taken the first step toward getting the job of your dreams by picking up this book!

Have fun reading it. It will help you prepare for a career you will truly love. Do not get discouraged, and do not give up on your goal. Every job you have teaches you something and is a stepping-stone to the job of your dreams.

Have faith and confidence in yourself. When you do get the job you have been dreaming about, I urge you to become a mentor, to share your knowledge and help others fulfill their dreams too.

I love to hear success stories about your career and how this book helped you. If you have a story and want to share it, go to www.shellyfield.com. I can't wait to hear from you!

Good luck.

Shelly Field

CASINO OPERATIONS AND THE GAMING AREA

CASINO MANAGER

Duties: Handling day-to-day casino operation; overseeing table games; supervising shift bosses and other casino management personnel; handling problems on the casino floor; taking care of customer complaints; promoting good customer service.

Alternate Title(s): Manager

Salary Range: $70,000 to $200,000+

Employment Prospects: Fair

Advancement Prospects: Fair

Best Geographical Location(s) for Position: Las Vegas, Reno, Laughlin, Lake Tahoe, Atlantic City, Biloxi, Baton Rouge, New Orleans, and Detroit offer most opportunities; other regions with land-based, riverboat, or Indian gaming facilities offer additional opportunities.

Prerequisites:

Education or Training—Minimum of high school diploma or equivalent and dealers training; college background helpful; see text.

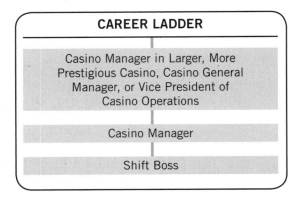

CAREER LADDER

Casino Manager in Larger, More Prestigious Casino, Casino General Manager, or Vice President of Casino Operations

Casino Manager

Shift Boss

Experience and Qualifications—Extensive experience in gaming.

Special Skills and Personality Traits—Supervisory skills; customer relations skills; organized; personable; knowledge of table games.

Special Requirements—State licensing required to work in gaming area.

Position Description

The Casino Manager holds an important position in the casino. The individual is in charge of handling the day-to-day management of the gaming area.

In order to run efficiently, casinos have operating policies formulated by the board of directors, CEO, or president of the company with the assistance of the executive vice president and the vice president of casino operations. The Casino Manager helps administer these policies.

The Casino Manager is responsible for overseeing the management of the table games in the casino. The individual must make sure all games are played in accordance with federal and state governmental regulations. He or she must also assure that all casino procedures and rules are followed.

The Casino Manager is in charge of overseeing those working in the gaming area and supervising casino management personnel. Depending on the structure of the casino, these may include the assistant Casino Manager, casino operations manager, assistant casino operations manager, casino administrator, casino credit manager, and shift bosses.

The individual is expected to build a good working relationship with casino employees, an essential ability for maintaining employee loyalty to the casino.

Other responsibilities of the Casino Manager may include:

- Assuring the security and protection of casino bankroll
- Promoting customer relations
- Assisting in the implementation of credit policies
- Handling problems on the gaming floor
- Dealing with customer complaints

Salaries

There is a great range of salaries for casino managers depending on a number of variables. Individuals may earn between $70,000 and $200,000 or more annually. Factors affecting earnings include the experience, training, and responsibilities of the individual as well as the geographic location, size, and prestige of the specific casino. In some facilities, casino managers may also receive bonuses above their annual salary.

Employment Prospects

Most casinos employ Casino Managers. Those that do not usually have someone in a similar position with a different name handling the same responsibilities. Casino Managers often work the swing shift because that is the usually the busiest time in the casino. Individuals may be required to work other shifts when necessary as well as weekends and holidays.

Las Vegas, Reno, Laughlin, Lake Tahoe, Atlantic City, Biloxi, Baton Rouge, New Orleans, and Detroit offer the greatest number of job possibilities. Other employment settings may include casino hotels in other areas of Nevada, Mississippi, New York, Louisiana, Colorado, Connecticut, Illinois, Arizona, California, and other regions where gambling is legal.

Other regions hosting Indian gaming and land-based or riverboat gaming facilities offer additional opportunities. New casinos and casino hotels are constantly under construction. More casinos and casino hotels are also opening every year as areas legalize gambling.

Advancement Prospects

Casino Managers may climb the career ladder in a number of ways. Some individuals obtain experience and then locate similar jobs in larger or more prestigious casinos. Others are promoted to positions such as casino general manager or the vice president of casino operations.

Education and Training

As a rule, Casino Managers are expected to have a minimum of a high school diploma or the equivalent. Individuals usually are trained as dealers in dealers school or gaming academies. They then obtain on-the-job training and experience as they move up the career ladder as floorpersons, pit bosses, and shift bosses. A college degree is helpful for many individuals in career advancement.

Special Requirements

State licensing is generally required for employees working in or around the gaming area in casinos. Generally, this license is issued by a regulatory agency, such as the specific state's casino control board or commission.

Each state has its own rules and regulations regarding which specific occupational licenses and permits are necessary for casino employees. In some states, for example, individuals must apply for and obtain a general gaming license. Some states have various levels of licensure and permits. Certain states may require a key employee license for those working in the management area of casinos.

The human resource department of casinos provide individuals with specific licensing requirements for each position.

Most states also have a minimum age requirement for this position.

Experience, Skills, and Personality Traits

Extensive experience working in the gaming industry is necessary for this position. As noted previously, most casino managers started out as dealers and then obtained experience as floorpersons, pit bosses, and shift bosses.

Casino Managers must have a total knowledge of table games. Supervisory skills are necessary. Communication skills are essential. Casino Managers must be personable people with the ability to promote good customer service. They must also be able to instill that ability in their employees.

Unions and Associations

There are no unions for Casino Managers. Individuals may obtain additional information from local gaming associations.

Tips for Entry

1. Job openings may be advertised in the classified sections of newspapers in areas hosting gaming. Look under classifications such as "Casinos/Gaming," "Casino Opportunities," "Casino Manager," or "Casinos."
2. Casinos often promote from within. Get experience as a floorperson, pit boss, and shift manager.
3. It is sometimes easier to seek employment as a Casino Manager in areas other than the gaming capitals.
4. Positions may be advertised on the Internet. They may be located via the home pages of casino hotels. They may also be found by doing a search of "Casino," "Casino Hotel," or "Gaming Job Opportunities."
5. Seek out search firms and recruiters that deal specifically in the gaming industry. (A selected listing is in the appendix of this book.)

DIRECTOR OF TABLE GAMES

CAREER PROFILE

Duties: Overseeing management of table games; supervising casino table staff; monitoring job performance of table staff; consulting and advising with management regarding casino.

Alternate Title(s): Director of Games; Director of Tables

Salary Range: $65,000 to $145,000+

Employment Prospects: Fair

Best Geographical Location(s) for Position: Las Vegas, Reno, Laughlin, Lake Tahoe, Atlantic City, Biloxi, Baton Rouge, New Orleans, Black Hawk, and Detroit offer most opportunities; other regions with land-based, riverboat, or Indian gaming facilities offer additional opportunities.

Prerequisites:

Education or Training—Minimum of high school diploma or equivalent; college degree may be preferred. Training in table games and gaming; see text.

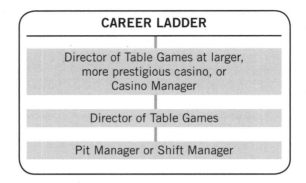

CAREER LADDER

Director of Table Games at larger, more prestigious casino, or Casino Manager

Director of Table Games

Pit Manager or Shift Manager

Experience and Qualifications—Supervisory experience in gaming; experience dealing.

Special Skills and Personality Traits—Supervisory skills; management skills; communication skills; training skills; people skills.

Special Requirements—State licensing required.

Position Description

The Director of Table Games is in charge of table gaming in the casino. This is an administrative position. Depending on the specific casino, the individual may also be referred to as the director of games or director of tables. Generally, there is one Director of Table Games in each casino.

The Director of Table Games is in charge of everything that goes on in the casino related to table games. The individual supervises the casino shift managers, who are directly under him or her, and has overall say involving the department. If there is a problem and it cannot be solved by the pit manager, the Director of Table Games must handle the situation.

The Director of Table Games is expected to supervise the casino table staff. He or she is also responsible for the scheduling, administration, and training of the table game staff. As part of his or her job, the Director of Table Games must continually monitor job performance of the department staff.

There is a great deal of responsibility in this type of job. Some of the other responsibilities include:

- Consulting and advising management regarding the casino

- Handling employee problems
- Handling customer complaints
- Ensuring and maintaining that the gaming in the casino is within state regulations
- Performing periodic analyses of operations of department action

Salaries

The Director of Table Games can earn between approximately $65,000 and $145,000 or more per year. Annual earnings for a Director of Table Games depend on the specific casino in which the individual is working, its size, prestige, and geographic location. Other variables might include the individual's experience and his or her responsibilities. Generally, individuals working in larger casinos in the gambling capitals will earn more than their counterparts in other areas.

Employment Prospects

Employment prospects are fair for those seeking positions as the Director of Table Games. The individual may find employment in casinos throughout the world. As noted previously, there is usually one Director of Table Games in each casino, so, while individuals may find employment in any casino in the world, most opportunities exist in areas where there are a large number of casinos.

Las Vegas, Reno, Laughlin, Lake Tahoe, Atlantic City, Biloxi, Baton Rouge, New Orleans, Black Hawk, and Detroit offer the greatest number of job possibilities. Other employment settings may include casino hotels in other areas of Nevada, Mississippi, New York, Louisiana, Colorado, Connecticut, Illinois, Arizona, and California.

Other regions hosting Indian gaming and land-based or riverboat gaming facilities offer additional opportunities. New casinos and casino hotels are constantly under construction. More casinos and casino hotels are also opening every year as areas legalize gambling.

Advancement Prospects

A Director of Table Games in a casino may advance his or her career by locating a similar position in a larger or more prestigious casino. This would result in increased responsibilities and earnings. The individual might also climb the career ladder by either moving into a position as a general manager or a position in the corporate area.

Education and Training

As in many casino jobs, the Director of Table Games does not necessarily need a formal education. Many casinos just require a minimum of a high school diploma or a GED. Some may give preference to individuals with a college degree. A complete knowledge of the gaming industry is required. Most people who hold this job began as dealers. They started from the ground up and learned everything there was to know about table games.

Depending on the casino, some have their own training schools. In other situations, individuals can learn by attending a gaming institute. These are located throughout the country.

Special Requirements

The Director of Table Games must be licensed in the state in which he or she works. This license is obtained from the state's gaming authority or commission.

Experience, Skills, and Personality Traits

The Director of Table Games must have a fair amount of experience in gaming with additional experience in a supervisory capacity. In many situations, the Director of Table Games had a prior job in the same casino as a shift manager.

Individuals need supervisory and administrative skills. In order to be effective, they also are required to have excellent verbal communications skills. Interpersonal skills are also needed. The Director of Table Games may be required to calm customers with complaints or deal with employee problems.

Unions and Associations

This is not a unionized position. The Director of Table Games may be a member of local gaming associations.

Tips for Entry

1. As most people in this type of position learn from the ground up, start off by getting skilled in dealing.
2. Casinos often recruit employees from gaming schools.
3. Positions for this type of job are often advertised in the newspaper classified section in areas where gaming is prevalent. Look under headings including "Director of Table Games," "Gaming," "Casinos," or "Table Games."
4. If you don't live in an area hosting gambling, consider subscribing to a newspaper in an area that does. You can also usually buy Sunday newspapers from different parts of the country in better bookstores and newspaper shops.
5. Contact search firms and recruiters that deal specifically in the gaming industry.
6. Don't forget to check out jobs online. Surf the net on traditional job sites like monster.com and hotjobs.com, as well as the sites specific to the gaming industry.

CREDIT MANAGER

CAREER PROFILE

Duties: Reviewing credit applications; creating and maintaining credit histories; supervising credit clerks; recommending credit limitations.

Alternate Title(s): Casino Credit Manager

Salary Range: $28,000 to $55,000+

Employment Prospects: Good

Advancement Prospects: Fair

Best Geographical Location(s) for Position: Las Vegas, Reno, Laughlin, Lake Tahoe, Atlantic City, Biloxi, Baton Rouge, New Orleans, and Detroit offer most opportunities; other regions with land-based, riverboat, or Indian gaming facilities offer additional opportunities.

Prerequisites:

Education or Training—Minimum of high school diploma or GED; college background or degree may be helpful or required; training in general business and/or accounting may be required; see text.

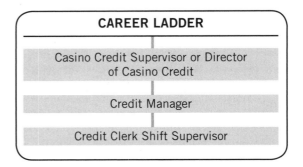

CAREER LADDER

Casino Credit Supervisor or Director of Casino Credit

Credit Manager

Credit Clerk Shift Supervisor

Experience and Qualifications—Experience in credit or collections.

Special Skills and Personality Traits—Supervisory skills; guest relations skills; communications skills; computer skills; diplomacy; tact.

Special Requirements—State licensing required.

Position Description

A Credit Manager in a casino is in charge of various casino credit functions. This is an administrative position. Depending on the specific casino, the individual may also be referred to as a credit executive. The Credit Manager may report to the credit supervisor, the vice president of casino operations, or the assistant general manager or v.p. of general finance depending on the structure of the individual facility.

The structure of each casino is different. Sometimes there is one Credit Manager. In other facilities, there may be a Credit Manager for each shift.

When people visit casinos to gamble, they often request credit. They may, for example, ask for a certain amount of credit or a loan. The Credit Manager is expected to check out each person's credit rating or worthiness before extending a line of credit. This includes the available credit a person may have as well as a credit history. To do this, the Credit Manager may check computer credit sources, fax banks, or get information from other casinos. If the Credit Manager finds that an individual's credit is good, he or she will extend a line of credit to be used in the casino. The amount extended will depend on the credit manager's recommendations or evaluation. If the Credit Manager finds that an indi-

vidual's credit is overextended, he or she must deny credit, and this must be done in a tactful manner.

There is a great deal of responsibility in this type of job. Some of the job functions include:

- Supervising credit clerks
- Monitoring job performance of the department staff
- Reviewing credit applications for completeness
- Creating and maintaining credit histories on guests
- Recommending credit limits based on credit checks
- Handling customer complaints regarding credit

Salaries

Casino credit managers can earn between $28,000 and $55,000 or more per year. Annual earnings depend on the specific casino the individual is working in, its size, prestige, and geographic location. Other variables include the individual's experience, responsibilities, training, and education. Generally, the larger or more prestigious the casino, the higher the earnings will be for this position.

Employment Prospects

Individuals may find employment in casinos throughout the world. Employment opportunities are good. This is an important job in every casino.

While individuals may find employment in any casino in the world, most opportunities exist in areas where there are a large number of casinos.

Las Vegas, Reno, Laughlin, Lake Tahoe, Atlantic City, Biloxi, Baton Rouge, New Orleans, and Detroit offer the greatest number of job possibilities. Other employment settings may include casino hotels in other areas of Nevada, Mississippi, New York, Louisiana, Colorado, Connecticut, Illinois, Arizona, and California.

Other regions hosting Indian gaming and land-based or riverboat gaming facilities offer additional opportunities. New casinos and casino hotels are constantly under construction. More casinos and casino hotels are also opening every year as areas legalize gambling.

Advancement Prospects

Casino Credit Managers can advance their careers by locating similar positions in larger or more prestigious casinos. They may also climb the career ladder by obtaining experience and becoming a credit supervisor or the director of casino credit.

Education and Training

Education and training requirements for Casino Credit Managers vary. In some positions, individuals need only have a high school diploma or GED and three to five years working in the credit or collection area. In other jobs, individuals may be required to have training in general business and/or accounting.

Many casino jobs also have on-the-job training programs. Some have their own in-house training programs. Community colleges, vocational technical schools, and gaming institutes throughout the country also offer training.

Individuals working in casinos must usually be licensed by the state in which they work.

Special Requirements

State licensing is generally required for employees working in or around the gaming area in casinos. Generally this license is issued by a regulatory agency such as the specific state's casino control board or commission.

Each state has its own rules and regulations regarding which specific occupational licenses and permits are necessary for casino employees. In some states individuals, for example, must apply for and obtain a general gaming license. In some there are various levels of licensure and permits. Certain states may require a key employee license for those working in the management area of casinos.

The human resource department of casinos provide individuals with specific licensing requirements for each position.

Most states also have a minimum age requirement for this position.

Experience, Skills, and Personality Traits

While the amount of experience varies, Casino Credit Managers are usually required to have a minimum of three to five years working in the credit or collection area. Supervisory experience is usually also required. Some facilities additionally require or prefer that applicants have cage or casino experience as well. There are Casino Credit Managers who started out working as slot booth cashiers and moved up to cage cashiers before working in the credit department. In other situations, the Credit Manager has worked as a credit clerk or credit clerk shift supervisor in the casino and been promoted from within.

Individuals need supervisory skills for this job. They must also have excellent verbal communication skills. Tact and diplomacy are also needed. Credit Managers should enjoy working with others and have good guest relations skills. Computer skills are necessary.

Unions and Associations

There are no bargaining unions for Casino Credit Managers. Individuals may belong to local gaming associations.

Tips for Entry

1. Look for a job as a credit clerk in a casino to obtain experience in this area.
2. Considering taking classes at a gaming institute to learn more about this job and to obtain a more thorough understanding of gaming.
3. If you do not live in an area hosting gambling and are thinking about moving, you might want to take a job working with a collection agency until you do. Ths will be good experience.
4. Positions for this type of job are often advertised in the newspaper classified section in areas where gaming is prevalent. Look under headings such as "Credit Manager," "Credit Executive," "Gaming," or "Casinos."
5. If you don't live in an area hosting gambling and are interested in looking for a job, consider subscribing to a newspaper in an area that does. You can also usually buy Sunday newspapers from different parts of the country in better bookstores and newspaper shops.
6. Positions are also advertised on the Internet. Put in search words including "Gaming," "Casinos," or the job title "Casino Credit Manager," or check out individual casino Web sites for employment listings.

CREDIT CLERK

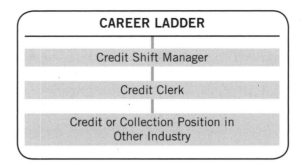
Position Description

The Casino Credit Clerk works in the casino's credit office. The individual is in charge of assisting others in the credit office perform their jobs. The Credit Clerk may report to the credit manager, Credit Clerk shift manager, or credit supervisor depending on the structure of the individual facility.

When people visit casinos to gamble, they often request a line of credit. In order to do this, they must visit the credit office and meet with a credit manager. The credit manager checks out each person's credit worthiness before extending a line of credit. There is often a great deal of paperwork involved in this task. The Credit Clerk takes care of this paperwork.

The individual is expected to handle general office duties. These include answering phones, filing, and typing correspondence. He or she may be required to organize incoming credit applications as well as perform data entry of information on credit applications.

Some of the other job functions include:

- Assisting credit manager with credit verifications
- Performing data entry of information for credit histories
- Processing completed credit applications
- Assisting in maintaining records and credit files

Salaries

As noted previously, credit clerks usually work on an hourly basis. They may earn between $7.00 and $20.00 per hour or more, depending on a number of variables. These include the specific casino in which the individual works as well as its size, prestige, and geographic location. Other factors may include the individual's responsibilities, training, and experience.

Generally, individuals working in larger casinos in the gambling capitals will earn higher salaries than their counterparts in smaller casinos or other geographic locations.

Employment Prospects

A Credit Clerk may find employment in casinos throughout the world. Employment opportunities are good. There are usually a number of credit clerks working in the credit office of every casino.

While individuals may find employment in any casino in the world, most opportunities exist in areas where there are a large number of casinos.

Las Vegas, Reno, Laughlin, Lake Tahoe, Atlantic City, Biloxi, Baton Rouge, New Orleans, and Detroit offer the greatest number of job possibilities. Other employment settings may include casino hotels in other areas of Nevada, Mississippi, New York, Louisiana, Colorado, Connecticut, Illinois, Arizona, and California.

Other regions hosting Indian gaming and land-based or riverboat gaming facilities or cruise ships offer additional opportunities. New casinos and casino hotels are constantly under construction. More casinos and casino hotels are also opening every year as areas legalize gambling.

Advancement Prospects

Credit Clerks working in casinos can climb the career ladder by obtaining experience. They may then land a position as a Credit Clerk shift supervisor. With more experience and training, individuals may also become a credit supervisor or the director of casino credit.

Education and Training

Education and training requirements for casino Credit Clerks vary. In some positions, individuals need only have a high school diploma or GED and three to five years working in the credit or collection area. In other jobs, individuals may be required to have training in general business and/or accounting. As in most jobs in casinos, experience may often be accepted in lieu of education.

Many casino jobs also have on-the-job training programs. Some have their own in-house training programs. Community colleges, vocational technical schools, and gaming institutes throughout the country also offer training.

Individuals working in casinos must usually be licensed by the state in which they work.

Special Requirements

State licensing is required for all employees working in or around the gaming area of casinos. Generally this license is issued by a regulatory agency, such as the specific state's casino control board or commission.

Experience, Skills, and Personality Traits

It is helpful for Credit Clerks to have some type of experience working in the credit or financial area. However, it is not always required.

Individuals need office and clerical skills for this position. They should be good on the phone and be able to use photocopy machines, faxes, and word processors. Data entry skills are essential. Organization is mandatory. Because individuals may deal with casino guests, customer relations skills are also important.

Unions and Associations

Casino Credit Clerks do not usually belong to any specific union. Contact a local community college offering courses in gaming, a gaming institute, or casino for more information on a job in this area.

Tips for Entry

1. The more you know and understand about the gaming industry and casinos in general, the more marketable you will be. Take a couple of classes at a gaming institute to learn more about the industry.

2. Positions for this type of job are often advertised in the newspaper classified section in areas hosting gaming. Look under headings such as "Credit Clerk," "Credit Department," "Gaming," or "Casinos."

3. If you don't live in an area hosting gambling and are interested in looking for a job, consider subscribing to a newspaper in an area that does. You can also usually buy Sunday newspapers from different parts of the country in better bookstores and newspaper shops.

4. Positions are also advertised on the Internet. Put in search words such as "Gaming," "Casinos," or the job title "Casino Credit Clerk."

5. Jobs in this area are often listed on casino job hotlines. These are frequently updated by recorded messages listing job availabilities. You can call each casino directly to get their job hotline phone number.

CAGE CASHIER

Duties: Perform accounting of casino cash and cash convertible inventory; redeem customers casino chips for cash; cash checks for customers; handle reconciliation of cage.

Alternate Title(s): Cashier

Salary Range: $7.00 to $20.00+ per hour

Employment Prospects: Excellent

Advancement Prospects: Fair

Best Geographical Location(s) for Position: Las Vegas, Reno, Laughlin, Lake Tahoe, Atlantic City, Biloxi, Baton Rouge, New Orleans, and Detroit offer most opportunities; other regions with land-based, riverboat, or Indian gaming facilities offer additional opportunities.

Prerequisites:

Education or Training—Minimum of high school diploma or GED; no formal training required.

CAREER LADDER

```
┌─────────────────────────────────────┐
│  Casino Cage Cashier Supervisor or   │
│             Shift Manager            │
└─────────────────────────────────────┘
                   │
┌─────────────────────────────────────┐
│             Cage Cashier             │
└─────────────────────────────────────┘
                   │
┌─────────────────────────────────────┐
│    Entry Level Cashier in Other      │
│    Industry, or Employee in Bank     │
└─────────────────────────────────────┘
```

Experience and Qualifications—Experience working in a bank or handling transactions with money is helpful.

Special Skills and Personality Traits—Ability to count money accurately; money-handling skills; data entry skills; bookkeeping skills.

Special Requirements—State licensing is required.

Position Description

The casino cage is similar to a bank. The Casino Cage Cashier position is similar to that of a teller in a bank. The cage is in charge of accounting for the financial activities that occur in the casino in each department for each shift.

The Cage Cashier issues money to the casino pits, hotel area restaurants, and bars. This money is used to handle customer sales in the gaming area, hotel, restaurants, and bars. Each department, in turn, sends their revenue to the Cage Cashier to be counted and verified. The Cage Cashiers then credit the correct department and place the monies in the cage cash inventory or a bank deposit.

Cage cashiers handle the issuance of credit to customers. They additionally are responsible for exchanging chips for money from customers who have won and want to "cash out" their chips.

The Casino Cage Cashier is responsible for a great deal of money. In addition to issuing money to casino departments the Casino Cage Cashier uses it to issue customer credits, to buy back chips, and to pay out jackpots.

The Casino Cage Cashier issues chips to the gaming tables. These transactions, too, must be recorded on fill slips or sheets so that the pit area can reimburse the cage to balance the transaction.

Casino Cage Cashiers are expected to count the casino bankroll or inventory as well as make an inventory of chips before and after each work shift. The Cage Cashier must perform an accounting *over* the entire casino bankroll or inventory. This includes money, chips, and markers, among other things. It also contains credits from those departments money has been issued to, debits from money received from other departments, and customer bank checks. All items that are cash or convertible back to cash are included when the accounting is taken.

Cage Cashiers record everything on paper. To do this, the individuals utilizes a cage cash count sheet as well as a bank control sheet. All information must be accounted for, recorded, and verified.

Other duties of the Cage Cashier may include:

- Redeeming chips or tokens that customers have won or have left over when they are done gambling
- Converting contents of Cage Cashier's drawer to cash currency in lieu of cash equivalents
- Obtaining currency fills from main banks if cage is running short
- Handling daily cage reconciliation for shift

Salaries

Hourly wages for casino Cage Cashiers can run from $7.00 to $20.00 or more depending on the specific casino in which the individual is working and the geographic location.

Employment Prospects

Because all casinos have Cage Cashiers, opportunities are excellent throughout the country, wherever casinos are located.

Cage Cashiers are usually hourly employees. Many casinos are open 24 hours a day and run in shifts. Individuals may work the day shift, swing shift or evening, graveyard shift, or overnight.

Shift hours may vary in different facilities. The day shift, for example, may run from 8 A.M. to 4 P.M., the swing shift from 4 P.M. to midnight, and the graveyard shift from midnight to 8 A.M. Some facilities may have overlapping shifts or different hours.

While individuals may find employment in any casino in the world, most opportunities exist in areas where there are a large number of casinos.

Las Vegas, Reno, Laughlin, Lake Tahoe, Atlantic City, Biloxi, Baton Rouge, New Orleans, and Detroit offer the greatest number of job possibilities. Other employment settings may include casino hotels in other areas of Nevada, Mississippi, New York, Louisiana, Colorado, Connecticut, Illinois, Arizona, and California.

Other regions hosting Indian gaming and land-based or riverboat gaming facilities or cruise ships offer additional opportunities. New casinos and casino hotels are constantly under construction. More casinos and casino hotels are also opening every year as areas legalize gambling.

Advancement Prospects

Casino Cage Cashiers can climb the career ladder by promotion to casino Cage Cashier supervisor or shift manager.

Education and Training

As in many jobs in casinos, the Casino Cage Cashier may receive on-the-job training. The individual might also attend gaming schools, academies, or institutes located throughout the country. These may be private or may be part of community colleges, four-year colleges, or universities. Many casinos also have their own training programs.

Special Requirements

Cage Cashiers must be licensed in the state in which they work. This license is generally issued by a regulatory agency such as the specific state's casino control board or commission.

Experience, Skills, and Personality Traits

Experience as a cashier or handling transactions with money is preferred for those seeking positions as Cage Cashiers. Money-handling and data entry skills are needed. The ability to count money accurately is essential.

Unions and Associations

While this may be a unionized position in a limited number of casinos, Cage Cashiers are not usually represented by any bargaining union. Individuals interested in a career in this field can get additional information by contacting casino human resources departments, gaming schools, institutes, or academies.

Tips for Entry

1. Stop by the human resources department of casinos to see if they have any job openings in this area.
2. Positions may be advertised in the classified section of newspapers in areas hosting gaming. Look under headings such as "Casinos/Gaming," "Casinos," or "Cage Cashier."
3. If you are not in an area hosting gaming, consider getting a short-term subscription to the newspaper in the area of your choice. The Sunday edition of many newspapers are also often available in larger bookstores.
4. Gaming is growing quickly throughout the country. You can often find an area building a gaming facility and get an application long before building is completed.
5. These jobs may be advertised on casino job hotlines. Call each casino to get their job hotline phone number.

HARD COUNT ATTENDANT

Duties: Collecting coins or electronic gaming device tokens; dropping coins into sorter; counting and accounting for coins; accounting for drop box contents.

Alternate Title(s): Hard Count Specialist; Drop Box Counter

Salary Range: $8.50 to $20.00+ per hour

Employment Prospects: Fair

Advancement Prospects: Fair

Best Geographical Location(s) for Position: Las Vegas, Reno, Laughlin, Lake Tahoe, Atlantic City, Biloxi, Baton Rouge, New Orleans, and Detroit offer most opportunities; other regions with land-based, riverboat, or Indian gaming facilities offer additional opportunities.

Prerequisites:

Education or Training—No specialized training; high school diploma or equivalent preferred.

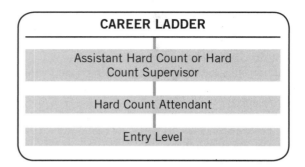

CAREER LADDER

Assistant Hard Count or Hard Count Supervisor

Hard Count Attendant

Entry Level

Experience and Qualifications—Experience requirements vary.

Special Skills and Personality Traits—Ability to count accurately; ability to lift heavy loads; ability to work in confined spaces; team player; money-handling skills.

Special Requirements—State licensing required to work in casinos.

Position Description

A great deal of money is gambled by customers every day in casinos. Thousands of coins are deposited daily in casino slot machines, games, and drop boxes. These coins must all be collected and counted. The employees who handle these duties are called Hard Count Attendants.

While some of the traditional slot machines that take coins have been replaced by paper tickets, there still are coin-operated machines. Some also take special tokens.

Hard Count Attendants may also be referred to as hard count specialists or drop box counters. They have a number of responsibilities. Hard count attendants must go to machines throughout the casino and empty the coins that have been deposited in them. Coins are collected in bags and placed on pushcarts. The Hard Count Attendants then move these into the count room or casino vault.

Once in the counting room, Hard Count Attendants lift the bags and drop them into coin sorters. Individuals then count all the coins.

Hard Count Attendants also are responsible for emptying drop boxes. Individuals usually record the contents of each drop box separately. They then record other pertinent information such as the date, shift, and table number of each drop box. In this manner, an accurate report can be made of what was collected each day, from each box, the specific shift and table.

As in other areas of the casino, there are numerous security measures and controls associated with this type of job. Surveillance cameras constantly record workers to make sure Attendants count and account for every coin they collect. The count room is locked until the Hard Count Attendants bring in uncounted boxes. It is also locked when individuals are sorting and counting money. No unauthorized employees may enter the count room.

Hard Count Attendants usually work as part of a team. Individuals are required to empty the drop box in view of the surveillance cameras as well as in front of the other members of the team.

Hard Count Attendants count the total value of each coin denomination. Often, a second member of the team may recount. A third member must compare both numbers and verify they are the same. If they are not, attendants must recount until all numbers match.

In some casinos, electronic gaming device tokens are used in lieu of coins. In these settings, the hard count attendants are expected to perform similar duties with the electronic gaming device tokens instead of coins.

Additional duties of Hard Count Attendants include:

- Scaling wrapped coins
- Ensuring drop box contents are counted and accurately accounted for
- Signing reports to verify they are correct

Salaries

Hard Count Attendants are paid an hourly wage ranging from $8.50 to $20.00. Factors affecting earnings include the geographic location, size, and prestige of the specific casino or casino hotel as well as the experience of the individual.

Employment Prospects

Employment prospects are fair for this position. All casinos use Hard Count Attendants. Many casinos have only one daily count. To keep monies as secure as possible, this is usually done at night when fewer people are likely to be around. While various shifts may be available, the most common shift for this job is the graveyard or overnight shift.

While individuals may find employment in any casino in the world, most opportunities exist in areas where there are a large number of casinos.

Las Vegas, Reno, Laughlin, Lake Tahoe, Atlantic City, Biloxi, Baton Rouge, New Orleans, and Detroit offer the greatest number of job possibilities. Other employment settings may include casino hotels in other areas of Nevada, Mississippi, New York, Louisiana, Colorado, Connecticut, Illinois, Arizona, and California.

Other regions hosting Indian gaming and land-based or riverboat gaming facilities or cruise ships offer additional opportunities. New casinos and casino hotels are constantly under construction. More casinos and casino hotels are also opening every year as areas legalize gambling.

Advancement Prospects

Hard Count Attendants may advance their careers in a number of ways. Some individuals are promoted to supervisory positions such as the assistant hard count or hard count supervisor. Others may take one or more classes in accounting and move into the clerical end of the department. Hard Count Attendants may also move into cage cashier positions.

Education and Training

There is no specialized training for this position. Most casinos and casino hotels prefer their Hard Count Attendants have a high school diploma or equivalent. Many casinos will assist employees in obtaining a GED if they do not have the minimum education.

Special Requirements

Hard Count Attendants must be licensed in the state in which they work. This license is generally issued by a regulatory agency such as the specific state's casino control board or commission.

Experience, Skills, and Personality Traits

Depending on the specific casino, this may be an entry level job or may require some experience in the hard count area. One of the most important qualifications of Hard Count Attendants is the ability to count coins accurately and precisely. Individuals must be able to lift heavy loads of coins. These are often 100 pounds or more. Hard Count Attendants should be team players. They must work easily with others.

Unions and Associations

Hard Count Attendants are usually not unionized. Those interested in learning more about careers in this field should contact the human resources department of casinos.

Tips for Entry

1. Stop by casino human resources departments to inquire about job openings.
2. Jobs may be advertised in the classified sections of newspapers in areas hosting gaming. Look under classifications such as "Casinos/Gaming," "Hard Count Attendant," "Hard Count Team Member," "Drop Box Counter," "Hard Count Specialist," or "Casino/Hotel Opportunities."
3. Openings are also often advertised on the Internet. They may be located via the home pages of casino hotels. Jobs may also be found doing a search of casino or casino hotel job opportunities. Look under key words in employment or career pages such as "Casinos," "Gaming," "Hospitality," "Entertainment," or "Hard Count Attendant."
4. Casino job fairs also may feature these jobs.

EXECUTIVE CASINO HOST

Position Description

The gaming industry is in large part a people business. There are many casinos that people can visit. Each casino tries to be the most hospitable to their clientele. The Executive Casino Host is in charge of welcoming guests to the facility.

This is usually a salaried position. It is the perfect job for someone who is friendly, likes people, enjoys socializing, and is good at it. The Executive Casino Host meets and greet customers who come to the casino. The individual has a high-visibility job. He or she walks around the casino, talks to guests, and answers questions regarding the facility.

Casinos often welcome people who are known in the industry as "high rollers," people who spend a great deal of money gambling in the casino. The Executive Casino Host is in charge of meeting with these individuals. When people spend a lot of money in casinos, the facility often "comps" goods or services for these individuals. (Comp is short for complimentary and means that the casino provides these items or services free.) A casino may, for example, comp rooms, meals, or drinks, depending on how much an individual is spending in the casino. The Executive Casino Host is often respon-

sible for tracking the high rollers, who are also known as high-limit customers. He or she can then authorize the complimentary amenities. One of the responsibilities of Executive Hosts is to actively develop players. The more revenue is gambled at a casino, the higher its returns, so depending on the specific job, Casino Executive Hosts are not only expected to meet with high rollers but often expected to actively seek them out.

In the gaming industry, extremely high rollers are also referred to as *whales*. These whales can significantly affect the bottom line of a casino. As a result, in order to attract these individuals to a specific casino, the host may offer extremely generous perks such as special "lavish high-roller suites," the use of private jets and limos, free tickets to the hottest shows, and meals at the top restaurants.

In addition to meeting with everyday casino customers and high-limit guests, the Executive Casino Host is in charge of meeting and greeting celebrities who visit the facility and gamble, stay at the hotel, or perform in the casino's showroom or nightclub.

In order to build up traffic in casinos, most facilities maintain players' clubs. These clubs offer various amenities and specials to people who are members.

The Executive Casino Host is expected to attend players' club functions and events designed to attract and keep members. As part of the duties of this job, the individual may explain players' club membership to new members.

The Executive Casino Host holds an important job in the casino. Some of the other job functions of the individual include:

- Assisting in the development of special promotions, events, and functions to attract new members to the players' club
- Assisting customers and players' club members with dinner and show arrangements
- Providing other guest services
- Answering questions regarding the casino

Salaries

Annual earnings vary from approximately $40,000 to $100,000 or more depending on a number of variables. These include the specific casino in which the individual works as well as its size, prestige, and geographic location. Other factors may include the individual's responsibilities, training, and experience.

Generally, individuals working in larger casinos in the major gambling capitals have higher earnings than their counterparts in smaller casinos or those in other geographic locations.

Employment Prospects

Casinos usually have a number of Executive Casino Hosts on staff. In many facilities there is one for each shift. Executive Casino Hosts may find employment in casinos throughout the world. Employment opportunities are good for qualified people.

While individuals may find employment in any casino in the world, most opportunities exist in areas where there are a large number of casinos.

Advancement Prospects

There are a number of different paths Executive Casino Hosts can take to career advancement. Some individuals obtain experience and move on to similar positions in larger or more prestigious facilities, resulting in increased responsibilities and earnings.

Other Executive Casino Hosts climb the career ladder by finding administrative or management positions in player development or other casino operations.

Education and Training

Education and training requirements for Executive Casino Hosts vary depending on the specific facility.

The educational requirement for some positions is a high school diploma or GED. Other facilities prefer that their employees in this position have gone through some sort of formal training. A college background or degree may be required or preferred. As in most jobs in casinos, experience may often be accepted in lieu of education. In this instance, experience dealing with the public would be extremely helpful.

Many casinos have on-the-job training programs. Some have their own in-house training programs. Community colleges, vocational technical schools, and gaming institutes throughout the country also offer training useful to jobs in the gaming industry.

Individuals working in casinos must be licensed by the state in which they work.

Special Requirements

State licensing is generally required for employees working in or around the gaming area in casinos. Generally this license is issued by a regulatory agency such as the specific state's casino control board or commission.

Each state has its own rules and regulations regarding which specific occupational licenses and permits are necessary for casino employees. In some states, for example, individuals must apply for and obtain a general gaming license. In some there are various levels of licensure and permits. Certain states may require a key employee license for those working in the management area of casinos.

The human resource department of casinos provide individuals with specific licensing requirements for each position.

Experience, Skills, and Personality Traits

The ideal candidate for this job will have had extensive experience dealing with the public as well as experience working in casinos in some capacity. Many Executive Casino Hosts were promoted from the position of casino host. Others worked in other areas of gaming.

A variety of skills are needed to be successful in this area. Customer service skills top the list. Individuals should be friendly, enthusiastic people who enjoy socializing with guests.

Excellent communications skills are essential. Organization skills are also helpful. A good memory for faces and names can be useful.

Unions and Associations

Usually this is not a unionized position. Individuals interested in learning more about this type of job should contact casinos or a local gaming institute, academy, or college offering classes in gaming.

Tips for Entry

1. Get experience dealing with the public by working as a receptionist or host in a restaurant or in customer service in retail.
2. The more you know and understand about the gaming industry and casinos in general, the more marketable you will be. Take classes at a gaming institute to learn more about the industry.
3. Positions for this type of job are often advertised in the newspaper classified section in areas hosting gaming. Look under headings such as "Executive Casino Host," "Casino Host," "Gaming," "Player Development," or "Casinos."
4. If you don't live in an area hosting gambling and are interested in looking for a job, consider subscribing to a newspaper in an area that does. You can usually buy Sunday newspapers from different parts of the country in better bookstores and newspaper shops.

CASINO HOST

Duties: Greeting guests; issuing and awarding comps and amenities; handling customer requests; handling customer relations; giving special treatment to guests.

Alternate Title(s): Host

Salary Range: $25,000 to $60,000+

Employment Prospects: Good

Advancement Prospects: Fair

Best Geographical Location(s) for Position: Las Vegas, Reno, Laughlin, Lake Tahoe, Atlantic City, Biloxi, Baton Rouge, New Orleans, and Detroit offer most opportunities; other regions with land-based, riverboat, or Indian gaming facilities offer additional opportunities.

Prerequisites:

Education or Training—Minimum of high school diploma or GED; no formal training required; on-the-job training may be offered.

Experience and Qualifications—Experience dealing with the public and working in casino environment.

CAREER LADDER

Casino Host in Larger, More Prestigious Casino or Executive Casino Host

Casino Host

Other Position in Casino or Position in Other Industry Dealing With Public

Special Skills and Personality Traits—Communications skills; organizational skills; personable; customer service skills; interpersonal skills; enthusiastic; enjoys dealing with public.

Special Requirement—State licensing required to work in casinos.

Position Description

Many casino customers choose a facility by the type of service they receive. The gaming industry, like others in the hospitality industry, is a people business. Casinos cater to guests in order to attract and keep them.

Casino Hosts are individuals who offer a variety of services to guests to make their stay more enjoyable. Responsibilities of Casino Hosts vary, depending on the specific casino and its structure.

Casino Hosts are responsible for providing special treatment to preferred guests, high rollers, high-limit guests, VIPs and invited guests, and celebrities. They may also provide special services for day-to-day customers.

Casino Hosts meet and greet customers at the casino. In some casinos, an executive casino host handles VIP guests and celebrities who visit the casino.

Casino Hosts are highly visible. They walk around the casino, answer questions, and talk to guests to make them feel good about being there.

Sometimes customers call Casino Hosts before a visit and request they make room reservations for them. Hosts are then responsible for obtaining the type of rooms with the amenities needed for the guest.

It is imperative to the success of the casino to keep all guests happy, especially premium customers and high rollers. Casino Hosts may assist premium guests in any number of ways, including securing accommodation, making dinner reservations, obtaining tickets to entertainment events, coordinating visits to the health club or spa, and so forth.

When people spend a great deal of money in casinos, the facility often "comps" goods or services for these individuals. (*Comp* is short for *complimentary* and means that the casino provides these items or services free.) The Casino Host may comp an array of amenities, including rooms, meals, drinks, or tickets to shows. The comps generally depend on the amount an individual is spending in the casino. The Casino Host can track the amount being spent by customers in order to know what type of comps should be authorized.

Casinos often maintain players' clubs designed to bring in and keep customers and build traffic. Membership entitles guests to various amenities, specials, and promotions. Casino Hosts are expected to explain players' clubs to guests and answer any questions they may have regarding membership.

Successful Casino Hosts keep in contact with their customers. They may invite them to parties and other special functions at the casino. Casino Hosts may call or write to customers to tell them about special promotions. Individuals may also send notes to guests who have visited the casino, thanking them for their business. These activities keep contact with premium guests and make sure they come back to the facility.

Casino Hosts may also be responsible for:

- Attending players' club functions
- Meeting and greeting individual bus tours and other groups entering the casino
- Authorizing rim credit, credit issued at the rim of the gaming table, for premium guests
- Providing special guest services
- Obtaining reservations for guests at either their casino or another casino hotel's restaurants or entertainment facilities

Salaries
Annual earnings vary from approximately $25,000 to $60,000 or more depending on a number of variables, including the specific casino in which the individual works as well as its size, prestige, and geographic location. Other factors may include the individual's responsibilities and experience.

Generally, individuals working in larger casinos in the major gambling capitals have higher earnings than their counterparts in smaller casinos or those in other geographic locations.

Employment Prospects
Employment opportunities are good for enthusiastic, outgoing individuals interested in jobs as Casino Hosts. While individuals may find employment in any casino in the world, most opportunities exist in areas where there are a large number of casinos.

Advancement Prospects
There are a number of different paths Casino Hosts take to career advancement. Some individuals obtain experience and move on to similar positions in larger or more prestigious facilities, resulting in increased earnings. Other Casino Hosts climb the career ladder by promotion to the position of casino executive host.

Education and Training
Education and training requirements for Casino Hosts vary depending on the specific facility. The educational requirement for most positions is a high school diploma or the equivalent. As in most jobs in casinos, experience may often be accepted in lieu of education.

Many casinos have on-the-job training programs. Some have their own in-house training programs. Community colleges, vocational technical schools, and gaming institutes throughout the country also offer training useful to jobs in this industry.

Special Requirements
State licensing is generally required for employees working in or around the gaming area in casinos. Generally this license is issued by a regulatory agency such as the specific state's casino control board or commission.

Each state has its own rules and regulations regarding which specific occupational licenses and permits are necessary for casino employees. In some states, for example, individuals must apply for and obtain a general gaming license. In some there are various levels of licensure and permits. Certain states may require a key employee license for those working in the management area of casinos.

The human resource department of casinos provide individuals with specific licensing requirements for each position.

Experience, Skills, and Personality Traits
In this position, experience dealing with the public is extremely helpful. Most Casino Hosts held prior jobs in the gaming industry.

Casino Hosts should be enthusiastic, friendly, personable people with customer service skills. Individuals should enjoy socializing with others. Hosts should be articulate people with good communications skills. The ability to remember names and faces is essential.

Unions and Associations
Contact casinos or a local gaming institute, academy, or college offering classes in gaming for more information on a job in this area. Individuals might also belong to local gaming associations in their area.

Tips for Entry
1. The more you know and understand about the gaming industry, the more marketable you will be. Consider taking one or more classes at a gaming institute or academy to learn more about the industry.
2. Positions for this type of job are often advertised in the newspaper classified in areas hosting

gaming. Look under "Casinos/Gaming," "Casino Hosts," "Gaming," or "Player Development."

3. If you don't live in an area hosting gambling and are-interested in looking for a job, consider subscribing to a newspaper in an area that does.

4. Many casinos have job hotlines advertising job availabilities. Call each casino to get its job hotline number.

PIT MANAGER

Duties: Overseeing pit area; assuring games are run smoothly; supervising operation of games; mediating disputes; opening and closing table games.

Alternate Title(s): Pit Boss

Salary Range: $35,000 to $75,000+

Employment Prospects: Good

Advancement Prospects: Good

Best Geographical Location(s) for Position: Las Vegas, Reno, Laughlin, Lake Tahoe, Atlantic City, Biloxi, Baton Rouge, New Orleans, and Detroit offer most opportunities; other regions with land-based, riverboat, or Indian gaming facilities offer additional opportunities.

Prerequisites:

Education or Training—Training at gaming academy, school, or institute.

Experience and Qualifications—Experience as floorperson or boxperson.

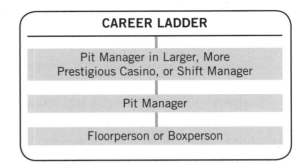

CAREER LADDER

Pit Manager in Larger, More Prestigious Casino, or Shift Manager

Pit Manager

Floorperson or Boxperson

Special Skills and Personality Traits—Supervisory skills; customer service skills; alert; knowledge of specific games in pit.

Special Requirements—State licensing required to work in and around gaming area; additional licensing requirements may be necessary.

Position Description

There is a lot of action on the casino gaming floor. The gaming area is usually separated into pits or groups of tables. The person in charge of overseeing the pit is called the Pit Manager.

A pit may consist of tables of one specific game such as craps or blackjack, or may have tables of different types of games grouped together. The Pit Manager must have an understanding of the games he or she is overseeing.

The Pit Manager works under the direction of the shift manager. The individual has a variety of responsibilities. First and foremost, the Pit Manager is expected to supervise the games in the pit and be sure they run smoothly. Games must be run properly and according to the policies of the casino. The Pit Manager must assure that regulations and procedures of the games are followed.

Pit Managers are in charge of pit personnel. Individuals are responsible for the conduct of employees in their pit. Pit Managers are expected to watch dealers to make sure they are dealing properly and not making mistakes. Pit Managers watch for any cheating on the part of dealers or other employees in the pit. Pit Man-

agers are additionally responsible for scheduling the breaks for all pit personnel.

The Pit Manager must be alert to players attempting to cheat the casino in any way. The individual watches players who seem more skilled than others, such as those who count blackjack cards.

Pit Managers deal with a certain amount of paperwork in the pit. This includes making out and authorizing cash-outs, fill, or credit slips. Individuals are also responsible for watching the play of high rollers and may award comps to players.

Other duties of the Pit Manager include:

- Settling disputes between players and casino employees
- Handling customer problems and complaints
- Calming down agitated customers
- Greeting players
- Opening and closing gaming tables

Salaries

Pit Managers are usually paid a weekly salary instead of an hourly wage. This can range between $35,000 and $75,000 or more annually. Factors affecting earnings include the geographic location, size, and prestige of the casino as well as the responsibilities and experience of the individual. Those with more experience working in large facilities in the gambling capitals may earn more than their counterparts in other areas.

Employment Prospects

Employment prospects are good for Pit Managers. Opportunities are available for qualified Pit Managers throughout the country or the world in a variety of settings. The greatest number of opportunities exist in areas where there are a large number of casinos.

Las Vegas, Reno, Laughlin, Lake Tahoe, Atlantic City, Biloxi, Baton Rouge, New Orleans, and Detroit offer the greatest number of job possibilities. Other employment settings may include casino hotels in other areas of Nevada, Mississippi, New York, Louisiana, Colorado, Connecticut, Illinois, Arizona, and California.

Other regions hosting Indian gaming and land-based or riverboat gaming facilities or cruise ships offer additional opportunities. New casinos and casino hotels are constantly under construction. More casinos and casino hotels are also opening every year as areas legalize gambling.

Advancement Prospects

Pit Managers can advance in two ways. After obtaining experience, some individuals locate similar positions in larger or more prestigious casinos, resulting in increased earnings. The other option for career advancement for Pit Managers is becoming a shift manager.

Education and Training

Pit Managers in casinos start out as dealers. They generally have gone through dealer training at gaming schools, academies, or institutes. Others have had similar training in community colleges, vocational technical schools, or casinos themselves. Some individuals have also taken casino-related training programs in-house to help prepare them for supervisory positions.

Special Requirements

Pit Managers, like all others working in the gaming area, must be licensed by the state regulatory gaming agency in the specific state in which they work. They may also be required to meet additional licensing requirements.

Experience, Skills, and Personality Traits

Experience in the gaming industry is necessary to become a Pit Manager. Individuals usually start out as dealers and move up to positions as boxpersons, floorpersons, or pit supervisors prior to becoming Pit Managers.

Pit Managers must be extremely alert so that they can watch everything that is going on in their pit. Supervisory and administrative skills are also necessary. A complete knowledge of the rules and procedures of the games in their pit is essential. Familiarity with the rules of the casino is also mandatory.

Unions and Associations

Individuals interested in learning more about careers in this area can contact gaming institutes, academies, and schools, as well as casino human resources departments. They may also belong to local gaming associations.

Tips for Entry

1. The more knowledgeable you are about a variety of games, and the more games you have experience with, the more marketable you will be.
2. Opportunities may be easier to obtain for individuals with less experience in casinos outside of the major gambling capitals of Las Vegas and Atlantic City.
3. Jobs are often advertised in the classified sections of newspapers in areas hosting gaming. Look under classifications such as "Casinos," "Casino Jobs," "Casino Opportunities," "Casino Executive," "Pit Manager," or "Gaming."
4. Visit the human resources department of casinos to inquire about job openings.
5. Look for new casinos under construction. Apply early.
6. Positions may be advertised on the Internet. Look under key words such as "Casinos," "Casino Jobs," "Gaming," or "Pit Manager." Many casino and casino hotel home pages also have employment opportunity sections.

PIT CLERK

CAREER PROFILE

Duties: Handling data entry; recording rim-credit transactions; communicating with cage, pit boss, and floor supervisors; updating players' credit standing; handling clerical duties.

Alternate Title(s): None

Salary Range: $15,000 to $23,000+

Employment Prospects: Good

Advancement Prospects: Good

Best Geographical Location(s) for Position: Las Vegas, Reno, Laughlin, Lake Tahoe, Atlantic City, Biloxi, Baton Rouge, New Orleans, Black Hawk, and Detroit offer most opportunities; other regions with land-based, riverboat, or Indian gaming facilities offer additional opportunities.

Prerequisites:

Education or Training—High school diploma or equivalent preferred; no formal training requirements; on-the-job training offered.

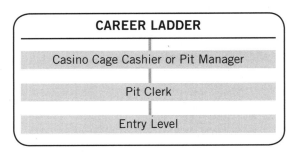

CAREER LADDER

Casino Cage Cashier or Pit Manager

Pit Clerk

Entry Level

Experience and Qualifications—No experience necessary.

Special Skills and Personality Traits—Data entry skills; clerical skills; detail-oriented.

Special Requirements—State licensing required.

Position Description

The gaming area is usually separated into pits or groups of tables. There are a number of different employees in the pit. These include dealers, pit bosses, supervisors, floorpeople, and Pit Clerks. The main function of the Pit Clerk is to sit in front of a computer terminal and input relevant data.

Pit Clerks handle a number of duties. They are responsible for recording rim-credit transactions. This type of credit is called rim because it is issued to players at the rim of a gaming table. Rim credit allows players to begin gambling without going to the cage to write a check to the casino. When rim credit is issued by a floorperson or pit boss, they notify the Pit Clerk to record the information in the pit terminal computer.

The casino must maintain records on the credit standings of individual casino customers. As new information becomes available, when customers request credit, the Pit Clerk is responsible for updating this data in the pit computer.

The individual often communicates with the cage cashier to get this and other information. Pit Clerks are expected to file all IOUs issued to players by casino executives. When players pay off IOUs at the cage, Pit

Clerks are informed so they can input the new data into the terminal. In this way the documentation will balance at the end of the shift.

Other duties of the Pit Clerk may include:

- Tracking player ratings
- Reporting and keeping track of comps awarded by floorpersons or pit bosses
- Answering pit telephones
- Handling additional clerical duties

Salaries

Pit Clerks earn an hourly wage ranging from approximately $7.00 to $10.00 or more, or roughly $15,000 to $23,000 or more for full-time clerks. Factors affecting earnings include the geographic location, size, and prestige of the casino as well as the experience of the individual.

Employment Prospects

Employment prospects are good for Pit Clerks. Opportunities are readily available in casinos throughout the country or the world. As casinos are often open 24 hours a day, individuals may work any shift. They may also be expected to work weekends or holidays.

While individuals may find employment in any casino in the world. the greatest number of opportunities exist in areas where there are a large number of casinos.

Las Vegas, Reno, Laughlin, Lake Tahoe, Atlantic City, Black Hawk, Biloxi, Baton Rouge, New Orleans, and Detroit offer the greatest number of job possibilities. Other employment settings may include casino hotels in other areas of Nevada, Mississippi, New York, Louisiana, Colorado, Connecticut, Illinois, Arizona, and California.

Other regions hosting Indian gaming and land-based or riverboat gaming facilities or cruise ships offer additional opportunities. New casinos and casino hotels are constantly under construction. More casinos and casino hotels are also opening every year as areas legalize gambling.

Advancement Prospects

In many instances, Pit Clerks positions are entry-level jobs, a way to get a foot in the door of the casino. Individuals may move up to positions working in the cage of the casino handling money and chips. Pit Clerks may also be promoted to pit managers.

Education and Training

Casinos prefer that Pit Clerks have a high school diploma or the equivalent. Many casinos will help individuals who do not have either the diploma or the equivalent obtain a GED.

There is no formal training for Pit Clerks. However, casinos usually offer on-the-job training for this position.

Special Requirements

Pit Clerks, like all others in the gaming industry, must be licensed by the state regulatory gaming agency in the specific state in which they work.

Experience, Skills, and Personality Traits

As noted previously, this is often an entry-level job, no experience is needed. Pit Clerks must have computer and data entry skills. A number of different computer software programs are used, so it is not necessary to be familiar with all software.

Unions and Associations

While there may be a limited number of casinos throughout the country where this is a unionized position, generally Pit Clerks are not represented by unions. Individuals interested in learning more about careers in this area can contact casino human resources departments. Pit Clerks may be members of local gaming associations.

Tips for Entry

1. Jobs are often advertised in the classified sections of newspapers in areas hosting gaming. Look under classifications such as "Casinos," "Casino Jobs," "Casino/Gaming Opportunities," or "Pit Clerk."
2. Visit the human resources department of casinos to inquire about job openings.
3. Most casinos have job hotlines. These are frequently updated messages listing job availabilities. You can call each casino directly to obtain its job hotline phone number.
4. Look for new casinos under construction. Apply early.
5. Positions may be advertised on the Internet. Look under key words such as "Casinos," "Casino Jobs," "Gaming," or "Pit Clerks." Many casino and casino hotel home pages also have employment opportunity sections.

FLOORPERSON

CAREER PROFILE

Duties: Overseeing table games and dealers.
Alternate Title(s): None
Salary Range: $30,000 to $47,000+
Employment Prospects: Fair
Advancement Prospects: Fair
Best Geographical Location(s) for Position: Las Vegas, Reno, Laughlin, Lake Tahoe, Atlantic City, Biloxi, Baton Rouge, New Orleans, and Detroit offer most opportunities; other regions with land-based, riverboat, or Indian gaming facilities offer additional opportunities.
Prerequisites:
    Education or Training—Dealer training at accredited gaming institute, academy, or college.

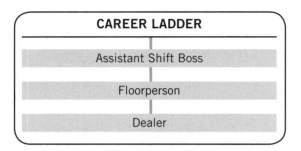

Experience and Qualifications—Experience as a dealer.
Special Skills and Personality Traits—Supervisory skills; alert; understanding of table games.
Special Requirements—State licensing required.

Position Description

A great deal of overseeing and supervision makes certain that everything that occurs in the casino area is watched and videotaped by banks of surveillance cameras. This protects both the casino and the player from possible cheating, stealing, or mistakes. In addition to surveillance cameras, several individuals oversee the games and the people who run the action.

Dealers in casinos work in what are known as pits. A Floorperson is the first-level supervisor in a pit. This is a management position.

The Floorperson supervises and oversees the dealers in his or her pit. for example, a blackjack pit consists of four tables and utilizes five dealers. The Floorperson oversees the four tables and the five dealers. In a pit with 16 tables, there would be four floorpeople.

The individual is in charge of overseeing the conduct of the games and the dealers. The Floorperson makes sure the dealers are not making mistakes and are running the games fairly. He or she is expected to check that the dealers are operating properly, counting accurately, and giving the proper payoffs. The individual must also check to see that bets are in place at the correct time. As part of the job, the Floorperson is additionally required to be on the lookout for patrons who attempt to cheat.

If there are any disputes between customers and dealers, the Floorperson is responsible for arbitrating the problem. He or she may take customers names, as

well track players' wins and losses. In some cases, the Floorperson may be required to go to a higher-level supervisor to settle the dispute. In other cases, the individual might just have to explain the rules of the game, the house, or the table to customers.

Depending on the specific casino, the Floorperson may have other duties. Dealers usually work for an hour and then break. The Floorperson is in charge of coordinating the scheduling of dealers. At times, the Floorperson may replace a dealer with a relief person if the dealer seems to be on a losing streak. Other responsibilities may include:

- Overseeing the conduct of games played at his or her tables
- Making sure rules and regulations of the gaming commission are followed
- Knowing the specific rules of the house and the table

Salaries

Because a Floorperson is considered part of the management team, he or she will usually be on salary. Individuals may have annual earnings ranging from $35,000 to $47,000 or more. Variables affecting salaries include the geographic location of the casino as well as the size and prestige of the facility. Other factors include the experience of the individual. While Floorpeople do not make tips, this position is the first step to a higher-paying management position.

Employment Prospects

Employment prospects are good for Floorpersons. Individuals are needed to oversee a variety of casino table games, including blackjack, craps, roulette, and keno. Positions may be located in all casinos hosting table games.

While individuals may find employment in any casino in the world, the greatest number of opportunities exist in areas where there are a large number of casinos.

Las Vegas, Reno, Laughlin, Lake Tahoe, Atlantic City, Biloxi, Baton Rouge, New Orleans, and Detroit offer the greatest number of job possibilities. Other employment settings include casino hotels in other areas of Nevada, Mississippi, New York, Louisiana, Colorado, Connecticut, Illinois, Arizona, and California.

Other regions hosting Indian gaming and land-based or riverboat gaming facilities offer additional opportunities. New casinos and casino hotels are constantly under construction. More casinos and casino hotels are also opening every year as areas legalize gambling.

Advancement Prospects

Floorpeople may advance their careers by obtaining experience and promotion to assistant shift boss, pit administrator, or pit boss, depending on the casino and game.

Education and Training

Floorpeople must usually be trained in dealing. Training requirements for Floorpeople vary depending on the specific state and casino. In certain areas, the Floorperson must be a graduate of an accredited gaming institute, academy, or dealer's school in order to get a job. In other areas, this training may not be required, but preferred. It is recommended that people interested in aspiring to a career in this field get formal training.

Special Requirements

Floorpeople, like all others working in casinos, must be licensed by the specific state's regulatory agency. Each state has its own standards and regulations.

Experience, Skills, and Personality Traits

The Floorperson must have prior dealing experience. Individuals should have supervisory skills. A complete knowledge and understanding of the rules of the games the individual supervises is essential.

Unions and Associations

Floorpeople do not usually belong to a union. Individuals may belong to local gaming associations and organizations geared to those in the casino industry.

Tips for Entry

1. Because Floorpeople must be dealers first, get trained in as many games as possible. This will make you more marketable.
2. Get job experience as a dealer. Many casinos promote from within.
3. Positions in this field are advertised in the newspaper classified section in areas hosting gambling facilities. Look under heading classifications such as "Floorperson," "Casinos," "Casino Jobs," or "Gaming."
4. Look for new casinos that are under construction. Get an application early.

BOXPERSON

Duties: Assuring crap game is run smoothly; supervising operation of craps table; overseeing conduct of craps dealers; mediating disputes; controlling chips.

Alternate Title(s): Boxman; Boxwoman

Salary Range: $33,000 to $60,000+

Employment Prospects: Good

Advancement Prospects: Fair

Best Geographical Location(s) for Position: Las Vegas, Reno, Laughlin, Lake Tahoe, Atlantic City, Biloxi, Baton Rouge, Black Hawk, New Orleans, and Detroit offer most opportunities; other regions with land-based, riverboat, or Indian gaming facilities offer additional opportunities.

Prerequisites:

Education or Training—Training at gaming academies, dealer schools or institutes; see text.

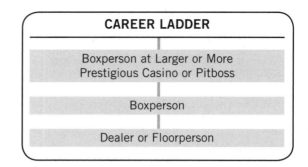

Experience and Qualifications—Experience as dealer and/or floorperson.

Special Skills and Personality Traits—Supervisory skills; customer service skills; alert; knowledge of craps.

Special Requirements—State licensing required; minimum age requirements.

Position Description

Craps is a fast, interesting, and exciting game in casinos because it is one of the games in which people can win or lose a great deal of money in a very short time. Craps is a game in which dice are thrown. Players often become very loud when this is occurring.

Craps tables are staffed with four dealers, one of whom is a replacement dealer. The table also has a Boxperson. Sometimes the action at a craps table is so hot and heavy there may be two side-by-side Boxpersons required. In these cases, each Boxperson will be in charge of one side of the tables. Although women may be employed in the Boxperson position, the job has in the past been referred to as a boxman.

The Boxperson is a casino executive who holds an important job at the craps table. He or she is the only executive in the casino who works at a gaming table. The individual has a number of responsibilities. The Boxperson is responsible for assuring that the game is run smoothly. The individual is in charge of overseeing the entire operation of the craps table and supervising the game. While dealers are expected to wear uniforms, the Boxperson usually wears a suit or sports jacket.

Originally, the Boxperson sat on a wooden crate or box and thereby acquired the name. Today, the Boxperson sits on a stool in the center of the craps table and remains seated during the course of the game.

The chips are stored directly in front of the Boxperson, who controls the casino chips during the game, thus protecting the casino's bankroll. The Boxperson is responsible for supplying chips to the dealers. He or she will also take back chips from dealers when they accumulate in front of them, and put them back in the casino's bankroll.

When customers want to buy chips, the Boxperson is in charge of collecting and counting the money. He or she then puts the money in an opening in the table called the drop box, the place all money and markers that have been collected during the shift go. The Boxperson must be sure that players who have bought casino chips receive the right amount of chips for their cash.

If there is any dispute between players and dealers, the Boxperson is expected to mediate it, with his or her decision usually final. Disputes may involve situations such as incorrect or alleged wrong payoffs or bets.

Other duties of the Boxperson may include:

- Examining dice for tampering or imperfections after dice have fallen or been thrown off the craps table and maintaining the integrity of equipment

- Watching the moves of the dealers
- Making sure payoffs made to players are correct
- Accepting or rejecting call and finger bets

Salaries

As noted previously, the Boxperson is a casino executive. He or she is therefore paid a salary in relation to an hourly wage. Boxpersons may have annual earnings ranging from $33,000 to $60,000+ or more. Factors affecting earnings include the geographic location, size, and prestige of the casino, as well as the experience of the individual. Those working in large facilities in the gambling capitals may earn more than their counterparts in other areas.

As a rule, a casino executive such as a Boxperson does not receive tips. One of the challenges for casinos is that many experienced dealers who would make great supervisors don't want to become casino executives because they generally lose the opportunity to make tips.

It should be noted that in 2007, Steve Wynn, CEO of Wynn Las Vegas, determined that frontline service might be improved if frontline supervisors such as the Boxperson received part of the tip pool. In casinos that follow this practice, earnings can significantly increase.

Employment Prospects

Employment prospects are good for Boxpersons and getting better as more and more casinos open throughout the country. Opportunities for a Boxperson may be found in any casino hosting craps tables. Because casinos are often open 24 hours a day, individuals may work during all shifts, including daytime, swing shift or evening, graveyard or overnight. Individuals may be expected to work weekends or holidays.

While individuals may find employment in any casino in the world, the greatest number of opportunities exist in areas where there are a large number of casinos.

Las Vegas, Reno, Laughlin, Lake Tahoe, Atlantic City, Biloxi, Baton Rouge, New Orleans, and Detroit offer the greatest number of job possibilities. Other employment settings include casino hotels in other areas of Nevada, Mississippi, New York, Louisiana, Colorado, Connecticut, Illinois, Arizona, and California.

Other regions hosting Indian gaming and land-based or riverboat gaming facilities or cruise ships offer additional opportunities. New casinos and casino hotels are constantly under construction. More casinos and casino hotels are also opening every year as areas legalize gambling.

Advancement Prospects

A Boxperson can advance his or her career by obtaining more experience and locating a similar position in a larger or more prestigious casino. Individuals may also move on to other management positions within the casino, including pit boss.

Education and Training

A Boxperson must have complete working knowledge of both the casino rules and the procedures of the game of craps. Depending on the specific casino, an individual in this position must be a graduate of an accredited gaming school, academy, or institute. In certain locations, community colleges, vocational technical schools, or the casinos themselves offer training.

Boxpersons, like all others working in the gaming area, must be licensed by the state gaming agency in the specific state in which they work.

Special Requirements

State licensing is generally required for employees working in or around the gaming area in casinos. Generally this license is issued by a regulatory agency such as the specific state's casino control board or commission.

Each state has its own rules and regulations regarding which specific occupational licenses and permits are necessary for casino employees. In some states, for example, individuals must apply for and obtain a general gaming license. In some there are various levels of licensure and permits. Certain states may require a key employee license for those working in the management area of casinos.

The human resource department of casinos provide individuals with specific licensing requirements for each position.

Most states also have a minimum age requirement for this position.

Experience, Skills, and Personality Traits

Experience as a dealer and/or a floorperson is necessary to become a Boxperson. The minimum amount of experience varies, but usually is approximately 1,200 to 1,500 hours.

A Boxperson must be extremely alert in order to watch everything that is going on at the table. Supervisory and administrative skills are also necessary.

Unions and Associations

Boxpersons working in casinos do not generally belong to a union. Individuals interested in learning more about careers in this area should contact gaming institutes, academies, and schools, as well as casino human resources departments.

Individuals may belong to local gaming associations and organizations.

Tips for Entry

1. Jobs are often advertised in the classified sections of newspapers in areas hosting gaming. Look under classifications such as "Casinos," "Casino Jobs," "Casino Opportunities," "Boxperson," "Boxman/woman," "Gaming."

2. Visit the human resources department of casinos to inquire about job openings.

3. Look for new casinos under construction. Apply early.

4. You may learn about job openings on casinos job hotlines. These are frequently updated messages listing job availabilities. You can call each casino directly to get its job hotline phone number.

CRAPS DEALER

CAREER PROFILE

Duties: Pushing dice to shooter; retrieving dice; calling game.

Alternate Title(s): Dealer; Stickman; Boxman; Stickperson; Boxperson

Salary Range: $30,000 to $110,000, plus tips

Employment Prospects: Good

Advancement Prospects: Good

Best Geographical Location(s) for Position: Las Vegas, Reno, Laughlin, Lake Tahoe, Atlantic City, Biloxi, Baton Rouge, New Orleans, and Detroit offer most opportunities; other regions with land-based, riverboat, or Indian gaming facilities offer additional opportunities.

Prerequisites:

Education or Training—Training at gaming academy, school, or institute

Experience and Qualifications—Experience dealing craps obtained through training.

CAREER LADDER

Craps Dealer at Larger, More Prestigious Casino, Dealer of other Game, or Floorperson or Boxperson

Craps Dealer

Student at Dealer School or Academy or Dealer in other Casino Game

Special Skills and Personality Traits—Manual dexterity; interpersonal skills; alert; math skills; knowledge of craps.

Special Requirements—State licensing required; minimum age requirements.

Position Description

A craps crew is usually composed of two standing Dealers, another Dealer called the stickperson, and a replacement Dealer, as well as one or two boxpersons. The stickperson stands in the middle of the craps table, pushing the dice around the table to the shooters. The boxperson is the casino executive in charge of overseeing the craps table.

Dealers usually work for 40 minutes and then go on break and are replaced by another Dealer. The Dealers at the craps table generally rotate positions in a counterclockwise direction looking down at the table. In this manner, every Craps Dealer at the table handles the position of the base Dealer as well as the position of stickperson.

Dealers stand during play. As a rule, they are expected to wear uniforms. The two standing Craps Dealers are each located at the base of one side or the other of the table. Each Dealer is responsible for the players in his or her section of the craps table.

Individuals have a number of responsibilities. They are responsible for changing a player's cash into chips. This is done by giving the money to the boxperson. The Dealer may also change a player's chips during the course of play to those worth either a higher or lower denomination. This is called changing color.

The Stickperson is in charge of pushing the dice to the shooter before his or her roll. The shooter must choose two dice from a choice of four to eight that are offered. The Stickperson must then put the non-selected dice back in a box that is kept in view in front of the individual at all times.

Another responsibility of the Stickperson is to "call the game." This happens when the Stickperson announces what each roll of the dice is as well as whether it is a winner or loser. Every Stickperson has his or her own way of calling a game, so that enthusiasm and excitement are generated at the table at all times—when the shooter is shaking the dice, when the dice have been rolled, and when the winning or losing bets are announced.

The Stickperson takes or books the proposition bets placed in the center of the craps table. The individual must verbally acknowledge every proposition wager. This is sometimes called advertising the bets. He or she will then point out the customers who win the standing dealers and announce the correct payoff for each person.

Standing Dealers are responsible for handling all the place bets as well as keeping track of them. This must be done in the proper order so that the right players are paid correctly if their numbers come up again.

Dealers are expected to move a plastic disk to a corner box number after a point has been established on the come-out roll of a shooter. This disk is called a buck. It indicates that the number in which the disk has been placed is the point. The disk may have a black and a white side. The white side of the buck in a box number indicates that number is the point.

Sometimes when a new shooter is coming out, the Dealer will move the disk to the "don't come" box. If the disk is black and in the "don't come" box, it indicates that no point has been established and the roll is a come-out roll.

The Dealer is responsible for placing even bets and odd bets in the correct box when "come" or "don't come" bets have been made. Winning bets are then paid off. Chips for losing bets are taken off and given back to the casino.

Other duties of the standing Dealer may include:

- Giving players chips to play with after their credit has been approved
- Paying off winning bets
- Removing losing bets made on the section of the craps table he or she is responsible for

Salaries

Craps Dealers earn an hourly wage ranging between $8.00 and $12.00 or more plus tips. Tips may also be referred to as tokes. Players who win often tip the Dealer, pushing their hourly wage in some cases to $50 or more. Some Dealers working at tables with high limits may earn $100 to $500 or more per hour in tips. Individuals may earn between $30,000 to $110,000 annually, or more with tips.

Employment Prospects

Employment prospects for Craps Dealers are good. Opportunities for Dealers may be located in any casino hosting craps tables. As casinos are often open 24 hours a day, individuals may work various shifts.

While individuals may find employment in any casino in the world, the greatest number of opportunities exist in areas where there are a large number of casinos.

Advancement Prospects

A Craps Dealer may take a number of different paths to career advancement. The individual can advance his or her career by obtaining more experience and finding a similar position in a larger or more prestigious casino, resulting in increased tips. Some Craps Dealers also obtain training and experience in dealing additional casino games. Individuals may also move on to management positions within the casino, including floorperson or boxperson.

Education and Training

A Craps Dealer must have complete working knowledge of both the casino rules and the procedures of the game of craps. According to many experts, craps is one of the most difficult casino games to work at as a Dealer. Individuals in this position should be trained in dealing craps at an accredited gaming school, academy, or institute. Community colleges, vocational technical schools, and casinos themselves also offer Dealer training.

Special Requirements

Craps Dealers, like all others working in a gaming area, must be licensed in the state in which they work. There are also minimum age requirements.

Experience, Skills, and Personality Traits

Individuals should be personable people who enjoy being around others. Showmanship is helpful. An enthusiastic patter is essential. Math skills are also needed, as is manual dexterity.

Unions and Associations

Craps Dealers do not usually belong to a union. Individuals interested in learning more about careers in this area should contact gaming institutes, academies, and schools, as well as casino human resources departments.

Tips for Entry

1. Visit the human resources department of casinos to inquire about job openings.
2. Craps Dealers, like most other casino game Dealers, often must audition for jobs. Get as much experience as possible while in training.
3. Jobs are often advertised in the classifieds in areas hosting gaming. Look under classifications such as "Casinos," "Casino Jobs," or "Dealers."
4. Look for new casinos under construction. Job opportunities may exist. Apply early.
5. Gaming institutes and schools often offer job placement.
6. Most casinos have job hotlines. Call casinos directly to get job hotline phone numbers.

BLACKJACK DEALER

CAREER PROFILE

Duties: Dealing cards for game of blackjack in a casino.
Alternate Title(s): Dealer
Salary Range: $30,000 to $110,000 plus tips
Employment Prospects: Excellent
Advancement Prospects: Good
Best Geographical Location(s) for Position: Las Vegas, Reno, Laughlin, Lake Tahoe, Atlantic City, Biloxi, Baton Rouge, New Orleans and Detroit offer most opportunities; other regions with land-based, riverboat, or Indian gaming facilities offer additional opportunities.
Prerequisites:
  Education or Training—Training at gaming academies, dealer schools, or institutes; see text.
  Experience and Qualifications—Experience at dealing blackjack gained through training.

CAREER LADDER

Blackjack or other Dealer at Larger or More Prestigious Casino, or Floorperson or Pit Manager

Blackjack Dealer

Student at Dealer School or Academy

Special Skills and Personality Traits—Dealing skills; math skills; manual dexterity; interpersonal skills.
Special Requirements—State licensing required; minimum age requirements.

Position Description

Blackjack is one of the most common table games offered at casinos throughout the world. In this game, the Blackjack Dealer deals cards to the players at the table and the house. The house is the casino, and the dealer represents the house.

The object of blackjack is to get a "blackjack or 21." A blackjack is an ace and a picture card or 10. If the player does not get a blackjack, he or she must beat the house. In order to do this, the player must get closer to 21 than the house without going over. In blackjack, aces count as one or 11, numbered cards equal their value, and picture cards count as 10. A tie means everybody is even.

The Blackjack Dealer waits for the bets to be placed by the players. The individual goes around the table from left to right and deals each player a card facedown as well as dealing one to the house. He or she then deals each player a card faceup. The players will then indicate to the dealer whether they want any other cards either verbally or by motioning. The players and dealer turn their cards over and see who beat the house. If one or more of the players did, the dealer gives them the payoff.

Blackjack Dealers work in what is known as a pit. There are four tables in each pit and five dealers. Blackjack Dealers usually work for an hour and then break.

The extra dealer is available to relieve the dealer who is on break.

Blackjack Dealers as well as everyone else in the casino are always being watched by others, including supervisors called floorpeople, pit clerks, and pit bosses. A supervisor may, for example, replace a dealer who is on a losing streak for the house. Everything that takes place in the gaming area is also screened and videotaped by banks of surveillance cameras. This procedure protects both the casino and the player from possible cheating or stealing.

The Blackjack Dealer must be able to deal from one or more decks of cards. He or she may also deal from a "shoe." This is a box that holds one or more decks of cards and dispenses them one by one. The individual must further understand the various options and procedures, including splitting pairs, doubling down, and insurance as it relates to the game.

The Blackjack Dealer is responsible for conducting the games at his or her table. In addition to mixing and dealing the cards, the individual is responsible for:

- Counting and tallying the cards of each player
- Determining the correct amount of chips the winner is entitled to
- Giving the payoff to the patron
- Knowing the specific rules of the house and the table
- Referring all customer problems to the floorperson

Salaries

Blackjack Dealers earn an hourly wage ranging between $8.00 and $12.00 or more. Most of their earnings, however, come from tips. Tips may also be referred to as tokes. Players who win often tip Blackjack Dealers, pushing their hourly wage in some cases to $50 or more. Blackjack Dealers working at tables with high limits may earn $100 to $500 or more an hour in tips. There are some individuals who earn approximately $30,000 annually and others who earn $110,000 or more including tips.

Employment Prospects

Because blackjack is one of the most common table games offered at casinos, Blackjack Dealers are always in demand. Employment prospects are excellent.

While individuals may find employment in any casino in the world, the greatest number of opportunities exist in areas where there are a large number of casinos.

Las Vegas, Reno, Laughlin, Lake Tahoe, Atlantic City, Biloxi, Baton Rouge, New Orleans, and Detroit offer the greatest number of job possibilities. Other employment settings include casino hotels in other areas of Nevada, Mississippi, New York, Louisiana, Colorado, Connecticut, Illinois, Arizona, and California.

Other regions hosting Indian gaming and land-based or riverboat gaming facilities or cruise ships offer additional opportunities. New casinos and casino hotels are constantly under construction. More casinos and casino hotels are also opening every year as areas legalize gambling.

Advancement Prospects

Blackjack Dealers may advance their careers by learning more games. The more games that individuals learn, the more money they will be able to earn. Some Blackjack Dealers climb the career ladder by becoming floorpeople, supervisors, or pit clerks.

Education and Training

While formal training is not required to become a Blackjack Dealer, many casinos prefer to hire applicants who have gone through a gaming school or institute or at least taken classes in dealing blackjack. Gaming schools are located in areas hosting gambling casinos.

Some casinos also have their own training facilities or offer on-the-job training.

Gaming schools offer classes during the day, evenings, and weekends to accommodate people working in the gaming industry. Some schools also offer classes after the midnight shift and on weekends to further accommodate workers.

Special Requirements

Blackjack Dealers, like most other casino employees, must usually be licensed in the state in which they work. There are also minimum age requirements.

Experience, Skills, and Personality Traits

Blackjack Dealers should be personable people who enjoy being around others. The ability to count and add quickly and accurately is essential to this job. Because cards are mixed and dealt in a certain manner, manual dexterity is also required.

Unions and Associations

Blackjack Dealers are not usually unionized in most casinos. There are cases, however, in which individuals working on riverboats or cruises may be members of a union.

Dealers may be members of local gaming trade associations and organizations.

Additional information regarding this career can be obtained from gaming institutes, academies, and schools as well as casino human resources departments.

Tips For Entry

1. As noted previously, formal training is not required. However, classes at a gaming institute, academy, or college will give you an edge over someone who has not been trained.
2. Learn how to deal multiple games. This will make you more marketable.
3. Positions in this field are advertised in the newspaper classified section in areas hosting gambling facilities. Look under heading classifications such as "Blackjack Dealer," "Dealers," "Casinos," "Casino Jobs," or "Gaming."
4. Stop in at the human resources department of casinos in which you might be interested in working to see if there are any openings.

ROULETTE DEALER

CAREER PROFILE

Duties: Overseeing roulette game; selling chips; spinning roulette wheel; releasing ball; paying off winning bets; collecting losing bets.

PR:**Alternate Title(s):** Dealer

Salary Range: $30,000 to $110,000 plus tips

Employment Prospects: Good

Advancement Prospects: Good

Best Geographical Location(s) for Position: Las Vegas, Reno, Laughlin, Lake Tahoe, Atlantic City, Biloxi, Baton Rouge, New Orleans, and Detroit offer most opportunities; other regions with land-based, riverboat, or Indian gaming facilities offer additional opportunities.

Prerequisites:

Education or Training—Training at gaming academy, school, or institute; see text.

Experience and Qualifications—Experience dealing roulette gained through training.

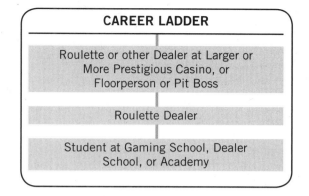

CAREER LADDER

Roulette or other Dealer at Larger or More Prestigious Casino, or Floorperson or Pit Boss

Roulette Dealer

Student at Gaming School, Dealer School, or Academy

Special Skills and Personality Traits—Manual dexterity; interpersonal skills; alert; skilled at dealing roulette; personable.

Special Requirements—State licensing required; minimum age requirements.

Position Description

Roullete is a casino game played on a large felt table on which players place wagers. These wagers are placed on portions of the table corresponding to numbers on which people want to bet.

The game features a roulette wheel, which includes a 31- or 32-inch bowl-shaped base that sits outside of the wheel. The bowl has a track with a one-inch-wide groove running around the circumference. This is where the Dealer spins the roulette ball.

The wheel head spins counterclockwise. It has 38 pockets separated with metal separators or frets. Eighteen pockets are red, eighteen are black, and the other two are green. Pockets are numbered 0 through 36. In America, the extra pocket is numbered 00. Pockets are numbered so that high, low, odd, and even numbers and red and black colors alternate.

Roulette tables may have single layouts or double-end tables with two layouts. The number of roulette dealers depends on which type of table is in use. A single layout table is staffed by two Roulette Dealers or a Dealer and an assistant. They are also called croupiers. The double-end tables may have three or four dealers.

Dealers usually work for 40 minutes, then go on break and are replaced by another Dealer. They stand during play. As a rule, they are expected to wear uniforms.

The Roulette Dealer is responsible for staffing the roulette table. The individual is expected to oversee the conduct of the game. On a single layout table one Dealer is responsible for selling chips to players. The individual must keep track of the value of the chips each player has on the table. The Dealer does this near the wheel by placing numbered buttons also known as lammers next to each color chip to illustrate the value. This is especially important when the player wants to cash out. In this manner the Dealer knows how much to pay each player.

The Dealer is in charge of spinning the roulette wheel. The individual may be called a wheel roller. The Dealer is also responsible for taking the ball from the last pocket in which it falls. He or she pushes the wheel to make sure it keeps moving. The individual then releases the ball in a clockwise manner onto the track.

The Dealer's responsibility is to call out something to the effect of "no more bets" just as the ball is ready to fall from the back track. At that time, the Dealer and players watch the ball settle into a numbered pocket. The Dealer announces the winning number and color.

The individual then pays off the winning bets as well as collecting all losing bets from the roulette table.

The other Dealer working the table is responsible for separating the losing chips. He or she must stack them after the other dealer sweeps them from the layout. This is done by stacking the chips in piles of 20 of the same color. These are then put into the chip rack on the apron of the roulette table.

Other duties of the Roulette Dealer may include:

- Placing a marker on the winning number of the felt
- Returning invalid bets to players

Salaries

The Roulette Dealer earns an hourly wage ranging between $8.00 and $12.00 or more. Most of his or her earnings, however, come from tips. Tips may also be referred to as tokes. Players who win often tip the Dealer, pushing their hourly wage in some cases to $30 or more. Some Dealers working at tables with high limits may earn $100 to $500 or more per hour in tips. There are some Roulette Dealers who earn approximately $30,000 annually, while others may earn $110,000 or more including tips.

Employment Prospects

Employment opportunities for Roulette Dealers are excellent and may be found in any casino hosting roulette tables. While individuals may find employment in any casino in the world, the greatest number of opportunities exist in areas where there are a large number of casinos.

Las Vegas, Reno, Laughlin, Lake Tahoe, Atlantic City, Biloxi, Baton Rouge, New Orleans, and Detroit offer the greatest number of job possibilities. Other employment settings include casino hotels in other areas of Nevada, Mississippi, New York, Louisiana, Colorado, Connecticut, Illinois, Arizona, and California.

Other regions hosting Indian gaming and land-based or riverboat gaming facilities or cruise ships offer additional opportunities. New casinos and casino hotels are constantly under construction. More casinos and casino hotels are also opening every year as areas legalize gambling.

Because casinos are often open 24 hours a day, individuals may work during the daytime, evening or swing shift, graveyard or overnight shift. Roulette Dealers may be expected to work weekends or holidays.

Advancement Prospects

A Roulette Dealer may take a number of different paths to career advancement. The individual can advance his or her career by obtaining more experience and locating a similar position in a larger or more prestigious casino, resulting in increased tips. Some Roulette Dealers also obtain training and experience in dealing additional casino games. Individuals may also get experience and move on to management positions within the casino, including floorpersons or pit bosses.

Education and Training

A Roulette Dealer must have complete working knowledge of both the casino rules and the procedures of the roulette game. Individuals in this position should be trained in dealing roulette at an accredited gaming school, academy, or institute. Community colleges, vocational technical schools, and casinos themselves may also offer Dealer training.

Gaming schools offer classes during the day, evenings, and weekends to accommodate people working in the gaming industry. Some schools also offer classes after the midnight shift and on weekends to further accommodate workers.

Special Requirements

Roulette Dealers, like most other casino employees, must usually be licensed in the state in which they work. There are also minimum age requirements.

Experience, Skills, and Personality Traits

Roulette Dealers should be personable people who enjoy being around others. Interpersonal skills are necessary for success in this career. Showmanship is helpful. Manual dexterity is essential.

Unions and Associations

Roulette Dealers are not usually unionized in most casinos, although individuals working on riverboats or cruises may be members of various unions.

Dealers may belong to local gaming-related trade associations and organizations.

Tips for Entry

1. Gaming institutes and schools often offer job placement. Check out the placement rate of various schools in the area before making a choice.
2. Stop by the human resources department of casinos to inquire about job openings.
3. Roulette Dealers, like most other casino game dealers, often must audition for jobs. Get as much experience as possible while in training.

4. Look for new casinos under construction. Apply early.
5. Most casinos have job hotlines. These are frequently updated messages listing job availabilities. Positions as Dealers are often included.
6. Jobs are often advertised in the classified sections of newspapers in areas hosting gaming. Look under classifications such as "Casinos," "Casino Jobs," "Casino Opportunities," "Roulette Dealers," "Dealers," or "Gaming."

BACCARAT DEALER

Position Description

Baccarat is a casino game played with cards. It was invented in Italy and became popular throughout Europe. Baccarat is a French word for the Italian term *baccarat* meaning zero. Zero refers to the face cards in a deck of jack, queen, king, and the 10 cards. In the game of baccarat these cards all have a zero value. Other cards, ace through nine, are valued according to their number.

A hand in baccarat consists of two or three cards. No hand can total more than nine. All hands totaling more than 10 have 10 subtracted from their value.

There are a number of versions of the game. In the American version of baccarat the casino plays against the participants at the gaming table. This includes the bet bank and the players. In the game of baccarat the player makes a bet on either the bank or the players.

Baccarat is a game that attracts bettors and high rollers. It is played on a large baccarat table. The baccarat area is often located in a separate area of the casino, roped off from other gaming tables.

Many people think baccarat is a glamorous game. Baccarat Dealers, like most other dealers in casinos, are expected to wear uniforms. However, the uniforms of these Dealers are often tuxedos, projecting a more glamorous image.

Baccarat is played at a special table on which numbers are printed. Fifteen people can participate at the table. The baccarat table is staffed by three Dealers.

At each table the rules are printed clearly, both for the participants' use as well as for the Dealers'. Dealers are in charge of knowing and enforcing the rules of the game. They make sure participants abide by the rules.

All three Dealers in baccarat cut, mix, and reshuffle the deck. One Dealer, referred to as the callman or callperson, stands between positions 1 and 15. Looking down at the table, this position is located at the bottom center of the table. This individual is responsible for receiving the cards. The callperson is also expected to place the cards in the appropriate boxes. The individual is also responsible, according to the written rules at the table, for deciding whether a hand should stand or draw a card. The callman or callperson is additionally expected to announce the winning hand after the final draw.

The other Dealers sit during play. After a winner is announced by the callman or callperson, the other Dealers pay off winning bets. They also must collect losing bets.

Other duties of Baccarat Dealers include:

- Keeping records of commissions due on wagers
- Collecting commissions when players leave the table or eight decks of cards are depleted

Salaries

A Baccarat Dealer earns an hourly wage ranging between $8.00 and $12.00. Most of his or her earnings, however, come from tips. Tips may also be referred to as tokes. Players who win often tip the Dealer, pushing their hourly wage in some cases to $50 or more. Some Dealers working at tables with high limits may earn $100 to $500 or more per hour in tips. There are some Baccarat Dealers who earn approximately $30,000 annually, while others may earn $110,000 or more including tips.

Employment Prospects

Employment opportunities for Baccarat Dealers are good and may be found in most casinos. Because some casinos may be open 24 hours a day, Baccarat Dealers might work various shifts including daytime, swing shift, graveyard shift or overnight. Individuals may also be required to work weekends or holidays.

While individuals may find employment in any casino in the world, the greatest number of opportunities exist in areas where there are a large number of casinos.

Las Vegas, Reno, Laughlin, Lake Tahoe, Atlantic City, Biloxi, Baton Rouge, New Orleans, and Detroit offer the greatest number of job possibilities. Other employment settings include casino hotels in other areas of Nevada, Mississippi, New York, Louisiana, Colorado, Connecticut, Illinois, Arizona, and California.

Other regions hosting Indian gaming and land-based or riverboat gaming facilities or cruise ships offer additional opportunities. New casinos and casino hotels are constantly under construction. More casinos and casino hotels are also opening every year as areas legalize gambling.

Advancement Prospects

A Baccarat Dealer may take a number of different paths to career advancement. The individual can advance his or her career by obtaining more dealing experience and locating a similar position in a larger or more prestigious casino, resulting in increased tips. Baccarat Dealers may also obtain training and experience in dealing additional casino games, making them more marketable. Individuals may also get experience and move on to management positions within the casino, including floorpersons or pit bosses.

Education and Training

A Baccarat Dealer must have complete working knowledge of both the casino rules and the procedures of the baccarat game. Individuals should be trained in dealing baccarat at an accredited gaming school, academy, or institute. Community colleges and vocational technical schools in areas hosting gaming and casinos themselves may also offer dealer training.

Special Requirements

Baccarat Dealers, like all others working in a gaming area, must be licensed in the state in which they work. There are also minimum age requirements.

Experience, Skills, and Personality Traits

Individuals should be personable people who enjoy being around others. The ability to deal with customers in a gracious, effective, and courteous manner is needed. Showmanship is helpful. Manual dexterity is also necessary.

Unions and Associations

Individuals may be members of local gaming-related trade associations and organizations.

Additional information regarding this career can be obtained from gaming institutes, academies, and schools, as well as casino human resources departments.

Tips for Entry

1. Baccarat Dealers, like most other casino game dealers, often must audition for jobs. Get as much experience as possible while being trained.
2. Gaming institutes and schools often offer job placement. Check out the placement rate of various schools in the area.
3. Stop by the human resources departments of casinos to inquire about job openings.
4. Look for new casinos under construction in gaming areas. Apply for jobs early.
5. Most casinos have job hotlines listing jobs available. These are frequently updated messages. You can call each casino directly to get its job hotline phone number.
6. Jobs are often advertised in the classified sections of newspapers in areas hosting gaming. Look under classifications such as "Baccarat," "Casinos," "Casino Jobs," "Casino Opportunities," "Baccarat Dealers," "Dealers," or "Gaming."

SLOT MANAGER

CAREER PROFILE

Duties: Formulating policies of slot department; overseeing slot operation; developing layout of floor; supervising slot personnel.

Alternate Title(s): Manager of Slots

Salary Range: $37,000 to $75,000+

Employment Prospects: Poor

Advancement Prospects: Fair

Best Geographical Location(s) for Position: Las Vegas, Reno, Laughlin, Lake Tahoe, Atlantic City, Biloxi, Baton Rouge, New Orleans, and Detroit offer most opportunities; other regions with land-based, riverboat, or Indian gaming facilities offer additional opportunities.

Prerequisites:

Education or Training—Training requirements vary; see text.

Experience and Qualifications—Experience working in slot department.

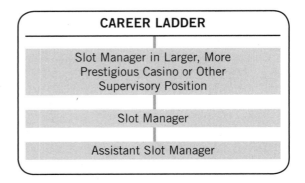

CAREER LADDER

Slot Manager in Larger, More Prestigious Casino or Other Supervisory Position

Slot Manager

Assistant Slot Manager

Special Skills and Personality Traits—Supervisory skills; administrative skills; marketing skills; analytical skills.

Special Requirements—State licensing required; slot mechanic license may be required.

Position Description

Slots generate a great deal of money for casinos. The person in charge overseeing the slot operation is called the Slot Manager. The individual holds an important administrative position and has a multitude of responsibilities.

The Slot Manager is responsible for formulating the policies and procedures used in the slot department. The individual is in charge of designing the layout for the slot floor. A lot of thought must go into this process. The Slot Manager must determine the width of aisles and location of booths, and decide where specific machines should physically be placed. The individual may also select the manufacturers and type and denominations of each machine used in the casino.

When designing the floor layout, the Slot Manager must find ways for machines to generate the maximum amount of business. Payoff schedules of machines must be developed to attract customers. The individual must decide which machines should have less frequent large payoffs and which should have smaller, more frequent jackpots.

The slot department has a number of employees. These may include an assistant slot manager, slot shift managers, attendant supervisors, slot attendants, slot repair managers, mechanics, floorpeople, cage cashiers, and change people. The Slot Manager is expected to oversee the slot employees and their activities.

The Slot Manager often works with the marketing and player development department designing promotions and special events to attract more players to the casino. These promotions may include events such as large slot tournaments.

Other duties of the Slot Manager may include:

- Attending staff and department head meetings
- Handling disputes on the floor between customers and employees
- Evaluating machines

Salaries

A Slot Manager may have annual earnings ranging from $37,000 to $75,000 or more. Factors affecting earnings include the geographic location, size, and prestige of the specific casino as well as the experience and responsibilities of the individual. Generally, those with the most experience working in larger, more prestigious casinos in the gambling capitals earn the highest salaries.

Employment Prospects

Employment prospects for Slot Managers may be limited in larger casinos located in the gambling capitals. In these facilities individuals may have to wait for an opening.

The greatest number of opportunities will be found in Las Vegas, Reno, Laughlin, Atlantic City, Biloxi, Baton Rouge, New Orleans, and Detroit. Other areas with land-based or riverboat gaming facilities offer additional job possibilities. As legalized gaming expands throughout the United States, opportunities in other locations will become available.

Advancement Prospects

Slot Managers can advance their careers by obtaining experience and locating similar positions in larger or more prestigious casinos. Individuals might also be promoted to other supervisory positions within the casino.

Education and Training

Training requirements vary at different casinos in various locations. Certain casinos require Slot Managers to have either completed an approved program in slot machine repair in at least two machines or be licensed as a slot mechanic in at least two types of machines. Other casinos may not have these requirements.

Courses or programs in casino-related training offered by gaming schools, academies, and institutes, as well as community colleges and vo-tech schools throughout the country may be useful.

Special Requirements

Slot Managers, like others working in a gaming area, must be licensed in the state in which they work. Depending on the specific job, individuals may also be required to be licensed as a slot mechanic in at least two different types of machines. Minimum age requirements generally apply.

Experience, Skills, and Personality Traits

Slot Managers are required to have from three to four years of experience working in the slot department prior to becoming Slot Managers. Some casinos require between 5,000 and 6,000 hours of experience working in the casino slot department to qualify for this job.

Supervisory skills, administrative skills, marketing skills, and analytical skills are necessary for success in this career.

Unions and Associations

Slot Managers in most casinos are not usually unionized. Individuals may belong to local gaming-related trade associations and organizations.

Additional information regarding this career can be obtained from gaming institutes, academies, and schools, as well as casino human resources departments.

Tips for Entry

1. Many casinos as well as gaming schools, academies, institutes, community colleges, and vo-tech schools in gaming areas offer casino-related training programs. These may not be necessary, but are helpful in attaining a high level of casino knowledge.
2. You may have to relocate to other gaming areas to find an opening as a Slot Manager.
3. Visit the human resources department of casinos and inquire about job openings.
4. Jobs are often advertised in the classified sections of newspapers in areas hosting gaming. Look under classifications such as "Slot Manager," "Casinos," "Casino Jobs," "Casino Opportunities," or "Gaming."
5. Check out specific casino Web sites. Many advertise employment openings directly on their sites.
6. New casinos under construction are a great place to look for employment. Stop at their human resources departments and ask for an application.
7. This is a position that is often promoted from within. Get your foot in the door and obtain as much as experience as possible in the slot department.

SLOT SHIFT MANAGER

Duties: Supervising slot personnel during shift.
Alternate Title(s): Shift Manager
Salary Range: $32,000 to $55,000+
Employment Prospects: Fair
Advancement Prospects: Fair
Best Geographical Location(s) for Position: Las Vegas, Reno, Laughlin, Atlantic City, Biloxi, Baton Rouge, New Orleans, and Detroit offer most opportunities; other regions with land-based, riverboat, or Indian gaming facilities offer additional opportunities.
Prerequisites:
Education or Training—Training requirements vary; see text.
Experience and Qualifications—Experience working in slot department.

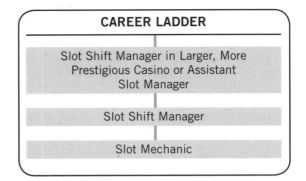

CAREER LADDER

Slot Shift Manager in Larger, More Prestigious Casino or Assistant Slot Manager

Slot Shift Manager

Slot Mechanic

Special Skills and Personality Traits—Supervisory skills; administrative skills; marketing skills; analytical skills; customer service skills.
Special Requirements—State licensing required; slot mechanic license may be required.

Position Description

Slots are a major moneymaker for casinos because it is easy for everyone to play. All people need to do is drop some coins into the machine and either pull a handle or press a button to start reels moving, then wait to see if they have won.

Many people work in the slot department. The Slot Shift Manager is responsible for supervising the slot personnel during the shift.

Slot personnel may include attendant supervisors, slot attendants, slot mechanics, floorpeople, cage cashiers, and change people. The Slot Shift Manager is expected to oversee the activities of these employees. The individual must make sure everyone is doing their job and assisting customers when needed. The Slot Shift Manager is also responsible for making sure employees take breaks when required.

Other duties of the Slot Shift Manager may include:

- Dealing with problems with employees
- Accounting for incidents during the shift
- Arbitrating decisions on payoffs

Salaries

Slot Shift Managers may have annual earnings ranging from $32,000 to $55,000 or more. Factors affecting earnings include the geographic location, size, and prestige of the specific casino, as well as the experience

and responsibilities of the individual. Generally, those with the most experience working in larger, more prestigious casinos in the gambling capitals earn the highest salaries.

Employment Prospects

Employment opportunities for Slot Shift Managers may be limited in larger casinos located in the gambling capitals of Las Vegas and Atlantic City. In these facilities, individuals may have to wait for someone to leave and openings to occur. There may be more opportunities in some of the newer gaming areas located throughout the country. Other opportunities will be found as gaming expands throughout the United States.

Slot Shift Managers may work various shifts, including daytime, evening or swing shift, overnight or graveyard shift. Individuals may also be expected to work weekends and holidays.

Advancement Prospects

Slot Shift Managers can advance their careers by obtaining more experience and locating similar positions in larger or more prestigious casinos. Individuals might also be promoted to the position of assistant slot manager.

Education and Training

Training requirements vary at different casinos in various locations. Certain casinos require Slot Shift Managers to either complete an approved program in slot machine repair in at least two machines or qualify to be licensed as a slot mechanic in at least two types of machines. Depending on the casino, some may not have these requirements and accept on-the-job training and experience.

Courses or programs in casino-related training offered by gaming schools, academies, and institutes, as well as community colleges and vo-tech schools throughout the country may be useful.

Special Requirements

Slot Shift Managers, like others working in the gaming area, must also meet specific state licensing requirements of the state gaming commission. Individuals may also be required to be licensed as a slot mechanic. Minimum age requirement may apply depending on the specific state.

Experience, Skills, and Personality Traits

Experience requirements, like training, vary. As noted previously, some casinos require that individuals complete an approved program in slot machine repair in at least two machines or be a licensed slot mechanic. Most positions require that Slot Shift Managers have at least two years or 2,500 to 3,000 hours of experience working in a casino slot department.

Slot Shift Managers should have both supervisory and administrative skills to be successful in this career. Marketing skills, analytical skills, and customer service skills are also essential.

Unions and Associations

Slot Shift Managers are not unionized. Individuals may be members of local gaming-related associations and organizations.

Additional information regarding this career can be obtained from gaming institutes, academies, and schools, as well as casino human resources departments.

Tips for Entry

1. Many casinos promote from within. Get your foot in the door and obtain as much as experience as possible in the slot department.
2. Stop by the human resources departments of casinos and inquire about job openings.
3. Some casinos as well as gaming schools, academies, institutes, community colleges, and vo-tech schools in gaming areas offer casino-related training programs. These may not be necessary, but are helpful in attaining a higher level of casino knowledge.
4. Jobs are often advertised in the classified sections of newspapers in areas hosting gaming. Look under classifications such as "Slot Shift Manager," "Slot Department," "Casinos," "Casino Jobs," "Casino Opportunities," or "Gaming."
5. New casinos under construction are a great place to look for employment. Visit their human resources departments as soon as they open and ask for an application.

SLOT FLOORPERSON

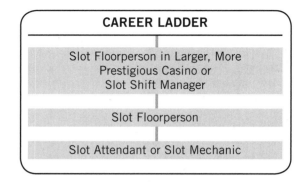

Position Description

The Slot Floorperson is responsible for overseeing the slot machines in a specified area of the casino. The individual has an array of responsibilities. The Slot Floorperson may also be called the slot supervisor.

The Slot Floorperson is responsible for supervising the activities of the slot attendants. The individual makes sure that they are doing their jobs when on the floor. The Floorperson makes certain that customers in the slot area who need help are being assisted.

The Slot Floorperson is responsible for protecting the slots in his or her area. The individual must keep an eye out for patrons attempting to cheat at the slots.

Another function of the Slot Floorperson is to handle all problems regarding the specific bank of slots assigned to him or her. The individual must look out for machines that are not working properly or those with coin jams, and then call a slot mechanic to take care of them immediately.

The Slot Floorperson is additionally responsible for helping slot customers who have won jackpots. The individual is in charge of either paying off a jackpot or verifying the jackpot has been paid by the change person.

Other duties of the Slot Floorperson may include:

- Assisting customers with casino credit
- Handling customer complaints and problems regarding slot personnel, machines, and disputes over payoffs

Salaries

Slot Floorpersons earn between $25,000 and $43,000 or more annually. Some casinos pay their Slot Floorpersons an hourly wage instead of a weekly salary. This may range from $12.00 to $20.00 per hour, but may run higher. Slot Floorpersons may also receive tips.

Factors affecting earnings include the geographic location, size, and prestige of the specific casino, as well as the experience and responsibilities of the individual. Generally, those with the most experience working in larger, more prestigious casinos in the gambling capitals earn the highest salaries.

Employment Prospects

Employment prospects are good for Slot Floorpersons. While individuals may find employment in any casino in the world, the greatest number of opportunities exist in areas where there are a large number of casinos.

Las Vegas, Reno, Laughlin, Lake Tahoe, Atlantic City, Biloxi, Baton Rouge, New Orleans, and Detroit offer the greatest number of job possibilities. Other employment settings include casino hotels in other areas of Nevada, Mississippi, New York, Louisiana, Colorado, Connecticut, Illinois, Arizona, and California.

Other regions hosting Indian gaming and land-based or riverboat gaming facilities offer additional opportunities. New casinos and casino hotels are constantly under construction. More casinos and casino hotels are also opening every year as areas legalize gambling.

Many casinos are open 24 hours a day. These operations run in shifts. Individuals may work the day shift, evening or swing shift, overnight or graveyard shift.

Shift hours may vary in different facilities. The day shift, for example, may run from 8 A.M. to 4 P.M.; the swing shift from 4 P.M. to midnight; and the overnight or graveyard shift from midnight to 8 A.M. Some facilities may have overlapping shifts or different hours.

Advancement Prospects

Slot Floorpersons, like most others working in casinos, have excellent opportunities to advance their careers by obtaining more experience and locating similar positions in larger or more prestigious casinos. They might also be promoted to the position of slot shift manager.

Education and Training

Training requirements for Slot Floorpersons vary at different casinos in various locations. Certain casinos require that Slot Floorpersons complete an approved program in slot machine repair. Some casinos do not have these requirements and accept on-the-job training and experience.

Courses or programs in casino-related training offered by gaming schools, academies, and institutes, as well as community colleges and vo-tech schools throughout the country may be useful.

Special Requirements

Slot Floorpersons, like others working in the gaming area, must also meet specific state licensing requirements of the state gaming commission. There are also generally minimum age requirements.

Experience, Skills, and Personality Traits

Experience requirements, like training requirements, vary for Slot Floorpersons. Most positions require or prefer that individuals have three to six months experience as either a slot attendant or slot mechanic.

Individuals in this position need supervisory and administrative skills. A knowledge of slot operations is mandatory. Customer service skills are also essential.

Unions and Associations

Slot Floorpersons in most casinos are not usually unionized. Individuals working on riverboats or cruises, however, may be members of various unions.

Slot Floorpersons may be members of local gaming-related trade associations and organizations.

Additional information regarding this career can be obtained from gaming institutes, academies, and schools, as well as casino human resources departments.

Tips for Entry

1. Most casinos have job hotlines. These are frequently updated messages listing jobs available. Call each casino directly to get its job hotline phone number.
2. Get your foot in the door in the slot department and obtain as much experience as possible. Most casinos promote from within.
3. Visit the human resources departments of casinos and inquire about job openings.
4. Jobs are often advertised in the classified sections of newspapers in areas hosting gaming. Look under classifications such as "Slot Floorperson," "Slot Department," "Casinos," "Casino Jobs," "Casino Opportunities," or "Gaming."
5. New casinos under construction are a great place to look for employment. Stop by their human resources departments as soon as you hear it is open and ask for an application.
6. Look for casino job and career fairs in areas hosting casinos. These offer good opportunities to find out about job openings.

SLOT REPAIR MANAGER

Duties: Overseeing and directing activities of slot mechanics; maintaining slot machines; converting machines; making recommendations for improvement of slots.

Alternate Title(s): Chief Slot Mechanic

Salary Range: $35,000 to $75,000+

Employment Prospects: Fair

Advancement Prospects: Fair

Best Geographical Location(s) for Position: Las Vegas, Reno, Laughlin, Lake Tahoe, Atlantic City, Biloxi, Baton Rouge, New Orleans, and Detroit offer most opportunities; other regions with land-based, riverboat, or Indian gaming facilities offer additional opportunities.

Prerequisites:

Education or Training—Attend approved training program for slot machine repair.

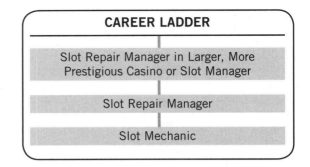

CAREER LADDER

Slot Repair Manager in Larger, More Prestigious Casino or Slot Manager

Slot Repair Manager

Slot Mechanic

Experience and Qualifications—Experience as slot mechanic or technician necessary.

Special Skills and Personality Traits—Supervisory skills; electronic skills; manual dexterity; detail-oriented.

Special Requirements—Licensing as slot mechanic; state licensing required to work in gaming area. Minimum age requirements.

Position Description

For many people who enjoy gambling, casinos mean slot machines. Casinos often have a great number of these electronic machines, which can be played with a nickel, quarter, dollar, and on up.

Slot machines, like all other electronic devices, sometimes break down. When machines are broken, they cannot be played and are not producing any revenue. Casinos, therefore, employ a staff of mechanics to keep the slots in working condition. The person in charge of overseeing the slot staff is called the Slot Repair Manager. Depending on the size of the casino and the number of slots, the Slot Repair Manager may supervise from eight to 20 employees or more. The individual may also be referred to as the chief slot mechanic.

The Slot Repair Manager has a number of duties in addition to supervising the slot staff. First and foremost, the individual is in charge of planning and directing activities within the slot department.

The Slot Repair Manager makes sure all machines within the casino are in working order. To do this, the individual makes sure regular maintenance is scheduled on all the machines.

Machines may not work properly for a number of reasons: programs may need readjusting; machines

may have been tilted; slots may require a fill; or parts may malfunction. The Slot Repair Manager must also be sure those in need of repair are fixed promptly.

Another important function of the Slot Repair Manager may be converting machines to different denominations. For example, the casino may want to convert machines from quarters to dollars or from nickels to quarters.

Other duties of the Slot Repair Manager may include:

- Modifying, testing, and correcting existing programs in machines to make sure they work properly
- Making recommendations for improvements in slot machines

Salaries

Slot Repair Managers earn between $35,000 and $75,000 or more annually. Factors affecting earnings include the geographic location, size, and prestige of the specific casino, as well as the experience and responsibilities of the individual.

Generally, those with the most experience working in larger, more prestigious casinos in the gambling capitals earn the highest salaries.

Employment Prospects

Employment prospects are fair for Slot Repair Managers. While many Indian gaming facilities do not host slots, almost every other casino has slot machines. Slot Repair Managers may find employment in any of these settings. Experienced and capable Slot Repair Managers are an asset to casinos.

While individuals may find employment in any casino in the world, the greatest number of opportunities exist in areas where there are a large number of casinos.

Las Vegas, Reno, Laughlin, Lake Tahoe, Atlantic City, Biloxi, Baton Rouge, New Orleans, and Detroit offer the greatest number of job possibilities. Other employment settings include casino hotels in other areas of Nevada, Mississippi, New York, Louisiana, Colorado, Connecticut, Illinois, Arizona, and California.

Other regions hosting Indian gaming and land-based or riverboat gaming facilities or cruise ships offer additional opportunities. New casinos and casino hotels are constantly under construction. More casinos and casino hotels are also opening every year as areas legalize gambling.

Advancement Prospects

Slot Repair Managers may find similar jobs in larger casinos, resulting in increased earnings. If openings exist and the Slot Repair Manager has enough experience, he or she might also move into the position of a slot manager.

Education and Training

Slot Repair Managers are usually required to complete an approved slot machine repair program. The program offers fundamentals of troubleshooting and repairing all models of electro-mechanical, electronic, and microprocessor-controlled slot machines. Additional courses may cover advanced troubleshooting in specific brands of microprocessor slot machines.

Experience, Skills, and Personality Traits

Individuals must usually have approximately three years of experience as a slot mechanic prior to obtaining positions as Slot Repair Managers.

Slot Repair Managers should have supervisory and administrative skills. Manual dexterity is also needed.

Special Requirements

Slot Repair Managers must usually be licensed as slot mechanics as well as meeting additional state licensing requirements necessary to work in the gaming area. Minimum age requirements generally apply.

Unions and Associations

Slot Repair Managers are not usually unionized. Individuals may belong to local gaming-related trade associations and organizations.

Those interested in learning more about careers in this area should contact gaming schools, academies, and community colleges offering training in slot machine repair, as well as human resources departments in casinos.

Tips for Entry

1. The more types of machines you are licensed in repairing, the more marketable you will be.
2. Continue taking classes in slot repair, advanced troubleshooting, and specific brands of slot machines.
3. Visit the human resources departments of casinos and inquire about job openings.
4. Jobs are often advertised in the classified sections of newspapers in areas hosting gaming. Look under classifications such as "Slot Repair Manager," "Chief Slot Mechanic," "Casinos," "Casino Jobs," "Casino Opportunities," or "Gaming."
5. Most casinos now have Web sites. Openings are often listed on their employment page.
6. New casinos under construction are a great place to look for employment. Stop at their human resources departments and ask for an application.

SLOT MECHANIC

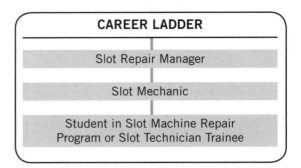

Position Description

Casinos are often full of slot machines of various denominations. Some can be played for a nickel, others for a quarter or a dollar, or even higher. Every slot is a possible generator of income for the casino. In order for slots to generate monies, they must be kept in proper working condition.

Slot machines, like all other electronic devices, sometimes break or malfunction. When this occurs, they cannot be played and do not produce any revenue. Casinos employ a staff of mechanics to keep the slots in working condition. The individuals responsible for handling the physical repair of the machines are called Slot Mechanics. They may also be referred to as slot repair mechanics or slot technicians. Depending on the size of the casino and the number of slots housed, there may be from eight to 20 mechanics or more employed by the casino.

The Slot Mechanic has a number of duties. The individual works under the supervision of the slot repair manager. The Slot Mechanic performs regular maintenance on slots in the casino and casino hotel area. Preventive maintenance keeps machines working longer with less extensive repair.

Slot Mechanics must also fix slots that are not working properly. Machines may not work correctly for a number of reasons: programs may need readjusting; machines might have been tilted; slots may require a fill; or parts may malfunction. The Slot Mechanic is responsible for fixing those machines that need repair promptly. This will often be done under the direction of the slot repair manager.

The Slot Mechanic may assist the slot repair manager in converting machines to different denominations. Casinos may find, for example, they want more quarter machines instead of nickel slots.

Other duties of the Slot Mechanic may include

- Resetting machines after jackpots
- Performing initial setup and checking out of new slot machines
- Responding to slot machines to resolve guest complaints about problems

Salaries

Slot Mechanics earn between $12.00 and $26.00 or more per hour or approximately $25,000 to $54,000 annually. Factors affecting earnings include the geographic location, size, and prestige of the specific casino, as well as the level of experience and responsibilities of the individual.

Generally, those with the most experience working in larger, more prestigious casinos in the gambling capitals earn the highest salaries.

Employment Prospects

A good Slot Mechanic is an asset to casinos. Opportunities are plentiful for skilled people. While individuals may find employment in any casino in the world, the greatest number of opportunities exist in areas where there are a large number of casinos.

Las Vegas, Reno, Laughlin, Lake Tahoe, Atlantic City, Biloxi, Baton Rouge, New Orleans, and Detroit offer the greatest number of job possibilities. Other employment settings include casino hotels in other areas of Nevada, Mississippi, New York, Louisiana, Colorado, Connecticut, Illinois, Arizona, and California.

Other regions hosting Indian gaming and land-based or riverboat gaming facilities or cruise ships offer additional opportunities. New casinos and casino hotels are constantly under construction. More casinos and casino hotels are also opening every year as areas legalize gambling.

Because many casinos are open 24 hours a day and machines must be fixed promptly, individuals may work various shifts. These include the day shift, evening or swing shift, overnight or graveyard shift.

Shift hours may vary in different facilities. The day shift, for example, may run from 8 A.M. to 4 P.M.; the swing shift from 4 P.M. to midnight; and the overnight or graveyard shift from midnight to 8 A.M. Some facilities may have overlapping shifts or different hours.

Advancement Prospects

Slot Mechanics can advance their careers by obtaining experience and locating similar positions in larger or more prestigious casinos. As casinos like to promote from within, with experience, Slot Mechanics also can advance to become slot repair managers.

Education and Training

Slot Mechanics must attend slot technicians school, a program in which individuals learn to repair and maintain slot machines. The program offers fundamentals of troubleshooting and repairing all models of electro-mechanical, electronic, and microprocessor-controlled slot machines. Additional courses may cover advanced troubleshooting in specific brands of microprocessor slot machines.

Special Requirements

Individuals must be licensed as Slot Mechanics as well as having state licensing for working in a gaming area. Minimum age requirements apply.

Experience, Skills, and Personality Traits

Depending on the specific job, individuals may start out as slot technician trainees. They may then move up to become full-fledged Slot Mechanics.

Slot Mechanics have manual dexterity and an understanding of electronics.

Unions and Associations

Slot Mechanics in most casinos are not usually unionized. Individuals working on riverboats or cruises, however, may be members of various unions.

Slot mechanics may be members of local gaming-related trade associations and organizations.

Those interested in learning more about careers in this area should contact gaming schools, academies, and community colleges offering training in slot machine repair, as well as the human resources departments in casinos.

Tips for Entry

1. Visit the human resources departments of casinos and inquire about job openings.
2. Become more marketable by obtaining training and licensing in a range of types of machines.
3. Continue taking classes in slot repair, advanced troubleshooting, and specific brands of slot machines.
4. Jobs are often advertised in the classified sections of newspapers in areas hosting gaming. Look under classifications such as "Slot Technician," "Slot Mechanic," "Casinos," "Casino Jobs," "Casino Opportunities," or "Gaming."
5. Positions may also be advertised on individual casino Web sites under employment opportunities.
6. New casinos under construction are a great place to look for employment. Stop at their human resources departments and ask for an application.
7. Most casinos have job hotlines. These are frequently updated messages listing job availabilities. You can call each casino directly to get its job hotline phone number.

SLOT BOOTH CASHIER

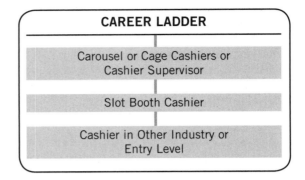

CAREER LADDER

Carousel or Cage Cashiers or Cashier Supervisor

Slot Booth Cashier

Cashier in Other Industry or Entry Level

Position Description

The Slot Booth Cashier has a number of responsibilities. The individual sits in a booth in the casino and is in charge of handling and accounting for coins and cash in a number of different areas.

When customers come to the booth, the Slot Booth Cashier sells them wrapped coins. For example, a customer may want to exchange a ten dollar bill for quarters, and the Slot Booth Cashier will give the patron one roll or 40 quarters.

Many casinos use coupons that offer a certain amount of money in coins as an incentive to attract customers. The casinos may mail these coupons, give them out to groups coming off buses, or use them as part of newspaper ads. The Slot Booth Cashier takes the coupons, validates them, then redeems them for the correct amount of coins.

When customers are done gambling, they bring their buckets or cups of coins that they have won or have left over to the Slot Booth Cashier, who then drops them into a counting machine and gives the customer the correct amount of bills in return. The counting machines deposit the money in bags that must be sealed, marked, and accounted for.

Other duties of the Slot Booth Cashier may include:

- Redeeming chips or tokens that customers have won or have left over when they are done gambling
- Dealing with people who work on the casino floor making change

Salaries

Slot Booth Cashiers, who may earn $15,000 to $31,000 or more annually, are usually hourly employees. Hourly wages can run from $7.50 to $15.00 or more depending on the specific casino the individual is working in and the geographic location. In some cases, Slot Booth Cashiers also receive tips when people have won.

Employment Prospects

Employment prospects are excellent for Slot Booth Cashiers. Every casino needs Slot Booth Cashiers, and most employ a number of people in this position.

While individuals may find employment in any casino in the world, the greatest number of opportunities exist in areas where there are a large number of casinos.

Las Vegas, Reno, Laughlin, Lake Tahoe, Atlantic City, Biloxi, Baton Rouge, New Orleans, and Detroit offer the greatest number of job possibilities. Other employment settings include casino hotels in other areas of Nevada,

Mississippi, New York, Louisiana, Colorado, Connecticut, Illinois, Arizona, and California.

Other regions hosting Indian gaming and land-based or riverboat gaming facilities or cruise ships offer additional opportunities. New casinos and casino hotels are constantly under construction. More casinos and casino hotels are also opening every year as areas legalize gambling.

Casinos that are open 24 hours a day run in shifts. Individuals may work the day shift, evening or swing shift, overnight or graveyard shift.

Shift hours may vary in different facilities. The day shift, for example, may run from 8 A.M. to 4 P.M.; the swing shift from 4 P.M. to midnight; and the overnight or graveyard shift from midnight to 8 A.M. Some facilities may have overlapping shifts or different hours.

Advancement Prospects

Slot Booth Cashiers, like most other employees working in casinos, have an excellent chance to advance their careers. Individuals can climb the career ladder by becoming carousel or cage cashiers. Others advance their careers by landing jobs as supervisors. This may require additional training and/or experience.

Education and Training

As in many jobs in casinos, the Slot Booth Cashier can receive on-the-job training or may attend any of the gaming schools, academies, or institutes located throughout the country. These may be private or may be part of community colleges, four-year colleges, or universities. Many casinos also have their own training programs or offer on-the-job training.

Often individuals who have received formal training from a gaming school, academy, or institute have an edge over their counterparts trained on the job.

Special Requirements

Slot Booth Cashiers must generally be licensed in the state in which they work. Most states have a minimum age requirement.

Experience, Skills, and Personality Traits

Because the Slot Booth Cashier deals with the public, the individual must have good interpersonal skills. Customer service skills are necessary. Other skills needed for this job include the ability to handle and count money quickly and accurately.

Unions and Associations

Slot Booth Cashiers in most casinos are not usually unionized. Individuals working on riverboats or cruises, however, may be members of various unions.

Additional information regarding this career can be obtained from gaming institutes, academies, and schools, as well as casino human resources departments.

Tips for Entry

1. Stop by the human resources departments of casinos to see if they have any job openings in this area.
2. These jobs are often listed on casino job hotlines. These hotlines are frequently updated messages listing jobs available.
3. Positions may be advertised in newspaper classified sections in areas hosting gaming. Look under heading classifications such as "Gaming," "Casinos," or "Slot Booth Cashier."
4. If you are not in an area hosting gaming, consider getting a short-term subscription to the newspaper in the area of your choice. Sunday editions of many newspapers are also often available in larger bookstores.
5. Gaming is growing quickly throughout the country. You can often get an application for a gaming facility being built long before it is finished.

CHANGE PERSON

Duties: Exchanging bills for coins; calling into dispatch for jackpots or broken machines.

Alternate Title(s): Change Girl; Change Man

Salary Range: $15,000 to $20,000 plus tips

Employment Prospects: Good

Advancement Prospects: Good

Best Geographical Location(s) for Position: Las Vegas, Reno, Laughlin, Lake Tahoe, Atlantic City, Biloxi, Baton Rouge, New Orleans, and Detroit offer most opportunities; other regions with land-based, riverboat, or Indian gaming facilities offer additional opportunities.

Prerequisites:

Education or Training—High school diploma or equivalent; on-the-job training; see text.

Experience and Qualifications—Experience handling money may be helpful, but not always required.

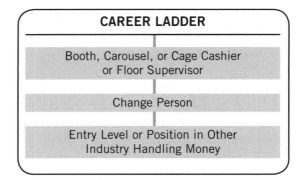

CAREER LADDER

Booth, Carousel, or Cage Cashier or Floor Supervisor

Change Person

Entry Level or Position in Other Industry Handling Money

Special Skills and Personality Traits—Money-handling skills; math skills; customer relations; interpersonal skills; pleasant; physical stamina.

Special Requirements—State licensing required to work in gaming area.

Position Description

For many people visiting casinos, slot machines are one of the most appealing ways to gamble. Casinos employ slot booth cashiers who sell wrapped coins in booths throughout the slot area. However, customers on a roll often do not want to leave their slot machines and go back to the booth to change bills for coins. In order to accommodate these customers, casinos hire Change Persons. Their main function is to give wrapped coins to patrons in exchange for bills.

The Change Person receives a bankroll of coins and bills. Depending on the casino, the bankroll may be worth from $200 to $2,000. Change Persons must sign a slip for the value of the bankroll they receive. They are totally responsible for this money. Individuals may store part of the bankroll in a drawer for which only they have a key.

The rest of the bankroll is placed either in a cart that the Change Person pushes or in an apron the individual wears as he or she walks around the slot area. When customers need coins, they motion to the Change Person, and the individual comes over and gives the patron the needed coins.

When customers hit small to medium jackpots, the Change Person may be called to issue the payoff. The individual signs and verifies that the customer is paid. In other situations, the individual signs and verifies that he or she observed a booth cashier issue the jackpot money to the customer. Usually two signatures are required. Larger jackpots are paid by slot supervisors or other casino executives.

In some settings, before the Change Person pays a winner, he or she slips blank jackpot sheets directly into the slot machine when a patron hits the jackpot. This is then stamped by the machine. In this manner the Change Person has a receipt stamped with needed information. The specialist must keep this receipt as proof the winner was paid.

The size of the bankroll the Change Person receives when signing in does not fluctuate throughout his or her shift because every transaction is always equally balanced in money or receipts. At the end of each individual's shift, the Change Person is expected to count down the bankroll with a shift manager or supervisor.

Other duties of the Change Person may include:

- Calling supervisors or dispatchers for jackpots
- Calling dispatchers to report malfunctioning machines
- Signing and verifying fill slips

Salaries

Change People earn between $7.00 and $9.50 per hour; sometimes more. Individuals also receive tips, also known as tokes, from winning patrons whom they service. Factors affecting earnings include the geographic location, size, and prestige of the specific casino, as well as the experience of the individual.

Employment Prospects

Employment opportunities for Change People are good. Individuals may find openings in most casinos. Because casinos are often open 24 hours a day, individuals may work various shifts, including days, swing shift or evening, overnight or graveyard. Change People may work on weekends and holidays as well.

While individuals may find employment in any casino in the world, the greatest number of opportunities exist in areas where there are a large number of casinos.

Las Vegas, Reno, Laughlin, Lake Tahoe, Atlantic City, Biloxi, Baton Rouge, New Orleans, and Detroit offer the greatest number of job possibilities. Other employment settings include casino hotels in other areas of Nevada, Mississippi, New York, Louisiana, Colorado, Connecticut, Illinois, Arizona, and California.

Other regions hosting Indian gaming and land-based or riverboat gaming facilities or cruise ships offer additional opportunities. New casinos and casino hotels are constantly under construction. More casinos and casino hotels are also opening every year as areas legalize gambling.

Advancement Prospects

Change People may advance in a number of ways depending on career aspirations. Some individuals move to jobs as booth, carousel, or cage cashiers. Others advance their careers by landing jobs as supervisors. Some Change People find employment in other areas of the slot operation. This may require additional training and/or experience.

Education and Training

Most casinos prefer their Change People to hold a high school diploma or the equivalent, although work experience may be accepted in lieu of education.

Training may be obtained on the job or in casino-related training programs offered at gaming academies, institutes, or schools or vocational technical schools and community colleges in areas hosting gaming. Many casinos often also have in-house training programs for employees.

Special Requirements

Change People working in casinos must be licensed by the state gaming commission in the specific state in which they work.

Experience, Skills, and Personality Traits

Positions may or may not require prior experience handling money. Change People should enjoy working around people and have customer service skills. Money handling and math skills are also needed.

Unions and Associations

Individuals interested in learning more about careers in this area should contact gaming schools, academies, and community colleges offering casino-related training programs, as well as the human resources departments in casinos.

Tips for Entry

1. Any experience handling money such as being a cashier will be useful. Remember to mention this information when seeking a job.
2. Visit the human resources departments of casinos and inquire about job openings.
3. Jobs are often advertised in the classified sections of newspapers in areas hosting gaming. Look under classifications such as "Change Person," "Change Specialist," "Slot Change Person," "Casinos," "Casino Jobs," "Casino Opportunities," or "Gaming."
4. Positions may also be advertised on the Internet. Look under key words in employment sections of the Internet and World Wide Web such as "Casinos," "Casino Jobs," "Gaming," "Slot Change Person," "Change Person," or "Change Specialist."
5. New casinos under construction are a great place to look for employment. Stop by their human resources departments and ask for an application.
6. Most casinos have job hotlines listing jobs available. You can call each casino directly to get its job hotline phone number.

KENO SUPERVISOR

CAREER PROFILE

Duties: Supervising Keno operation; verifying winners; training staff.

Alternate Title(s): None

Salary Range: $25,000 to $40,000+

Employment Prospects: Fair

Advancement Prospects: Good

Best Geographical Location(s) for Position: Las Vegas, Reno, Laughlin, Lake Tahoe, Atlantic City, Biloxi, Baton Rouge, New Orleans, and Detroit offer most opportunities; other regions with land-based, riverboat, or Indian gaming facilities offer additional opportunities.

Prerequisites:

Education or Training—On-the-job training or Keno training at gaming school, academy, institute, or casino.

Experience and Qualifications—One to three years experience as Keno writer.

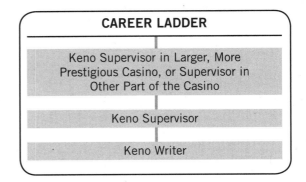

CAREER LADDER

Keno Supervisor in Larger, More Prestigious Casino, or Supervisor in Other Part of the Casino

Keno Supervisor

Keno Writer

Special Skills and Personality Traits—Supervisory skills; interpersonal skills; customer service skills; math skills.

Special Requirements—State licensing required to work in gaming area. Minimum age requirements generally apply.

Position Description

Keno is played with 80 numbered Ping-Pong balls. The balls are mixed with circulated air in a large plastic bowl. Using air pressure, 20 balls are randomly forced up through tubes called gooses. Selected balls are referred to as the draw.

Keno is a fast-moving game. Participants buy Keno game tickets in which they select between one and 15 numbered spots. Certain games may allow players to choose up to 20 spots. Players win by having the numbered balls that are selected match the number they have chosen. The payout is related to the number of spots selected, the number of balls matching the spots, and the price of the ticket. The numbers that match the player's card are called catch spots. Once the balls are selected, the game is over and a new one begins.

Keno Supervisors are expected to oversee the Keno operation. They have a number of responsibilities. When people bring their winning tickets to Keno writers, the writers must calculate the payoff. The Supervisor is responsible for checking the ticket to make sure it is valid and to verify the amount of the payoff.

Keno Supervisors are also responsible for the training of the Keno staff. Some staff members including runners and writers may have completed Keno train-

ing at gaming schools, institutes, or academies. Others may need on-the-job training. No matter where or how people were trained, the Supervisor trains the staff in the manner in which the specific casino runs its Keno operation.

A Keno Supervisor is also responsible for overseeing and supervising the Keno staff. If there are any problems with employees in this area, it is up to the Keno Supervisor to handle them appropriately.

Keno Supervisors sit at the Keno counter desk. They may also work on the floor. Supervisors collect the inside tickets from each of the Keno writers' bins. When doing this, individuals must check the floor and counters to be sure they have every inside ticket that was written. Tickets must be moved to the Keno counter desk after a game is closed and before numbers are drawn.

Other duties of the Keno Supervisor may include:

- Dealing with any customer problems or complaints
- Lighting the "closed" sign to indicate a game is closed and tickets will no longer be accepted for the current game
- Examining microfilm camera results to prevent fraud

Salaries

A Keno Supervisor can earn between $25,000 and $40,000 or more annually. Factors affecting earnings include the geographic location, size, and prestige of the specific casino, as well as the experience and responsibilities of the individual.

Employment Prospects

Employment prospects are fair for Keno Supervisors. Opportunities may be found in casinos hosting Keno. Because casinos are often open 24 hours a day, individuals may be expected to work the daytime, swing or evening, graveyard or overnight shift. Supervisors are also expected to work weekends and/or holidays.

While individuals may find employment in any casino in the world, the greatest number of opportunities exist in areas where there are a large number of casinos.

Las Vegas, Reno, Laughlin, Lake Tahoe, Atlantic City, Biloxi, Baton Rouge, New Orleans, and Detroit offer the greatest number of job possibilities. Other employment settings include casino hotels in other areas of Nevada, Mississippi, New York, Louisiana, Colorado, Connecticut, Illinois, Arizona, and California.

Other regions hosting Indian gaming and land-based or riverboat gaming facilities or cruise ships offer additional opportunities. New casinos and casino hotels are constantly under construction. More casinos and casino hotels are also opening every year as areas legalize gambling.

Advancement Prospects

Keno Supervisors may advance their careers by obtaining experience and/or additional training. Some may locate similar positions in larger or more prestigious casinos, resulting in increased earnings. Others move into other positions in the casino gaming area.

Education and Training

Most casinos require or prefer individuals to hold a minimum of a high school diploma or the equivalent. Work experience may be accepted in lieu of education. Some Keno Supervisors receive on-the-job training in Keno prior to becoming supervisors and move up the career ladder. Others have Keno training at gaming schools, academies, or institutes, as well as at community colleges, or vocational technical schools in areas hosting gaming, and in casinos themselves.

Special Requirements

Keno Supervisors, like all others working in a gaming area, must usually be licensed in the state in which they work. There are also minimum age requirements in most states.

Experience, Skills, and Personality Traits

Experience is required for this position. One to three years working in Keno is necessary to become a Keno Supervisor. Most Keno Supervisors have been Keno writers and were promoted.

Individuals should be personable people who enjoy being around others. Supervisory and training skills are necessary for this position. Excellent customer service skills are essential. Math skills are also needed.

Unions and Associations

There are no bargaining unions for Keno Supervisors. Individuals interested in learning more about careers in this area can contact gaming institutes, academies, and schools, as well as casino human resources departments.

Tips for Entry

1. Jobs are often advertised in the classified sections of newspapers in areas hosting gaming. Look under classifications such as "Casinos," "Casino Jobs," "Casino Opportunities," "Keno," "Keno Supervisors," "Casino Supervisory Opportunities," or "Gaming."
2. The human resources department of a casino is the place to visit to inquire about job openings. Stop by and fill out an application.
3. Look for new casinos under construction. There are a multitude of positions to fill.
4. Positions may be advertised on the Internet. Look under key words in employment sections of the Internet and World Wide Web such as "Casinos," "Casino Jobs," "Gaming," "Keno," or "Keno Supervisors."

KENO WRITER

Duties: Writing Keno tickets; collecting bets; making payoffs.

Alternate Title(s): Writer

Salary Range: $15,000 to $21,000 plus tips

Employment Prospects: Good

Advancement Prospects: Fair

Best Geographical Location(s) for Position: Las Vegas, Reno, Laughlin, Lake Tahoe, Atlantic City, Biloxi, Baton Rouge, New Orleans, and Detroit offer most opportunities; other regions with land-based, riverboat, or Indian gaming facilities offer additional opportunities.

Prerequisites:

Education or Training—On-the-job training or Keno training at gaming school, academy, institute, or casino.

Experience and Qualifications—Experience requirements vary.

CAREER LADDER

```
Keno Writer in Larger, More Prestigious
Casino, or Keno Supervisor

Keno Writer

Entry Level or Keno Runner
```

Special Skills and Personality Traits—Data entry skills; interpersonal skills; customer service skills; money-handling skills; math skills.

Special Requirements—State licensing required to work in gaming area. Minimum age requirements.

Position Description

Keno is a casino game played with 80 numbered Ping-Pong balls that are mixed with air in a plastic or glass bowl. Twenty balls are forced up with air at random through tubes, much like procedures in bingo or state lotteries. The selected balls are known as the draw.

Participants buy Keno game tickets. On each ticket players select between one and 15 numbered spots. In some games players choose as many as 20 numbered spots. These will relate to the numbered balls they think will come up for the game. The payout is correlated to the number of spots selected, the number of balls that match the spots, and the price of the ticket. The numbers that match the player's card are called catch spots.

Keno Writers work at a Keno counter. They take the customer tickets, which are referred to as the inside tickets, mark them and make a copy. This is called writing Keno tickets. The copy called the outside ticket is given back to the player. Keno runners often deliver tickets from within the casino to Keno Writers to handle. Another responsibility of the Keno Writer is to collect bets from players. Depending on the ticket, players may place straight bets or combination tickets.

Keno Writers exchange winning tickets for the payoff. They calculate the payoff, stamp winning tickets

"paid," and write the amount of the payoff on the outside of the ticket.

Salaries

The Keno Writer earns an hourly wage ranging between $7.00 and $10.00 per hour plus tips. Tips may also be referred to as tokes. Players who win often tip the writer, pushing the hourly wage in some cases to $25 or more.

Employment Prospects

Employment prospects are good for Keno Writers. Opportunities may be found in all casinos hosting Keno. The greatest number of opportunities exist in areas where there are a large number of casinos.

Las Vegas, Reno, Laughlin, Lake Tahoe, Atlantic City, Biloxi, Baton Rouge, New Orleans, and Detroit offer the greatest number of job possibilities. Other employment settings include casino hotels in other areas of Nevada, Mississippi, New York, Louisiana, Colorado, Connecticut, Illinois, Arizona, and California.

Other regions hosting Indian gaming and land-based or riverboat gaming facilities or cruise ships offer additional opportunities. New casinos and casino hotels are constantly under construction. More casinos and casino hotels are also opening every year as areas legalize gambling.

Advancement Prospects

Keno Writers can advance their careers by obtaining experience and/or additional training. Some may locate similar positions in larger or more prestigious casinos, resulting in increased earnings and tips. Others may become Keno supervisors.

Education and Training

Most casinos require or prefer individuals to hold a minimum of a high school diploma or the equivalent. Work experience may be accepted in lieu of education. Some Keno Writers receive on-the-job training. Others take Keno training at gaming schools, academies, or institutes, as well as at community colleges, or vocational technical schools in areas hosting gaming, and in casinos themselves.

Special Requirements

Keno Writers, like all others working in a gaming area, must usually be licensed in the state in which they work. There are also minimum age requirements.

Experience, Skills, and Personality Traits

Individuals should be personable people who enjoy being around others. Excellent customer service skills are essential. Data entry skills, the ability to handle money, and math skills are also necessary.

Experience requirements vary. In some situations, individuals move up from positions as Keno runners, while in others, this is an entry-level position.

Unions and Associations

Individuals interested in learning more about careers in this area can contact gaming institutes, academies, and schools, as well as casino human resources departments.

Tips for Entry

1. Jobs are often advertised in the classified sections of newspapers in areas hosting gaming. Look under classifications such as "Casinos," "Casino Jobs," "Casino Opportunities," "Keno Writers," or "Gaming."
2. Stop by the human resources departments of casinos to inquire about job openings.
3. These jobs are often listed on casino job hotlines. These are frequently updated messages listing jobs available. You may call each casino directly to get its job hotline phone number.
4. Look for new casinos under construction. Apply early.
5. Positions may be advertised on the Internet. Look under key words in employment sections of the Internet and World Wide Web such as "Casinos," "Casino Jobs," "Gaming," "Keno," or "Keno Writers." Opportunities may also be found on specific casino Web sites.
6. Look for casino job fairs in areas hosting casinos.

KENO RUNNER

Duties: Getting money for Keno tickets from customers; collecting tickets; bringing tickets back to customers; getting payoffs for winning tickets.

Alternate Title(s): None

Salary Range: $15,000 to $19,000 plus tips

Employment Prospects: Good

Advancement Prospects: Fair

Best Geographical Location(s) for Position: Las Vegas, Reno, Laughlin, Lake Tahoe, Atlantic City, Biloxi, Baton Rouge, New Orleans, and Detroit offer most opportunities; other regions with land-based, riverboat, or Indian gaming facilities offer additional opportunities.

Prerequisites:

Education or Training—On-the-job training or Keno training at gaming school, academy, institute, or casino.

Experience and Qualifications—Experience requirements vary.

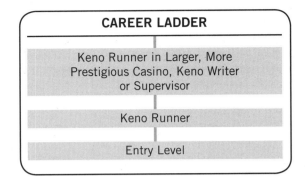

CAREER LADDER

Keno Runner in Larger, More Prestigious Casino, Keno Writer or Supervisor

Keno Runner

Entry Level

Special Skills and Personality Traits—Interpersonal skills; customer service skills; money-handling skills; physical stamina.

Special Requirements—State licensing required to work in casinos. Minimum age requirements.

Position Description

Keno is a casino game that resembles state lotteries. Eighty numbered Ping-Pong balls are used in a Keno game. Twenty balls are chosen at random for each game. Balls are mixed by air and then forced up through tubes. Keno drawings are shown on electronic displays shown throughout the casino.

Players select between one and 15 or 20 spots on a Keno game ticket. The payout is related to the number of spots selected, the number of balls that match the spots, and the price of the ticket.

Casinos have Keno lounges. Players do not have to be in the Keno lounge to play or win this game. They must, however, turn in winning tickets before the next game is called or their prize will be forfeited.

Keno Runners service customers throughout the casino-and casino hotel facilities. They do not usually-handle customers within the casino lounge. Keno Runners increase the casino's Keno business by finding customers who are busy in other areas of the casino and then selling these people tickets. Players might be gambling at other games, sipping drinks at the bar, or eating in a restaurant.

Keno Runners have a number of responsibilities. Individuals get the money from customers to purchase Keno tickets. They must also collect the tickets from these players.

Keno Runners deliver the tickets to Keno writers. After the tickets are written, the runners return the outside tickets to the customers who purchased them. Players can then watch the game with their tickets.

Other duties of the Keno Runner may include:

- Collecting payoffs for winning customers
- Returning invalid bets to players

Salaries

The Keno Runner earns an hourly wage ranging between $7.00 and $9.00 plus tips. Tips may also be referred to as tokes. Players who win often tip the runner, pushing their hourly wage in some cases to $25 or more.

Employment Prospects

Employment prospects are good for Keno Runners. Opportunities may be found in casinos hosting Keno. Because casinos are often open 24 hours a day, individuals may work during daytime, swing shift or evening, graveyard shift or overnight. Individuals may also be expected to work weekends or holidays.

The greatest number of opportunities exist in areas where there are a large number of casinos. Las Vegas, Reno, Laughlin, Lake Tahoe, Atlantic City, Biloxi, Baton Rouge, New Orleans, and Detroit offer the greatest number of job possibilities. Other employment settings include casino hotels in other areas of Nevada, Mississippi, New York, Louisiana, Colorado, Connecticut, Illinois, Arizona, and California.

Other regions hosting Indian gaming and land-based or riverboat gaming facilities offer additional opportunities. New casinos and casino hotels are constantly under construction. More casinos and casino hotels are also opening every year as areas legalize gambling.

Advancement Prospects

Keno Runners can advance their careers by obtaining experience and/or additional training. Some may locate similar positions in larger or more prestigious casinos, resulting in increased earnings and tips. Others may become Keno writers or supervisors.

Education and Training

Most casinos require or prefer individuals to hold a minimum of a high school diploma or the equivalent. Work experience may be accepted in lieu of education. Some Keno Runners receive on-the-job training. Others take Keno training at gaming schools, academies, or institutes, as well as at community colleges or vocational technical schools in areas hosting gaming, and in casinos themselves.

Special Requirements

Keno Runners, like all others working in a gaming area, must usually be licensed in the state in which they work. There are also minimum age requirements.

Experience, Skills, and Personality Traits

Individuals should be personable people who enjoy being around others. Customer service skills are essential. Physical stamina is necessary. The ability to handle money is also needed.

Unions and Associations

Keno Runners are not usually unionized. Individuals interested in learning more about careers in this area can contact gaming institutes, academies, and schools, as well as casino human resources departments.

Tips for Entry

1. Stop by the human resources departments of casinos to inquire about job openings.
2. Look for new casinos under construction. Apply early.
3. Positions may be advertised on the Internet. Look under key words in employment sections of the Internet and World Wide Web such as "Casinos," "Casino Jobs," "Gaming," or "Keno Runners."
4. Call casino job hotlines. Most casinos have them. These are frequently updated messages listing jobs available. You can call each casino directly to get its job hotline phone number.
5. Jobs are often advertised in the classified sections of newspapers in areas hosting gaming. Look under classifications such as "Casinos," "Casino Jobs," "Casino Opportunities," "Keno Runners," or "Gaming."
6. Look for casino job fairs in areas hosting casinos.

POKER ROOM MANAGER

Duties: Developing and instituting policies of poker room; overseeing operation of poker room; supervising floor supervisors and shift supervisors.

Alternate Title(s): None

Salary Range: $30,000 to $55,000+

Employment Prospects: Good

Advancement Prospects: Good

Best Geographical Location(s) for Position: Las Vegas, Reno, Laughlin, Lake Tahoe, Atlantic City, Biloxi, Baton Rouge, New Orleans, and Detroit offer most opportunities; other regions with land-based, riverboat, or Indian gaming facilities offer additional opportunities.

Prerequisites:

Education or Training—Training at gaming academy, school, or institute.

Experience and Qualifications—Four to seven years experience working in poker rooms.

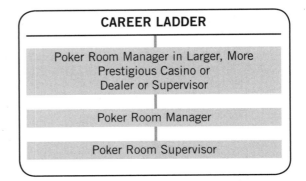

CAREER LADDER

Poker Room Manager in Larger, More Prestigious Casino or Dealer or Supervisor

Poker Room Manager

Poker Room Supervisor

Special Skills and Personality Traits—Supervisory skills; administrative skills; interpersonal skills; customer service skills; alert; knowledge of rules and procedures of card games.

Special Requirements—State licensing required to work in gaming area; additional licensing may be necessary; minimum age requirements.

Position Description

Most casinos have a separate room set off from the rest of the casino specifically for poker. The person in charge of overseeing the operation of the poker room is called the Poker Room Manager. There are a number of others employed in the poker room; these may include floor supervisors, dealers, and brushpersons.

A number of different types of poker are played in casinos. These include seven-card stud, pai gow poker, Caribbean stud, seven-card low, low-ball, Texas hold'em, Omaha hold'em, and high-low split. The Poker Room Manager must know the rules and regulations of each game in order to properly oversee the room.

The Poker Room Manager is in charge of developing and instituting policies in the poker room. The individual often works with other casino executives on this task.

The Poker Room Manager helps make the poker room profitable. In the game of poker, customers wager against each other instead of against the house. The casino makes money in the poker room by charging players for running the games. This may be done in a number of ways. One method takes a commission from each pot, commonly referred to as taking a rake of the chips. Another method the casino uses to make money

in poker rooms is by charging a specific amount of money for each player as a time charge. This method is usually used in high-limit or no-limit games. The Poker Room Manager may develop programs to assure the room will be full of games and players. In this manner, the profitability of the room can be increased.

The Poker Room Manager is responsible for overseeing the employees of the poker room. On a day-to-day basis, the individual provides administrative supervision over the floor supervisor, who in turn oversees the rest of the employees.

Other duties of the Poker Room Manager may include:

- Overseeing floor supervisors
- Handling customer problems and disputes
- Ensuring rules and regulations are followed

Salaries

Poker Room Managers are usually part of the executive staff and therefore receive a weekly salary instead of an hourly wage. Individuals may earn between $30,000 and $55,000 or more annually depending on a number of factors. These include the geographic location, size, and prestige of the specific casino, size of the room, and the experience and responsibilities of the individual.

Employment Prospects

Employment prospects for qualified individuals are good. Poker Room Managers may find positions throughout the country in areas hosting card rooms, land-based casinos, dockside or floating riverboat casinos, and Indian gaming facilities.

Advancement Prospects

Poker Room Managers may obtain more experience and find similar positions in larger or more prestigious facilities. This will result in increased responsibilities and earnings. As with other jobs in casinos, advancement depends to a great extent on the area in which the individual wishes to work. Poker Room Managers with training and experience in other areas of gaming may find other executive-type positions.

Education and Training

A Poker Room Manager must have complete knowledge of the procedures of the poker games. The individual should also have an understanding and knowledge of the casino rules and regulations.

The best training can be obtained at an accredited gaming school, academy, or institute. Community colleges, vocational technical schools, and casinos themselves may also offer training in this area.

Special Requirements

Poker Room Managers, like all others working in a gaming area, must usually be licensed in the state in which they work. There may also be specific licensing and age requirements.

Experience, Skills, and Personality Traits

Experience requirements for Poker Room Managers can range from four to seven years, depending on the specific casino. Usually, larger, more prestigious casinos prefer more experience.

Individuals should have supervisory and administrative skills. They should be personable people who enjoy being around others. Interpersonal and customer service skills are mandatory.

Unions and Associations

Poker Room Managers are not unionized. Those interested in learning more about careers as Poker Room Managers should contact gaming institutes, academies, and schools, as well as casino human resources departments.

Tips for Entry

1. Jobs may be advertised in the classified sections of newspapers in areas hosting gaming. Look under classifications such as "Casinos/Gaming," "Poker Room Manager," "Poker Room," or "Casino Opportunities."
2. Visit the human resources departments of casinos and inquire about job openings.
3. Check out specific casino Web sites to see what employment opportunities casinos offer.

POKER BRUSHPERSON

Duties: Calling out available poker games to customers; posting game information; explaining rules to customers.

Alternate Title(s): Brushman

Salary Range: $15,000 to $25,000 plus tips.

Employment Prospects: Good

Advancement Prospects: Fair

Best Geographical Location(s) for Position: Las Vegas, Reno, Laughlin, Lake Tahoe, Atlantic City, Biloxi, Baton Rouge, New Orleans, and Detroit offer most opportunities; other regions with land-based, riverboat, or Indian gaming facilities offer additional opportunities.

Prerequisites:

Education or Training—Training at gaming academy, school, or institute.

Experience and Qualifications—Experience requirements vary from casino to casino.

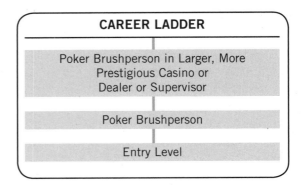

Special Skills and Personality Traits—Interpersonal skills; customer service skills; alert; knowledge of rules of poker game.

Special Requirements—State licensing required to work in gaming area; additional licensing may be necessary.

Position Description

Poker is a card game. There are a number of different types of poker played in casinos. One of the most popular is called seven-card stud. Other popular games include seven-card low, low-ball, Texas hold'em, Omaha hold'em, and high-low split.

Poker is the only game in the casino in which customers wager against each other instead of against the house. The casino charges customers for running the games. This may be done by taking a commission from each pot, sometimes referred to as taking a rake of the chips. Sometimes, with high-limit or no-limit games, the casino charges a specific amount of money to each player for a time charge.

Most casinos have a separate room set off from the rest of the casino specifically for poker. A number of different employees in the poker room may include the poker room manager, floor supervisor, dealers, and Brushpersons.

The Brushperson has a number of responsibilities. The individual keeps poker seats filled. In order to accomplish this, the Brushperson waits for potential customers to walk by the poker room and then calls out the games that are available. This often may occur,

for example, after the showroom breaks. The Poker Brushperson may also post poker game information for guests so that they know about games.

The individual is responsible for explaining the rules of the various games to customers. This is important so that new players will understand the games.

The Poker Brushperson will seat customers, and this is often done at the direction of the floor supervisor, who may direct customers to games. In some settings, the Poker Brushperson may handle the exchange of chips and money. In other situations, this function may be done by another employee.

Other duties of the Poker Brushperson may include:

- Ordering drinks for players
- Handling customer problems and disputes

Salaries

Poker Brushpersons may earn between $7.50 and $12.00 or more per hour plus tips. Factors affecting earnings include the geographic location, size, and prestige of the specific casino, as well as the experience and responsibilities of the individual.

Employment Prospects

Employment prospects for Poker Brushpersons are good. Opportunities are abundant in Las Vegas, Reno, Atlantic City, Biloxi, Baton Rouge, and New Orleans. Other regions with land-based or riverboat gaming and Indian gaming facilities offer additional job prospects.

Because casinos often are open 24 hours a day, individuals may work any shift. Employees in these positions often are scheduled to work on weekends and holidays.

Advancement Prospects

Individuals may climb the career ladder in a number of ways. Some obtain experience and find similar positions in larger or more prestigious facilities. Others may move up to other positions in the card room, such as dealers or floor supervisors. With the proper training, individuals may work in other areas of the casino as well.

Education and Training

The Poker Brushperson must have a complete knowledge of the procedures of the poker games. The individual should also have an understanding and knowledge of the casino rules and regulations.

The best training can be found at an accredited gaming school, academy, or institute. Community colleges, vocational technical schools, and casinos themselves may also offer training in this area.

Special Requirements

Poker Brushpersons, like all others working in a gaming area, must usually be licensed in the state in which they work. There may also be additional licensing and age requirements.

Experience, Skills, and Personality Traits

Experience requirements for Poker Brushpersons vary depending on the casino. More prestigious casinos may prefer more experience.

Individuals should be personable people who enjoy being around others. Interpersonal and customer service skills are essential.

Unions and Associations

Those interested in learning more about careers as Poker Brushpersons should contact gaming institutes, academies, and schools, as well as casino human resources departments.

Tips for Entry

1. Call casino job hotlines. Most casinos have these and update them regularly with current job openings. You can call each casino directly to get its job hotline phone number.
2. Get your foot in the door of a casino. Most promote from within. Obtain experience and move up the career ladder.
3. Jobs may be advertised in the classified sections of newspapers in areas hosting gaming. Look under classifications such as "Casinos/Gaming," "Poker Brushperson," "Poker Room Employees," or "Casino Opportunities."
4. Stop by the human resources departments of casinos and inquire about job openings.
5. Look for new casinos under construction. Apply early.
6. Check out casino job fairs. These offer an opportunity to interview and be hired quickly.

BINGO MANAGER

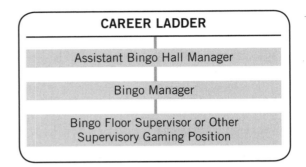
Position Description

Bingo, a game used for fund-raising purposes throughout the country in many not-for-profit institutions such as churches, synagogues, and schools, is also featured in many casinos. The game attracts a variety of people who enjoy games that can be played for a minimum amount and for an extended period of time.

Players buy one or more bingo cards to participate in a game. Each card has five rows of five squares each. One letter, either B, I, N, G, or O is printed above each vertical column. Each square has a number with the exception of the center square. The center square is known as a free square or free play.

Casinos hosting bingo usually have large rooms known as bingo parlors. The bingo operation employs a number of staff people. These include bingo floor workers, floor supervisors, paymasters, callers, and package preparers. The individual who is in charge of overseeing the bingo operation is called the Bingo Manager. He or she also has an assistant to help with the duties of the job.

The Bingo Manager supervises the bingo staff. He or she is responsible for overseeing training of employees within the department. The individual may pass this duty on to the assistant bingo manager.

The Bingo Manager is expected to develop and formulate policies and procedures used within the bingo area. The individual further develops programs that will help maximize the profits of the bingo operation within the casino.

Other duties of the Bingo Manager may include:

- Handling customer problems or complaints
- Attending department head meetings
- Recommending promotions within the bingo operation
- Implementing programs and policies within department

Salaries

The Bingo Manager's salary can range from approximately $30,000 to $40,000 annually. Factors affecting earnings include the geographic location, size, and prestige of the specific casino, as well as the experience and responsibilities of the individual.

Employment Prospects

Employment prospects are fair for Bingo Managers. Individuals may find employment at casinos hosting bingo. It should be noted, however, that every casino does not have this game. Individuals may find employment in settings such as casinos, dockside and floating riverboat casinos, and Indian gaming facilities.

Advancement Prospects

Bingo Managers may advance their careers by obtaining experience. They may then locate similar positions in other more prestigious casinos, resulting in increased earnings.

Education and Training

Most casinos require or prefer individuals to hold a minimum of a high school diploma or the equivalent. Work experience may be accepted in lieu of education. Bingo Managers are usually trained within the casino. Much of the training is picked up as individuals move up the career ladder in the bingo area. Most have worked as floor workers, floor supervisors, and assistant bingo managers.

Special Requirements

Bingo Managers must be licensed by the gaming commission in the state in which they work.

Experience, Skills, and Personality Traits

Experience is required for Bingo Managers. Depending on the casino, individuals may need four to six years of experience working in gaming. Some of that experience needs to be working in the bingo area. One to two years supervisory experience is also required.

Individuals must have a total understanding and knowledge of the rules, regulations, and procedures of the casino and those of bingo operations.

Unions and Associations

Bingo Managers are not represented by a union. Additional information regarding this career can be obtained from casino human resources departments.

Tips For Entry

1. Jobs are often advertised in the classified sections of newspapers in areas hosting gaming. Look under classifications such as "Casinos," "Casino Jobs," "Casino Opportunities," "Bingo Manager," "Bingo Operations," or "Gaming."
2. Casinos often promote from within when openings exist. Keep up with what is happening in the bingo operations area.
3. Visit the human resources departments of casinos to find out about job openings.
4. Look for new casinos under construction. Stop at their human resources departments and ask for an application. Apply early.
5. Positions may be advertised on the Internet. Look under key words in employment sections of the Internet and World Wide Web such as "Casinos," "Casino Jobs," "Gaming," or "Bingo Managers."

BINGO FLOOR SUPERVISOR

Duties: Oversee bingo activities on floor; supervise games; handle customer problems.

Alternate Title(s): Supervisor

Salary Range: $23,000 to $33,000+

Employment Prospects: Fair

Advancement Prospects: Fair

Best Geographical Location(s) for Position: Indian gaming facilities and bingo halls throughout the country offer most opportunities; regions with land-based or riverboat gaming facilities offer additional opportunities.

Prerequisites:

Education or Training—On-the-job training.

Experience and Qualifications—Experience working in bingo operation necessary.

CAREER LADDER

Assistant Bingo Hall Manager

Bingo Floor Supervisor

Bingo Caller, Assistant Floor Supervisor

Special Skills and Personality Traits—Supervisory skills; interpersonal skills; knowledge of bingo game rules and regulations.

Special Requirements—State licensing required.

Position Description

Casinos with bingo parlors have a number of employees to run the operation. These include bingo managers, assistant bingo managers, floor workers, paymasters, bingo callers, package preparers, and Floor Supervisors.

The Bingo Floor Supervisor oversees everything that occurs on the bingo floor. This includes supervising floor workers as well as the bingo paymaster. The individual may assign floor workers to various parts of the bingo room. The Floor Supervisor also makes sure the floor workers are doing their job and assisting players when needed. The individual must be sure the floor workers go to players who have winning cards when they shout "Bingo."

Another duty of the Bingo Floor Supervisor is to make sure the bingo paymaster goes to winning players and pays them the correct amounts.

The Bingo Floor Supervisor works under the direction of the assistant bingo manager. The individual assists in carrying out programs that help maximize the profits of the casino. Within the scope of the job, the individual is in charge of supervising the games. The Floor Supervisor makes sure all gaming rules and regulations are complied with on the bingo floor.

Other duties of the Bingo Floor Supervisor may include:

- Handling customer problems or complaints
- Scheduling workers

Salaries

Bingo Floor Supervisors earn between $23,000 and $33,000 or more annually. Factors affecting earnings include the geographic location, size, and prestige of the specific casino, as well as the experience and responsibilities of the individual.

Employment Prospects

Employment prospects for Bingo Floor Supervisors are fair. Individuals may find employment opportunities at casinos with bingo games. Depending on when casinos hold bingo sessions, individuals may work shifts, including daytime, swing shift or evening, graveyard or overnight. Bingo Floor Supervisors may also have to work weekends and holidays.

Advancement Prospects

With experience, Bingo Floor Supervisors may advance their careers through promotion to the job of assistant bingo manager.

Education and Training

Generally, casinos require or prefer individuals to hold a minimum of a high school diploma or the equivalent. Work experience may be accepted in lieu of education.

Bingo Floor Supervisors usually receive on-the-job training within the casino. A great deal of the training needed is picked up in prior jobs in bingo operations.

Special Requirements

Bingo Floor Supervisors must be licensed by the gaming commission in the state in which they work.

Experience, Skills, and Personality Traits

Experience working in bingo operations is necessary to become a Bingo Floor Supervisor. Depending on the specific casino, this may range from one to three years. Supervisory experience in some capacity is also usually required. Individuals must have total understanding and knowledge of the rules, regulations, and procedures of bingo operations.

Unions and Associations

Bingo Floor Supervisors are not generally unionized. Additional information regarding this career can be obtained from gaming schools, as well as from casino human resources departments.

Tips For Entry

1. Visit the human resources departments of casinos to find out about job openings.
2. Many casinos promote from within. If you are working in the bingo area as a floor worker, keep up with developments in your department.
3. Jobs are often advertised in the classified sections of newspapers in areas hosting gaming. Look under classifications such as "Casinos," "Casino Jobs," "Casino Opportunities," "Bingo Floor Supervisor," "Bingo Operations," or "Gaming."
4. Positions may also be advertised on the Internet and World Wide Web. Look under key words in employment sections of the Internet such as "Casinos," "Casino Jobs," "Gaming," or "Bingo Floor Supervisors."
5. Look for new casinos under construction. Stop at their human resources departments and ask for an application.
6. These positions may be listed on casino job hotlines. These are frequently updated messages listing jobs available. You can call each casino directly to get its job hotline phone number.

BINGO PAYMASTER

Duties: Paying bingo prizes to winners; recording winnings.
Alternate Title(s): Paymaster
Salary Range: $18,000 to $25,000
Employment Prospects: Fair
Advancement Prospects: Fair
Best Geographical Location(s) for Position: Indian gaming facilities and bingo halls throughout the country offer most opportunities; regions with land-based or riverboat gaming facilities offer additional opportunities.
Prerequisites
　Education and Training—On-the-job training.
　Experience/Qualifications—Cashier experience helpful.

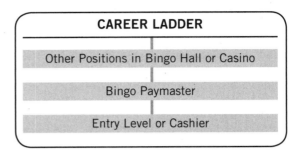

CAREER LADDER

Other Positions in Bingo Hall or Casino

Bingo Paymaster

Entry Level or Cashier

Special Skills and Personality Traits—Money-handling skills; cashier skills; math skills; knowledge of bingo game rules and regulations.
Special Requirements—State licensing required.

Position Description

The game of bingo is popular in many casinos due to its simplicity of play and the fact that every game has at least one winner. As bingo callers announce more and more numbers and the game progresses, excitement builds. For the players at least, the most exciting part of a bingo game is hearing the last number needed for winning.

When a player covers all the required numbers on his or her card and shouts "Bingo," a floor worker reads the numbers on the card and verifies it is a winner. Once the card is declared a winner, the floor person indicates the individual to a staff member called the Bingo Paymaster.

The Bingo Paymaster is responsible for paying the lucky winner. If there is more than one winner, the Bingo Paymaster must determine what the prize will be for each person.

The Paymaster pays each winner the correct amount of money. The individual is responsible for recording each bingo prize paid out.

Other duties of the Bingo Paymaster may include:

- Accounting for cash and winnings at the end of each shift
- Congratulating winners
- Providing customer service for guests

Salaries

Bingo Paymasters earn between $8.50 and $12.00 or more per hour or about $18,000 to $25,000 annually. They may also receive tips. Factors affecting earnings include the geographic location, size, and prestige of the specific casino, as well as the experience of the individual.

Employment Prospects

Employment prospects are fair for Bingo Paymasters. Individuals may find employment opportunities at casinos hosting bingo games. Depending on when casinos hold bingo sessions, individuals may work daytime, swing or evening, graveyard or overnight shifts. Bingo Paymasters may be expected to work weekends and holidays.

Advancement Prospects

Depending on career aspirations, Bingo Paymasters can obtain experience and move into other areas of the bingo operation or other areas of the casino for advancement opportunities.

Education and Training

Generally, casinos require or prefer individuals to hold a minimum of a high school diploma or the equivalent. Work experience may be accepted in lieu of education.

Bingo Paymasters usually receive on-the-job training within the casino.

Special Requirements

Individuals must generally be licensed by the gaming commission in the state in which they work.

Experience, Skills, and Personality Traits

Depending on the specific position, casinos may require from six months to one year of cashier experience.

Individuals must have math and money-handling skills. The ability to record prizes in an accurate fashion is also necessary. Knowledge of the rules, regulations, and procedures of bingo operations is needed.

Unions and Associations

Bingo Paymasters are not represented by a union. Additional information regarding this career can be obtained from gaming schools as well as from casino human resources departments.

Tips for Entry

1. Stop by the human resources departments of casinos and inquire about job openings.

2. Jobs are often advertised in the classified sections of newspapers in areas hosting gaming. Look under classifications such as "Casinos," "Casino Jobs," "Casino Opportunities," "Bingo Paymaster," "Bingo Operations," or "Gaming."

3. Positions may also be advertised on the Internet. Look under key words in employment sections of the Internet and World Wide Web such as "Casinos," "Casino Jobs," "Gaming," or "Bingo Paymasters."

4. New casinos under construction are a great place to look for employment. Stop at their human resources departments and ask for an application.

5. Experience working as a cashier is often necessary. This experience can be obtained anywhere in or out of the casino.

6. Most casinos have job hotlines. These are frequently updated messages listing job available. You can call each casino directly to get its job hotline phone number.

BINGO CALLER

CAREER PROFILE

Duties: Calling letter and number of bingo balls during bingo games; verifying winners.

Alternate Title(s): Caller

Salary Range: $15,000 to $21,000+

Employment Prospects: Fair

Advancement Prospects: Fair

Best Geographical Location(s) for Position: Indian gaming facilities and bingo halls throughout the country offer most opportunities; regions with land-based or riverboat gaming facilities offer additional opportunities.

Prerequisites:

Education or Training—On-the-job training.

Experience and Qualifications—No experience necessary.

CAREER LADDER

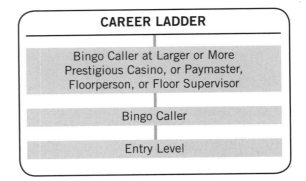

Bingo Caller at Larger or More Prestigious Casino, or Paymaster, Floorperson, or Floor Supervisor

Bingo Caller

Entry Level

Special Skills and Personality Traits—Clear speaking voice; ability to speak in public; manual dexterity; personable.

Special Requirements—State licensing required.

Position Description

Many casinos offer bingo as an attractive gambling game. Bingo does not have difficult rules to follow, and there is always at least one if not more winners in every game. In order to induce players, many casinos offer large super jackpots or special bingo promotions.

Players buy one or more bingo cards to participate in a game. Depending on the casino and game, these may be made of cardboard, paper, or plastic. Each card has five rows of five squares each. One letter, either B, I, N, G, or O is printed above each vertical column. Each square has a number with the exception of the center square, which is known as a free square or free play.

There are a number of ways to win in bingo, depending on the game. Players might play a game in which five numbers in a straight vertical, horizontal, or diagonal line must be covered. Other games require players to cover four numbers at the four corners of their bingo card, to cover eight numbers surrounding the center square, or to cover all the numbers on the card.

Bingo uses 75 Ping-Pong balls, each imprinted with a number from one to 75 and lettered with one of the letters B, I, N, G, or O. The balls are placed in a bingo bowl, cage, or bingo blower. Some casinos have a special colored ball in the mix, which can be used as a wild ball when a number is needed to win. Randomly, one by one, balls are chosen or forced out by air into a pocket or the neck of a tube.

The Bingo Caller is responsible for taking the ball that has been selected and showing it to the audience. The individual must then announce the number and letter of the ball. The Bingo Caller places each announced ball onto a board that corresponds to the number and letter that have been called. The Bingo Caller continues selecting and announcing ball numbers and letters until someone shouts "Bingo," indicating a winner. Electronic numbered boards are often used that light up when a number is selected so that the playing audience can clearly see the numbers that have been picked.

A Bingo Caller is responsible for verifying the winning ticket. This is done by a floorperson going to the winning player and reading out loud the numbers that have been covered. The Bingo Caller checks the numbers that are read against the numbers that have been selected. He or she may also verify the ticket number. The Bingo Caller announces a winner and the payoff.

The Bingo Caller may be responsible for operating the bingo equipment. He or she may turn the machine on and off. In some games there may be two Callers. One turns on the machine and hands the ball that comes out to the second Bingo Caller. In other games one Bingo Caller handles both functions.

Other duties of the Bingo Caller may include:

- Releasing balls back into machine after end of game
- Announcing type of game, rules, and payoffs before game begins.

Salaries

A Bingo Caller is paid an hourly wage ranging from $7.00 to $10.00 or about $15,000 to $21,000, or possibly more, annually. Factors affecting earnings include the geographic location, size, and prestige of the specific casino, as well as the experience of the individual.

Employment Prospects

Employment prospects for Bingo Callers are fair. Opportunities may be located in casinos hosting bingo parlors. Because casinos are often open 24 hours a day, individuals may be asked to work during various shifts including daytime, evening or swing shift, graveyard or overnight. Individuals may also work weekends or holidays.

Advancement Prospects

Bingo Callers may advance their careers by obtaining experience and/or additional training. They may then locate similar positions in larger or more prestigious casinos, resulting in increased earnings. Depending on training, experience, and qualifications, individuals may move into other positions in this area such as bingo paymasters, floorpersons, or floor supervisors.

Education and Training

Most casinos require or prefer individuals to hold a minimum of a high school diploma or the equivalent. Work experience may be accepted in lieu of education. On-the-job training is usually offered at casinos.

Special Requirements

Bingo Callers, like others working in a gaming area, must be licensed in the state in which they work. There are also minimum age requirements in most states.

Experience, Skills, and Personality Traits

In most positions, no prior experience is necessary for this job. An individual should have a clear speaking voice, and the ability to speak into a microphone and talk in front of an audience is necessary.

Unions and Associations

Bingo Callers are not represented by a union. Additional information regarding this career can be obtained from gaming schools as well as from casino human resources departments.

Tips For Entry

1. While experience isn't usually required, it never hurts and might give you an edge over another applicant. You might want to obtain experience volunteering at church, synagogue, or school bingo games as a Bingo Caller.
2. Jobs are often advertised in the classified sections of newspapers in areas hosting gaming. Look under classifications such as "Casinos," "Casino Jobs," "Casino Opportunities," "Bingo Callers," or "Gaming."
3. Visit the human resources departments of casinos to inquire about job openings.
4. Read newspapers from areas where gaming is legal. Look for articles on new casinos under construction. Apply early.

BINGO FLOOR WORKER

Duties: Listening for shouts of "Bingo"; selling bingo cards to players; reading numbers to bingo caller to verify winning card; assisting and servicing bingo players.

Alternate Title(s): Floorperson

Salary Range: $15,000 to $18,000 plus tips

Employment Prospects: Fair

Advancement Prospects: Fair

Best Geographical Location(s) for Position: Indian gaming facilities and bingo halls throughout the country offer most opportunities; regions with land-based or riverboat gaming facilities offer additional opportunities.

Prerequisites:

Education or Training—On-the-job training.

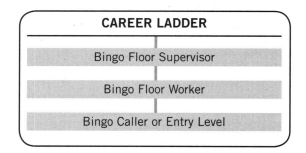

CAREER LADDER

Bingo Floor Supervisor

Bingo Floor Worker

Bingo Caller or Entry Level

Experience and Qualifications—No experience necessary.

Special Skills and Personality Traits—Interpersonal skills; customer service skills; physical stamina.

Special Requirements—State licensing required. Minimum age requirements.

Position Description

Bingo is offered in many casinos. The game often attracts players who enjoy gambling with a relatively minimum amount of money for a long period of time. The game has simple rules, is easy to play, and guarantees one or more winners every time. Bingo in casinos is played like bingo games in not-for-profit facilities throughout the country such as churches, synagogues, and schools.

Players buy one or more bingo cards to participate in a game. Each card has five rows of five squares each. One letter, either B, I, N, G, or O. is printed above each vertical column. Each square has a number with the exception of the center square, which is known as a free square or free play.

Bingo parlors are often large rooms. Bingo Floor Workers are assigned a section of the room and are responsible for assisting players in their area.

Bingo Floor Workers may also be called bingo floor attendants, bingo attendants, or bingo floorpeople in different casinos. Responsibilities vary depending on the specific casino. A Bingo Floor Worker explains to participants the various games and how they are played.

Bingo games may be won in various ways. It might be a game in which five numbers in a straight vertical, horizontal, or diagonal line must be covered. Other games might require players to cover four numbers at the four corners of their bingo card, to cover eight numbers surrounding the center square, or to cover all the numbers on the card. Players may, for example, need an explanation of what a small round robin looks like.

As the bingo caller announces numbers and the game progresses, players cover the designated spots on their cards. The Bingo Floor Workers walk around their designated area, listening for a player to call out "Bingo!" When that occurs, the Floor Worker takes the card from the player, reads the numbers that have been covered aloud to the bingo caller, and verifies the card as a winner. The individual may also verify the ticket or card number. Once a card is declared a winner, the floorperson indicates the individual to the bingo paymaster, who pays the lucky person.

Bingo Floor Workers in some casinos may be responsible for selling additional bingo cards, packages, and specials to players in their areas. In other casinos, other workers handle this function.

Other duties of the Bingo Floor Worker may include:

- Seating players
- Assisting and servicing players throughout games

Salaries

The Bingo Floor Worker is paid an hourly wage ranging from $7.50 to $8.50. Individuals may also receive tips.

Factors affecting earnings include the geographic location, size, and prestige of the specific casino.

Employment Prospects

Employment prospects for Bingo Floor Workers are fair. Individuals may work at any casino hosting bingo parlors. It should be noted, however, that all casinos do not have bingo. A number of Bingo Floor Workers are needed for each game. Bingo Floor Workers work various shifts, depending on when the casino schedules games. These may include daytime, swing shift or evening, graveyard or overnight. Individuals may also work weekends or holidays.

Advancement Prospects

Bingo Floor Workers may advance their careers by obtaining experience and/or additional training. Some may move into other positions in the bingo area such as bingo floor supervisors. Others may locate positions in other areas of the casino.

Education and Training

Most casinos require or prefer individuals to hold a minimum of a high school diploma or the equivalent. Work experience may be accepted in lieu of education. On-the-job training is usually offered for this type of position at casinos hosting bingo parlors.

Experience, Skills, and Personality Traits

In most positions, no prior experience is necessary for this job. Individuals should be personable, friendly people. Interpersonal skills and customer service skills are mandatory. Physical stamina and the ability to stand for periods of time are necessary.

Special Requirements

Bingo Floor Workers must be licensed by the gaming commission in the state in which they work. Most states also have minimum age requirements.

Unions and Associations

Bingo Floor Workers are not represented by a union. Additional information regarding this career can be obtained from casino human resources departments.

Tips For Entry

1. As noted previously, experience is not usually necessary, but it can't hurt. Experience working on the bingo floor at a church, synagogue, or school should be noted when applying for jobs.
2. Jobs are often advertised in the classified sections of newspapers in areas hosting gaming. Look under classifications such as "Casinos," "Casino Jobs," "Casino Opportunities," "Bingo Floor Workers," "Bingo Floor People," or "Gaming."
3. Visit the human resources departments of casinos to find out about job openings. You might want to check newspapers first to see which casinos in the area offer bingo.
4. Look for new casinos under construction. Stop at their human resources departments and ask for an application. Apply early.

CASINO AND CASINO HOTEL MARKETING, PUBLIC RELATIONS, AND SALES

DIRECTOR OF CASINO MARKETING

Position Description

Those interested in visiting casinos have numerous choices depending on the location, size, and atmosphere they are seeking. In order to increase their market share, therefore increasing profitability, casinos develop programs to market their facilities.

The Director of Casino Marketing is in charge of the development and implementation of the casino's marketing plan. The individual often works under the direction of the vice president of marketing for the entire facility.

The Director of Casino Marketing develops different promotions designed to attract business, brings in new customers, and brings back those who have previously visited the facility. The individual often works in conjunction with staff people in the public relations, publicity, advertising, and sales departments to attain the goals.

As part of the job, the Director of Casino Marketing must not only conceptualize and plan innovative programs, promotions, and special events, but implement them as well. These might include a variety of promotions as well as tournaments, bus tour programs, and junkets. The individual is responsible for taking these projects from inception to fruition. It is essential that these marketing efforts build customer loyalty and increase the existing player base.

The Director of Casino Marketing is responsible for developing the concepts and campaigns that detail how the casino lets potential customers know about the facility and its programs. He or she decides how much and what type of advertising, promotion, public relations, and selling will be most effective.

The individual also determines the most effective techniques to market the casino and its services. The Director will often determine the viability of introducing new promotions, games, clubs, or markets to the casino. In some cases, after attempting to market a new promotion, the Director of Casino Marketing may find the idea is not financially viable. In these cases the Director scraps the particular program in favor of another.

The Director of Casino Marketing may direct marketing efforts toward various segments of the population — those who visit casinos on bus tours or junkets, and those who play the slots or other popular games at the casino.

The Director of Casino Marketing often works on marketing programs involving special events and functions for customers, bringing new players into the casino and keeping prior guests coming back.

Other duties of the Director of Casino Marketing include:

- Overseeing the casino marketing staff
- Handling player development
- Developing direct mail marketing
- Coordinating database marketing efforts
- Performing research for marketing efforts and results

Salaries

Directors of Casino Marketing earn between $65,000 and $160,000 or even more annually. Factors affecting earnings include the geographic location, size, and prestige of the specific casino, as well as the track record, experience, education, and responsibilities of the individual. Generally, those with a proven track record working in larger, more prestigious casinos in the gambling capitals earn the highest salaries.

Employment Prospects

Employment prospects for the Director of Casino Marketing are limited because each casino has only one person in this position. Because casinos promote from within, jobs can be secured by talented and creative individuals who move up the career ladder.

The largest number of opportunities can be found in Las Vegas, Reno, Laughlin, Atlantic City, Biloxi, Baton Rouge, New Orleans, Detroit, and Black Hawk. Other regions with land-based or riverboat gaming facilities offer additional opportunities. As other areas begin to host gaming, more positions will become available.

Advancement Prospects

The Director of Casino Marketing may climb the career ladder by promotion to vice president of marketing. However, a more common method of advancement is finding a similar position in a larger or more prestigious facility. This results in increased responsibilities and earnings.

Education and Training

Most casinos and casino hotels prefer their Director of Casino Marketing to hold a bachelor's degree in marketing, public relations, communications, business management, or a related field.

Courses, workshops, and seminars in marketing, sales, and the gaming and hospitality industries are also useful.

Special Requirements

The Director of Casino Marketing will generally be required to hold state licensing.

Experience, Skills, and Personality Traits

Casinos expect their Director of Casino Marketing to have a proven track record and marketing credentials in the casino gaming and hospitality industry.

The Director of Casino Marketing needs a wide array of skills. The individual must be a self-starter. He or she should also be creative, with the ability to develop innovative ideas for marketing casinos. Excellent writing and communication skills are essential. Marketing, public relations, and sales skills are necessary in this position. Strategic-planning skills are also needed.

A complete knowledge and understanding of the gaming and hospitality industries are mandatory.

Unions and Associations

Those interested in learning more about careers as the Director of Casino Marketing can obtain additional information by contacting the Hotel Sales and Marketing Association International (HSMA), the Public Relations Society of America (PRSA), or the human resources departments in casino hotels.

Tips for Entry

1. Some employment agencies and recruitment firms deal specifically in the field of marketing, as well as in the hospitality industry.
2. Get your foot in the door of a casino hotel. Most promote from within. Start out in the marketing or sales department, obtain experience, and climb the career ladder.
3. Jobs may be advertised in the classified sections of newspapers in areas hosting gaming. Look under classifications such as "Casino/Gaming Opportunities," "Director of Casino Marketing," "Casino Marketing Director," "Marketing," or Casino Opportunities."
4. Read trade journals and the business news in areas hosting gaming. Look for articles on people who have been promoted. This often means job openings.

CASINO MARKETING COORDINATOR

Duties: Sending out mailings; answering phones; making phone calls; inputting information into computers; assisting in handling details for special events, parties, and functions; assisting in coordinating details for junkets and bus programs.

Alternate Title(s): Marketing Assistant

Salary Range: $17,000 to $33,000

Employment Prospects: Good

Advancement Prospects: Good

Best Geographical Location(s) for Position: Las Vegas, Reno, Laughlin, Lake Tahoe, Atlantic City, Biloxi, Baton Rouge, New Orleans, and Detroit offer the greatest number of job possibilities. Other employment settings include casino hotels in other areas of Nevada, Mississippi, New York, Louisiana, Colorado, Connecticut, Illinois, Arizona and California.

Other regions hosting Indian gaming and land-based or riverboat gaming facilities offer additional opportunities.

Prerequisites:

Education or Training—High school diploma or equivalent; on-the-job training.

Experience and Qualifications—Experience in gaming, hospitality, or marketing helpful, but not required.

Special Skills and Personality Traits—Customer service skills; computer literate; telephone skills; communications skills; detail-oriented.

Special Requirements—State licensing may be required.

Position Description

Casinos put a great deal of emphasis on their marketing programs to increase their market share and profitability. The casino director of marketing is expected to develop programs to market the facility effectively. The marketing program often consists of a great many promotions, special events, player parties, and tournaments. Marketing efforts also include bus programs, junkets, and player development promotions.

Casino Marketing Coordinators assist in handling many of the details of these events and programs. For example, Casino Marketing Coordinators help set up the parties and other functions held for high rollers, slot tournaments, or V.I.P. guests.

Individuals work under the direction of marketing managers, supervisors, and administrators. Marketing Coordinators are required to handle a great deal of the clerical work associated with this department. For example, they may be responsible for collating direct mail brochures and letter responses directed toward

prior or potential customers. Individuals must also prepare direct mail pieces for distribution.

Marketing Coordinators are responsible for inputting a variety of data into computers for use in the marketing office. This may include names, addresses, and phone numbers of customers who call, visit, or fill in forms from advertisements.

Marketing Coordinators may be required to input and tabulate data regarding specific programs and promotions the marketing department has held. This information will then be used to analyze and track those that have been effective or ineffective.

The Casino Marketing Coordinator handles the phones in the marketing office. The individual answers questions from callers regarding upcoming promotions and special events in the casino. The Coordinator additionally is responsible for sending callers information and mailings on specific promotions upon request. The Coordinator might also be required to make calls to customers to see if they are attending functions or to tell them about upcoming events in the facility.

Other duties of the Casino Marketing Coordinator include:

- Tabulating questionnaires and other research
- Inputting data regarding player tracking
- Assisting in player tracking
- Sending invitations to customers for events, promotions, parties, and other functions

Salaries

Casino Marketing Coordinators earn an hourly wage ranging from $8.00 to $16.00. Wages may run higher; factors affecting earnings include the geographic location, size, and prestige of the specific casino, as well as the experience and responsibilities of the individual.

Employment Prospects

Every casino, no matter how small, has Casino Marketing Coordinators. Casino marketing is extremely important to all casinos, so employment opportunities are good for Casino Marketing Coordinators. The greatest number of jobs are located in the gambling capitals and other areas hosting larger casinos, including cities such as Las Vegas, Reno, Laughlin, Lake Tahoe, Atlantic City, Biloxi, Baton Rouge, New Orleans, and Detroit. Other areas with land-based or riverboat gaming facilities offer additional job possibilities. As legalized gaming expands throughout the United States, opportunities in other locations will become available.

Advancement Prospects

Casinos like to promote from within. This is a great position to start with if you are interested in casino marketing. Casino Marketing Coordinators may climb the career ladder by promotion to casino marketing supervisors or marketing office administrators. With additional education and experience, individuals may move into other positions in the casino marketing area.

Education and Training

Casino Marketing Coordinators are often trained on the job. Most casinos and casino hotels prefer their Marketing Coordinators to hold a minimum of a high school diploma or its equivalent. Many casinos help individuals who do not have the minimum education obtain a GED. Work experience may be accepted in lieu of education.

Special Requirements

Individuals in this position generally are required to be licensed by the specific state in which they work.

Experience, Skills, and Personality Traits

In most casinos, this is an entry-level job. Any experience in marketing, gaming, or the hospitality industry will be helpful.

There is a great deal of customer service needed in this job. Marketing coordinators should be detail-oriented individuals. Excellent telephone and communication skills are necessary. Office skills such as data entry and typing are also mandatory. Individuals should also have computer skills.

Unions and Associations

Additional information regarding this career can be obtained from gaming institutes, academies, and schools, as well as casino and casino human resources departments.

Tips for Entry

1. This is a good position to get your foot in the door of casino marketing. Learn what you can, get some experience, and move up the career ladder.
2. Jobs are often advertised on casino job hotlines. These are recorded messages put out by casinos announcing current job openings as well as required skills. Call individual casinos to get their job hotline phone numbers.
3. Openings may be also advertised in the classified sections of newspapers in areas hosting gaming. Look under classifications such as "Casino/Gaming Opportunities," "Casino Marketing," "Casino Marketing Coordinator," "Marketing," or "Casino Opportunities."
4. Stop by casino human resources departments and inquire about job openings.
5. Look for casino job fairs in areas hosting casinos.

PLAYER'S CLUB REPRESENTATIVE

Duties: Handles enrollment into casino's player's club program; assists guest with questions or information that they need regarding player's club or casino; helps provide club members with service to ensure guest satisfaction.

Alternate Title(s): Player's Club Rep; Loyalty Club Representative

Salary Range: $20,000 to $34,000+

Employment Prospects: Good

Advancement Prospects: Good

Best Geographical Location(s) for Position: Positions located in areas hosting gaming; Las Vegas, Reno, Laughlin, Lake Tahoe, Atlantic City, Biloxi, Baton Rouge, New Orleans, Detroit, and Black Hawk offer most opportunities; other regions with land-based riverboat or Indian gaming facilities offer additional opportunities.

Prerequisites:

Education or Training—Minimum of a high school diploma or equivalent.

CAREER LADDER

```
┌─────────────────────────────────────────┐
│  Player's Club Shift Supervisor or        │
│  Player's Club Supervisor, Player's Club  │
│  Coordinator                              │
└─────────────────────────────────────────┘
                   │
┌─────────────────────────────────────────┐
│  Player's Club Representative             │
└─────────────────────────────────────────┘
                   │
┌─────────────────────────────────────────┐
│  Guest Services Representative, Position  │
│  in Customer Service or Entry Level       │
└─────────────────────────────────────────┘
```

Experience—Experience requirements vary; see text.

Special Skills and Personality Traits—Enthusiastic; people skills; customer service skills; problem solving skills; communication skills; computer skills.

Special Requirements—State licensing from gaming commission or gaming authority necessary; minimum age requirements.

Position Description

In order to develop a loyalty to their property, casinos generally offer loyalty programs also known as player's clubs to their guests. These player's clubs give casino guests a chance to earn valuable rewards based on the amount of money they spend on both slots and table game play. In some cases, the time casino guests play table games is also factored into the player's club accounts.

Rewards vary from property to property, but may include things such as cash back, coupons, complimentary rooms, show tickets, and meals at the casino's restaurants. Other rewards may include branded merchandise as well as invitations to exclusive casino promotions and special events.

It should be noted that while casinos want to reward guests for their loyalty, one of the other reasons they offer loyalty programs is because it gives them the opportunity to track what types of games guests play, when they play them, and how much they spend. This information can be very valuable in casino marketing.

In order to join player's clubs, casinos have player's club booths or kiosks located throughout the gaming area. Individuals called Player's Club Representatives man these booths.

Player's Club Representatives are responsible for handling the enrollment into the casino's player's club program. When guests come to the booth, the Player's Club Representative tells them all about the casino's player's club and what membership can offer. Individuals explain how the program works and what type of rewards are available. Membership to these programs is generally free.

If the guest is interested, the Player's Club Representative will ask for a photo ID to assure the guest is of legal gambling age and sign him or her up. In order to do this, the Player's Club Representative will take the guest's pertinent information from the photo ID, such as his or her name, address, phone number, birthday, and so on, and enter this in the casino's computer system.

The computer then generates a player's club card, which looks much like a credit card. A guest can then use that card by swiping it in each slot machine he or she plays. This tracks the amount of money the guest is spending in each machine. If the guest plays table games, he or she may give it to the pit boss to insure that credit is given for game play.

Signing people up to the player's club is just part of the job. A good part of the job of Player's Club Representatives is dealing with people who are already player's club members. Some of these individuals may have questions that they want to ask regarding the player's club policies, casino promotions, or events. The Player's Club Representative is expected to answer all questions courteously, making each guest feel that he or she is valued as a casino customer.

In many situations, guests lose their player's cards or want extra cards so that they can play more machines simultaneously. After checking their photo ID, Player's Club Representatives will then issue customers new or extra cards.

Many casinos have special promotions and events for player's club members. The Player's Club Representative is often called upon to evaluate a guest's information to determine if his or her qualifications have met the criteria needed for these various casino promotions. Depending on the specific structure of the casino's players club, the individual may be responsible for evaluating what type of promotions the guest will be offered. This will depend, of course, on the amount of money he or she has spent gambling at the facility.

The Player's Club Representative is often responsible for issuing coupons or cash vouchers associated with player's club promotions to guests or swiping guest's player's cards for entry into drawings for casino prizes. Player's Club Representatives may direct guests to various features of the casino including the cashier, hosts, change booths, restaurants, restrooms, or the hotel. They are expected to be goodwill ambassadors for the casino.

Customer service skills are extremely important in this job. It is essential that the Player's Club Representative always make the guest feel that he or she is a valued customer. At no time can the Player's Club Representative make the guest feel that the casino is doing the guest a favor by providing a voucher or coupon.

Casino guests with complaints or problems may stop at the player's club booth to vent, voice their displeasure, or try to get a resolution. The Player's Club Representative is expected to listen attentively and try to find a way to satisfy the guest. He or she may enlist the help of supervisors to accomplish this task.

Additional responsibilities of a Player's Club Representative working in a casino include:

- Assisting hosts with guest inquires
- Providing accurate and complete information to guests regarding casino events and promotions
- Keeping the player's club booth neat and orderly
- Communicating with supervisors regarding any guest complaints
- Promoting the player's club on the casino floor

Salaries

Earnings for Player's Club Representatives working at casinos can range from approximately $20,000 to $34,000 annually. Factors affecting earnings include the specific casino as well as its size, prestige, and geographic location. Other factors affecting earnings include the responsibilities and experience of the individual. Those working in larger casinos in gaming capitals will generally earn more than their counterparts at smaller casinos in areas with few casinos.

Employment Prospects

Employment prospects are good for Player's Club Representatives. As player's clubs are very important to casinos, facilities generally have a fair number of individuals working in this position every shift. Additionally, larger casinos generally have a number of player's club booths located throughout the facility.

The greatest number of opportunities exist in areas where there are large numbers of casinos. Las Vegas, Reno, Laughlin, Lake Tahoe, Atlantic City, Biloxi, Baton Rouge, New Orleans, Detroit, and Black Hawk offer the largest number of jobs. Other employment settings include casinos and casino hotels in other areas of Nevada, Mississippi, New York, Louisiana, Colorado, Connecticut, Illinois, Arizona, and California. Other regions hosting Indian gaming and land-based or riverboat gaming facilities, racinos, and bingo will offer additional opportunities.

Advancement Prospects

Advancement prospects are good for Player's Club Representatives. Individuals may become player's club shift supervisors or player's club supervisors or coordinators. After obtaining some experience, other individuals may move into either hosting positions or other jobs in the marketing department.

Education and Training

Most casinos require that their Player's Club Representatives hold a minimum of a high school diploma or the equivalent. A college background or degree may be helpful in career advancement.

Special Requirements

Player's Club Representatives needs to be licensed by the state in which they work. This is done through a state gaming authority or commission. Individuals must also meet minimum age requirements. Depending on the specific state, Player's Club Representatives may also need to either have TIPS (Training for Intervention Procedures) or another alcohol awareness certification.

Experience, Skills, and Personality Traits

Experience requirements for this position vary from casino to casino. In some facilities, this is an entry-level position. Other casinos prefer some sort of experience in the customer service area of the casino.

In order to be successful in this type of job, individuals should be enthusiastic people with excellent customer service skills. Good communications skills are essential to this type of job. Organizational skills are a must. The ability to multitask without getting flustered is helpful.

Computer skills and the ability to type are necessary. Problem solving skills are critical. The ability to deal well with guests is essential.

Unions and Associations

Individuals interested in a career in this field should contact gaming institutes and schools and casino human resources department.

Tips for Entry

1. If you are still in school, seek out an apprenticeship in the casino marketing or player's club development department of a casino or casino hotel.
2. Positions in this field are advertised in the newspaper classified section in areas hosting casinos. Look under the headings of "Casinos," "Gaming," "Player Club Development," "Player's Club Representative," etc. You might also look under the name of a specific casino or casino hotel.
3. Jobs may also be located online. Check out the Web sites of casinos and casino hotels. Many post openings on their sites.
4. Don't forget to check traditional job sites such as www.monster.com and www.hotjobs.com, as well as job sites specific to the gaming industry.
5. Many casinos also have job hotlines that may advertise openings in this area.
6. Send your résumé to casino hotel human resources departments.

PUBLIC RELATIONS DIRECTOR

CAREER PROFILE

Duties: Publicizing and promoting casino and casino hotel as well as their theaters, showrooms, and restaurants; publicizing promotional and special events.

Alternate Title(s): Director of Public Relations

Salary Range: $40,000 to $85,000+

Employment Prospects: Fair

Advancement Prospects: Good

Best Geographical Location(s) for Position: Las Vegas, Reno, Laughlin, Lake Tahoe, Atlantic City, Biloxi, Baton Rouge, New Orleans, and Detroit offer most opportunities; other regions with land-based, riverboat, or Indian gaming facilities offer additional opportunities.

Prerequisites:

Education or Training—Bachelor's degree generally required; see text.

Experience and Qualifications—Experience in public relations or the hospitality industry helpful.

CAREER LADDER

Public Relations Director in Larger, More Prestigious Casino, V.P. of Public Relations, or Director of Marketing

Public Relations Director

Public Relations Coordinator, Assistant Director of Public Relations, or Publicist in Other Industry

Special Skills and Personality Traits—Writing skills; communication skills; marketing skills; creativity; organization; interpersonal skills; customer service skills.

Special Requirements—State licensing may be required.

Position Description

Casinos and casino hotels employ a Public Relations Director to publicize the facility. The individual is responsible for promoting everything in the resort including the hotel, casino, showrooms, nightclubs, restaurants, and theaters. The Public Relations Director also publicizes any promotional and special events held at the casino or hotel.

The P.R. Director tries to develop various angles and conceive different methods to promote the facility. The P.R. Director often has a staff that assists in many of the individual's responsibilities.

The Public Relations Director is responsible for developing and writing press releases for media distribution. Targets include print, television, and radio. Stock press releases must be prepared, as well as releases on hotel and casino news and events. The P.R. Director must also make sure fact sheets on all areas of the casino and hotel are prepared. These might include interesting facts such as the number of eggs or steaks or shrimp served per year in one of the restaurants, the ratio of employees to rooms, or the amount of quarters won in slots annually.

The difference between advertising and publicity is that advertising has a cost factor. A full page ad in a major newspaper or magazine, or a commercial on national television can cost thousands of dollars. While it often costs money to generate publicity, there generally is no charge to get feature stories and articles written in the print media or have stories appear on television. The Public Relations Director generates publicity ideas so that editors and producers find the concepts interesting and want to do articles or stories.

The Public Relations Director acts as a liaison between the casino hotel and the media. A great many events occur at any one time in a casino hotel. A big slot tournament might be scheduled, as well as the opening of a well-known celebrity act in the showroom, a major boxing show, interesting new slot machines, or a major convention. The Public Relations Director must know which media to call for specific events—sports editors, entertainment writers, gaming media, and hotel or hospitality columnists. The P.R. Director must have a good working relationship with all media, print as well as television, cable, and radio.

The casino hotel P.R. Director works with the facility's marketing and advertising department. Together, they may develop and implement a variety of special events designed to promote the facility and its activities. These might include press conferences, parties, extravaganzas, promotions, or tournaments.

Because guests often travel to casinos and casino hotels from other areas, the Public Relations Director must generate both local and national media exposure.

Other duties of the casino hotel Public Relations Director may include:

- Supervising the public relations staff
- Developing special projects and promotional events to promote the facility
- Building relationships with media editors, producers, and writers

Salaries

Casino and casino hotel Public Relations Directors earn around $40,000 to $85,000 or more annually. Factors affecting earnings include the geographic location, size, and prestige of the specific casino hotel, as well as the experience and responsibilities of the individual. Generally, those with the most experience working in larger, more prestigious casinos hotels, in the gambling capitals earn the highest salaries.

Employment Prospects

Employment prospects for casino and casino hotel Public Relations Directors are fair. Jobs can be found throughout the country in locations hosting casinos.

The greatest number of opportunities exist in areas where there are a large number of casinos. Las Vegas, Reno, Laughlin, Lake Tahoe, Atlantic City, Biloxi, Baton Rouge, New Orleans, and Detroit offer the greatest number of job possibilities. Other employment settings include casino hotels in other areas of Nevada, Mississippi, New York, Louisiana, Colorado, Connecticut, Illinois, Arizona, and California. Other regions hosting Indian gaming and land-based or riverboat gaming facilities offer additional opportunities.

Advancement Prospects

Individuals may climb the career ladder in a number of ways. Some people gain experience and professional reputations and locate similar positions in larger or more prestigious facilities. This results in increased responsibilities and earnings.

Public Relations Directors may also advance their careers by being promoted to positions such as vice president of P.R., Corporate Public Relations Director, or Director of Marketing.

Education and Training

Generally, most casinos and casino hotels prefer their Public Relations Directors to have a bachelor's degree. Good majors include public relations, marketing, communications, journalism, English, or liberal arts.

Courses, workshops, and seminars in publicity, writing, and the hospitality industry are useful.

Special Requirements

The Public Relations Director working in a casino or casino hotel may be required to be licensed by the state.

Experience, Skills, and Personality Traits

Experience working in public relations is required to become a casino or casino hotel Public Relations Director. Some individuals start out as journalists or publicists. They then move up to positions as assistant directors of public relations prior to their appointment as P.R. Director. Experience working in the hospitality industry, hotels, or casinos is required or preferred.

Public Relations Directors are creative individuals with excellent writing and communication skills. They enjoy working with the public and are outgoing and articulate.

Unions and Associations

Those interested in learning more about careers as casino hotel publicists can obtain additional information by contacting the Hotel Sales and Marketing Association International (HSMA), the Public Relations Society of America (PRSA), or the human resources departments in casino hotels.

Tips for Entry

1. You might also want to check out recruitment and search firms dealing in the public relations or hospitality industries.
2. Get your foot in the door of a casino hotel. Most promote from within. You might have to start as a publicist, but you can obtain experience and move up the career ladder.
3. Jobs may be advertised in the classified sections of newspapers in areas hosting gaming. Look under classifications such as "Hotel Public Relations Director," "Casino Hotel Public Relations Director," "Director of Public Relations," "Public Relations," "Communications," or "Casino Opportunities."
4. Skills are transferable. If you have worked as a P.R. Director in another industry, you might have a good shot if you are in the right place at the right time.

HOTEL PUBLICIST

Position Description

Casino hotels usually have public relations and marketing departments. Depending on the facility, there may be one or more Hotel Publicists working within the department, as well as Publicists who handle the publicity for the casino.

The Casino Hotel Publicist has varied duties. The major function, of course, is to publicize the facility. This often overlaps with the duties of the casino publicist or marketing people.

The individual is responsible for developing and writing informative press releases about the facility. The Publicist also prepares press releases regarding special events and promotions of the casino hotel.

The Publicist may also be responsible for either taking photographs or arranging for photos of the hotel, as well as special events and promotions that take place at the facilities.

The Hotel Publicist also puts together fact sheets and develops press kits about the facility. These will be provided to the various media.

The casino Hotel Publicist also works with travel agents. The individual may work with others in the department, setting up "FAM" or familiarization programs. These are designed so travel agents visit the facility and then recommend the hotel to their clients.

The casino Hotel Publicist is generally responsible for publicizing events and celebrities that bring bookings to the facility or just keep the name of the hotel in the public eye. The casino Hotel Publicist often works with publicists for entertainers appearing in the facility's showroom. They also work with publicists of sports figures, such as world champion fighters starring in boxing shows at the hotel.

Other duties of the casino Hotel Publicist may include:

- Developing relationships with print feature editors, television and radio producers, and other media personnel
- Compiling media lists for the travel and gaming trade, as well as for the general press
- Working on special projects and promotional events within the casino hotel

Salaries

Casino Hotel Publicists earn between $24,000 and $48,000 or more annually, depending on a number of factors, including the geographic location, size, and prestige of the specific casino hotel, as well as the experience and responsibilities of the individual. Generally, those with the most experience working in larger, more prestigious casinos hotels in the gambling capitals earn the highest salaries.

Employment Prospects

Employment prospects for casino Hotel Publicists are fair. Jobs can be found throughout the country. The greatest number of employment opportunities are be found in Las Vegas, Reno, Laughlin, Lake Tahoe, Atlantic City, Biloxi, Baton Rouge, New Orleans, and Detroit. Other regions hosting Indian gaming and land-based or riverboat gaming facilities offer additional opportunities.

As more areas begin to legalize gambling, more opportunities will become available.

Advancement Prospects

Casino Hotel Publicists may advance their careers in a number of ways. Depending on career aspirations, individuals may find positions as the assistant director of public relations, public relations manager, special events assistant director, or director. Some individuals may also move into the casino marketing area. Experience and additional training are generally required for career advancement.

Education and Training

Educational requirements vary at different casino hotels. While every position does not require a college degree, one is recommended. Good majors include journalism, public relations, marketing, communications, English, or liberal arts.

Courses, workshops, and seminars in publicity, writing, and the hospitality industry are useful.

Special Requirements

Depending on the specific state and casino, individuals may be required to be licensed by the state.

Experience, Skills, and Personality Traits

Experience requirements, like educational requirements, vary. Most employers require or prefer individuals to have some sort of experience writing or handling publicity or public relations. Some casino hotels may have training programs or internships for those with no experience.

Casino Hotel Publicists should have excellent writing and communication skills. They should enjoy working with the public and be outgoing, articulate individuals.

Unions and Associations

Those interested in learning more about careers as casino Hotel Publicists can obtain additional information by contacting the Hotel Sales and Marketing Association International (HSMA), the Public Relations Society of America (PRSA), or the human resources departments in casino hotels.

Tips for Entry

1. Get your foot in the door of a casino hotel. Most promote from within. You might have to start as a trainee, but if you work hard, you will move up the career ladder.
2. Stop by the human resources departments of casinos and inquire about job openings. You might also consider sending a résumé and a short cover letter.
3. Jobs may be advertised in the classified sections of newspapers in areas hosting gaming. Look under classifications such as "Hotel Publicist," "Casino Hotel Publicist," "Publicist," "Public Relations," or "Casino Opportunities."
4. Check out casino and casino hotel Web sites. Many list openings on their sites.

ADVERTISING COORDINATOR

Duties: Assisting in the development of advertising campaigns; creating promotional ads, sales pieces, and commercials; supporting casino's marketing and public relations efforts.

Alternate Title(s): Advertising Assistant; Media Coordinator

Salary Range: $22,000 to $35,000+

Employment Prospects: Fair

Advancement Prospects: Good

Best Geographical Location(s) for Position: Las Vegas, Reno, Laughlin, Lake Tahoe, Atlantic City, Biloxi, Baton Rouge, New Orleans, and Detroit offer the greatest number of opportunities; other regions hosting Indian gaming and land-based or riverboat gaming facilities offer additional opportunities.

Prerequisites:

Education or Training—Bachelor's degree preferred, but not always required.

Experience and Qualifications—Experience in advertising, marketing, or public relations neces-

---

CAREER LADDER

Advertising Director or Other Position in Marketing or Public Relations Department

↑

Advertising Coordinator

↑

Advertising Assistant in Other Industry or Advertising Intern

---

sary; experience in the gaming or hospitality industry a plus.

Special Skills and Personality Traits—Creativity; communication skills; copywriting skills; ability to work on multiple projects at one time; knowledge of graphics and typefaces.

Special Requirements—State licensing may be required.

Position Description

More and more casinos are being constructed every year. Casinos and casino hotels are different sizes, have different atmospheres, and offer an array of amenities, games, foods, entertainment, and themes. Casinos market and advertise their facilities to attract customers.

The marketing department constantly develops different promotions designed to attract new customers and keep those who have previously visited the facility. Within this department are sub areas such as public relations, publicity, and advertising. These departments work in conjunction with marketing to help attain the goals. The Advertising Coordinator creates themes, campaigns, and single advertisements that support the casino and casino hotel's marketing efforts. This individual may also be referred to as an advertising assistant.

The Advertising Coordinator assists in the creation of advertising campaigns. The individual works with an advertising director or under the supervision of the director of marketing. In some settings, casinos and casino hotels utilize the services of outside advertising agencies. In these cases, the Advertising Coordinator

often acts as a liaison between the agency and the facility in developing advertising campaigns.

In addition to working on the advertising campaigns, the Coordinator also creates individual promotional ads that may be needed for special promotions and events in both the casino and the casino hotel. These may include hotel and restaurant specials, entertainment events, slot parties and tournaments, nationally televised attractions, sporting events, and many other promotions.

Keeping these goals in mind, the Advertising Coordinator must reach the proper markets. The Coordinator must know in which geographic area it is best to advertise, as well as the proper media. This may include radio, television, newspapers, consumer and business publications, and billboards.

The Advertising Coordinator also prepares direct mail advertising pieces aimed at former customers and potential guests. This type of advertising is often used in casinos to promote specials and giveaways during slow seasons.

The Advertising Coordinator performs a variety of research projects in the job. The individual must determine the most effective type of ads, as well as media and locations in which to place them in order to reach the market the facility is aiming for.

The Advertising Coordinator might be required to do the actual copywriting, graphics, and audiovisual components of advertising, or to farm out some of these duties to freelance people. If the facility is working with an outside advertising agency, the Coordinator may develop the ideas instead of doing the actual writing and artwork.

Other duties of a casino or casino hotel Advertising Coordinator may include:

- Obtaining current demographics and rate information from media
- Assisting in the development of the advertising budget
- Helping develop other marketing pieces

Salaries

Advertising Coordinators working in casinos and casino hotels earn between $22,000 and $35,000 or more annually. Factors affecting earnings include the geographic location, size, and prestige of the specific casino or casino hotel, as well as the education, experience, and responsibilities of the individual.

Employment Prospects

Employment prospects are fair for people seeking this position and will increase as gaming expands throughout the country. Opportunities exist in the marketing departments of many gaming facilities. As noted, some facilities utilize the services of independent advertising agencies. However, these casinos and hotels often employ an Advertising Coordinator to work with the outside agency.

Advancement Prospects

One of the great things about working in casinos and casino hotels is that they like to promote from within. Once you're in, if you are a good employee, your opportunities are limitless.

The Advertising Coordinator may take a number of different steps toward advancement depending on career aspirations. Individuals may become the advertising director of the casino or casino hotel if the facility has such a position. With experience, education, and training advertising coordinators may also be promoted to other jobs in the marketing and public relations area.

Special Requirements

Depending on the specific state and casino, individuals may be required to be state licensed.

Education and Training

Educational requirements vary for Advertising Coordinators at casinos and casino hotels. Most prefer candidates to hold a bachelor's degree with a major in advertising, marketing, public relations, communications, or liberal arts. In some cases, work experience is accepted in lieu of education.

Experience, Skills, and Personality Traits

Experience working in advertising, marketing, public relations, or a related field is usually necessary. Any experience in the hospitality or gaming industry is a plus.

Advertising Coordinators should be creative individuals with copywriting and graphics skills. An understanding of the hospitality and gaming industries is needed. Good communication skills are also necessary. The Advertising Coordinator must have the ability to work on several multiple projects at one time without getting flustered.

Unions and Associations

Those interested in learning more about careers in this field can contact the Hotel Sales and Marketing Association (HMA) and the American Advertising Federation (AAF).

Tips for Entry

1. Many casinos have job hotlines for available jobs. Call casinos directly to obtain their job hotline phone numbers.
2. Get your foot in the door of a casino hotel. Most promote from within. If you have experience in advertising or marketing, see what positions are open, then move up the career ladder.
3. Jobs may be advertised in the classified sections of newspapers in areas hosting gaming. Look under classifications such as "Casino/Casino Hotel Advertising Coordinator," "Casino/Casino Hotel Advertising Assistant," "Advertising," "Marketing," or "Casino/Hotel Opportunities."
4. Openings are often advertised on the Internet. They may be located via the home pages of casino hotels.
5. Check out opportunities online. Many casinos list openings on their Web sites.

PROMOTIONS COORDINATOR

Position Description

Casinos often plan a multitude of special events and promotions to attract new customers. The programs are designed to keep those who have already visited the facility as well as to generate publicity for the casino. The Promotions Coordinator is employed by the casino to assist with the development and implementation of promotions and special events.

Depending on the specific facility and its structure, the Promotions Coordinator works in conjunction with the marketing director, special events director, or manager of entertainment.

Casinos generally plan promotions well in advance. Most casinos prepare an annual calendar of events and attractions for customers via direct mail, as well as promotion in the casino and casino hotel and media advertising.

In order to be successful, promotions must be novel, workable ideas. The individual assists in the development of innovative promotions for the facility. In some settings these promotions are the result of brainstorming efforts of others in the marketing, public relations, special events, entertainment, and advertising departments.

The Promotions Coordinator assists in working out the details of the promotion. The individual is often responsible for putting together a basic outline of the event. He or she is expected to locate people, places, and items necessary for making the promotion a success.

The Promotions Coordinator must be extremely organized, and every detail of the promotion must be coordinated. The Promotions Coordinator is responsible for notifying all department heads of the promotion and explaining what, if any, their participation will be. The individual must also coordinate all activities in the casino necessary to execute promotions.

The Promotions Coordinator is expected to work with the media by arranging interviews, articles, feature stores, photo opportunities, and broadcasts to garner publicity and media attention for the promotion and therefore the facility.

The individual may also be required to prepare press releases and other publicity on upcoming events or on parts of a promotion that have already occurred.

Other duties of a casino or casino hotel Promotions Coordinator may include:

- Assisting in the preparation of a budget for the promotion

- Working with advertising department creating promotional ads and direct mail advertising pieces
- Helping develop marketing materials such as ads and brochures

Salaries

Promotions Coordinators working in casinos and casino hotels earn between $24,000 and $42,000 or more annually. Factors affecting earnings include the geographic location, size, and prestige of the specific casino or casino hotel, as well as the education, experience, and responsibilities of the individual.

Employment Prospects

Employment prospects are good for Promotions Coordinators. Opportunities exist in most gaming facilities. The greatest number of opportunities exist in areas where there are a large number of casinos.

Las Vegas, Reno, Laughlin, Lake Tahoe, Atlantic City, Biloxi, Baton Rouge, New Orleans, and Detroit offer the greatest number of job possibilities. Other employment settings include casino hotels in other areas of Nevada, Mississippi, New York, Louisiana, Colorado, Connecticut, Illinois, Arizona, and California.

Other regions hosting Indian gaming and land-based or riverboat gaming facilities offer additional opportunities. New casinos and casino hotels are constantly under construction. More casinos and casino hotels are also opening every year as areas legalize gambling.

Advancement Prospects

The Promotions Coordinator may take a number of different steps toward advancement depending on career aspirations. Individuals may climb the career ladder through promotion to positions such as entertainment and special events coordinator or manager. Others may move into another area of the marketing or public relations department.

Education and Training

Educational requirements vary for Promotions Coordinators at casinos and casino hotels. Most prefer candidates to hold a bachelor's degree with a major in marketing, public relations, communications, or liberal arts. In some cases, work experience is accepted in lieu of education.

Special Requirements

Depending on the specific state and casino in which the individual works, the Promotion Coordinator may be required to be state licensed.

Experience, Skills, and Personality Traits

Experience working in marketing, public relations, entertainment, or a related field is usually necessary. Any experience in the hospitality or gaming industry is a plus.

Promotions Coordinators should be creative, detail-oriented, organized individuals. They must have the ability to work on a variety of projects at one time without becoming confused. Excellent communication skills, both verbal and written, are needed. An understanding of the hospitality and gaming industries is helpful.

Unions and Associations

Those interested in learning more about careers in this field can contact the Public Relations Society of America (PRSA). Other information may be obtained by contacting the human resources departments of casino hotels.

Tips for Entry

1. Jobs may be advertised in the classified sections of newspapers in areas hosting gaming. Look under classifications such as "Casino/Casino Hotels," "Casino/Gaming," "Casino Promotions Coordinator," "Promotions Coordinator," or "Marketing."
2. Many casinos have job hotlines for jobs available. Call casinos to get the job hotline phone number.
3. Get your foot in the door of a casino hotel. Most promote from within. If you have experience in marketing, public relations, entertainment, special events, or promotions, see what positions are open, then move up the career ladder.
4. Openings are often advertised on the Internet. They may be located via the home pages of casinos and casino hotels.

GROUP/CONVENTION SALES MANAGER

CAREER PROFILE

Duties: Soliciting and booking convention and group sales; negotiating rates; assigning leads to salespeople; maintaining wholesale accounts.

Alternate Title(s): Sales Manager

Salary Range: $50,000 to $95,000+

Employment Prospects: Good

Employment Prospects: Fair

Best Geographical Location(s) for Position: Las Vegas, Reno, Laughlin, Lake Tahoe, Atlantic City, Biloxi, Baton Rouge, New Orleans, and Detroit offer most opportunities; other regions with land-based, riverboat, or Indian gaming facilities offer additional opportunities.

Prerequisites:

Education or Training—Bachelor's degree required or preferred; see text.

Experience and Qualifications—Experience in convention or group sales.

CAREER LADDER

Group/Convention Sales Manager in Larger, More Prestigious Casino Hotel or Director of Sales

Group/Convention Sales Manager

Group Sales Manager in Other Industry

Special Skills and Personality Traits—Sales ability; communication skills; organization; detail-oriented; administrative ability; interpersonal skills; customer service skills; aggressive; negotiation skills.

Position Description

Convention sales can substantially increase business in casino hotels during slow periods at the facilities. In order to keep rooms filled, casino hotels often market their facilities to conventions, conferences, and other groups. Many hotels have constructed their own private convention facilities. Some areas hosting gaming also have centrally located major convention centers. As a result, casino hotels have become important convention destinations.

The Convention or Group Sales Manager is responsible for seeking out groups looking for locations to hold their meetings. The hotel often sells rooms at a reduced price to these groups because they are buying blocks of rooms. In addition to selling rooms, the Sales Manager offers groups food and beverage service for meetings and banquets, meeting rooms, ballrooms, and convention facilities.

The Sales Manager is responsible for maintaining established accounts. He or she must also look for new business by contacting representatives of government, business, or social groups to solicit convention or conference business for the casino hotel. The individual is responsible for analyzing the requirements of the group. He or she will then develop a proposal outlining the services and quoting prices the casino hotel can offer.

The Sales Manager is responsible for developing marketing packages, telemarketing, and direct mail promotions to attract new group business. The individual may work with others in advertising, marketing, and public relations on these projects.

The individual works closely with other departments to make sure groups that are booked receive proper service. Once a group is booked, the Sales Manager alerts the convention services manager about the contract to assure that groups' needs are taken care of and that they are satisfied with their visit.

The Group or Convention Sales Manager may be required to go on the road on occasion to make contact with groups, to meet important clients, and to attend trade shows and sales meetings.

The Sales Manager makes calls to prospective clients or has sales packages sent to potential clients. The individual works with hotel sales representatives in closing deals.

Other duties of a Casino Hotel Convention or Group Sales Manager may include:

- Conducting training seminars and workshops for salespeople
- Assigning leads to salespeople
- Drawing up contracts and obtaining required signatures

Salaries

Group/Convention Sales Managers working in casino hotels earn between $50,000 and $95,000 or more annually. Individuals in some facilities may earn bonuses or commissions on business brought into the hotel or business over and above that which has been forecast.

Factors affecting earnings include the geographic location, size, and prestige of the specific casino or casino hotel, as well as the experience, responsibilities, and professional reputation of the individual.

Employment Prospects

Employment prospects for talented Group Sales Managers are good. Casino hotels, like others in the hospitality industry, are always on the lookout for individuals who can produce.

The greatest number of opportunities can be found in Las Vegas, where countless casino hotels and new mega resorts are being built. Other good opportunities can be found in Reno, Laughlin, Lake Tahoe, Atlantic City, Biloxi, Baton Rouge, New Orleans, and Detroit. Other regions hosting Indian gaming and land-based or riverboat gaming facilities offer additional job possibilities.

Advancement Prospects

Group/Convention Sales Managers may advance their careers by locating similar positions in larger, more prestigious casino hotels. Some individuals may be promoted to the position of director of sales if the facility has such a job. Depending on the career aspirations and training of the individual, he or she may also move into the marketing department.

Education and Training

A bachelor's degree is usually required or preferred by most casino hotels for Group or Convention Sales Managers. In some settings, work experience may be accepted in lieu of formal education.

Good choices for majors include marketing, sales, public relations, communications, or hotel management and administration.

Experience, Skills, and Personality Traits

Group/Convention Sales Managers need experience in hotel sales, group or convention sales, or tours and travel. Some individuals also have held similar positions with hotels not involved in the gaming industry prior to being employed at a casino hotel.

Sales Managers should be personable, pleasantly aggressive people with sales ability. Communication skills are necessary. Individuals should be organized and detail-oriented. The ability to negotiate is mandatory.

Unions and Associations

Those interested in learning more about careers as Group/Convention Sales Managers may obtain additional information from the American Hotel and Lodging Association (AH&LA).

Tips for Entry

1. Casinos often promote from within. If you have sales ability, start as a sales representative and work your way up the career ladder.
2. Send, fax, or visit the human resources departments of casino hotels to inquire about job openings. You might also consider sending or faxing a résumé and a short cover letter.
3. Jobs may be advertised in the classified sections of newspapers in areas hosting gaming. Look under classifications such as "Casino/Gaming Opportunities," "Convention Sales Manager," "Group Sales Manager," "Hotel Sales," or "Casinos/Casino Hotels."
4. Openings are often advertised on the Internet. They may be located via the home pages of casino hotels. They may also be found by doing a search of "Casino," "Casino Hotel," or "Gaming Job Opportunities."

HOTEL SALES REPRESENTATIVE

Duties: Contacting groups; soliciting and booking convention and group sales; preparing proposals; negotiating rates; servicing groups.

Alternate Title(s): Sales Rep; Convention Sales Representative

Salary Range: $23,000 to $48,000+

Employment Prospects: Good

Advancement Prospects: Fair

Best Geographical Location(s) for Position: Las Vegas, Reno, Laughlin, Lake Tahoe, Atlantic City, Biloxi, Baton Rouge, New Orleans, and Detroit offer most opportunities; other regions with land-based, riverboat, or Indian gaming facilities offer additional opportunities.

Prerequisites:

    Education or Training—Educational requirements vary; see text.

    Experience and Qualifications—Experience in convention hotel sales preferred, but not always required.

CAREER LADDER

Advertising Director or Other Position in Marketing or Public Relations Department

⬆

Casino Hotel Sales Representative

⬆

Sales Position in Other Industry or Entry Level

Special Skills and Personality Traits—Sales ability; communication skills; organization; detail-oriented; interpersonal skills; negotiation skills; persuasiveness; customer service skills.

Position Description

Casino hotels seek out groups looking for locations to hold meetings, conferences, and conventions. The facility often sells rooms at a reduced price to these groups because they are buying blocks of rooms as well as food and beverage service, meeting rooms, ballrooms, and/or convention facilities.

Casino Hotel Sales Representatives are responsible for soliciting and booking groups, conferences, and conventions into the facility. These groups often substantially increase the business of a casino hotel, especially during slow periods of the year.

In order to attract group business, Casino Hotel Sales Representatives actively seek out and contact groups. They contact groups that have previously visited the facility, or they are assigned leads by the convention and group sales manager.

Sales Representatives deal with potential customers on the telephone or set up and meet with prospective clients at the facility. Some Sales Representatives also meet outside the hotel with clients.

Sales Representatives must have complete knowledge of the casino hotel and all the services and amenities it offers. They must be able to discuss every detail of the facility comfortably and knowledgeably. While doing this, the Casino Hotel Sales Representative is responsible for explaining how the services and facilities offered meet the potential client's needs. For example, the Sales Representative may be required to discuss availability of types of rooms and packages, as well as options in catering meals, breaks, and meetings.

The individual is also expected to answer any questions the client may have. While doing this, the Sales Representative attempts to overcome objections or problems of potential clients, persuading these customers to choose their hotel instead of another.

The Sales Representative often gives tours of the facility to prospective customers. He or she shows rooms, convention facilities, the gaming area, health clubs, and restaurants. The Sales Representative may also show customers sample menus for food service.

The Casino Hotel Sales Representative must constantly follow up. He or she schedules additional visits, writes additional letters, or makes more phone calls to prospective customers.

The Sales Representative negotiates rates and services with groups. Generally, individuals have some sort of leeway in handling these negotiations, although they may need approval from the sales manager.

Other duties of Casino Hotel Sales Representatives may include:

- Servicing groups
- Preparing proposals
- Obtaining required signatures
- Sending sales packages to clients

Salaries

Casino Hotel Sales Representatives earn between $23,000 and $48,000 or more annually. Individuals may be compensated in a variety of ways, ranging from straight salary, salary plus commissions, or salary plus bonuses on business brought into the hotel over and above what was forecast.

Factors affecting earnings include the geographic location, size, and prestige of the specific casino or casino hotel, as well as the experience, responsibilities, and professional reputation of the individual.

Employment Prospects

Employment opportunities for Casino Hotel Sales Representatives are very good. Casino hotels, like all others in the hospitality industry, are always on the lookout for talented people who can produce sales.

Sales Representatives work in various settings, including land-based casino hotels, Indian gaming facilities with on-site hotels, and dockside or floating riverboat casinos with hotel facilities.

Advancement Prospects

Casino Hotel Sales Representatives may climb the career ladder by locating similar positions in larger, more prestigious casino hotels. Others may advance through promotion to the position of convention sales manager.

Education and Training

Educational requirements vary for Casino Hotel Sales Representatives. Some facilities require just a high school diploma or the equivalent. Others prefer a col-lege background or degree. Good choices for majors include marketing, sales, public relations, communications, or hotel management and administration. Work experience may be accepted in lieu of formal education. In many casino hotels, the convention or group sales manager conducts training seminars and workshops for Sales Representatives.

Experience, Skills, and Personality Traits

Experience requirements, like education requirements, vary. In some casino hotels, this may be an entry-level position. Others require experience in hotel sales.

Sales Representatives should be pleasantly aggressive, personable people with sales ability. Communication and phone skills are necessary. Individuals should be organized, detail-oriented, and have the ability to negotiate.

Unions and Associations

Those interested in learning more about careers as Casino Hotel Sales Representatives can obtain additional career information from the American Hotel and Lodging Association (AH&LA) or casino hotel human resources departments.

Tips for Entry

1. Send or fax your résumé to the human resources departments of casino hotels with a short cover letter inquiring about job openings. Include any sales experience you have had in any capacity on your résumé.
2. You can also stop by the human resources departments of casino hotels with this same information.
3. Many casinos offer these jobs on their job hotlines. These are recorded messages giving jobs available at the casino hotel. Call the casino to get its job hotline phone number.
4. Jobs are often advertised in the classified sections of newspapers in areas hosting gaming. Look under classifications such as "Casino/Gaming Opportunities," "Convention Sales," "Group Sales," "Casino Hotel Sales," "Casinos/Casino Hotels," or "Sales Rep."

CONVENTION SERVICES MANAGER

Position Description

Organizations, corporations, and associations often plan group meetings and annual conventions at casino hotels. These groups have a variety of needs and requirements. The person in charge of coordinating all the details for these groups is called the Convention Services Manager.

The individual has a wide array of duties. His or her job starts when a group is booked. The Convention Services Manager talks to the group's representative or meeting planner to discuss special needs, such as display space, meeting rooms, stages, podiums, audiovisual equipment, food service, and break schedules. The Convention Services Manager also arranges for special permits from fire and/or health departments. The individual also may have to deal with the various unions whose members may work in a hotel setting.

The Convention Services Manager is responsible for notifying other departments in the hotel of arrangements being made or requirements that must be met.

The Convention Services Manager directs workers in preparing special rooms for guests. These may include meeting rooms, banquet halls, and convention rooms. The individual also supervises workers or exhibition companies in erecting displays and exhibits for conventions. The Convention Services Manager inspects rooms and displays to make sure they conform to the needs and desires of the group.

The Convention Services Manager may arrange publicity for the group and/or their meeting. The individual handles this function directly or assigns the task to the hotel's public relations or publicity department.

Convention Services Managers meet with the group's representatives before and during their stay to assure that everything is going as scheduled and that any problems are taken care of. The Convention Services Manager may also contact the group's representative after their stay to be sure the group was satisfied, helping to secure the group's return business.

Other duties of Convention Services Manager may include:

- Promoting good will between the hotel and the group
- Handling complaints and problems
- Arranging special functions

Salaries

Convention Services Managers in casino hotels work on salary. Individuals have annual earnings ranging from $30,000 to $60,000 or more. Factors affecting earnings include the geographic location, size, and prestige of the facility. Other variables include the experience and responsibilities of the individual. Those working in large facilities in the gambling capitals usually earn more than their counterparts in other hotels.

Employment Prospects

Employment prospects are fair for Convention Services Managers. Individuals can find employment in areas hosting casino hotels. The largest number of opportunities are available in areas with more casino hotels: Las Vegas, Reno, Laughlin, Lake Tahoe, Atlantic City, Biloxi, Baton Rouge, New Orleans, and Detroit. Other regions with land-based, riverboat, or Indian gaming facilities offer additional opportunities.

Advancement Prospects

Convention Services Managers working in casino hotels can advance their careers in a number of ways. Individuals may find similar jobs in larger or more prestigious hotels, resulting in increased responsibilities and earnings. Depending on career aspirations, education, and experience, Convention Services Managers may also move on to positions in convention or group sales.

Education and Training

Education and training requirements vary from job to job. For some positions, a high school diploma or its equivalent is required. For others, a college background or degree may be needed. Work experience is often accepted in lieu of education.

Experience, Skills, and Personality Traits

Depending on the specific casino hotel, this job may require from three to 10 years' experience working in a hotel or other area of the hospitality industry. Some individuals gain experience working in the convention services office in various positions, including assistant convention services manager. Others may have prior experience in other departments of the hotel.

Unions and Associations

Individuals interested in learning more about careers in this area can contact the human resources departments of casino hotels. Other information may be available from the American Hotel and Lodging Association (AH&LA).

Tips for Entry

1. Jobs are often advertised in the classified sections of newspapers in areas hosting gaming. Look under classifications such as "Casino," "Casino Hotels," "Hotels," "Convention Services," "Convention Services Manager," "Casino Hotel Opportunities," or "Hospitality."
2. If you are still in school, consider an internship offered by a hotel to obtain experience and make contacts.
3. Stop by the human resources departments of casino hotels to inquire about job openings.
4. Send your résumé to directors of human resources at casino hotels.
5. Look for new casino hotels that are under construction. Apply early.
6. Check out casino home pages to see if the casino hosts an employment site. Openings may be listed.

TOUR AND TRAVEL MANAGER

CAREER PROFILE

Duties: Developing programs to attract bus business; creating promotions.

Alternate Title(s): Travel Manager

Salary Range: $38,000 to $65,000+

Employment Prospects: Fair

Advancement Prospects: Fair

Best Geographical Location(s) for Position: Las Vegas, Reno, Laughlin, Lake Tahoe, Atlantic City, Biloxi, Baton Rouge, New Orleans, and Detroit offer most opportunities; other regions with land-based, riverboat, or Indian gaming facilities offer additional opportunities.

Prerequisites:

Education or Training—College degree preferred; see text.

Experience and Qualifications—Experience working in tour and travel, marketing, or other related area.

CAREER LADDER

Tour and Travel Manager in Larger, More Prestigious Casino or Position in Marketing or Sales

Tour and Travel Manager

Tour and Travel Coordinator or Assistant or Public Relations, Marketing, or Convention Sales Position

Special Skills and Personality Traits—Communication skills; marketing skills; creativity; organization.

Position Description

Bus tour trade for casinos grows annually. Each facility vies for customers by offering promotions, giveaways, and special prices for bus customers.

Some casinos themselves own buses, which leave from a central location on a scheduled basis and bring excited guests to the facility. Many bus lines also work in conjunction with casinos, scheduling daily trips to the various casinos. Some groups of people and organizations charter buses for visits to the gaming area.

The individual responsible for developing bus programs to attract customers to the casino is called the Tour and Travel Manager. Bus promotions have become very popular with casinos. For many guests, the bus is an ideal method of visiting a casino. To garner bus customers for their casino, Tour and Travel Managers must constantly create new promotions.

These promotions, for example, provide guests with some sort of monetary reimbursement, such as a roll of quarters or equivalent coupon to use for slots, food, or entertainment. They may also include coupons for reduced prices on meals in casino restaurants and entertainment in showrooms. In order to assure repeat business, promotions may also involve coupons for future trips. Some promotions involve contests, giveaways, or entertainment. Promotions might include

books of coupons for a wide array of items such as free souvenirs, slot machine pulls, or drinks.

Most bus customers are slot players. Therefore, the Tour and Travel Manager also works with the slot and marketing departments on slot promotions designed to attract bus customers. Together the departments create, market, and implement bus tour programs.

The Tour and Travel Manager may work with private bus lines as well as charter groups in order to develop new markets for service to the casino.

With a successful bus program, the casino may have 100 or more buses pulling up to the facility daily. The Tour and Travel Manager must create a working operating system so that total mayhem does not occur at the casino hotel's arrival and departure area.

The individual must work out a reservation system for charter buses, as well as a timetable for daily scheduled bus lines. The Tour and Travel Manager must also develop procedures for bus drivers regarding discharging arriving passengers, loading them at departure time, and parking.

Other duties of the casino Tour and Travel Manager may include:

- Overseeing and training tour and travel staff
- Developing promotional literature for bus programs

Salaries

Tour and Travel Managers working in casinos earn between $38,000 and $65,000 or more annually. Factors affecting earnings include the geographic location, size, and prestige of the casino, as well as the importance placed on its bus program. Other variables include the experience and responsibilities of the individual.

Employment Prospects

Employment prospects for Tour and Travel Managers are fair. Casinos are always looking for talented, creative people who can produce in this job. Opportunities for Tour and Travel Managers can be found in facilities hosting bus programs. Areas with a large number of casinos hosting bus programs have more opportunities. These include land-based casinos, dockside and floating riverboat casinos, and Indian gaming facilities.

Advancement Prospects

Advancement opportunities for Tour and Travel Managers depend to a great extent on the area in which the individual desires to work. Some Tour and Travel Managers climb the career ladder by locating similar positions in larger casinos or properties placing more emphasis on bus programs. Depending on career aspirations and training, the individual may also move into an administrative position in a marketing or convention sales department.

Education and Training

A bachelor's degree is usually required or preferred by most casinos for the position of Tour and Travel Manager. In some settings, work experience may be accepted in lieu of formal education.

Good choices for majors include marketing, public relations, communications, liberal arts, or hotel management and administration. Courses and seminars on various aspects of casinos administration and marketing are offered in many areas hosting gaming.

Experience, Skills, and Personality Traits

Two to four years' experience working in tour and travel or marketing, public relations, travel, or hospitality are necessary for most positions in casinos as a Tour and Travel Manager. Individuals must be creative with good marketing and communication skills. An understanding of the gaming and tour and travel industries is essential.

Unions and Associations

Those interested in learning more about careers in this area can obtain additional information by contacting the American Hotel and Lodging Association (AH&LA) or the human resources departments of casinos.

Tips for Entry

1. Many casinos promote from within. If you are interested in this type of job, see what openings exist in the department. Learn what you can and move up the career ladder.
2. Jobs may be advertised in the classified sections of newspapers in areas hosting gaming. Look under classifications such as "Casino/Gaming Opportunities," "Casino Tour and Travel," or "Tour and Travel Manager."
3. Send, fax, or visit the human resources departments of casino hotels to inquire about job openings. You might also send or fax a résumé and a short cover letter.
4. Call casinos job hotline numbers. These offer current job opportunities available at the facility. You can call casinos directly to obtain their job hotline phone numbers.
5. Check out individual casino Web sites. Many casinos now list job openings on an employment page within their web sites.

TOUR HOST

Position Description

Every day people pile on buses for scheduled trips to casinos. While there are bus trips that include overnight stays, most visitors stay only for the day. Guests who take these trips are often called day-trippers.

In keeping with their goal of providing excellent customer service, casinos often employ Tour Hosts to meet incoming buses. Tour Hosts wait in the area where buses pull up. The Hosts either get on the bus to say hello to guests, or greet each guest as he or she gets off the bus.

Tour Hosts provide brochures, literature, and other written material on the facility and its restaurants, games, and other amenities. Tour Hosts also give out coupons for coin reimbursement, meals, and other giveaways.

Tour Hosts orient the guests to the property, including directing guests to the gaming area, restaurants, gift shops, and rest rooms. They also answer questions regarding the casino, hotel, or any of the facilities located on the property.

Individuals often escort guests to specific parts of the casino such as the slot area. Tour Hosts show guests where the various denominations of slots can be played. They also escort patrons to change booths and cages.

In some cases, bus tour leaders make arrangements for meals in one of the casino restaurants. The Tour Host escorts the group to the restaurant, makes sure they are seated and that everything moves along satisfactorily. During the meal, the individual talks to guests to see if they need anything. After the meal, the Tour Host escorts guests to the gaming area.

Other duties of the casino bus Tour Host may include:

- Telling guests when and where to meet the bus for departure
- Wishing guests well on departure
- Promoting good customer service to guests

Salaries

Casino Tour Hosts are usually paid an hourly wage. This can range between $7.50 and $12.00 or more, approximately $15,000 to $25,000 annually. Individuals may also receive tips. Factors affecting earnings include the geographic location, size, and prestige of the specific casino hotel, as well as the experience and responsibilities of the individual.

Employment Prospects

Employment prospects are good for casino Tour Hosts. Opportunities can be found in casinos with active bus programs. Some larger casinos bring in over 100 buses or more daily. Individuals may work either full or part time.

Land-based casinos, dockside and floating riverboat casinos, and Indian gaming facilities all use active bus programs and are potential employment possibilities.

Advancement Prospects

Advancement opportunities depend to a great extent on the area in which the individual desires to work. This is often an entry-level position and a good way to get in the door of the casino. Individuals can then move into a variety of other areas with experience and the proper training. Some Tour Hosts go into public relations or marketing.

Some Tour Hosts obtain additional training or education and experience and are promoted within the tour and travel department. Others move into other areas of customers service such as VIP hosts, slot hosts, and other hosting positions.

Education and Training

Most casinos and casino hotels prefer Tour Hosts to have a minimum of a high school diploma or the equivalent. Many facilities help those who do not have a high school diploma obtain a GED.

Special Requirements

Depending on the specific state, Tour Hosts may be required to be state licensed.

Experience, Skills, and Personality Traits

As noted, this job is usually an entry-level position. Any experience in the hospitality industry will be helpful, as well as experience dealing with the public.

Tour Hosts should be personable, enthusiastic, outgoing people who enjoy being around others. They should be articulate with good communication skills. Customer and guest service skills are mandatory.

Unions and Associations

Those interested in learning more about careers as casino Tour Hosts can obtain additional information by contacting the human resources departments in casinos and casino hotels.

Tips for Entry

1. While experience is not necessary in most situations, it is always useful. Be sure to mention any retail sales experience or any experience in hospitality or food service when seeking a job.

2. Many casinos have job hotline numbers. These offer current job opportunities available at the facility. Call each casino directly to obtain its job hotline phone number.

3. This is a great job to get your foot in the door of a casino. Most promote from within. Obtain experience and move up the career ladder.

4. Jobs may be advertised in the classified sections of newspapers in areas hosting gaming. Look under classifications such as "Casino/Gaming Opportunities," "Casino Tour Host," "Bus Tour Host," "Travel/Tour Program Host," "Casino Bus Program," or "Tour Host."

5. Stop by the human resources departments of casinos and inquire about job openings. You might also send or fax a résumé and a short cover letter.

6. Look for casino job or career fairs. These jobs are often available at fairs.

7. This a great job for college students on summer vacation or retired people looking for part-time employment.

EXECUTIVE DIRECTOR, GAMING TRADE ASSOCIATION

Duties: Oversee operations of trade association; manage business affairs of organization; implement programs; develop budgets.

Alternate Title(s): Association Executive; Trade Association Director

Salary Range: $26,000 to $85,000+

Employment Prospects: Fair

Advancement Prospects: Fair

Best Geographical Location(s) for Position: Positions located in areas hosting gaming and/or gaming related industries; some positions may be located in or around Washington, D.C.

Prerequisites:

Education or Training—Most positions require or prefer minimum of four-year college degree.

Experience—Experience with public relations, grant writing, administration, and gaming industry.

CAREER LADDER

```
Executive Director of Larger, More
Prestigious Gaming Trade Association or
Trade Association in Other Industry
              |
Executive Director, Gaming Trade
Association
              |
Trade Association Assistant Director,
Public Relations Director, Grant Writer or
Administrator, or Journalist
```

Special Skills and Personality Traits—Management skills; grant-writing skills; fund-raising skills; creativity; personable; excellent verbal and written communications skills; understanding of gaming industry.

Position Description

The gaming industry, like other industries, has a large number of trade groups, associations, and organizations geared at promoting their particular segment of the industry. These trade associations cover a wide array of areas, including those that deal with casinos, casino employees, employers, educators, casino machines and equipment, state and local gaming, gaming hotels, restaurants, entertainment, and regulatory issues.

The individual in charge of overseeing the operations of these groups is called the Executive Director. In some instances, he or she may also be called the trade association director.

Trade associations generally are not-for-profit organizations. The main function of the Executive Director is to manage the affairs of the organization. Responsibilities can vary greatly depending on the specific organization, its mission, size, structure, prestige, and budget. In smaller organizations, the Executive Director may handle everything alone or perhaps with the help of committees of volunteers. In larger trade associations, the Executive Director may have a large staff and assistants to help handle the various duties.

The Executive Director works with the board of directors of the organization to establish the direction in which the trade association will go. The individual is also expected to determine what types of programs the association will undertake.

The Executive Director is heavily involved in the budget and finances of the organization. One of the responsibilities of the individual may be the preparation of an annual budget. Depending on the size and structure of the organization, this may be difficult because many of these organizations work with limited budgets.

In order to help increase the funds of the association, the Executive Director is often responsible for fund-raising. The individual may develop, implement, and execute a number of special events during the year to raise needed money. These events may include dinners, membership drives, auctions, galas, and golf tournaments. If the association is large, there may a fund-raising director who handles this function.

Grants are another source of funds that trade associations depend on to sustain themselves. The Executive Director is responsible for locating grants from federal, state, or local agencies and from private industry. He or she must then write and prepare the grant application. If the individual is successful in securing a grant, he or she must then make sure that all rules and regulations of the grant are adhered to. In some situations the Executive Director will oversee a grant writer and administrator who handles these tasks.

The Executive Director is expected to either personally handle or oversee the association's public relations and advertising. This may include public relations and advertising efforts directed toward the public as well as internally within the organization's membership.

As part of this responsibility press releases, calendar schedules, and newsletters must be developed and prepared. In addition, brochures, leaflets, and booklets must be developed and designed to promote the organization. In smaller organizations, the Executive Director may handle these tasks himself. In larger organizations, the Executive Director is responsible for overseeing the public relations and publications department and staffers.

Many trade associations depend on the help of volunteers within their membership. The Executive Director is responsible for coordinating the efforts of all volunteer groups and committees within the association membership.

A big responsibility for the Executive Director of trade associations in the gaming industry is scheduling conferences, conventions, and other educational and networking activities. The Executive Director is expected to either handle these activities and events personally, or delegate the duties to a committee or conference coordinator.

The Executive Director of the trade association must be the champion of the organization. He or she is expected to attend meetings and events on behalf of the association. This may include industry events as well as community meetings. The individual will often be the liaison between the association and community groups often serving on boards of community and civic organizations.

Other responsibilities of the Executive Director of a gaming industry trade association might include:

- Developing new membership drives and handling membership applications and renewals
- Assisting with lobbying efforts
- Supervising staff
- Dealing with issues significant to the associations
- Attending industry meetings, conferences, and conventions on behalf of the association

Salaries
Earnings for Executive Directors of gaming industry trade associations can range from approximately $26,000 to $85,000, and may run higher, depending on a number of factors. These include the size, structure, prestige, and budget of the specific trade association. Other factors affecting earnings include the responsibilities, professional reputation, and experience of the individual.

Employment Prospects
Employment prospects are fair for individuals seeking positions as Executive Directors of gaming, industry trade associations. Individuals may find employment in a wide array of areas dealing with gaming, which might include casinos, casino employees, employers, educators, casino machines and equipment, state and local gaming, gaming hotels, restaurants, entertainment, regulatory issues, and more. It should be noted that individuals may need to relocate for positions.

Advancement Prospects
Advancement prospects are fair for Executive Directors of gaming industry trade associations. Advancement is often dependent to a great extent on the level the individual has currently achieved in his or her career.

The Executive Director of a gaming industry trade association may climb the career ladder by finding similar positions at larger or more prestigious gaming or gaming related trade associations. In some cases, the Executive Director may also seek advancement by successfully building his or her trade association into a larger, more prestigious association. In these situations, this will often result in increased responsibilities and earnings. Some Executive Directors also advance their careers by moving into similar positions in larger or more prestigious associations outside of the gaming industry. There are others who move into corporate positions in the gaming industry.

Education and Training
Education and training requirements vary for Executive Directors of gaming industry trade associations. Most large associations require or prefer their applicant have at minimum a four-year college degree. There are, however, smaller associations that may accept an applicant with an associate's degree or even a high school diploma coupled with experience.

Courses, seminars, and workshops in fund-raising, grant writing, public relations, business management, and presentation techniques will be useful in honing skills and making new contacts.

Experience, Skills, and Personality Traits

Experience requirements depend, to a great extent, on the size, structure, and prestige of the specific trade association. Individuals seeking positions with large, prestigious gaming associations will generally be required to either have a minimum of two to three years' experience working with trade associations in some manner or working at a high-level corporate job within the industry. Experience in public relations, journalism, grant writing, and working with not-for-profit organizations will also be helpful.

Individuals in this position need to be well-spoken with excellent written and verbal communication skills. An understanding of grant writing is usually necessary, as is the ability to develop and adhere to budgets. People skills are essential.

Those who are creative and visionaries for the particular trade association will be especially successful in this type of job. Management and supervisory skills are also crucial.

An understanding and knowledge of the specific area of the industry that the association serves is essential.

Unions and Associations

Individuals interested in careers as Executive Directors of gaming industry trade associations may want to contact the Center for Association Leadership in Washington, D.C. They should also join other professional associations representing the gaming industry.

Tips For Entry

1. Get experience working with not-for-profit organizations by volunteering with a local civic or community organization.
2. Look for job openings in areas hosting gaming companies. Heading titles might be under key words such as "Trade Association," "Trade Association Executive Director," "Executive Director," "Gaming Trade Association," or "Association Executive." Jobs may also be advertised under the name of the specific gaming trade association.
3. Openings may be listed on the Web sites of specific gaming trade associations.
4. Network as much as you can in the industry. Go to conferences, conventions, and educational seminars and workshops to meet industry insiders.
5. Offer to do the publicity or fund-raising for a local not-for-profit organization. It doesn't matter if the organization is related to the gaming industry or not. If you can do publicity or fund-raising for one organization, you can do it for any type of group.
6. Read trade publications. They often advertise openings.

CASINO AND CASINO HOTEL SECURITY AND SURVEILLANCE

DIRECTOR OF SECURITY

Position Description

Many people feel that casinos are one of the safest places in the world to visit. Because legalized gaming must adhere to strict state and government regulations, and in order to keep things legal and safe, most casinos have very extensive security and surveillance departments.

While many think these two departments are the same, there are tremendous differences. The surveillance department consists of officers who are generally not seen by those outside of the surveillance department. Additionally, surveillance officers are not usually known or visible to other employees of the casino. They usually work in an isolated area of the casino observing the casino gaming area and other surroundings via closed-circuit cameras.

The security department, on the other hand, is visible. While there may be a number of security officers who are non-uniformed or in plain clothes, the depart-

ment mainly consists of large number of security officers who are uniformed and identifiable in the casino.

The individual in charge of overseeing the security department and its operations throughout the casino or casino hotel is called the Director of Security or security director. Within the scope of the job, the individual has a great many responsibilities.

The Director of Security in a casino or casino hotel is expected to lead the department in providing security and protection for guests, employees, and casino property. As part of this responsibility, he or she assures that the security staff protects all areas of the casino and casino hotel, including the gaming area, retail outlets, restaurants, bars, etc., as well as protecting its customers and employees against theft and vandalism.

The Director of Security must assure that the security department and the various areas of the casino and casino hotel are in compliance with federal, state, and local laws and regulations. Additionally, if the casino is part of an Indian gaming facility, the individual must be sure that all of the tribal rules, regulations, and laws are met and adhered to.

A big part of the job of the Director of Security in a casino is developing, updating, and implementing procedures and polices for the department. He or she must also periodically review the security measures throughout the facility as well as analyzing procedures and policies to ascertain that they are working effectively for the casino.

The Director of Security is responsible for supervising any investigations that are carried out by members of the security staff. The individual is also expected to oversee any internal investigations regarding illegal activity on the part of employees.

He or she is responsible for reporting illegal activities of employees or customers to the proper authorities. The individual will often be the contact between state, federal, and local agencies regarding security issues in or around the casino, casino hotel, or other external areas of the property.

A huge part of the job of the Director of Security is the staffing of the department. Depending on the specific casino and its structure, he or she may select and hire new employees for the department or sit in during parts of the interviewing process with members of the human resources department.

The individual is expected to coordinate the activities of the security staff, scheduling security officers and giving them their assignments. At times, he or she may need to schedule more officers for busy weekends, special events, or on days when big conventions are expected in town.

Assignments may include scheduling staff for routine patrolling of the casino floor, casino restaurants, stores, hotel, and any other additional areas within the property. The Director of Security may also assign security staff to accompany those transporting money to the cages or the count room.

The Director of Security is responsible for assuring that all security personnel are trained in accordance with the casino's policies and procedures. It is essential that while following these procedures, the security staff have the ability to handle security issues with a customer service attitude.

In addition to making sure that all staff are properly trained, the Director of Security also is expected to train qualified members of the department for supervisory positions.

As part of his or her responsibilities, the Director of Security is responsible for evaluating employees of the department. After performing these evaluations, the director of the department may terminate employees who are not performing their jobs effectively. He or she may also recommend promotions when warranted.

The individual is responsible for reviewing daily reports prepared by the security staff regarding activities that occurred during their shifts. He or she is also responsible for reviewing any incidents and actions that were taken as a result of theft, cheating, or embezzlement by either customers or employees. As part of this task, the Director of Security must be sure that every incident on the property is accurately documented. The individual is further responsible for assuring that all departmental records and reports of any kind are maintained.

The Director of Security is responsible for advising corporate management of incidents and actions that were taken. This is generally done with written reports, but may also be done verbally. In cases where the police are involved, such as in incidents where there is drug trafficking or theft, the director may be the one responsible for providing the evidence necessary for conviction.

Additional responsibilities of the Director of Security at a casino and casino hotel include:

- Directing emergency management
- Preparing annual budgets
- Maintaining relationship with police agencies
- Preparing reports for police
- Reporting any incidents to the appropriate parties
- Handling employee disciplinary actions

Salaries

Earnings for the Director of Security at casinos and casino hotels can vary greatly. Individuals may have salaries ranging from approximately $45,000 to $100,000 or more. Factors affecting earnings include the specific facility and its size, prestige, and geographic location. Other factors affecting earnings include the responsibilities and experience of the individual.

Employment Prospects

Employment prospects are fair for individuals seeking positions as the Director of Security at a casino or casino hotel. The greatest number of opportunities exist in areas where there are large numbers of casinos.

Las Vegas, Reno, Laughlin, Lake Tahoe, Atlantic City, Biloxi, Baton Rouge, New Orleans, Detroit, and Black Hawk offer the largest number of jobs. Other employment settings include casinos and casino hotels in other areas of Nevada, Mississipi, New York, Louisiana, Colorado, Connecticut, Illinois, Arizona, and

California. Other regions hosting Indian gaming and land-based or riverboat gaming facilities, racinos, and bingo will offer additional opportunities.

Advancement Prospects

Advancement prospects are fair for the Director of Security at a casino and casino hotel. Individuals may follow a number of different paths to climb the career ladder. The most common method for career advancement is finding a similar position at a larger, more prestigious casino, resulting in increased responsibilities and earnings. Other individuals advance their careers by being promoted to positions as corporate director of security or vice president of security. Some individuals strike out on their own and become security consultants for gaming companies.

Education and Training

Education and training requirements vary for the Director of Security at casinos and casino hotels. Positions generally require a minimum of a high school diploma or the equivalent. Some positions may require or prefer a bachelor's degree in criminal justice, law, or a related field.

Courses, seminars, or workshops in casino operations, games protection, fraud detection and prevention, and security will be helpful.

Training may have been done in-house as the individual goes through the ranks in the security department, or may be more formal. Some states require all members of the security department—including the director—to go through a specified training program as well as an annual in-service course to update individuals about changes in the security field and gaming regulations.

Special Requirements

The Director of Security at a casino and casino hotel, like others working in casinos, needs to be licensed by the state in which they work. This may be done either through the state's gaming authority or commission or another regulatory agency. A clean criminal record is essential. Before being hired, the Director of Security will generally also need to go through a complete background check.

Most states additionally have minimum age requirements. Those who carry firearms will require a special permit. Depending on the state individuals may also need to a certificate indicating they have gone through an alcohol awareness program or have TIPS (Training for Intervention Procedures) certification.

Experience, Skills, and Personality Traits

The Director of Security at a casino or casino hotel will be required to have a number of years of experience working in gaming security. The amount of experience often depends on the size and prestige of the casino in which the employee aspires to work and can range from five to 10 years in the field.

The Director of Security must be a responsible individual with excellent judgment and good communications skills. The ability to supervise others effectively is essential. Organizational skills are also necessary.

A knowledge of the gaming industry is needed. Problem solving skills, customer service skills, and the ability to deal with guests, employees, corporate management, and law enforcement agencies is critical.

Unions and Associations

Individuals interested in a career in this field should contact gaming institutions schools and casino human resources department.

Tips for Entry

1. Prior experience in police work, the military, or security is helpful.
2. Positions in this field are advertised in the newspaper classified section in areas hosting casinos. Look under the headings of "Casinos," "Gaming," "Director of Security," "Security Director," or "Casino Security." You might also look under the name of a specific casino or casino hotel.
3. Jobs may also be located online. Check out the Web sites of casinos and casino hotels. Many post openings on their sites.
4. Don't forget to check traditional job sites such as www.monster.com and www.hotjobs.com as well as job sites specific to the gaming industry.
5. You might also check out recruiters and search firms that specialize in the casino and gaming industry.
6. Send your résumé to casino and casino hotel human resources departments.
7. Try to attend casino conferences and conventions. They provide a wealth of networking opportunities.

SECURITY OFFICER

CAREER PROFILE

Duties: Patrolling, inspecting, and protecting casino and casino hotel property, guests, and employees; enforcing regulations; handling loss prevention.

Alternate Title(s): Security Guard

Salary Range: $19,000 to $39,000+

Employment Prospects: Good

Advancement Prospects: Fair

Best Geographical Location(s) for Position: Las Vegas, Reno, Laughlin, Lake Tahoe, Atlantic City, Biloxi, Baton Rouge, New Orleans, and Detroit offer most opportunities; other regions with land-based, riverboat, or Indian gaming facilities offer additional opportunities.

Prerequisites:

Education or Training—High school diploma or equivalent; on-the-job training; additional training may be required; see text.

Experience and Qualifications—Good moral character.

CAREER LADDER

Security Shift Commander or Seargent

Security Officer

Entry-Level or Private Security Officer, Police Officer, Member of the Military

Special Skills and Personality Traits—Good judgment; responsible; interpersonal skills; leadership; alert; deals well with others; customer relations skills; communication skills.

Special Requirements—Clean criminal record. State licensing required; minimum age requirement.

Position Description

Casinos and casino hotels take security very seriously. These facilities are among the safest places to visit. Properties have large security departments to assure the safety and protection of customers, guests, and employees.

Security Officers protect the casino and casino property. The security department should not be confused with the surveillance department, whose main responsibility is monitoring the activities in the gaming area, count rooms, and cages. One of the major ways security officers can be distinguished from surveillance officers is that Security Officers are usually visible. While there may be some plainclothes or non-uniformed security employees, security officers generally wear uniforms and can be identified. Surveillance officers, on the other hand, are not identifiable. They are not usually seen by those outside the surveillance office.

Security Officers are responsible for patrolling the casino and the rest of the facility. They walk around the casino and maintain a presence. Security Officers are assigned designated areas to patrol. It is up to them to identify potentially dangerous situations and act on them in an effective manner.

Security Officers keep the peace. Individuals are responsible for calming situations if customers become loud or boisterous. They may be required to evict guests acting in a disorderly fashion. Individuals also handle any other disturbances within the casino gaming areas and hotel.

Security Officers are responsible for protecting against theft and vandalism. Individuals must be alert to everything going on around them. They must observe the actions and activities of both customers and employees. Individuals may have to handle thefts in the casino area, as well as in any retail or food establishments in the facility. Security Officers patrol the common areas of the hotel as well to assure guest safety.

Individuals must be alert for unusual situations. This may include players who are attempting to cheat the house or employee improprieties such as embezzlement.

Gaming is a regulated industry. Security Officers are required to enforce all casino rules, as well as state gaming regulations and controls.

Some Security Officers are armed, while others are not. In the event of problems requiring police assistance, security officers may be required to detain people until the outside law enforcement agency arrives.

Security Officers often use two-way radios to keep in contact with their supervisor and vice versa. Individuals must be able to handle emergency situations such as holdups, power outages, and weather problems.

Security Officers file daily shift reports detailing any incidents or accidents that occur during shifts. All unusual activities within the casino complex must be documented.

Other duties of the casino or casino hotel Security Officer may include:

- Escorting casino employees when money or chips are being transferred
- Transporting cash and chips to designated areas
- Answering guests' questions regarding the facility
- Following state-regulated security duties
- Providing for loss prevention within the casino

Salaries

Security Officers working in casinos and casino hotels earn between $8.00 and $19.00 or more per hour. Some Security Officers earn $17,000, while others earn $39,000 or more annually. Factors affecting earnings include the geographic location, size, and prestige of the specific casino or casino hotel, as well as the education, experience, and responsibilities of the individual.

Employment Prospects

Employment prospects for Security Officers in casinos are good. The greatest number of opportunities exist in areas where there are a large number of casinos.

Advancement Prospects

With experience and/or additional training, Security Officers may be promoted to supervisory positions within the security department. Individuals may, for example, advance to positions such as shift commander or sergeant.

Education and Training

Most casinos and casino hotels prefer their Security Officers to have a high school diploma or the equivalent. Training requirements vary from state to state. In house, on-the-job training is usually provided. Individuals with no experience may start out on the graveyard shift and learn the ropes.

Certain states require individuals working as Security Officers in casinos to complete either an in-house training program or another specified training program offered in the area. Some states or casinos require an annual in-service course to refresh or update officers in changes in the security field or gaming regulations.

Armed officers must complete a firearms training course, usually involving both classroom instruction and a specified number of hours on the firing range.

Special Requirements

State licensing is required for casino security guards. Individuals who carry guns must also complete firearms training. There are also minimum age requirements for this position.

Experience, Skills, and Personality Traits

In some casinos, entry-level positions may be open. However, experience working in private security, the military, or civil service police is useful.

Many states require that Security Officers working in casinos be registered with the state. Security Officers who are armed usually also must be registered with the state to carry arms.

Security Officers require many skills. Individuals should be responsible people with good judgment. Interpersonal and customer relations skills are essential. Communication skills are mandatory.

Unions and Associations

Those interested in learning more about careers in this field can contact casino human resources departments.

Tips for Entry

1. Some community colleges, universities, and vocational technical schools offer courses for Security Officers interested in working in casinos and casino hotels. These courses may be useful in career advancement.
2. Jobs may be advertised in the classified sections of newspapers in areas hosting gaming. Look under classifications such as "Casinos/Gaming," "Casino Security," "Gaming Security," "Security Officer/Gaming," or "Casino/Hotel Opportunities."
3. Most casinos have job hotlines. These are updated messages listing jobs available. Call each casino directly to obtain its job hotline phone number.
4. Get your foot in the door of a casino hotel. Most promote from within. If you have experience in security, whether in the military or civil service, see what positions are open, get in, and then move up the career ladder.

DIRECTOR OF SURVEILLANCE

Position Description

Casinos deal with tremendous amounts of money and large numbers of customers, guests, and employees. While the majority of people visiting casinos are honest, any time there are big sums of money around, there may be those who think there is an easy way to get it. They may come up with simple or elaborate schemes and techniques to cheat either the casino or other guests and customers.

Legalized gaming must adhere to strict state and government regulations. In order to keep everything legal and safe, casinos have very extensive security and surveillance departments. The security department is filled with security officers who are uniformed, visible, and identifiable in the casino. Members of the surveillance department, on the other hand, are not usually seen by those outside the surveillance office. As a matter of fact, in most cases, the surveillance officers are not even known or visible to other employees of the casino, with members of the surveillance department generally working in an isolated area of the casino.

The individual in charge of overseeing the surveillance department and its operations throughout the casino is called the Director of Surveillance. Within the scope of the job, the individual has a great many responsibilities.

The main responsibility of the surveillance department is to observe the activities in the gaming areas, count rooms, and cages. In order to do this, the casino places hundreds and sometimes thousands of closed-circuit video cameras strategically throughout the casino gaming area. Some of these cameras are focused on gaming tables. Others follow people throughout the casino.

Many casinos build catwalks above the gaming tables and gaming area so surveillance can be conducted via these closed-circuit camera screens. These cameras are often referred to as "the eye in the sky."

The surveillance room is full of banks of TV screens that allow the workers in the surveillance department to see the gaming tables as well as the people in the casino and the casino hotel.

Members of the surveillance department monitor the video from these cameras in a surveillance room to determine if there are any wrongdoings, illegal activities, or problems occurring in the casino.

The Director of Surveillance coordinates the activities of the entire surveillance staff to assure that the casino and its customers are protected. He or she is responsible for making sure that there is extensive protection in the gaming area against cheating and theft.

Within the scope of the job, the Director of Surveillance is also responsible for ensuring that people within the casino are safe. He or she additionally must make certain that surveillance officers watch for errors made by dealers in the ways games are dealt, played, or paid off.

The surveillance director insures that his or her department watches for cheating at all table games including roulette, craps, blackjack, and baccarat, as well as slots, bingo, keno, and so on. This is generally done by viewing the closed-circuit camera screens in the surveillance office.

The Director of Surveillance must assure that surveillance officers or observers are watching the activities of cages and cashiers. In doing this, the individual can watch to see if employees are embezzling, making accounting errors, or giving out incorrect amounts of money or chips.

The Director of Surveillance will often go to seminars, conferences, and workshops to learn about new ways people might attempt to cheat or embezzle money.

The Director of Surveillance is expected to select and recommend the hiring of new employees for the department. He or she may sit in on the interviewing process with the human resources director or may handle this process alone.

The individual is expected to coordinate the surveillance staff, scheduling surveillance officers and giving them their assignments. At times, he or she may need to schedule more officers for special circumstances, such as holiday weekends or on days when a big convention is expected in town. The individual may also schedule more staff when there is a known cheater or card counter in town.

The Director of Surveillance is responsible for training all surveillance personnel. It is essential that each employee knows what to look for when reviewing tapes and what procedures need to be followed. The individual is also expected to train qualified department employees for supervisory positions.

As part of his or her responsibilities, the Director of Surveillance performs evaluations of all employees. He or she may recommend promotions when warranted or

be expected to terminate employees who are not performing effectively.

The Director of Surveillance is also expected to review the surveillance measures in the facility. He or she may make changes or recommend improvements in the surveillance procedures being utilized to make them more effective.

The individual is responsible for reviewing daily reports prepared by the surveillance staff regarding activities that occurred during their shift, such as theft, cheating, or embezzlement from either customers or employees. He or she is also responsible for reviewing any actions that were taken as a result of these activities.

The Director of Surveillance is responsible for advising corporate management of incidents and actions. This is generally done with written reports, but may also be done verbally. In cases where the police are involved, the director may be the one responsible for providing the evidence necessary for conviction.

Additional responsibilities of the Director of Surveillance at a casino or casino hotel include:

- Reporting any incidents to the appropriate parties
- Making sure all departmental reports and records are maintained
- Handling employee disciplinary actions
- Making sure employees follow company policy
- Leading investigations in game protection concerning cheating by customers and employees
- Preparing reports for police

Salaries

Salaries the Director of Surveillance for casinos and casino hotels can range from approximately $42,000 to $100,000, but may be higher. Factors affecting earnings include the specific facility and its, prestige, size, and geographic location. Other factors affecting earnings include the responsibilities and experience of the individual.

Employment Prospects

Employment prospects are fair for Directors of Surveillance for casinos and casino hotels. The greatest number of opportunities exist in areas where there are large numbers of casinos.

Las Vegas, Reno, Laughlin, Lake Tahoe, Atlantic City, Biloxi, Baton Rouge, New Orleans, Detroit, and Black Hawk offer the largest number of jobs. Other employment settings include casinos and casino hotels in other areas of Nevada, Mississipi, New York, Louisiana, Colorado, Connecticut, Illinois, Arizona, and

California. Other regions hosting Indian gaming and land-based or riverboat gaming facilities, racinos, and bingo will offer additional opportunities.

Advancement Prospects

Advancement prospects are fair for Directors of Surveillance at casinos and casino hotels. Individuals may climb the career ladder in a number of ways. The most common method for career advancement is finding a similar position at a larger, more prestigious casino, resulting in increased responsibilities and earnings. Other individuals advance their careers by being promoted to positions as corporate director of surveillance or vice president of security and surveillance. Some individuals strike out on their own and become surveillance consultants for the casino industry.

Education and Training

Education and training requirements vary for the Director of Surveillance at casinos and casino hotels. Most casinos require a minimum of a high school diploma or the equivalent. Additional requirements generally include formal training in a number of different casino games. This is usually done at either a dealer school or gaming academy.

In certain states the Director of Surveillance must also go through an approved surveillance school course of study. These are offered in gaming schools as well as in some community colleges, vocational technical schools, and trade schools, in areas that host gambling. Some casinos also offer surveillance training internally.

Special Requirements

The Director of Surveillance at a casino needs to be licensed by the state in which he works. This is done through a state gaming authority or commission. Before being hired, the Director of Surveillance will generally also need to go through a complete background check.

Experience, Skills, and Personality Traits

The Director of Surveillance at a casino must have a number of years of experience working in the casino surveillance department. Generally, the larger and more prestigious the casino, the more experience will be required. Some casinos may require four or five years of experience in the field, while others may want 10 years or more.

Experience as a dealer is also needed so individuals can have a better knowledge of games and techniques people might use to cheat.

Supervisory experience is necessary. This may come from a prior position as a floorperson or pit boss.

The Director of Surveillance needs to be a responsible individual with excellent judgment, good communications skills, and the ability to solve problems. A total knowledge of casino games, facility policies, and state gaming rules and regulations is essential. An understanding and awareness of methods and techniques used by customers and employees for cheating is critical to success in this type of job.

Unions and Associations

Individuals interested in a career in this field should contact gaming institutions or academies, gaming schools, and casino human resources department.

Tips for Entry

1. Prior experience in surveillance, police work, the military, or security is helpful.
2. Positions in this field are advertised in the newspaper classified section in areas hosting casinos. Look under the headings of "Casinos," "Gaming," "Director of Surveillance," "Surveillance Director," or "Casino Surveillance." You might also look under the name of a specific casino or casino hotel.
3. Jobs may also be located online. Check out the Web sites of casinos and casino hotels. Many post openings on their sites.
4. Don't forget to check traditional job sites such as www.monster.com and www.hotjobs.com, as well as job sites specific to casinos.
5. You might also check out recruiters and search firms that specialize in the casino and gaming industry.
6. Send your résumé to casino hotel human resources departments.

SURVEILLANCE OFFICER

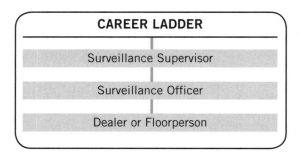

Position Description

The gaming industry must adhere to strict state and government regulations. In addition, casinos deal with a great many customers and employees and a great deal of money. In order to keep everything legal, casinos have very extensive security and surveillance departments.

The security department makes a casino one of the safest places in the world to visit. This department ensures the safety and protection of customers, guests, and employees. Security officers are visible in the casino, and most are uniformed and readily identifiable.

Members of the surveillance department work in an isolated area of the casino, apart from other employees and customers. Surveillance Officers, also called surveillance observers, are not usually seen by those outside the surveillance office and are not identifiable in the casino. The main responsibility of the surveillance department is to observe the activities in the gaming areas, count rooms, and cages.

The most visible part of surveillance are the closed-circuit video cameras located throughout the property. Surveillance Officers monitor these cameras to determine if there are any wrongdoings, illegal activities, or problems occurring in the casino.

Many casinos build catwalks above the gaming tables, where surveillance can be conducted, as well as the observation of the action in the gaming areas via the closed-circuit screens. Surveillance Officers are responsible for extensive game protection. They must watch for cheating at all table games, including roulette, craps, blackjack, and baccarat. Individuals look for cheating by both customers and employees. For example, a customer may have a $50 bet down in blackjack, looks at the hand, sees it is not good, and tries to take back some chips when a dealer looks away. An employee may try to steal chips or money from the drop box, the betting area, or other locations. Surveillance Officers also watch over the activity at the slots, Bingo, Keno, and all other gaming activities.

Surveillance Officers must be alert for unusual situations. They must be on the lookout for the various ways people attempt to cheat. Individuals also watch for errors made by dealers in the ways games are dealt, played, or paid off.

Surveillance Officers monitor the activities of the cages and cashiers. They look for improprieties like embezzlement or errors such as giving out incorrect amounts of money or chips.

Surveillance Officers must observe employees entering, working in, and leaving the count room. This is the area where the contents of drop boxes as well as the money from slots and cashiers are counted and accounted for.

Other duties of casino Surveillance Officers include:

- Reporting illegal activities of employees and customers
- Initiating enforcement procedures
- Observing to assure all casino rules and state gaming regulations and controls are followed

Salaries
Surveillance Officers working in casinos earn between $10.00 and $30.00 or more per hour. Factors affecting earnings include the geographic location, size, and prestige of the specific casino, as well as the experience and responsibilities of the individual.

Generally, Surveillance Officers working in larger, more prestigious casinos in the gaming capitals earn more than their counterparts working in other settings.

Employment Prospects
Employment prospects for Surveillance Officers in casinos are good. The greatest number of opportunities exist in areas where there are a large number of casinos. Las Vegas, Reno, Laughlin, Lake Tahoe, Atlantic City, Biloxi, Baton Rouge, New Orleans, Black Hawk, and Detroit offer the greatest number of job possibilities. Other employment settings include casino hotels in other areas of Nevada, Mississippi, New York, Louisiana, Colorado, Connecticut, Illinois, Arizona, and California.

Other regions hosting Indian gaming and land-based or riverboat gaming facilities offer additional opportunities. New casinos and casino hotels are constantly under construction. More casinos and casino hotels are also opening every year as areas legalize gambling.

Surveillance Officers work various shifts and may be expected to work weekends and holidays.

Advancement Prospects
With experience, Surveillance Officers may be promoted to supervisory positions in the surveillance department. Individuals can also find similar positions in larger, more prestigious casinos.

Education and Training
Most casinos and casino hotel prefer Surveillance Officers to have a high school diploma or the equivalent. Individuals must also be formally trained in at least one if not more casino games, usually at a dealers or gaming school. Additional training requirements vary

from state to state. In most areas, Surveillance Officers must complete an approved surveillance school course of study. These are offered in gaming schools as well as in some community colleges, vo-tech, and trade schools in areas hosting gaming. In some areas, especially those new to gaming, casinos may offer surveillance training programs themselves.

Experience, Skills, and Personality Traits
Experience as a dealer is usually necessary for this position. Casinos may prefer some supervisory experience, such as that of a floorperson.

Surveillance Officers must usually undergo a complete background check.

Surveillance Officers should be alert, responsible people with good judgment. They must have total understanding and knowledge of the rules of the casino and its games, as well as government regulations. Individuals must also be aware of cheating techniques and methods used by employees and casino customers. Individuals must be licensed by the specific state gaming authority in which they work.

Special Requirements
Surveillance Officers must be licensed by the specific state in which they work. This is done through a state gaming authority or gaming commission. Before being hired, individuals may also have to undergo a background check.

Unions and Associations
Those interested in learning more about careers in this field should contact gaming institutes, academies, and schools, as well as casino human resources departments.

Tips for Entry
1. Prior experience in surveillance, police work, or security may be helpful.
2. Jobs may be advertised in the classified sections of newspapers in areas hosting gaming. Look under classifications such as "Casinos/Gaming," "Casino/Hotel Opportunities," "Casino Surveillance," "Gaming Surveillance," "Surveillance Officer/Gaming," or "Surveillance Observer."
3. Openings are often advertised on the Internet. They may be located via the home pages of casino hotels. They may also be found by doing a search of "Casino," "Casino Hotel," or "Gaming Job Opportunities."
4. Make sure you are trained in as many table games as possible, making you more marketable.

CASINO HOTELS

CASINO HOTEL GENERAL MANAGER

CAREER PROFILE

Duties: Overseeing operations of hotel; supervising staff; assigning tasks to department heads; developing budgets.

Alternate Title(s): Manager; Hotel GM

Salary Range: $65,000 to $250,000+

Employment Prospects: Fair

Advancement Prospects: Fair

Best Geographical Location(s) for Position: Las Vegas, Reno, Laughlin, Lake Tahoe, Atlantic City, Biloxi, Baton Rouge, New Orleans, and Detroit offer most opportunities; other regions with land-based, riverboat, or Indian gaming facilities offer additional opportunities.

Prerequisites:

Education or Training—College degree in hotel or hospitality administration management required; see text.

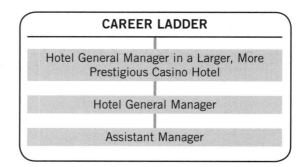

CAREER LADDER

Hotel General Manager in a Larger, More Prestigious Casino Hotel

Hotel General Manager

Assistant Manager

Experience and Qualifications—Administrative and supervisory experience working in hospitality industry.

Special Skills and Personality Traits—Administrative skills; supervisory skills; management skills; communication skills; organization.

Position Description

There are many types of casino hotels. Some, in Las Vegas for example, have hundreds of rooms, while others have accommodations for thousands. Many are like cities unto themselves. Others are smaller. A large number of casino hotels have themes or special attractions that touch upon every part of the hotel operation. The one thing all casino hotels have in common is a casino on-site.

People visit casino hotels for a number of reasons—many come to gamble, some to watch others gamble or to be a part of the excitement. Guests schedule stays at casino hotels for the lavish entertainment, the food, and the fun.

The Casino Hotel General Manager has an important job. He or she is responsible for overseeing the day-to-day operation of the facility. Specific duties vary depending on the job. The individual's main functions, however, are to make sure the establishment runs smoothly, efficiently, and profitably.

Hotels run 24 hours a day. The General Manager is responsible for supervising other managers in the facility. Depending on the specific hotel, there may be one or more assistant managers, shift managers, customer

service managers, and guest service managers in the hotel. Every hour is covered. All managers and administrative personnel report to the General Manager.

Most casino hotels are part of corporate conglomerates. In some the General Manager works in conjunction with the corporate structure, setting room rates, and developing services for guests and standards for housekeeping and food service. In others these responsibilities are handled by the president, chief executive officer (CEO), chief operating officer (COO), or executive vice president. Whoever formulates the standards, once they are set, the General Manager makes sure everything is continually up to par.

While casino hotels, like other large facilities in the hospitality industry, employ customer service and guest service managers, the General Manager has ultimate responsibility in dealing with problems or complaints. Maintaining good customer relations is important to every hotel, but especially to casino hotels where repeat business both in the hotel and the casino is imperative.

The General Manager often works with other departments, including food and beverage, marketing, public relations, promotions, and sales to find ways to bring in new customers as well as to maintain a repeat business.

The General Manager develops budgets for the entire facility or specific departments for approval by the CEO, COO, president, or executive vice president. The General Manager has the power to authorize certain expenses and approve expenditures.

Individuals in this position work long, hard hours. All problems that occur in the hotel become his or her responsibility. The individual must constantly monitor activities in the facility and take care of any problems or situations that crop up. Other responsibilities of the General Manager may include:

- Representing the hotel at public or private functions
- Participating in community affairs
- Evaluating performance of supervisory and administrative staff

Salaries

Annual earnings can range from $65,000 to $250,000 or more for Casino Hotel General Managers. Factors affecting earnings include the geographic location, size, and prestige of the specific casino hotel. Other variables include the experience, education, and responsibilities of the individual. Those working in larger, more prestigious facilities in the gambling capitals usually earn more than their counterparts in other hotels.

Employment Prospects

Employment prospects are fair for those seeking positions as Casino Hotel General Managers. Individuals can find employment in all areas hosting gaming. Individuals may work in large, luxury casino hotels, smaller casino hotels, and theme casino hotels.

Regions hosting Indian gaming and land-based or riverboat gaming facilities offer additional opportunities. New casinos and casino hotels are constantly under construction.

Advancement Prospects

Casino Hotel General Managers can advance their careers by obtaining experience and landing jobs in larger or more prestigious casino hotels, resulting in increased responsibilities and earnings. Depending on experience, education, and career aspirations, individuals may also be promoted to other administrative positions.

Education and Training

While educational requirements vary from job to job, recommended education for Casino Hotel General Managers is a minimum of bachelor's degree in hotel administration or management. In some cases, experience will be accepted in lieu of education requirements.

Some individuals move through the ranks in hotels owned by major corporations to General Manager positions, as do those who have participated in management training programs sponsored by hotels.

Experience, Skills, and Personality Traits

Casino Hotel General Managers must have a fair amount of experience working in administrative and supervisory positions within the hospitality industry. Experience working in the casino industry is also useful.

Some Casino Hotel General Managers obtain prior experience as hotel assistant managers or as General Managers in smaller hotels.

Casino Hotel General Managers should be well-spoken, articulate people with good communication skills. Supervisory, management, and administrative skills are essential. Complete understanding of the hospitality industry is mandatory.

Individuals should be organized and have the ability to prioritize projects.

Unions and Associations

Individuals interested in pursuing careers in casino hotel management can obtain additional information by contacting the American Hotel and Lodging Association (AH&LA) or the Educational Institute of the American Hotel & Lodging Association (EIAH&LA) for more information.

Tips for Entry

1. Many hotel chains offer training programs in this field. These are excellent ways to get training, and experience.
2. Jobs are often advertised in the classified sections of newspapers in areas hosting gaming. Look under classifications such as "Casino Hotels," "Casino Hotel General Manager," "Hotel General Manager," "Hospitality Careers," or "Management-Casino Hotels."
3. Contact recruitment firms specializing in the hospitality or gaming industries.

RESERVATIONS MANAGER

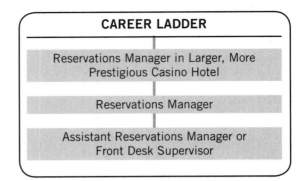

Position Description

The reservations department of a casino hotel is responsible for making sure rooms are available for guests when they arrive. Guests of casino hotels usually make reservations prior to arriving at the facilities. The Reservations Manager of a casino hotel is in charge of overseeing the entire reservations department. The individual has a vast array of duties.

The Reservations Manager supervises and coordinates the activities of the reservations clerks in the front office. The individual makes sure room clerks answer phones to take, record, and, if necessary, cancel reservations.

The Reservations Manager trains new clerks in reservations methods used by the hotel. This may include training clerks in the correct method for taking telephone reservations, as well as operating computer terminals and printers. The individual may also pass these training duties on to an assistant.

Some reservations arrive by mail. Room Reservations Managers are in charge of sorting reservations received and giving them to clerks so that this information may be input into the computer system.

The Reservations Manager is given information from sales representatives or the sales director regarding contracts detailing room allotments for conventions. This information, too, must be input into the computer system.

The Reservations Manager makes sure that room clerks at the front desk have daily printouts listing arriving guests. The individual must also verify that guests' folios are given to the front desk personnel.

The Reservations Manager devises schedules for reservations clerks. The individual may also reschedule workers to accommodate arrivals of large conventions and other groups.

Other duties of Reservations Managers may include:

- Recommending promotion and/or termination of reservations clerks
- Corresponding with individuals, groups, and travel agents to answer special requests for rooms and rates
- Handling guest problems or complaints about room reservations

Salaries

Reservations Managers working in casino hotels are usually on salary. Annual earnings range from $29,000 to $56,000 or more. Factors affecting earnings include the geographic location, size, and prestige of the facility. Other variables include the experience and responsibilities of the individual. Those working in facilities with a large number of rooms in the gambling capitals usually earn more than their counterparts in other hotels.

Employment Prospects

Employment prospects are fair for Reservations Managers in casino hotels. Individuals have more opportunities in areas with larger numbers of casino hotels.

Las Vegas, Reno, Laughlin, Lake Tahoe, Atlantic City, Biloxi, Baton Rouge, New Orleans, and Detroit offer the greatest number of job possibilities. Other employment settings include casinos and casino hotels in other areas of Nevada, Mississippi, New York, Louisiana, Colorado, Connecticut, Illinois, Arizona, and California.

Other regions hosting Indian gaming and land-based or riverboat gaming facilities offer additional opportunities. New casinos and casino hotels are constantly under construction. More casinos and casino hotels are also opening every year as areas legalize gambling.

Advancement Prospects

Reservations Managers working in casino hotels can advance their careers by finding similar positions in larger casino hotels, resulting in increased responsibilities and earnings.

Education and Training

Education and training requirements for Reservations Managers vary from job to job. Usually, a high school diploma or its equivalent is required. However, work experience may be accepted in lieu of education.

Experience, Skills, and Personality Traits

Reservations Managers must have experience in either the reservations or front desk departments of hotels. The length of experience needed varies from two to three years depending on the specific hotel. Individuals must have supervisory experience as well, often obtained through positions as assistant reservations manager or supervisor.

Complete knowledge of the front office and/or reservations departments is needed. Additionally, individuals should be computer competent.

Unions and Associations

Individuals interested in learning more about careers in this area can contact the human resources departments of casino hotels. Other information may be available from the American Hotel and Lodging Association (AH&LA).

Tips for Entry

1. Jobs are often advertised in the classified sections of newspapers in areas hosting gaming. Look under classifications such as "Casinos," "Casino Hotels," "Hotels," "Reservations," "Casino Hotel Opportunities," "Reservations Manager," "Room Reservations," or "Hospitality."
2. If you are still in school, consider an internship offered by a hotel to obtain experience and to make contacts.
3. Stop by the human resources departments of casino hotels to inquire about job openings.
4. Send your résumé to the directors of human resources at casino hotels.
5. Look for new casino hotels that are under construction. Apply early.
6. Positions may be advertised on the Internet. Look under keywords such as "Hospitality," "Hotels," and "Casinos." Also check out casino hotel home pages for employment listings.

ROOM RESERVATIONS CLERK

Position Description

Potential guests of casino hotels usually make reservations prior to arriving at facilities. Room Reservations Clerks are in charge of taking, recording, and canceling these reservations.

Room Reservations Clerks have a number of duties. They answer incoming calls from people who are interested in knowing about room rates and availability. Individuals may also be asked about specials, promotions, activities, or other events being held in the hotel or casino. Room Reservations Clerks also answer questions regarding conventions and meetings scheduled at the hotel.

Reservations Clerks retrieve information regarding room rates and availabilities. With this information Clerks can help guests choose the type of room and room rates needed.

When people decide to make reservations, the Room Reservations Clerk must obtain certain information, such as names, addresses, and phone numbers. Other information includes the number of people in the party, the date guests are arriving, and the number of nights they expect to stay. Reservations Clerks must also find out if there are any special requests, such as king-size beds, cribs, smoking, or nonsmoking sections.

Reservations Clerks then input all information into the computer, including credit card information to guarantee reservations. Clerks then usually provide confirmation numbers to guests.

Some people call to cancel reservations made previously. After Room Reservations Clerks cancel a guest's reservation, they give the individual a confirmation cancellation number to use in case they are inadvertently charged on their credit card.

Often when people call hotels, they request brochures or other written information on the facility. Room Reservations Clerks take people's names and addresses so that requested material may be forwarded to them.

Other duties of Room Reservations Clerks may include:

- Performing any additional clerical duties regarding making and canceling room reservations
- Referring guest problems or complaints about room reservations to the reservations assistant manager, manager, or supervisor

Salaries

Room Reservations Clerks working in casino hotels are paid an hourly salary. Individuals earn $16,000 to

$30,000 or more annually or between $8.00 and $14.00 or more per hour. Factors affecting earnings include the geographic location, size, and prestige of the facility. Other variables include the experience and responsibilities of the individual. Those working in larger or more prestigious facilities in the gambling capitals usually earn more than their counterparts in other hotels.

Employment Prospects

Employment prospects for Room Reservations Clerks are excellent. Individuals can find employment in locations where casino hotels are located. The number of Reservation Clerks employed by each hotel depends on the size of the facility.

Reservation Clerks work various shifts depending on the structure of the hotel. Las Vegas, Reno, Laughlin, Lake Tahoe, Atlantic City, Biloxi, Baton Rouge, New Orleans, and Detroit offer the greatest number of job possibilities. Other employment settings include casino hotels in other areas of Nevada, Mississippi, New York, Louisiana, Colorado, Connecticut, Illinois, Arizona, and California.

Other regions hosting Indian gaming and land-based or riverboat gaming facilities offer additional opportunities. New casinos and casino hotels are constantly under construction. More casinos and casino hotels are also opening every year as areas legalize gambling.

Advancement Prospects

Reservations Clerks can advance their careers by obtaining experience working in the reservations or front desk department of the hotel. Individuals may be promoted to assistant reservations managers, reservations managers, or room reservations supervisors.

Education and Training

Education and training requirements vary from job to job. Usually, a high school diploma or its equivalent is required. However, work experience may be accepted in lieu of education. On-the-job training is often available for this position.

Experience, Skills, and Personality Traits

Experience requirements, like education, vary for Reservations Clerks. In some hotels, this is an entry-level position. In others, prior experience in the reservations department is required or preferred. General understanding of the workings of the front office and/or reservations department is helpful.

Reservations Clerks should have data-entry and retrieval skills. A pleasant phone manner and customer service skills are essential.

Unions and Associations

This may or may not be a unionized position, depending on the specific casino hotel. In unionized casino hotels in Las Vegas, for example, Reservations Clerks may be members of the Teamsters Local #995 union.

Individuals interested in learning more about careers in this area can contact the human resources departments of casino hotels. Other information may be available from the American Hotel and Lodging Association (AH&LA).

Tips for Entry

1. While experience may not be required, experience usually gives one applicant an edge over another. Any experience working with reservations, whether it be with a hotel, travel agent, or airline, is useful.
2. Stop by the human resources departments of casino hotels to inquire about job openings.
3. Jobs are often advertised in the classified sections of newspapers in areas hosting gaming. Look under classifications such as "Casinos," "Casino Hotels," "Hotels," "Reservations," "Casino Hotel Opportunities," "Reservations Clerk," "Room Reservations Clerk," or "Hospitality."
4. Many casinos and casino hotels have job fairs. Look for these in the local paper in areas hosting casinos.

FRONT OFFICE MANAGER

CAREER PROFILE

Duties: Overseeing front office; supervising employees; estimating volume of reservations; overseeing guests' check-in and check-out.

Alternate Title(s): None

Salary Range: $35,000 to $60,000+

Employment Prospects: Fair

Advancement Prospects: Fair

Best Geographical Location(s) for Position: Las Vegas, Reno, Laughlin, Lake Tahoe, Atlantic City, Biloxi, Baton Rouge, New Orleans, and Detroit offer most opportunities; other regions with land-based, riverboat, or Indian gaming facilities offer additional opportunities.

Prerequisites:

Education or Training—Bachelor's degree preferred; see text.

CAREER LADDER

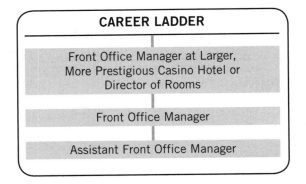

Experience and Qualifications—Experience working in front office operation.

Special Skills and Personality Traits—Organized; communication skills; administrative and supervisory skills; customer service skills.

Position Description

On any given day, successful casino hotels have a large volume of guests checking in and out. It is essential that the hotel have a system for making sure that guests who are arriving can check in easily, and those who are departing can leave in a timely manner without incident. The person in charge of overseeing these functions is the Front Office Manager.

This individual has a great deal of responsibility. The Front Office Manager oversees everything that occurs in the department, including supervising the front office staff. Employees in the front office include an assistant front office manager, front desk managers, front office shift supervisors, front office agents or representatives, front office cashiers, mail and information clerks, reservation and assistant reservations managers, and reservations clerks. In some hotels the Front Office Manager is also responsible for customer relations managers, concierges, and the bell staff.

The Front Office Manager trains the front desk staff to make sure they deal with guests in a courteous and efficient manner.

The Front Office Manager coordinates reservations and room assignments. It is imperative that the individual know how many of each room type are available

at all times. The Front Office Manager must also know approximately how many reservations are firm, assuring that hotel rooms are not overbooked.

The Front Office Manager develops systems for guest information. In most hotels, information is entered into a computer system. The hotel must know exactly who is registered in each room, the number of guests, and the length of their stay.

The Front Office Manager sees that departments are in contact with one another to make sure rooms are available when needed.

Other duties of the casino hotel Front Office Manager may include:

- Resolving guest complaints and problems
- Handling guests' requests for special services

Salaries

A Front Office Manager earns between $35,000 and $60,000 or more annually. Factors affecting earnings include the geographic location, size, and prestige of the specific casino hotel, as well as the experience and responsibilities of the individual. Generally, those with the most experience working in larger or more prestigious casinos hotels in the gambling capitals earn the highest salaries.

Employment Prospects

Employment prospects for casino hotel Front Office Managers are fair and may be found throughout the country. Las Vegas, Reno, Laughlin, Lake Tahoe, Atlantic City, Biloxi, Baton Rouge, New Orleans, and Detroit offer the greatest number of job possibilities.

Other employment settings include casinos and casino hotels in other areas of Nevada, Mississippi, New York, Louisiana, Colorado, Connecticut, Illinois, Arizona, and California.

Other regions hosting Indian gaming and land-based or riverboat gaming facilities offer additional opportunities. New casinos and casino hotels are constantly under construction. More casinos and casino hotels are also opening every year as areas legalize gambling.

Advancement Prospects

Casino hotel Front Office Managers may climb the career ladder by obtaining more experience and/or training. Individuals may find similar positions in larger, more prestigious casino hotels, resulting in increased earnings. A casino hotel Front Office Manager may also advance his or her career by locating a position as a director of rooms.

Education and Training

Educational requirements vary at different casino hotels. While every position does not require college, a bachelor's degree is recommended. Good majors include hotel management, marketing, sales, or liberal arts. Some hotels accept experience in lieu of education.

Courses, workshops, and seminars in the hospitality and gaming industry are useful.

Experience, Skills, and Personality Traits

Prior to hiring someone as a Front Office Manager, casino hotels usually require three to four years experience working in various areas of the front office.

Casino hotel Front Office Managers should be very organized and have administrative and supervisory skills. Communication skills and customer service skills are essential.

Unions and Associations

Those interested in learning more about careers as casino hotel Front Office Managers can obtain additional information by contacting the Council on Hotel, Restaurant and Institutional Education (CHRIE), Hotel Sales and Marketing Association International (HSMA), or the human resources departments in casino hotels.

Tips for Entry

1. Get your foot in the door of a casino hotel. Most promote from within. You might have to start out as a trainee, but if you work hard, you will move up the career ladder.
2. Stop by the human resources departments of casino hotels and inquire about job openings. You might also consider sending a résumé and a short cover letter.
3. Jobs may be advertised in the classified sections of newspapers in areas hosting gaming. Look under classifications such as "Hotel Front Office Manager," "Casino Hotel Front Office Manager," "Front Office Manager," "Front Office," or "Casino Opportunities."
4. A number of search firms deal exclusively with positions in the hospitality industry. A few deal with jobs in gaming related to the hospitality industry.
5. Surf the net looking for openings. Many casinos and casino hotels list their openings on a special employment or job section of their Web sites.
6. Don't forget to check out job sites like www.monster.com and www.hotjobs.com.

FRONT DESK MANAGER

CAREER PROFILE

Duties: Overseeing front desk clerks.

Alternate Title(s): None

Salary Range: $28,000 to $42,000+

Employment Prospects: Fair

Advancement Prospects: Fair

Best Geographical Location(s) for Position: Las Vegas, Reno, Laughlin, Lake Tahoe, Atlantic City, Biloxi, Baton Rouge, New Orleans, and Detroit offer most opportunities; other regions with land-based, riverboat, or Indian gaming facilities offer additional opportunities.

Prerequisites:

Education or Training—High school diploma or equivalent; on-the-job training; see text.

Experience and Qualifications—Experience working in front office operation.

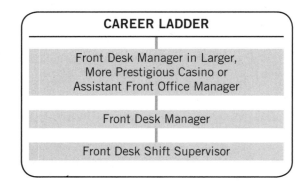

CAREER LADDER

Front Desk Manager in Larger, More Prestigious Casino or Assistant Front Office Manager

Front Desk Manager

Front Desk Shift Supervisor

Special Skills and Personality Traits—Organization; supervisory skills; communication skills; computer skills; customer service skills.

Position Description

The front desk is the place in the casino hotel where guests check in and check out. To run this area in an efficient manner, the hotel employs front office or front desk clerks. The individual responsible for overseeing these employees is called the Front Desk Manager. In some casino hotels the person is called the front desk supervisor.

The Front Desk Manager supervises all activities of the front desk clerks. He or she is responsible for making sure the clerks are properly trained. The Front Desk Manager makes certain that clerks welcome guests when they arrive and treats each one in a courteous and pleasant manner.

The Front Desk Manager is responsible for handling problems that may occur with guests' reservations. This might include, for example, a reservation that somehow is not in the computer. The Front Desk Manager does everything possible to keep guests happy. This can mean upgrading a room or offering some type of amenity. In some cases, these decisions may have to be authorized by the front office manager.

The Front Desk Manager assists clerks in solving difficulties with credit cards or in handling check cashing or other monetary transactions.

The Front Desk Manager assists clerks with guests' problems at checkout. These might include charges guests think are incorrect or were supposed to be "comped" or provided at no charge.

Other duties of the casino hotel Front Desk Manager may include:

- Handling customer complaints and problems
- Recommending front office clerks for promotion

Salaries

Depending on the specific casino hotel, Front Desk Managers are paid an hourly wage or a weekly salary. Individuals may earn between $12.00 and $20.00 or more per hour or be paid annual salaries ranging from $28,000 and $42,000 plus.

Factors affecting earnings include the geographic location, size, and prestige of the specific casino hotel, as well as the experience and responsibilities of the individual.

Employment Prospects

Employment opportunities for casino hotel Front Desk Managers are fair. Las Vegas, Reno, Laughlin, Lake Tahoe, Atlantic City, Biloxi, Baton Rouge, New Orleans, and Detroit offer the greatest number of job possibilities. Other employment settings include casinos and casino hotels in other areas of Nevada, Mississippi, New York, Louisiana, Colorado, Connecticut, Illinois, Arizona, and California.

Other regions hosting Indian gaming and land-based or riverboat gaming facilities offer additional opportunities. New casinos and casino hotels are constantly under construction. More casinos and casino hotels are also opening every year as areas legalize gambling.

Advancement Prospects

Casino hotel Front Desk Managers may climb the career ladder by obtaining more experience and/or training. They may then locate similar positions in larger, more prestigious casino hotels, resulting in increased earnings. With additional experience and training an individual may also be promoted to the job of assistant front office manager.

Education and Training

Most hotels require individuals to hold a high school diploma or the equivalent. Experience may be accepted in lieu of education. Individuals are usually trained on the job for this position.

Experience, Skills, and Personality Traits

Generally, Front Desk Managers must have at least one year of experience working in the front office of a hotel. Individuals must be organized, detail-oriented, and have supervisory skills. Computer skills and customer service skills are essential in this job.

An understanding of the front office and the hospitality industry is also necessary.

Unions and Associations

Those interested in learning more about careers as casino hotel Front Desk Managers can obtain additional information by contacting the Council on Hotel, Restaurant and Institutional Education (CHRIE), Hotel Sales and Marketing Association International (HSMA), or the human resources departments in casino hotels.

Tips for Entry

1. If you do not live in a gaming area and aspire to work in a casino hotel, get experience in the front office of a luxury hotel before you move.
2. The human resources departments of casino hotels will tell you of any job openings.
3. Most casinos have job hotlines. These are frequently updated messages listing jobs available. You can call each casino directly to get its job hotline phone number.
4. Jobs are often advertised in the classified sections of newspapers in areas hosting gaming. Look under classifications such as "Hotel Front Desk Manager," "Casino Hotel Front Desk Manager," "Front Desk Manager," "Hospitality Industry," or "Casino Hotel Opportunities."
5. Check out casino and casino hotel Web sites for openings.
6. You might also want to surf the net for openings on traditional job sites like www.monster.com and www.hotjobs.com.
7. There are Web sites dedicated specifically to jobs on the casino industry. Check out the appendix for some of them.

FRONT OFFICE CLERK

Position Description

When guests arrive at a casino hotel, they usually expect to check in quickly and efficiently. Front Office Clerks are the individuals responsible for making sure this happens. Front Office Clerks may also be called front office agents or front desk clerks.

Front Office Clerks welcome guests and check their reservations, often by computer. Information regarding the reservation is retrieved from the computer by the Front Office Clerk, who then registers the guest.

The Front Office Clerk usually asks the guest for identification such as a driver's license or credit card. In many situations the individual makes an imprint of the guest's credit card to guarantee payment.

The Front Office Clerk checks the computer to see what type of room has been reserved and assigns the guest to his or her room. Information regarding guests must also be input into the computer system.

The Front Office Clerk issues the guest one or more room keys. In some situations, hotels use computerized cards instead of keys. The Front Office Clerk may be responsible for explaining how such cards work.

The Front Office Clerk assists guests when they check out. The individual asks if the guest had a pleasant stay. During this time, the Front Office Clerk brings up the necessary computer information regarding guest charges.

The Front Office Clerk must deal with guests in a courteous and efficient manner at all times.

Other duties of the casino hotel Front Office Clerk may include:

- Cashing checks or handling other monetary transactions for guests
- Accepting payment for guest charges, including rooms, room service, restaurant and bar bills, and other amenities

Salaries

Casino hotel Front Office Clerks are paid an hourly wage. Individuals may earn between $8.00 and $14.00 or more per hour or about $17,000 to $28,000 annually. Factors affecting earnings include the geographic location, size, and prestige of the specific casino hotel, as well as the experience and responsibilities of the individual. In some hotels, Front Office Clerks may also receive tips.

Employment Prospects

Employment opportunities for casino hotel Front Office Clerks are plentiful. They may be found throughout the country.

Las Vegas, Reno, Laughlin, Lake Tahoe, Atlantic City, Biloxi, Baton Rouge, New Orleans, and Detroit offer the greatest number of job possibilities. Other employment settings include casinos and casino hotels in other areas of Nevada, Mississippi, New York, Louisiana, Colorado, Connecticut, Illinois, Arizona, and California.

Other regions hosting Indian gaming and land-based or riverboat gaming facilities offer additional opportunities. New casinos and casino hotels are constantly under construction. More casinos and casino hotels are also opening every year as areas legalize gambling.

Advancement Prospects

Casino hotel Front Office Clerks may climb the career ladder by obtaining more experience and/or training. They may then locate similar positions in larger, more prestigious casino hotels, resulting in increased earnings. With additional experience and training, individuals may also be promoted to front office shift supervisor.

Education and Training

Educational requirements vary with different casino hotels. Most hotels require individuals to hold a high school diploma or the equivalent. Experience may be accepted in lieu of education. Individuals are usually trained on the job for this position.

Experience, Skills, and Personality Traits

Depending on the hotel, this may be an entry-level position. Individuals must be organized and detail-oriented. Customer service and interpersonal skills are essential.

Understanding of hotel front office activities and the hospitality industry is useful.

Unions and Associations

Depending on the specific casino, this may or may not be a unionized position. In unionized hotels in Las Vegas, for example, Front Office Clerks may be members of the Teamsters Local #995.

Those interested in learning more about careers as casino hotel Front Office Clerks can obtain additional information by contacting the Council on Hotel, Restaurant and Institutional Education (CHRIE), Hotel Sales and Marketing Association International (HSMA), or the human resources departments in casino hotels.

Tips for Entry

1. This is a good job to get your foot in the door of a casino hotel. Remember that most facilities promote from within. Learn as much as you can and work hard to move up the career ladder.
2. Visit the human resources departments of casino hotels and inquire about job openings.
3. At casino job fairs in areas hosting gaming these types of positions are often available.
4. Jobs may be advertised in the classified sections of newspapers in areas hosting gaming. Look under classifications such as "Hotel Front Office Clerk," "Casino Hotel Front Office Clerk," "Front Office Clerk," "Front Office," or "Casino Opportunities."
5. Most casinos have job hotlines. These are frequently updated messages listing jobs available. You can call each casino directly to get its job hotline phone number.
6. Openings are often advertised on the Internet. They may be located via the home pages of casino hotels. They may also be found by doing a search of "Casino," "Casino Hotel," or "Gaming Job Opportunities."

CONCIERGE

CAREER PROFILE

Duties: Providing special assistance and service to casino hotel guests.

Alternate Title(s): None

Salary Range: $25,000 to $50,000+

Employment Prospects: Good

Advancement Prospects: Good

Best Geographical Location(s) for Position: Las Vegas, Reno, Laughlin, Lake Tahoe, Atlantic City, Biloxi, Baton Rouge, New Orleans, and Detroit offer most opportunities; other regions with land-based, riverboat, or Indian gaming facilities offer additional opportunities.

Prerequisites:

Education or Training—Minimum of high school diploma or equivalent; on-the-job training; some employees may prefer or require a college background or degree.

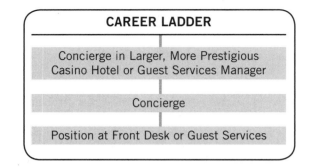

CAREER LADDER

Concierge in Larger, More Prestigious Casino Hotel or Guest Services Manager

Concierge

Position at Front Desk or Guest Services

Experience and Qualifications—Experience working in hospitality industry.

Special Skills and Personality Traits—Customer service skills; service-oriented; communication skills; personable; detail-oriented; ingenuity; articulate; computer skills.

Position Description

Casino hotels, especially the larger, more luxurious ones, pride themselves on customer service. The more the hotel staff can do to accommodate guests' needs, the better. These hotels employ a person called the Concierge to provide special assistance and service to hotel guests.

The Concierge performs a variety of services. He or she may, for example, help a guest obtain tickets to a show either in the hotel or at another hotel's showroom. Sometimes the Concierge is asked to obtain tickets to sold-out events or shows for which tickets are no longer available.

Guests may be looking for a restaurant that serves a specific type of food. The Concierge tells the guests about the restaurants in the area and may recommend one or two. He or she may even get a sample menu for guests to look over before they visit the restaurant.

The Concierge may be asked to find babysitters, nannies, or other child care services for guests. The individual might also make arrangements for guests to take a tour of the casino, the area, or special attractions nearby.

The Concierge assists guests who need courier services, cell phone or beeper rentals, fax or computer rentals, or secretarial services.

The Concierge helps guests requiring other types of special services. For example, a guest wants to talk to a casino representative who speaks another language so that the rules of a game can be explained in the guest's native tongue.

The Concierge may be asked to find a shop that sells a specific brand of clothing or to find an after-hours pharmacy. The individual might additionally be required to recommend a physician, dentist, or optician close by.

The Concierge gives information to guests when they are looking for something interesting to do in the area. The individual may make arrangements for transportation such as limos or car service, or recommend various entertainment activities.

Depending on the hotel, the concierge may be responsible for attending to the needs of VIP guests or may be expected to handle the special needs of all guests. The individual sometimes has an office on a special floor of the hotel, or may be found at a desk in the lobby.

In order to be effective, Concierges must have a great many contacts both in and out of the casino hotel. They must know every inch of the area or city in which they are located.

Other duties of the casino hotel Concierge may include:

- Introducing hotel guests to casino personnel
- Assisting guests with other services

Salaries

Depending on the specific casino hotel, Concierges are usually paid an hourly wage ranging from $15.00 to $25.00, but may be higher. The Concierge also often receives tips from hotel guests. Individuals may have annual earnings ranging from $25,000 to $50,000 or more including tips.

Factors affecting earnings include the geographic location, size, and prestige of the specific casino hotel, as well as the experience and responsibilities of the individual. A major factor affecting earnings is the ability to provide the services guests are seeking.

Employment Prospects

Employment opportunities for casino hotel Concierges are good. Jobs may be found throughout the country in larger, prestigious, and luxury casino hotels, as well as in many of the smaller ones.

Las Vegas, Reno, Laughlin, Lake Tahoe, Atlantic City, Biloxi, Baton Rouge, New Orleans, and Detroit offer the greatest number of job possibilities. Other employment settings include casinos and casino hotels in other areas of Nevada, Mississippi, New York, Louisiana, Colorado, Connecticut, Illinois, Arizona, and California.

Other regions hosting Indian gaming and land-based or riverboat gaming facilities offer additional opportunities. New casinos and casino hotels are constantly under construction. More casinos and casino hotels are also opening every year as areas legalize gambling.

Advancement Prospects

Casino hotel Concierges may climb the career ladder by obtaining more experience and locating similar positions in larger or more prestigious hotels, resulting in increased earnings. With additional training and experience Concierges can be promoted to customer relations managers.

Education and Training

Most hotels require Concierges to hold a minimum of a high school diploma or the equivalent. Experience may be accepted in lieu of education. College training in hotel management is a plus. Concierges are usually trained on the job for this position.

Experience, Skills, and Personality Traits

Generally, Concierges working in a casino hotel are required to have some experience working in a hotel. Some individuals have worked in guest services or at the front desk.

To be successful, Concierges must have customer service skills, be personable, and like to help people. Individuals should have a great deal of ingenuity and creativity in order to "do the impossible." They should also be organized and detail-oriented.

Understanding of the hospitality industry is also necessary.

Unions and Associations

Those interested in learning more about careers as Concierges can obtain additional information by contacting the Council on Hotel, Restaurant and Institutional Education (CHRIE) or the human resources departments in casino hotels.

Tips For Entry

1. If you are not currently living in a gaming area and aspire to work in such a region, get experience in some capacity working in a luxury hotel before you move.
2. Stop by the human resources departments of casino hotels to learn of job openings.
3. Jobs may be advertised in the classified sections of newspapers in areas hosting gaming. Look under classifications such as "Hotels," "Concierge," "Hospitality Industry," "Casino Hotels," or "Casino Hotel Opportunities."
4. Look for new casino hotels under construction. Apply early for the best positions.
5. Surf the net. Job openings may be located on casino and casino hotel Web sites as well as on traditional job sites.

BELL CAPTAIN

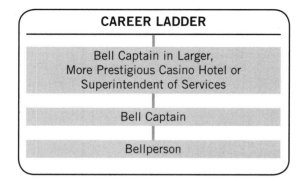

Special Skills and Personality Traits:—Interpersonal skills; customer service skills; supervisory skills; organization; friendly; courteous; ability to carry heavy baggage.

Position Description

Thousands of guests check in and out of casino hotels every day. Those who help guests carry their luggage in and out of the hotel are called bellpersons or bellhops. The person who supervises these individuals is called the Bell Captain.

Depending on the hotel, the Bell Captain reports to the customer relations manager or the superintendent of services. In some hotels, the Bell Captain also handles the duties of a superintendent of services.

Bell Captains have a number of responsibilities. They are in charge of the bellhops. When guests arrive at a casino hotel and are given rooms, the Bell Captain assigns a bellperson to escort guests to their rooms, transporting their luggage as well.

When guests are ready to depart, they often make a call to the service desk, requesting a bellperson. Bell Captains assign bellpersons to go to guests' rooms to bring luggage to the checkout area or to transport it to the guests' vehicles.

Bell Captains may also be responsible for supervising the hotel's front door staff, the employees who assist arriving and departing guests, open doors, welcome guests, call taxis, and help guests with public transportation needs.

Casino hotel guests arrive by car, limo, public transportation, or by chartered or scheduled bus. The Bell Captain is additionally responsible for overseeing the baggage handlers who load, unload, and sort guests' luggage for movement to and from rooms.

Bell Captains answer questions regarding activities and facilities in the casino and hotel, as well as questions about attractions in the area, and public transportation.

Bell Captains must have an understanding of the duties of the bellpersons, door attendants, and baggage handlers. When these employees are busy with guests leaving, arriving, or in need of service, the Bell Captain may be required to step in to perform their duties.

Other duties of the Bell Captain may include:

- Scheduling bell persons, door attendants, and baggage handlers
- Handling special requests for guests
- Taking care of guest complaints regarding bellpersons, door people, and baggage handlers.

Salaries

Bell Captains working in hotel casinos are usually paid an hourly salary. Individuals may earn between $7.00

and $15.00 per hour or more plus tips. Bell Captains may earn between approximately $29,000 and $52,000 annually, including tips. Factors affecting earnings include the geographic location, size, and prestige of the casino hotel. Other variables include the experience and responsibilities of the individual. Those working in larger or more prestigious facilities in the gambling capitals usually earn more than their counterparts in other hotels.

Some Bell Captains receive a salary instead of an hourly wage.

Employment Prospects

Employment prospects are good for Bell Captains in casino hotels. Individuals can find employment wherever casino hotels are located. There usually is one Bell Captain per shift. Because casinos hotels operate 24 hours a day, individuals may work the day shift, swing or evening shift, overnight or graveyard shift.

Las Vegas, Reno, Laughlin, Lake Tahoe, Atlantic City, Biloxi, Baton Rouge, New Orleans, and Detroit offer the greatest number of job possibilities. Other employment settings include casinos and casino hotels in other areas of Nevada, Mississippi, New York, Louisiana, Colorado, Connecticut, Illinois, Arizona, and California.

Other regions hosting Indian gaming and land-based or riverboat gaming facilities offer additional opportunities. New casinos and casino hotels are constantly under construction. More casinos and casino hotels are also opening every year as areas legalize gambling.

Advancement Prospects

There are a number of ways Bell Captains can advance their careers. Individuals can find similar positions in larger or more prestigious hotels, resulting in increased responsibilities and earnings. Bell Captains may also be promoted to other supervisory positions, including superintendent of services, or customer relations manager. These promotions usually require that the individual obtain additional experience.

Education and Training

Education and training requirements vary from job to job. Usually, a high school diploma or its equivalent is required. However, work experience may be accepted in lieu of education.

Experience, Skills, and Personality Traits

Experience requirements, like education, vary for Bell Captains. In many positions, Bell Captains are promoted from the ranks of bellpersons.

To be successful, Bell Captains should be friendly, courteous individuals with excellent customer service and interpersonal skills. Ability to carry heavy baggage is necessary, as is understanding of the service and hospitality industries.

Unions and Associations

Individuals interested in learning more about careers in this area can contact the human resources departments of casino hotels. Other information may be available from the American Hotel and Lodging Association (AH&LA).

Tips for Entry

1. Get experience as a bellperson in a casino hotel. Management often promotes from within.
2. Stop by human resources departments to inquire about job openings.
3. Jobs are often advertised in the classified sections of newspapers in areas hosting gaming. Look under classifications such as "Casinos," "Casino Hotels," "Hotels," "Bell Captain," "Casino Hotel Opportunities," and "Gaming."
4. Job openings may also be listed on casino and casino hotel Web sites.

BELLPERSON

CAREER PROFILE

Duties: Escorting hotel guests to rooms; assisting with luggage; inspecting guests' rooms to ensure guest satisfaction.

Alternate Title(s): Bellman; Bellwoman; Bellhop; Bell Attendant

Salary Range: $18,000 to $29,000+

Employment Prospects: Excellent

Advancement Prospects: Fair

Best Geographical Location(s) for Position: Las Vegas, Reno, Laughlin, Lake Tahoe, Atlantic City, Biloxi, Baton Rouge, New Orleans, and Detroit offer most opportunities; other regions with land-based, riverboat, or Indian gaming facilities offer additional opportunities.

Prerequisites:

Education or Training—High school diploma or equivalent; see text.

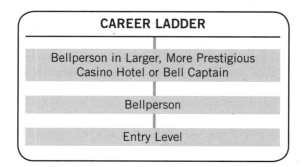

CAREER LADDER

Bellperson in Larger, More Prestigious Casino Hotel or Bell Captain

Bellperson

Entry Level

Experience and Qualifications—Experience in hospitality industry useful.

Special Skills and Personality Traits—Interpersonal skills; customer service skills; friendly; courteous; ability to carry heavy baggage.

Position Description

Casino hotels, like all other hotels, are part of the hospitality industry. In order to make guests happy, hotels provide a great deal of service. Bellpersons, also known as Bell Attendants or Bellhops, are the individuals who escort incoming hotel guests to their rooms after they check in.

Bellpersons serve casino hotel guests in a variety of ways. Individuals load luggage onto carts. They also assist with hand luggage. While escorting guests to their rooms, the bellperson answers any questions regarding the hotel and its facilities.

Once the Bellperson gets to the correct room with a guest, he or she opens the door, shows the guest in, and inspects the room. The individual must be sure the room is in order and the guest is satisfied. Sometimes after guests see a room, they decide they want a king-size bed instead of a queen or that they want a room with a different view. The Bellperson calls down to the desk to get the guest a more satisfactory room.

The Bellperson explains the features of the room, such as the operation of the locks, thermostat, air conditioner, or in-room Jacuzzi. The Bellperson also shows guests where exits are located.

Bellpersons may also deliver packages, additional luggage, trunks, and flowers to guest rooms.

Bellpersons in many casino hotel assist guests with local information about points of interest and entertainment attractions.

When guests are ready to depart, they often call the service desk to request that a Bellperson bring their luggage downstairs. Individuals may transport luggage to the checkout area or to guests' vehicle.

Other duties of the Bellperson may include:

• Delivering messages to guests
• Handling special requests for guests
• Bringing guests room keys

Salaries

Bellpersons earn an hourly salary ranging from minimum wage to approximately $9.00 or more plus tips. Individuals' annual salaries including tips can range from $18,000 to $29,000 or more annually. Factors affecting earnings include the geographic location, size, and prestige of the casino hotel. Those working in larger or more prestigious facilities usually earn more than their counterparts in other hotels.

Employment Prospects

Employment opportunities for Bellpersons are excellent. Individuals can find employment wherever casino hotels are located. Usually a number of Bellpersons work each shift. Because casino hotels operate 24 hours a day, individuals may work various shifts.

Las Vegas, Reno, Laughlin, Lake Tahoe, Atlantic City, Biloxi, Baton Rouge, New Orleans, and Detroit offer the greatest number of job possibilities. Other employment settings include casinos and casino hotels in other areas of Nevada, Mississippi, New York, Louisiana, Colorado, Connecticut, Illinois, Arizona, and California.

Other regions hosting Indian gaming and land-based or riverboat gaming facilities offer additional opportunities. New casinos and casino hotels are constantly under construction. More casinos and casino hotels are also opening every year as areas legalize gambling.

Advancement Prospects

Bellpersons may move up the career ladder by locating similar positions in larger or more prestigious hotels, resulting in increased earnings and tips. If a position opens up, and individuals have experience, they may also be promoted to bell captain.

Education and Training

Usually casino hotels prefer applicants to hold a high school diploma or its equivalent. Many casinos assist people who do not hold a high school diploma to get a GED. Work experience may be accepted in lieu of education.

Experience, Skills, and Personality Traits

In most casino hotels this is an entry-level position. Any experience in the hospitality or service industries will be useful.

Bellpersons must be able to carry heavy luggage. Individuals should be friendly, courteous, and personable. Excellent customer service and interpersonal skills are mandatory in this job.

Unions and Associations

Individuals interested in learning more about careers in this area can contact the human resources departments of casino hotels. Other information may be available from the American Hotel and Lodging Association (AH&LA).

Tips for Entry

1. Human resources departments in casino hotels are good places to find out about job openings.
2. Call each casino directly to obtain its job hotline phone number.
3. Jobs are also advertised in the classified sections of newspapers in areas hosting gaming. Look under classifications such as "Casinos," "Casino Hotels," "Hotels," "Bellperson," "Bellhop," "Bell Attendant," and "Casino Hotel Opportunities."
4. Many casinos and casino hotels host job fairs. Look for these in the classified section of the newspaper in areas where casinos are located.

DOORPERSON

CAREER PROFILE

Duties: Helping guests get in and out of their cars; welcoming guests to facility; opening doors; loading and unloading guests' luggage from vehicles; calling taxis.

Alternate Title(s): Doorman; Doorwoman

Salary Range: $16,000 to $35,000+

Employment Prospects: Good

Advancement Prospects: Fair

Best Geographical Location(s) for Position: Las Vegas, Reno, Laughlin, Lake Tahoe, Atlantic City, Biloxi, Baton Rouge, New Orleans, and Detroit offer most opportunities; other regions with land-based, riverboat, or Indian gaming facilities offer additional opportunities.

Prerequisites:

Education or Training:—High school diploma or equivalent preferred; see text.

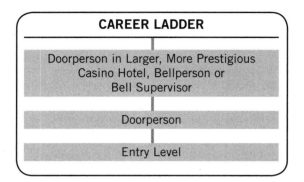

CAREER LADDER

Doorperson in Larger, More Prestigious Casino Hotel, Bellperson or Bell Supervisor

Doorperson

Entry Level

Experience and Qualifications—Experience in hospitality industry preferred, but not required.

Special Skills and Personality Traits—Interpersonal skills; customer service skills; friendly; courteous.

Position Description

Casinos and casino hotels are very customer-oriented. When guests arrive at a casino, a Doorperson is often one of the first people to greet and welcome them.

Sometimes called a door attendant, the individual opens guests' car doors and helps them out of the vehicle.

The Doorperson is stationed near the main casino or casino hotel door so the individual can open the door for guests each time they enter and depart from the facility.

The Doorperson assists guests with hand luggage, packages, and other items. The individual also unloads guests' luggage onto a cart. In some facilities, the Doorperson moves the luggage inside the hotel. In others, baggage handlers or bellhops handle interior luggage movement.

Doorperson duties extend to assisting guests when they are leaving as well as upon arrival. Individuals load luggage into guests' vehicles. They also open the patrons' car doors, help them in, and close the doors. Doorpersons converse with guests on departure, asking if they enjoyed their stay and inviting them back to the facility.

Other duties of the Doorperson may include:

- Assisting guests with local information
- Calling or hailing taxis
- Helping guests with public transportation

Salaries

Doorpersons earn an hourly salary ranging from $8.00 to $8.50 or more plus tips. Individuals may earn between $16,000 and $35,000 or more, depending on the tips they receive. Tips will be best for personable, customer-oriented individuals. Factors affecting earnings include the geographic location, size, and prestige of the casino hotel. Those working in larger or more prestigious facilities usually earn more than their counterparts in other hotels.

Employment Prospects

Employment opportunities for Doorpersons are good for customer- and guest-oriented individuals. Because casinos and casino hotels operate 24 hours a day, individuals may work various shifts.

Las Vegas, Reno, Laughlin, Lake Tahoe, Atlantic City, Biloxi, Baton Rouge, New Orleans, and Detroit offer the greatest number of job possibilities. Other employment settings include casinos and casino hotels in other areas of Nevada, Mississippi, New York, Louisiana, Colorado, Connecticut, Illinois, Arizona, and California.

Other regions hosting Indian gaming and land-based or riverboat gaming facilities offer additional opportunities. New casinos and casino hotels are constantly under construction. More casinos and casino hotels are also opening every year as areas legalize gambling.

Advancement Prospects
Doorpersons may move up the career ladder in a number of ways. Some individuals move into the guest service area, while others become bellpersons or bell supervisors.

Education and Training
Usually casino hotels prefer applicants to hold a high school diploma or its equivalent. Casinos often assist employees who do not hold either of these to obtain a GED.

Experience, Skills, and Personality Traits
In many casinos and hotels this job is an entry-level position. However, experience in the hospitality industry is useful.

Doorpersons must be personable, friendly, and courteous individuals who like being around others. Customer service skills are essential to this type of job.

Unions and Associations
Depending on the specific casino, this may or may not be a unionized position. Individuals interested in learning more about careers in this area can contact the human resources departments of casino hotels.

Tips for Entry
1. Most casinos have job hotlines. These are frequently updated messages listing jobs availables. You can call each casino directly to get its job hotline phone number.
2. Stop by the human resources departments in casino hotels to inquire about job openings.
3. Jobs are advertised in the classified sections of newspapers in areas hosting gaming. Look under classifications such as "Casinos/Gaming," "Casino Hotels," "Hotels," "Doorperson," "Door Attendant," and "Casino Hotel Opportunities."
4. Attend casino job fairs in areas hosting gaming.

VALET ATTENDANT

Duties: Parking and retrieving guest vehicles.
Alternate Title(s): Valet
Salary Range: $16,000 to $40,000+ including tips
Employment Prospects: Excellent
Advancement Prospects: Fair
Best Geographical Location(s) for Position: Las Vegas, Reno, Laughlin, Lake Tahoe, Atlantic City, Biloxi, Baton Rouge, New Orleans, and Detroit offer most opportunities; other regions with land-based, riverboat, or Indian gaming facilities offer additional opportunities.
Prerequisites:
Education or Training—High school diploma or equivalent; see text.
Experience and Qualifications—Ability to drive; experience working in valet department may be required for some positions.

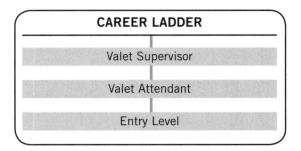

CAREER LADDER

Valet Supervisor

Valet Attendant

Entry Level

Special Skills and Personality Traits—Ability to drive; customer service skills; pleasant; interpersonal skills; friendly; courteous.
Special Requirements—Valid, clean driver's license.

Position Description

Guests who drive to casinos and casino hotels often prefer valet parking so that they do not have to park their own cars in a distant lot or garage and walk back to the facility.

With valet parking, guests get out of their cars at the main entrance of the casino, leave their keys in the vehicles, and have their cars parked for them.

As guests drive up to the facility, Valet Attendants welcome them, opening car doors for guests and helping them out of their vehicles.

The Valet Attendant ascertains the length of a guest's stay to determine where the vehicle should be parked. Many facilities have different parking areas for guests just staying for the day and for those staying overnight.

Two-piece tickets with numbers are usually used in valet parking. One side of the ticket is given to the customer to retrieve the automobile later. The other portion is either placed on the windshield of the auto or kept with the guest's keys. In some casinos, the Valet Attendant may be expected to write information on the parking ticket, stating the make, model, color, and license of the guest's automobile, as well as the location in which the car is to be parked. In others, a valet supervisor handles this responsibility. The Valet Attendant or supervisor also stamps the ticket with the time and

date. This information is used to determine any parking charges levied by the facility.

The Valet Attendant is responsible for driving the guest's car to the correct lot and parking the car. The individual will then bring the keys back to the valet parking office for storage.

When guests are ready to leave, they give their valet ticket to the valet supervisor. The Valet Attendant must then go to the parking area, retrieve the car, and drive it back to the casino hotel and turn it over to the guest.

Other duties of the casino or casino hotel Valet Attendant may include:

- Retrieving items for guests from their parked cars
- Bringing vehicles to a garage or service center to be cleaned or serviced
- Giving directions to guests
- Directing customers to spaces to park their own vehicles

Salaries

Valet Attendants working in casinos and casino hotels are paid an hourly wage ranging between $7.00 and $8.50 or more plus tips. In unionized casinos, the union will negotiate minimum wages.

Many Valet Attendants earn $40,000 or more annually with tips.

Employment Prospects

Employment prospects for Valet Attendants in casinos and casino hotels are excellent. There are usually openings at most facilities. Individuals may work full-time or part-time during various shifts.

Las Vegas, Reno, Laughlin, Lake Tahoe, Atlantic City, Biloxi, Baton Rouge, New Orleans, and Detroit offer the greatest number of job possibilities. Other employment settings include casinos and casino hotels in other areas of Nevada, Mississippi, New York, Louisiana, Colorado, Connecticut, Illinois, Arizona, and California.

Other regions hosting Indian gaming and land-based or riverboat gaming facilities offer additional opportunities. New casinos and casino hotels are constantly under construction. More casinos and casino hotels are also opening every year as areas legalize gambling.

Advancement Prospect

Valet Attendants may be promoted to supervisory positions within the valet department. These may include valet supervisor or valet cashier. Individuals may also find similar jobs at larger or more prestigious facilities, resulting in increased earnings and tips.

Education and Training

Casinos and casino hotels usually prefer Valet Attendants to have a high school diploma or the equivalent. Many hotels assist individuals who do not have this education in obtaining a GED.

Special Requirements

All Valet Attendants must possess a valid driver's license.

Experience, Skills, and Personality Traits

In many casino hotels, no experience is required for this position. In others, experience working in a valet department may be preferred.

Valet Attendants must hold a valid driver's license. Individuals should be careful drivers with clean driving records. Valets should be courteous, personable people with good customer service skills.

Unions and Associations

Depending on the specific hotel and its location, Valets may be represented by a union. Unionized casino hotels in different parts of the country have different union representation. In Las Vegas, for example, Valets may be represented by the Teamsters Local #995.

Those interested in learning more about jobs in this area should contact the human resources departments of casinos and casino hotels to learn about specific opportunities.

Tips for Entry

1. Visit the human resources departments of casinos and casino hotels to learn of job openings.
2. Most casinos have job hotlines. These are frequently updated messages listing jobs available. You can call each casino directly to obtain its job hotline phone number.
3. Jobs are often advertised in the classified sections of-newspapers in areas hosting gaming. Look under-classifications such as "Casinos/ Gaming," "Casinos/Hotels," "Valet Attendants," or "Valet Department."
4. If you don't like being confined to an office and enjoy dealing with people and moving around during your shift, this job may be a good opportunity.
5. Look for casino and casino hotel job fairs in areas hosting gaming.

BAGGAGE HANDLER

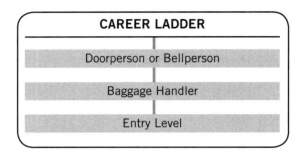

Position Description

A great many guests arrive daily at casino hotels. Some come by cars or limos. Others arrive on bus tours or in vans from airport junkets. Baggage Handlers are responsible for loading and unloading guests' luggage from vehicles.

After Baggage Handlers unload guests' luggage, they bring it into the hotel. Bellhops can then transport the luggage to the correct room.

When guests arrive in groups on buses or vans, Baggage Handlers are responsible for sorting the luggage, tagging it with the guests' names.

In some situations, Baggage Handlers are required to get guests' room assignments and bring their luggage to the rooms. In other situations, Baggage Handlers just carry luggage into the hotel. Bellhops are then responsible for getting the correct luggage to the proper rooms.

Other duties of the Baggage Handler may include:

- Loading baggage back into vehicles
- Transporting trunks, packages, and other baggage to loading areas, using luggage cart or handtruck

Salaries

Baggage Handlers earn an hourly wage ranging from minimum wage up to approximately $8.00. Tips can increase their earnings dramatically. Factors affecting earnings include the geographic location, size, and prestige of the casino hotel. Those working in larger or more prestigious facilities usually earn more than their counterparts in other hotels.

Employment Prospects

Employment prospects for Baggage Handlers in casino hotels are good. Individuals may find employment whereever casino hotels are located. Hotels usually hire a number of Baggage Handlers per shift.

Las Vegas, Reno, Laughlin, Lake Tahoe, Atlantic City, Biloxi, Baton Rouge, New Orleans, and Detroit offer the greatest number of job possibilities. Other employment settings include casinos and casino hotels in other areas of Nevada, Mississippi, New York, Louisiana, Colorado, Connecticut, Illinois, Arizona, and California.

Other regions hosting Indian gaming and land-based or riverboat gaming facilities offer additional opportunities. New casinos and casino hotels are constantly under construction. More casinos and casino hotels are also opening every year as areas legalize gambling.

Advancement Opportunities

Baggage Handlers may be promoted to either doorpersons or bellpersons. These positions often provide increased earnings through tips.

Education and Training

Casino hotels prefer applicants to hold a high school diploma or its equivalent. Work experience may be accepted in lieu of education.

Experience, Skills, and Personality Traits

This is an entry-level position. No experience is necessary. Individuals must be able to carry heavy luggage. They should also be friendly, courteous, and personable. Excellent customer service and interpersonal skills are essential.

Unions and Associations

Individuals who want to know more about careers in this field should contact the human resources departments of casino hotels. Additional information may be available from the American Hotel and Lodging Association (AH&LA).

Tips for Entry

1. Visit the human resources departments in casino hotels and ask about job openings.
2. Jobs are often advertised in the classified sections of newspapers in areas hosting gaming. Look under classifications such as "Casinos," "Casino Hotels," "Hotels," "Hospitality," "Baggage Handler," and "Casino Hotel Opportunities."
3. Most casino hotels have job hotlines that are updated frequently. You can call each casino directly to obtain its job hotline phone number.
4. Look for job fairs in areas hosting casino and casino hotels.

EXECUTIVE HOUSEKEEPER

CAREER PROFILE

Duties: Supervising housekeeping staff; making sure guest rooms, banquet rooms, and public areas are clean and well maintained; training staff; inspecting rooms.

Alternate Title(s): None

Salary Range: $37,000 to $75,000+

Employment Prospects: Fair

Advancement Prospects: Fair

Best Geographical Location(s) for Position: Las Vegas, Reno, Laughlin, Lake Tahoe, Atlantic City, Biloxi, Baton Rouge, New Orleans, and Detroit offer most opportunities; other regions with land-based, riverboat, or Indian gaming facilities offer additional opportunities.

Prerequisites:

Education or Training—Bachelor's degree in hotel administration preferred; experience may be accepted in lieu of education.

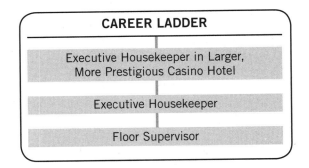

Experience and Qualifications—Experience in hotel housekeeping.

Special Skills and Personality Traits—Supervisory skills; management skills; communication skills; detail-oriented; organized.

Position Description

It is essential to the success of hotels that guests feel comfortable and find their stay enjoyable and pleasant. The first thing guests often notice at hotels is the cleanliness or lack of cleanliness of their room. The Executive Housekeeper at a casino hotel is in charge of keeping guest rooms, meeting rooms, banquet rooms, and public areas of the hotel clean, orderly, and well maintained. The individual has a number of responsibilities depending on the specific hotel, and its size and structure.

An Executive Housekeeper may be expected to physically clean rooms on occasion. Most of the time, however, the Executive Housekeeper supervises others on the housekeeping staff. The individual inspects rooms that others in the staff have cleaned, making sure everything is up to hotel standards. When inspecting rooms, the Executive Housekeeper must check the condition of the rooms to make sure needed repairs are made.

The Executive Housekeeper is responsible for training all other housekeeping personnel. The individual explains cleaning procedures and hotel policies.

The Executive Housekeeper is also responsible for devising work schedules for housekeepers, as well as for assigning individual rooms to clean. The Executive Housekeeper must keep an accurate record of which rooms are clean and ready for guests.

Casino hotels usually provide a number of amenities to guests such as shampoos. bubble baths, body lotions, shower caps, mouthwash, soaps, chocolates, stationery, and postcards. The Executive Housekeeper makes sure that there is an adequate supply of these amenities and that they are distributed to each guest room. The individual must also ensure that room service menus and other literature regarding the hotel, casino, and restaurants are stocked and distributed to each guest room.

In many casino hotels, the Executive Housekeeper also must supervise laundry and valet services provided by the facility for guests.

Other duties of the Executive Housekeeper might include:

- Ordering cleaning supplies
- Making sure there are enough clean linens and towels for guest rooms
- Making sure uniforms for housekeeping staff are cleaned and distributed
- Preparing budget for department

Salaries

Annual earnings for Executive Housekeepers working in casino hotels can range from $37,000 to $75,000 or more annually. Factors affecting earnings include the specific hotel, number of rooms, prestige, and geographic location. Other variables include the individual's responsibilities, education, and experience. In addition to salaries, Executive Housekeepers may also receive annual bonuses.

Individuals with the most education, working in the largest, most prestigious hotels generally make the most money.

Employment Prospects

Employment prospects for Executive Housekeepers in casino hotels are fair. All hotels large or small require housekeepers, and most utilize an Executive Housekeeper.

Las Vegas, Reno, Laughlin, Lake Tahoe, Atlantic City, Biloxi, Baton Rouge, New Orleans, and Detroit offer the greatest number of job possibilities. Other employment settings include casinos and casino hotels in other areas of Nevada, Mississippi, New York, Louisiana, Colorado, Connecticut, Illinois, Arizona, and California.

Other regions hosting Indian gaming and land-based or riverboat gaming facilities offer additional opportunities. New casinos and casino hotels are constantly under construction. More casinos and casino hotels are also opening every year as areas legalize gambling.

Advancement Prospects

Executive Housekeepers can advance their careers by obtaining experience. They may then locate similar positions in larger or more prestigious hotels, resulting in increased responsibilities and earnings. Individuals may also climb the career ladder by finding employment in hotels in other supervisory positions.

Education and Training

Educational requirements for Executive Housekeepers vary. While some hotels accept experience in lieu of education, individuals with a formal college education usually are more marketable.

Recommended education for this position is a four-year college degree. A good major is hotel administration. There are also a number of technical schools, community, and junior colleges offering majors or courses in hotel housekeeping. The International Executive Housekeepers Association (IEHA) works with schools and colleges, putting together courses in this area.

Continuing education as well as home study courses are also offered through the Educational Institute of the American Hotel and Lodging Association (AH&LA).

Experience, Skills, and Personality Traits

Executive Housekeepers need excellent supervisory and administrative skills. They must have the ability to work well with others while directing their activities.

In order to be successful in this field, individuals should have excellent communication skills. They need to be organized, detail-oriented, and have a great deal of pride in their work.

Executive Housekeepers are usually required to have several years' experience in supervisory housekeeping. This is often obtained through prior positions as assistant executive housekeepers, or as night or evening housekeeping supervisors.

Unions and Associations

Organizations that provide additional information regarding a career as Executive Housekeeper include the International Executive Housekeepers Association (IEHA) and the American Hotel and Lodging Association (AH&LA).

Tips for Entry

1. Continue your education. Contact trade associations to see what courses or seminars are offered in your area.
2. Positions in this field are advertised in the newspaper classified sections in the casino capitals of the country. Look under headings such as "Casino Hotels," "Casinos," "Hotels," and "Executive Housekeeper."
3. Subscribe to newspapers in Atlantic City, Las Vegas, Reno, Laughlin, Lake Tahoe, Detroit, or any other city where there are casino hotels. Don't forget other areas hosting gambling throughout the country. Your local newspaper or bookstore can often get you Sunday newspapers from various areas in the country. Look in the classified section to see what openings are available.
4. If you can't get Sunday newspapers from areas hosting gaming, check out newspapers on the Web. Some have their classified section online.

GUEST ROOM ATTENDANT

CAREER PROFILE

Duties: Cleaning and preparing hotel guest rooms; replenishing supplies and amenities.

Alternate Title(s): Housekeeper

Salary Range: $21,000 to $31,000+ plus tips

Employment Prospects: Excellent

Advancement Prospects: Fair

Best Geographical Location(s) for Position: Las Vegas, Reno, Laughlin, Lake Tahoe, Atlantic City, Biloxi, Baton Rouge, New Orleans, and Detroit offer most opportunities; other regions with land-based, riverboat, or Indian gaming facilities offer additional opportunities.

Prerequisites:

Education or Training—On-the-job training.

Experience and Qualifications—Prior experience in service industry helpful.

Special Skills and Personality Traits—Detail-oriented; organized; physical stamina.

CAREER LADDER

```
Floor Supervisor or Guest Room
Attendant in Larger, More Prestigious
Casino Hotel

        ↑

Guest Room Attendant

        ↑

Guest Room Attendant in Non-Casino
Hotel or Entry Level
```

Position Description

Guest Room Attendants are responsible for cleaning guest rooms in casino hotels. They also clean and maintain public areas such as hallways on guest floors.

Guest Room Attendants have a number of duties. Individuals are usually assigned rooms to clean. Their responsibilities include changing linens and making the beds in guest rooms. They also are expected to dust, wipe up any spills, and vacuum.

The Guest Room Attendant must thoroughly clean the bathroom shower, tub, and toilet, as well as make sure counters and floor are spotless. The individual also clears any room service dishes and trays from the room.

The Guest Room Attendant empties waste baskets and cleans ashtrays in the rooms. He or she replenishes drinking glasses as well as stationery, postcards, matches, room service menus, and magazines. Casino hotels usually offer an array of cosmetic amenities including shampoos, soaps, shower caps, body creams, conditioners, and bubble baths. The Guest Room Attendant makes sure each room is fully supplied with the required amenities. The individual also places clean towels in the bathroom and replenishes any other bathroom supplies.

The Guest Room Attendant makes sure the room is well maintained. He or she must check to see no light bulbs are out, that blankets and bedspreads are clean and not worn, and that drapes are not ripped.

Guest Room Attendants' responsibilities may also include:

- Turning down beds in the evening
- Placing candy or cookies on turned-down beds
- Bringing guests extra towels, pillows or other requested amenities
- Transporting trash to disposal area
- Stocking housekeeping cart

Salaries

Guest Room Attendants earn between $10.00 and $15.00 or more per hour plus tips or about $21,000 to $31,000 annually. Factors affecting earnings include the geographic location, size, type, and prestige of the specific casino hotel, as well as the experience and responsibilities of the individual.

In unionized settings, the union may negotiate minimum earnings.

Employment Prospects

Employment opportunities for Guest Room Attendants are abundant. Las Vegas, Reno, Laughlin, Lake Tahoe, Atlantic City, Biloxi, Baton Rouge, New Orleans, and Detroit offer the greatest number of job possibilities. Other employment settings include casinos and casino hotels in other areas of Nevada, Mississippi, New York, Louisiana, Colorado, Connecticut, Illinois, Arizona, and California.

Other regions hosting Indian gaming and land-based or riverboat gaming facilities offer additional opportunities. New casinos and casino hotels are constantly under construction. More casinos and casino hotels are also opening every year as areas legalize gambling.

Advancement Prospects

Guest Room Attendants working in casino hotels can advance their careers by locating similar jobs in larger, more prestigious facilities. This may result in increased earnings and/or tips.

Some Guest Room Attendants climb the career ladder through promotion to positions such as floor supervisor.

Education and Training

On-the-job training is usually provided for Guest Room Attendants. Individuals who have prior experience in this area may be preferred.

Experience, Skills, and Personality Traits

Experience requirements vary. In many casino hotels this is an entry-level position. As noted, some hotels prefer or require applicants to have prior experience working in either the service or hospitality industry.

Unions and Associations

Depending on the specific hotel and its location, Guest Room Attendants may be represented by a union. Casinos in different parts of the country have different union representation. In Las Vegas, for example, Guest Room Attendants may be members of the Culinary Workers Local #226 union. In Atlantic City casino hotels, Guest Room Attendants are represented by Local #54 of the Hotel Employees and Restaurant Employees International Union. It is important to note that many casinos in the country are not unionized.

Individuals interested in jobs as Guest Room Attendants may obtain additional career information by contacting human resource directors of casino hotels. Additional information may be obtained by writing to the International Executive Housekeepers Association (IEHA).

Tips for Entry

1. While this is often an entry-level position, the ability to demonstrate a stable work history will be helpful.
2. Jobs are often advertised in the classified sections of newspapers in areas hosting gaming. Look under classifications such as "Guest Room Attendants," "Hotel Housekeepers," "Hospitality Industry Jobs," and "Casino Hotels."
3. Call casino job hotlines for openings in this area. These are frequently updated messages listing jobs available. Call each casino directly to get its job hotline phone number.
4. Visit the human resources departments of casino hotels to inquire about job openings.
5. Look for casino job fairs. They often have openings in this area.

PBX OPERATOR

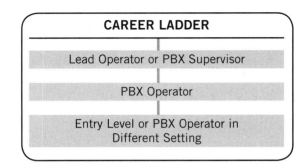

Position Description

The first contact many people have with casinos or casino hotels is the telephone operator who answers calls. The individual is referred to as the PBX Operator, PBX Attendant, or Operator.

PBX stands for private branch exchange. These are the type of switchboards used in casinos and casino hotels. PBX Operators answer calls and connect them to the correct party. Individuals are often responsible for determining the specific department or individual to which a caller should be transferred.

In order to connect callers to the proper person, PBX Operators are responsible for finding room numbers of guests, as well as extensions of departments and personnel. This may be accomplished by retrieving data from computers or consulting lists or other written information.

The success of casinos and casino hotels depends on good customer service skills. Operators in these facilities should be very pleasant and helpful in making customers feel good about calling. Individuals answer questions, give directions, and provide a great deal of information regarding the hotel, and casino facilities.

PBX Operators are responsible for connecting inter-office or house calls. They also relay or connect outgoing calls.

Other duties of casino or casino hotel PBX Operators may include:

- Assisting guests in placing calls
- Handling related clerical duties

Salaries

PBX Operators working in casinos and casino hotels earn between $8.00 and $17.00 or more per hour or about $16,500 to $35,000 annually. In unionized situations, the union will negotiate minimum earnings. Factors affecting earnings include the geographic location, size, and prestige of the specific casino or casino hotel, as well as the training, experience, and responsibilities of the individual.

Employment Prospects

Employment opportunities for PBX operators in casinos are good. Individuals work various shifts, including daytime, swing shift or evening, or graveyard or overnight shift.

Las Vegas, Reno, Laughlin, Lake Tahoe, Atlantic City, Biloxi, Baton Rouge, New Orleans, and Detroit offer the greatest number of job possibilities. Other employment settings include casinos and casino hotels in other areas of Nevada, Mississippi, New York, Louisiana, Colorado, Connecticut, Illinois, Arizona, and California.

Other regions hosting Indian gaming and land-based or riverboat gaming facilities offer additional opportunities. New casinos and casino hotels are constantly under construction. More casinos and casino hotels are also opening every year as areas legalize gambling.

Advancement Prospects

With experience and/or additional training, PBX Operators may be promoted to supervisory positions within the communications department. Individuals may advance to positions such as lead operator or PBX supervisor.

Education and Training

Most casinos and casino hotels prefer PBX Operators to have a high school diploma or the equivalent. Many facilities assist individuals who do not have this education in obtaining a GED.

On-the-job training in handling routine calls and equipment is usually provided for PBX Operators. Individuals are also usually trained in providing customer service to callers.

Experience, Skills, and Personality Traits

In some casinos, entry-level positions may be open. Many facilities, however, prefer to hire individuals with prior PBX experience.

PBX Operators must have a clear speaking voice and good telephone skills. Individuals must be courteous, and pleasant and have good customer service skills.

Unions and Associations

Depending on the specific hotel and its location, this may or may not be a unionized position. In unionized casinos and casino hotels in Las Vegas, for example, PBX Operators may be members of the Teamsters Local #995 union.

Those interested in learning more about careers in as PBX Operators can obtain information from the Communications Workers of America (CWA) as well as the human resources departments of casinos.

Tips For Entry

1. Get experience as a PBX operator at an office, large retail establishment, or hotel.
2. Jobs may be advertised in the classified sections of newspapers in areas hosting gaming. Look under classifications such as "Casinos/Gaming," "PBX Operator," "PBX Clerk," "Operator," "Communications Department," or "Casino/Hotel Opportunities."
3. Openings are often advertised on the Internet via the home pages of casino hotels. They may also be found by doing a search of "Casino," "Casino Hotel," or "Gaming Job Opportunities."
4. Get your foot in the door of a casino hotel. Most promote from within.
5. Stop by the human resources departments of casinos and casino hotels to learn about job openings.
6. Most casinos have job hotlines. These are frequently updated messages listing jobs available. You can call each casino directly to obtain its job hotline phone number.
7. Look for new casinos under construction. Some may need PBX operators before opening.

CASINO AND CASINO HOTEL ENTERTAINMENT

DIRECTOR OF ENTERTAINMENT

CAREER PROFILE

Duties: Overseeing the operation, development, and implementation of the entertainment at a casino or casino hotel; developing new and innovative shows and entertainment events; sourcing out and negotiating terms for shows, events, and entertainment vendors.

Alternate Title(s): Entertainment Director

Salary Range: $45,000 to $125,000+

Employment Prospects: Fair

Advancement Prospects: Fair

Best Geographical Location(s) for Position: Positions located in areas hosting gaming; Las Vegas, Reno, Laughlin, Lake Tahoe, Atlantic City, Biloxi, Baton Rouge, New Orleans, Detroit, and Black Hawk offer most opportunities; other regions with land-based riverboat or Indian gaming facilities offer additional opportunities.

Prerequisites:

Education or Training—Minimum of a high school diploma or equivalent; training and educational requirements vary; see text.

Experience—Experience and background in entertainment and gaming industries.

CAREER LADDER

```
Director of Entertainment for a Larger
and More Prestigious Casino, Corporate
Entertainment Director, or Vice President
of Casino Entertainment

            │

Director of Entertainment

            │

Assistant Director of Entertainment or
Position as Entertainment Director in
Other Field
```

Special Skills and Personality Traits—Creative; innovative; people skills; customer service skills; negotiating skills; problem solving skills; Supervisory skills; good judgment; organization skills; responsible; knowledge of entertainment contracts; knowledge of gaming and entertainment industries; communication skills.

Special Requirements—State licensing may be required.

Position Description

With the fierce competition to attract guests to casinos and casino hotels, it is essential today that facilities offer an all-encompassing entertainment experience. While for some a trip to the casino gaming floor is entertainment enough, others want more.

By bringing guests into the casino property for various forms of entertainment, the facility increases the odds of having people gamble, eat in their restaurants, drink in their bars and clubs, purchase items in their retail outlets, and stay in the hotel. All of this results in increased revenue for the casino.

Depending on the specific facility, casinos may offer a variety of entertainment options ranging from lounge singers to megastars, major sports events to Broadway style production shows, and everything in between. The facility may host one or more lounges, nightclubs, arenas, and showrooms.

The individual responsible for entertainment at the casino and casino hotel is called the Director of Enter-

tainment. He or she may also be referred to as the entertainment director.

Within the scope of the job, this individual has a great many duties. He or she is first and foremost responsible for the development of the entertainment concepts and events for the casino. Entertainment might include events such as weekly boxing matches, periodic major championship boxing matches, major megastar concerts, or traditional entertainment such as piano bars, singers, or bands in lounges and bars, karaoke nights, comedy clubs, magic shows, Broadway-style theatrical plays, huge production shows, and nightclub shows.

Depending on the specific casino and its structure, entertainment might be held in various areas of the casino property including bars, lounges, and clubs on the property, theaters, showrooms, arenas, and public areas.

The Director of Entertainment at casinos and casino hotels has an interesting challenge when developing and booking events and entertainment. He or she must try to bring in entertainment that will attract fans who will spend money in the casino, book rooms, and eat in the property's restaurants. What that means is that the individual cannot just book an act based on its reputation or even if the act has a hit tune on the charts. If the act's fans won't drop money into the slots or play table games, the most famous act in the world is not a good "buy" for the casino, even if they do sell out the seats.

Conversely, the Director of Entertainment might bring in an event like a championship boxing match where general admission tickets are given away gratis. While under normal circumstances this might be considered a loss, but when people watching these boxing shows go into the gaming area after the event and gamble huge sums of money, eat at the casino's better restaurants, or visit its clubs, it is quite another story. What this could mean potentially is that even if an event such as a big fight ends up losing money in ticket sales, the casino can experience a really good night financially, resulting in a huge profit.

The Director of Entertainment deals with a great many different people in his or her job. These may include booking agents, casino talent buying services, concert promoters, touring artists and attractions, event product vendors, managers, attorneys, public relations and publicity people, press agents, marketing people, special event producers, and those working in various areas of production.

While of course, there is always standard classic entertainment such as lounge singers or piano bars, the Director of Entertainment is also expected to develop new, exciting, and innovative shows and entertainment events for the casino. Once this is accomplished, the individual must find the perfect entertainers to make the shows happen and then negotiate terms. In some cases, the Director of Entertainment may outsource some of these events or shows. He or she may, for example, develop a deal for a show to be brought into the casino and then work with a concert promoter or production company.

In order to choose the best entertainment and entertainment events, the individual must have a total knowledge and understanding of not only the entertainment industry, but the gaming and hospitality industries as well. What will work? What type of entertainment do casino visitors enjoy? Can the event be cross-marketed? What will end up ultimately making the casino the most money?

The Director of Entertainment must have the ability to forecast revenue projections as well as managing costs for the proposed entertainment. To do this, the Director of Entertainment will be expected to perform a risk analysis for every show and entertainment event.

Will building a new multimillion-dollar showroom for a star bring in enough money to make it financially worthwhile? Can the facility sustain ticket sales for a long enough to pay for the facility and the megastar? These are all questions that need to be answered.

The Director of Entertainment is responsible for overseeing the day-to-day activities of the entertainment department, its staff, its entities, and any subcontractors and vendors. He or she will generally work with one or more assistants handling this task.

The Director of Entertainment often works with both the casino marketing and public relations departments in marketing, promoting, and publicizing all casino entertainment and events to ensure maximum visibility and attendance. The individual may also work in partnership with the management, marketing reps, and publicists of any acts or entertainment events to help promote the entertainment at the casino.

The Director of Entertainment is expected to oversee the operational and production logistics for each entertainment event. After events are completed, he or she is also responsible for writing reports to assure that all logistical as well as financial objectives were met.

Additional responsibilities of the Director of Entertainment at a casino and casino hotel include:

- Preparing annual budgets
- Maintaining relationship with local police agencies, local authorities, trade associations, and unions
- Obtaining necessary licenses, permissions, and protocols
- Reporting any incidents to the appropriate parties
- Handling employee disciplinary actions
- Overseeing logistical needs of entertainers
- Preparing and reviewing entertainment contracts
- Working with the marketing department to develop marketing strategies in regard to casino entertainment events
- Preparing reports for corporate management

Salaries

Earnings for the Director of Entertainment at casinos and casino hotels can vary greatly. Individuals may have salaries ranging from approximately $45,000 to $125,000; salaries may run higher. Factors affecting earnings include the specific casino and casino hotel as well as its size, prestige, and geographic location. Other factors affecting earnings include the responsibilities, experience, and professional reputation of the individual.

Individuals employed by large casinos or gaming corporations in gaming capitals will earn more than their counterparts at smaller facilities.

Employment Prospects

Employment prospects are fair for qualified individuals seeking positions as the Director of Entertainment at casinos and casino hotels. The greatest number of opportunities exist in areas where there are large numbers of casinos. Las Vegas, Reno, Laughlin, Lake Tahoe, and Atlantic City, Biloxi, Baton Rouge, New Orleans, Detroit, and Black Hawk, offer the largest number of jobs. Other employment settings include casinos and casino hotels in other areas of Nevada, Mississippi, New York, Louisiana, Colorado, Connecticut, Illinois, Arizona, and California. Other regions hosting Indian gaming and land-based or riverboat gaming facilities, racinos, and bingo will offer additional opportunities.

In some situations, positions in this area may be available with large gaming corporations handling the entertainment functions for more than one casino property.

Advancement Prospects

Advancement prospects are fair for innovative and creative Directors of Entertainment. Individuals may follow a number of different paths to climb the career ladder. The most common method for career advancement is to find a similar position at a larger and more prestigious casino, resulting in increased responsibilities and earnings.

Some individuals advance their careers by being promoted to positions such as the corporate entertainment director or vice president of casino entertainment. Other individuals climb the career ladder by locating positions with large gaming corporations, where they become responsible for the entertainment at a number of properties.

Education and Training

Education requirements vary for casino and casino hotel Directors of Entertainment. Most positions require a minimum of a high school diploma or the equivalent. A college background or degree may be preferred or required. In most situations, however, educational requirement will generally be waived in lieu of experience.

Courses, seminars, or workshops in various areas of the entertainment, sports, music, theater, contracts, and gaming industries will be helpful.

Special Requirements

Some states may require individuals in this position to hold a license from the state gaming commission or authority.

Experience, Skills, and Personality Traits

Experience in some aspect of the entertainment industry is necessary for those seeking a position as the Director of Entertainment in casinos and casino hotels. Individuals may come from prior positions as booking agents, publicists, personal managers, club managers, show production personnel, or entertainment directors in other industries. Some individuals also obtain their experience by working in various areas of the casino entertainment department and moving up through the ranks. The amount of experience needed for this position generally depends on the size and prestige of the casino in which the employee aspires to work, and can range from five to 10 years or more in the entertainment field. Experience working in the gaming industry may also either be preferred or required.

Successful Directors of Entertainment working in casinos and casino hotels need to be driven individuals with an innate sense of what will work in entertainment for a specific property.

Good communication skills, both verbal and written, are essential to this type of job. Organizational skills are necessary. The Director of Entertainment needs to have a thorough understanding of contracts and negotiations.

The Director of Entertainment must be a responsible individual with excellent judgment and the ability to multitask effectively. The ability to supervise others is essential. Organizational skills are also necessary.

Problem solving skills, customer service skills, and the ability to deal well with guests, employees, entertainers, their management, and corporate management are critical.

Unions and Associations

Individuals interested in a career in this field might look to join the International Association of Corporate Entertainment Producers (IACEP) or the American Gaming Association (AGA).

Tips for Entry

1. Prior experience in some aspect of the entertainment industry will be helpful.
2. If you are still in school, seek out an apprenticeship in the entertainment department of a casino or casino hotel.

3. Many people move up the ranks to get this position. If you don't have a lot of experience, seek out a position as a coordinator or assistant in a casino entertainment department.
4. Positions in this field are advertised in the newspaper classified section in areas hosting casinos. Look under the headings of "Casinos," "Gaming," "Director of Entertainment," "Entertainment Director," or "Casino Entertainment." You might also look under the name of a specific casino or casino hotel.
5. Jobs may also be located online. Check out the Web sites of casinos and casino hotels. Many post openings on their sites.
6. Don't forget to check traditional job sites such as www.monster.com and www.hotjobs.com as well as job sites specific to the gaming industry.
7. You might also check out recruiters and search firms that specialize in the casino and gaming industry.
8. Send your résumé to casino hotel human resources departments.
9. Try to attend casino conferences and conventions. They provide a wealth of networking opportunities.

STAGE MANAGER

CAREER PROFILE

Duties: Overseeing and supervising activities occurring onstage and backstage during performances.

Alternate Title(s): None

Salary Range: $30,000 to $75,000+

Employment Prospects: Poor

Advancement Prospects: Fair

Best Geographical Location(s) for Position: Las Vegas, Reno, Laughlin, Lake Tahoe, Atlantic City, Biloxi, Baton Rouge, New Orleans, and Detroit offer the greatest number of opportunities; other regions hosting Indian gaming and land-based or riverboat gaming facilities offer additional opportunities.

Prerequisites:

Education or Training—Educational requirements vary; see text.

Experience and Qualifications—Experience working backstage.

CAREER LADDER

```
┌─────────────────────────────────────┐
│  Stage Manager in Larger, More       │
│  Prestigious Casino                  │
└─────────────────────────────────────┘
                  │
┌─────────────────────────────────────┐
│  Stage Manager                       │
└─────────────────────────────────────┘
                  │
┌─────────────────────────────────────┐
│  Assistant Stage Manager, Sound      │
│  Technician, Intern or Apprentice    │
└─────────────────────────────────────┘
```

Special Skills and Personality Traits—Supervisory skills; organizational skills; knowledge of lighting and sound technology.

Special Requirements—Minimum age requirements may apply.

Position Description

Many casinos and casino hotels have big showrooms where a variety of entertainment and production shows are presented. The Stage Manager is in charge of supervising and overseeing everything occurring onstage and backstage during a performance. This is an important job in the entertainment end of the casino industry. The Stage Manager performs a vast array of duties and usually has one or more assistants. He or she is responsible for supervising the backstage staff, including sound people, lighting people, and electricians.

The Stage Manager is required to attend sound checks, rehearsals, and performances. Individuals in this position do not work normal business hours. Instead, they generally work split shifts.

The Stage Manager works closely with the entertainers and artists appearing at the facility. In some cases, the casino or casino hotel produces its own elaborate stage shows. In other situations, entertainers and artists are booked to appear at the facility. The Stage Manager works closely with all of these people. He or she works with the crew of the artists and entertainers appearing at the facility. When performers travel with their own sound and light crews, the Stage Manager assists and advises them.

Backstage areas be kept as clear as possible. The Stage Manager must find out ahead of time who is allowed backstage. This list can be obtained from the performer's management or road manager. In addition to performers, singers, musicians, and crew members, others on a backstage list might include business associates, journalists, friends and/or family members. The Stage Manager issues backstage passes to each person authorized to be in that area before and during a performance. The individual is in charge of making sure that everyone backstage has proper permission.

This is a job with a great deal of responsibility. During a performance, the Stage Manager makes sure everyone does their job properly. Before the show begins, the Stage Manager determines the length of the show, when any intermissions will be held and when the curtain must be opened and closed. Additional information may also be needed to cue sound and lighting people.

Other duties of the Stage Manager may include:

- Assigning dressing rooms
- Making sure any required amenities are available
- Advising performers how much time remains before they must appear
- Advising performers exactly what time they must go onstage

- Handling all emergencies and problems occurring during shows
- Documenting accidents or injuries that take place before or during a performance

Salaries

Annual earnings for Stage Managers in casinos and casino hotels can range from $30,000 to $75,000 or more. Factors affecting earnings include the size, prestige, and location of the specific facility, and the size and prestige of the theater or showroom. Other factors affecting earnings include the responsibilities, qualifications, and experience of the individual. In unionized settings, Stage Managers' minimum salaries are negotiated by a union.

Employment Prospects

Employment prospects for Stage Managers are poor. While jobs may be available in casinos throughout the country, only the larger facilities have more than one individual in this position. That doesn't mean jobs aren't available at all; it just means you may have to look a little harder to find one.

Look for jobs in Las Vegas, Reno, Laughlin, Lake Tahoe, Atlantic City, Biloxi, Baton Rouge, New Orleans, and Detroit. Other employment settings include casinos and casino hotels in other areas of Nevada, Mississippi, New York, Louisiana, Colorado, Connecticut, Illinois, Arizona, and California.

Other regions hosting Indian gaming and land-based or riverboat gaming facilities offer additional opportunities. Casino hotels are constantly under construction. More casinos and casino hotels are opening every year as new areas legalize gambling.

Advancement Prospects

Stage Managers can advance their careers by locating similar positions in larger, more prestigious facilities, resulting in increased earnings and responsibilities. Some Stage Managers climb the career ladder by going into other types of facilities and becoming facility managers or directors. Others make contacts and move to positions in other areas in the entertainment industry.

Education and Training

Educational requirements for Stage Managers working in casino showrooms and theaters varies greatly. In some situations, individuals work as apprentices, interns, or assistant stage mangers to obtain training.

Others acquire training by watching those working in sound, lighting, and/or electronics. Many Stage Managers today have college or drama-school backgrounds or degrees in stage management.

Experience, Skills, and Personality Traits

Experience as an assistant stage manager is helpful. Some people obtain experience in school or local community theater and performing arts productions.

Stage Managers should be very organized, detail-oriented people. Supervisory and interpersonal skills are necessary to be successful.

Knowledge of lighting, sound, and electronics is important.

Unions and Associations

Depending on the specific casino, this may or may not be a unionized position. Individuals interested in becoming Stage Managers can obtain additional information by contacting the International Alliance of Theatrical Stage Employees (IATSE).

Tips for Entry

1. Look for internships in this field to give you on-the-job training. You will also make valuable contacts.
2. Positions may be advertised in newspaper classified sections. Look under headings such as "Stage Manager," "Casinos," "Casino Hotels," "Stage Director," "Entertainment," or "Production Shows."
3. Get experience by offering to act as the Stage Manager in your school or community theater, music, or performing arts production.
4. Consider getting other experience in small clubs and facilities. These venues usually experience a high employee turnover rate as people often move on quickly for career advancement.
5. A summer or part-time job assisting a Stage Manager will also give you good hands-on experience, as well as additional opportunities to make contacts.
6. Send your résumé and a short cover letter to human resources directors of casinos and casino hotels. Inquire about openings and ask that your résumé be kept on file.
7. Take as many workshops, seminars, and courses as you can regarding lighting, sound, electronics, and staging techniques. The more skills you have, the more marketable you will be.

SOUND TECHNICIAN

Duties: Overseeing sound requirements of showroom or club.

Alternate Title(s): Sound Person; Soundman/woman; Sound Tech

Salary Range: $24,000 to $48,000+

Employment Prospects: Good

Advancement Prospects: Fair

Best Geographical Location(s) for Position: Las Vegas, Reno, Laughlin, Lake Tahoe, Atlantic City, Biloxi, Baton Rouge, New Orleans, and Detroit offer the greatest number of opportunities; other regions hosting Indian gaming and land-based or riverboat gaming facilities offer additional opportunities.

Prerequisites:

Education or Training—Formal or self-taught electronic or sound training.

Experience and Qualifications—Experience using sound equipment and working soundboards.

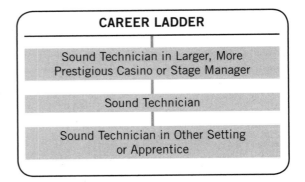

Special Skills and Personality Traits—Ability to use soundboard; knowledge of electronics; dependable.

Special Requirements—Minimum age requirements may apply.

Position Description

Casinos and casino hotels host a wide array of showrooms and nightclubs. The individual responsible for overseeing the sound requirements of these rooms is called the Sound Technician. The individual has a multitude of responsibilities and duties.

Every room has different sound requirements depending on the size and structure. Different types of performances also require varying sound requirements. The Sound Technician oversees the setup of the sound equipment. If there are acoustical problems, the Sound Technician determines what they are and finds solutions including moving equipment to different spots in the room or adjusting controls on the soundboard.

One of the most important duties of the Sound Technician is running the sound control board during performances. The individual sits at the board during a performance and makes adjustments so the sound is properly balanced and regulated. The Technician also adjusts the board for any special sound effects required.

In some cases, performers bring their own sound equipment. In these situations the resident Sound Technician works with the performers' sound people, advising and assisting them. Sound Technicians must attend rehearsals, sound checks, and performances. Working with performers and their crews, individuals can determine the type of sound required.

Other duties of the Sound Technician include:

- Keeping the sound equipment in perfect working condition
- Checking equipment after each performance for problems
- Advising supervisors if equipment cannot be repaired

Salaries

Earnings for resident Sound Technicians range from $24,000 to $48,000 or more annually. Factors affecting earnings include the specific hotel or casino, its facility, size, prestige, and geographic location. Other variables include the experience and responsibilities of the individual.

Sound Technicians working in unionized settings may have their minimum earnings negotiated by the union.

Employment Prospects

Employment prospects are good for Sound Technicians aspiring to work in casinos and casino hotels. Opportunities can be found in all gaming facilities hosting entertainment.

Las Vegas, Reno, Laughlin, Lake Tahoe, Atlantic City, Biloxi, Baton Rouge, New Orleans, and Detroit offer the greatest number of job possibilities. Other employment settings include casinos and casino hotels in other areas of Nevada, Mississippi, New York, Louisiana, Colorado, Connecticut, Illinois, Arizona, and California.

Other regions hosting Indian gaming and land-based or riverboat gaming facilities offer additional opportunities. New casinos and casino hotels are constantly under construction. More casinos and casino hotels are also opening every year as new areas legalize gambling.

Advancement Prospects

Advancement prospects for Sound Technicians include locating similar positions in larger, more prestigious casinos or casino hotels. Some Sound Technicians obtain experience and become a facility's stage manager. As the Sound Technician works with a variety of performers, he or she may climb the career ladder by making contacts and locating a position on the road with a major touring artist.

Education and Training

Sound Technicians must have some type of training in electronics and sound. This may be obtained through attendance at vocational and technical schools or may be self-taught. Many people pick up the skills of the trade by apprenticing or watching others.

Special Requirements

Depending on the specific facility and whether or not alcohol is being served, there may be minimum age requirements for this job.

Experience, Skills, and Personality Traits

Sound Technicians should have complete knowledge of electronics and sound. Experience working the soundboards and other sound equipment is required.

Unions and Associations

Depending on the specific casino or casino hotel, this position may or may not be unionized. Those interested in learning more about this job can contact the International Alliance of Theatrical Stage Employees (IATSE).

Tips for Entry

1. Find an apprenticeship in this area by contacting clubs, halls, theaters, and other facilities. Ask a sound technician if you can apprentice with him or her.
2. Offer to handle the sound requirements for a local musical group. It will provide good experience.
3. Another way to learn skills and gain experience is by taking part in your school or local community theater productions. Volunteer to work with people handling the sound requirements.
4. Stop in at casino and casino hotel human resources departments to inquire about job openings in this area.
5. If you don't live in a gaming area and are interested in finding employment in a casino or casino hotel, send your résumé with a short cover letter.
6. Job openings are often advertised in the newspaper classified section in areas hosting gaming. Look under headings such as "Sound Technician," "Audio Technician," "Sound Engineer," "Casinos," "Casino Hotels," or "Entertainment."
7. Check out the Web sites of casinos and casino hotels. Many list job openings on a special employment section of their site.

LIGHTING TECHNICIAN

Duties: Working light board during performances in main showroom or nightclub.

Alternate Title(s): Lighting Person; Light Man/woman; Lighting Tech.

Salary Range: $24,000 to $115,000+

Employment Prospects: Good

Advancement Prospects: Fair

Best Geographical Location(s) for Position: Las Vegas, Reno, Laughlin, Lake Tahoe, Atlantic City, Biloxi, Baton Rouge, New Orleans, and Detroit offer the greatest number of opportunities; other regions hosting Indian gaming and land-based or riverboat gaming facilities offer additional opportunities.

Prerequisites:

Education or Training—Educational requirements vary; training through internships, apprenticeships, or hands-on training as assistant.

CAREER LADDER

Lighting Technician in Larger, More Prestigious Casinos or Lighting Designer

Lighting Technician

Lighting Technician in Other Industry or Apprentice

Experience and Qualifications—Experience working with lighting.

Special Skills and Personality Traits—Electronics skills; communication skills; reliable.

Special Requirements—Minimum age requirements may apply.

Position Description

Casino hotels are often known for their entertainment. In large facilities there may be a showroom featuring major entertainment and one or more small nightclubs hosting lesser-known acts. Smaller facilities may have just one club. Many productions in large casino showrooms are elaborately staged with dramatic lighting and special effects.

Lighting Technicians are responsible for handling the lighting requirements for a facility's entertainment. Some lighting requirements are fairly simple and just involve spotlights and other lighting so the audience can see the entertainers better. In other situations, elaborate lighting plans have been developed by a lighting designer to increase the excitement of shows. These are often documented in writing so the Lighting Technician can follow them precisely. The documentation describes exactly what the Lighting Technician must do in order to duplicate the lighting effects created by the lighting designer. Various lights, filters, and colors create an array of lighting effects.

The Lighting Technician is responsible for working the lighting control board during the performance. The individual follows the cue schedule provided by the lighting designer. These cues alert the lighting technician to which lights are used at specific times during the performance.

Other responsibilities of the Lighting Technician include:

- Performing lighting checks before each performance
- Making sure all lights and equipment are working properly
- Checking that all lights, bulbs, and filters are in the proper position
- Discussing lighting changes or requirements with entertainers if there is no lighting designer

Salaries

Earnings for lighting people range from $450 to $2,200 or more weekly or from $24,000 to $115,000 or more annually. In some casino hotels, this is a union position. Depending on the specific situation, those working in a unionized setting have their minimum weekly earnings negotiated and set by the International Alliance of Theatrical Stage Employees (IATSE), the United Scenic Artists (USA), or the International Brotherhood of Electrical Workers (IBEW). Individuals working in nonunionized settings negotiate their own salaries.

Factors affecting earnings include the specific facility, its size, prestige, and geographic location. Other factors include the specific responsibilities, experience, and professional reputation of the Lighting Technician.

Additionally, earnings depend on the type of stage productions the individual handles.

Employment Prospects

Employment prospects are good for Lighting Technicians. As noted previously, many casino hotels host showrooms as well as nightclubs. Usually there are a number of Lighting Technicians working in all but the smallest facilities.

Las Vegas, Reno, Laughlin, Lake Tahoe, Atlantic City, Biloxi, Baton Rouge, New Orleans, and Detroit offer the greatest number of job possibilities. Other employment settings include casinos and casino hotels in other areas of Nevada, Mississippi, New York, Louisiana, Colorado, Connecticut, Illinois, Arizona, and California.

Other regions hosting Indian gaming and land-based or riverboat gaming facilities offer additional opportunities. New casinos and casino hotels are constantly under construction. More casinos and casino hotels are opening every year as new areas legalize gambling.

Advancement Prospects

Lighting Technicians can advance their careers in a couple of ways. Individuals may either locate similar jobs in larger facilities or handle lighting for more elaborate productions. Some Lighting Technicians climb the career ladder by becoming lighting designers for major stage extravaganzas.

Education and Training

Educational requirements vary from job to job. While formal education may not be required, training is necessary and can be acquired through apprenticeships, internships, or work as an assistant to other Lighting Technicians or lighting designers. Other valuable training includes classes in lighting and electronics often offered in school or through vocational programs.

Special Requirements

Depending on the specific facility and whether or not alcohol is being served there may be minimum age requirements.

Experience, Skills, and Personality Traits

Experience in lighting is necessary in this job. As noted previously, experience can be obtained through apprenticeships, internships, or work as an assistant to a Lighting Technician or lighting designer. Experience may also be acquired by assisting lighting people handle lights in school or community theater productions.

Some Lighting Technicians work in the music industry handling lighting requirements for entertainers on the road before they settle down for a career in one place. Others work in small nightclubs as lighting people prior to jobs in casino hotels.

Knowledge of lighting, staging, and electronics is imperative.

Unions and Associations

Depending on the casino, this position may or may not be unionized. Individuals interested in becoming a Lighting Technician can obtain additional information by contacting the International Alliance of Theatrical Stage Employees (IATSE), the United Scenic Artists (USA), or the International Brotherhood of Electrical Workers (IBEW).

Tips for Entry

1. Consider breaking into the field on a small scale. Get experience working the lights in a local club.
2. Consider a short stint handling lights for a local rock group.
3. Obtain experience is by volunteering to handle the lighting for school and community theater productions.
4. Take workshops and seminars in theatrical and entertainment lighting and staging. You can hone skills, learn new ones, and make valuable contacts.
5. Watch lighting people at work, take classes, and read relevant books. The more you know, the more marketable you will be.
6. Contact hotels, clubs, theaters, and production companies to find internships and apprentice or training programs.
7. Jobs may be advertised in trade papers or local newspapers in areas hosting gaming. Look under heading classifications such as "Lighting Technician," "Lighting," "Lighting Person," "Lightman/woman," "Entertainment," "Showroom," or "Nightclubs."
8. Call casino human resources offices to see if they have openings in this area.

ENTERTAINER

Duties: Performing in casino or casino hotel nightclubs, lounges, or showrooms.

Alternate Title(s): Singer; Comedian; Dancer; Magician; Musician; Show Group

Salary Range: Impossible to determine due to nature of the job.

Employment Prospects: Good

Advancement Prospects: Fair

Best Geographical Location(s) for Position: Las Vegas, Reno, Laughlin, Lake Tahoe, Atlantic City, Biloxi, Baton Rouge, New Orleans, and Detroit offer the greatest number of opportunities; other regions hosting Indian gaming and land-based or riverboat gaming facilities offer additional opportunities.

Prerequisites:

Education or Training—No formal educational or training requirements.

CAREER LADDER

Entertainer in Bigger Showrooms or Larger, More Prestigious Casinos

Entertainer

Entertainer in Different Setting

Experience and Qualifications—Prior performing experience.

Special Skills and Personality Traits—Talent; ability to perform in front of audience; stage presence; charisma.

Special Requirements—Minimum age requirements may apply.

Position Description

Entertainment is a big attraction at many casinos and casino hotels. Facilities may have a variety of entertainment venues. These include showrooms, lounges, and nightclubs of different sizes utilizing various types of entertainment.

A wide array of Entertainers are booked at casinos and casino hotels, including singers, magicians, dancers, jugglers, and comedians.

While showrooms often host big-name entertainers and/or major extravaganzas to attract patrons, lounges and nightclubs feature a combination of talent to entertain guests. Some Entertainers are well known through television, movies, radio, and records. However, lesser-known people may be equally talented.

Entertainers put together a show to entertain a seated audience. The set may be any combination of music, songs, dancing, jokes, ad libs, and skits.

Entertainers may also utilize light shows, special effects, and costumes to create elaborate productions or shows with a great deal of excitement.

Other duties of Entertainers performing in a casino hotel showroom, lounge, or nightclub may include:

- Involving the audience in the show
- Obtaining bookings

Salaries

It is difficult to determine earnings of Entertainers. The range can be tremendous. Earnings depend to a great extent on the popularity and reputation of the entertainer. A popular singer or singing group earns more than a singer or group that is lesser known. In certain areas, minimum earnings are set by the presiding union.

Employment Prospects

Employment opportunities for Entertainers in casinos and casino hotels are good. As noted previously, these facilities utilize a wide variety of Entertainers.

In addition to working in nightclubs, lounges, and showrooms, Entertainers may be booked to work in other settings, including special events, players' club parties, VIP parties, or corporate events.

Las Vegas, Reno, Laughlin, Lake Tahoe, Atlantic City, Biloxi, Baton Rouge, New Orleans, and Detroit offer the greatest number of job possibilities. Other employment settings include casinos and casino hotels in other areas of Nevada, Mississippi, New York, Louisiana, Colorado, Connecticut, Illinois, Arizona, and California.

Other regions hosting Indian gaming and land-based or riverboat gaming facilities offer additional opportunities. New casinos and casino hotels are constantly under construction. More casinos and casino hotels are opening every year as new areas legalize gambling.

Advancement Prospects

Entertainers working in casinos and casino hotels can climb the career ladder by earning more popularity and building a following. Entertainers who are professional and exciting can find employment in larger and more prestigious casinos and casino hotels.

Education and Training

There is no formal educational or training requirement for Entertainers. Individuals may have music, voice, or dance training, or may be self-taught.

Special Requirements

Depending on the specific facility, and whether or not alcohol is being served there may be minimum age requirements.

Experience, Skills, and Personality Traits

Generally, Entertainers working in casinos and casino hotels have had prior experience performing. Often individuals or groups perform in other venues before finding employment in these facilities.

In order for Entertainers to be successful, they must be talented, energetic, charismatic individuals with a great deal of stage presence.

Unions and Associations

Entertainers working in casinos may be members of various unions, including the American Federation of Musicians (AFM).

Those interested in learning more careers in entertainment at casinos and casino hotels should contact the directors of entertainment, house bookers, or musical directors at these facilities.

Tips for Entry

1. You often are required to be a member of the appropriate union to perform in a casino.
2. Contact casino and casino hotel house bookers and directors of entertainment.
3. Openings are often advertised in the classified sections of newspapers in areas hosting gaming. Look under classifications such as "Entertainment," "Casinos/Casino Hotels," "Casino Hotel Entertainment," "Singer," "Comedian," "Dancer," "Entertainer," "Magician," and so on.
4. Jobs may also be located in trade publications such as *Billboard*.
5. Make sure you have professional 8 X 10 glossy photographs, bios, and press kits.
6. Retain an agent to help you find work.
7. Get booking commitments in writing. You might want to engage an attorney to put together a standard contract.

CASINO AND CASINO HOTEL FOOD AND BEVERAGE SERVICE

HOTEL FOOD AND BEVERAGE MANAGER

CAREER PROFILE

Duties: Overseeing kitchen operations in food service outlets in facility; supervising sous chefs and pastry chefs; creating menus; devising recipes; developing budgets.

Alternate Title(s): None

Salary Range: $45,000 to $150,000+

Employment Prospects: Fair

Advancement Prospects: Fair

Best Geographical Location(s) for Position: Las Vegas, Reno, Laughlin, Lake Tahoe, Atlantic City, Biloxi, Baton Rouge, New Orleans, and Detroit offer most opportunities; other regions with land-based, riverboat, or Indian gaming facilities offer additional opportunities.

Prerequisites:

Education or Training—Education and training requirements vary.

Experience and Qualifications—Supervisory experience in hotel and food service necessary; cost-control experience; complete knowledge of food and beverage departments.

Special Skills and Personality Traits—Detail-oriented; organization; management and administrative skills; budgeting; negotiating skills; communication skills; supervisory skills.

Special Requirements—State license and/or health card may be required.

CAREER LADDER

Food and Beverage Manager in Larger, More Prestigious Casino or Casino Hotel

Food and Beverage Manager

Assistant Food and Beverage Manager or Chef

Position Description

Hotels and hotel casinos realize a great deal of their profits in their food and beverage departments. The Food and Beverage Manager holds the important position of being in charge of directing the food services of the hotel. Within the scope of the job, there is a vast array of responsibilities.

The Food and Beverage Manager is ultimately responsible for the quality of the service in all food establishments in the facility. He or she oversees the operation of all the hotel's restaurants, room service, cocktail lounges, and bars. The individual is additionally responsible for the food and beverage service for banquets, meeting facilities, conferences, and receptions.

As part of the job, the Food and Beverage Manager is responsible for monitoring the supervisory staff in charge all the food and beverage preparation. The Food and Beverage Manager works with a staff that includes assistants, managers, and other service workers. He or she may be responsible for hiring and scheduling them or may assign this task to an assistant. The individual may also be responsible for training staff or developing training programs.

Generally, each restaurant or bar within the facility has a separate manager. The Food and Beverage Manager is responsible for the service and profits in each establishment, making sure they are the best possible. The individual schedules meetings on a regular basis to discuss these and other topics.

The Food and Beverage Manager and the managerial staff of the various food establishments in the hotel are responsible for planning menus, including those for special celebrations, events, or hotel happenings and promotions, as well as those for special foods and drinks. They may develop themes within the food establishments, including decorations and wait staff costumes, as well as related food and drink items.

To make sure the food establishments are as profitable as possible the Food and Beverage Manager must know how to estimate food costs. The individual often deals with food suppliers, negotiating prices. Menus may then be adjusted to reflect seasonal and bountiful foods.

This position carries a great deal of responsibility and it is not usually a nine-to-five job. The Food and Beverage Manager is on call whenever a problem arises and he or she is needed.

As part of this job, the Food and Beverage Manager is responsible for:

- Working closely with various food establishment managers
- Establishing standards for each restaurant in the facility
- Working with managers on any emergencies that arise
- Keeping in close contact with all managers to make sure everything is taking place as scheduled and problems are solved as they occur

Salaries
Earnings for Food and Beverage Managers in these settings can range from approximately $45,000 to $150,000 or more, depending on a number of variables. These include the specific facility, type, size, and geographic location. Other factors affecting earnings include the responsibilities, training, and experience of the individual. Many employment settings provide an annual bonus in addition to salary, depending on profits.

Employment Prospects
More states are allowing gambling facilities every year. Establishments and locations where people can gamble are on the increase. Employment opportunities are fair for quality people seeking this position. The best-trained individuals will be the most marketable.

Advancement Prospects
Food and Beverage Managers can advance their careers by locating similar positions in larger or more prestigious facilities. This results in increased responsibilities and earnings. Some individuals also climb the career ladder by moving into other hotel management positions.

Education and Training
As noted previously, the better an individual's training, the more marketable he or she will be. A number of different educational paths lead to this position.

A bachelor's degree in hotel management or hotel and restaurant administration is often required or pre-

ferred. Some individuals have moved into this position with a liberal arts degree coupled with related hotel and restaurant experience.

There are also programs offered at community and junior colleges leading to associates' degrees, as well as formal programs at technical institutes, vocation and trade schools, and other institutions in hotel and restaurant management. These programs plus experience in food service and hotel management may also be acceptable.

Some Food and Beverage Managers are trained in food preparation at culinary institutes or have worked as apprentices in food service.

Special Requirements
Depending on the specific state that the individual works, he or she may be required to be state licensed and/or hold a health card.

Experience, Skills, and Personality Traits
Individuals interested in pursuing a career in this field should have a vast amount of experience working in food service. Ideally, but not always, this includes experience in management and cooking. Some Food and Beverage Managers worked as chefs prior to their current position. Others worked in a variety of hotel management jobs.

Depending on the specific position and an individual's education, applicants may be required to have from five to 15 years of experience working in the hospitality industry before landing a job such as this.

Successful individuals need the ability to deal with a variety of people on different levels. They should be organized and detail-oriented. Administrative and management skills are necessary. Problem-solving skills are mandatory. A tremendous wealth of knowledge of every area of food service and management is necessary to be successful in this career.

Unions and Associations
Additional career information may be obtained by contacting the Council on Hotel, Restaurant and Institutional Education, the American Hotel and Lodging Association (AH&LA), the American Culinary Federation (ACF), and the American Institute of Wine and Food (AIWF).

Tips for Entry
1. If you are still in school, look for an internship to learn skills, make contacts, and network.

2. Positions in this field are advertised in newspaper classified sections under the headings such as "Food and Beverage Manager," "Casino Hotels," "Casino Restaurants," "Food Service," and "Food and Beverage."

3. Join trade associations. They usually hold annual conferences that are invaluable for learning and making contacts.

4. Look for executive search firms specializing in the hospitality and gaming industry.

CASINO HOTEL EXECUTIVE CHEF

Duties: Overseeing kitchen operations in food service outlets in facility; supervising sous chefs and pastry chefs; creating menus; devising recipes; developing budgets.

Alternate Title(s): Restaurant Outlet Manager

Salary Range: $45,000 to $150,000+

Employment Prospects: Fair

Advancement Prospects: Fair

Best Geographical Location(s) for Position: Las Vegas, Reno, Laughlin, Lake Tahoe, Atlantic City, Biloxi, Baton Rouge, New Orleans, and Detroit offer most opportunities; other regions with land-based, riverboat, or Indian gaming facilities offer additional opportunities.

Prerequisites:

Education or Training—Training in culinary school, academy, institute, or apprenticeship.

Experience and Qualifications—Prior experience required; see text.

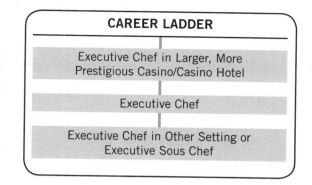

Special Skills and Personality Traits—Supervisory skills; culinary skills; administrative skills; organization; budgeting skills; knowledge of a variety of cuisines; food creativity.

Special Requirements—Health card from local public health department may be required.

Position Description

Casinos and casino hotels host a variety of restaurants serving different types of food. The Executive Chef in a casino or casino hotel is responsible for the kitchen operations of all the food outlets in the facility. The individual sets the mood for each of the restaurants in the facility and is responsible for their culinary reputation.

The Executive Chef has a variety of responsibilities. He or she is responsible for hiring and training the kitchen staff. The individual is further responsible for directing the training and apprenticeship programs of chefs and other cooks working in the hotel. The Executive Chef handles this alone, or may assign this duty to an executive sous chef.

The individual must be a talented Chef with excellent culinary skills. He or she makes sure that food is appetizing and prepared in an attractive, efficient, and profitable manner. The Executive Chef plans menus by knowing the probable number of guests or customers and the popularity of various dishes, thus being able to estimate food consumption and requisition the necessary food and kitchen supplies from the purchasing manager.

The Executive Chef creates new and special recipes. These menus and recipes often reflect the theme or flavor of the particular casino, casino hotel, or restaurant. They may also take things into account such as food surpluses, local specialities, or seasonal items. Once recipes and dishes are created for inclusion on the menu, the Executive Chef develops recipe specifications. Sous chefs must then be trained in the preparation of each dish.

The Executive Chef also reviews menus, analyzes recipes, and determines food, labor, and overhead costs. With this information in mind, the Chef may be responsible for assigning prices to various items on the menu.

While the Executive Chef may on occasion prepare dishes, this job is mostly an administrative position. The individual supervises the culinary skills of the other chefs. The Executive Chef, for example, may taste food in various stages of preparation to make sure the food preparation is in line with his or her specifications.

The Executive Chef is additionally responsible for the following functions:

- Representing casino or hotel in food-related benefit functions

- Coordinating the activities of the sous chefs and pastry chefs in the kitchen
- Developing budgets for food and payroll

Salaries

Executive Chefs in casinos and casino hotels earn from $45,000 to $150,000 or more depending on a number of factors, including the geographic location, size, and prestige of the specific facility. Other variables include the experience, training, professional reputation, and responsibilities of the individual. Those working in larger, more prestigious facilities in the gambling capitals usually earn more than their counterparts in other hotels.

Employment Prospects

Employment prospects are fair for Executive Chefs seeking employment in casinos and casino hotels.

Las Vegas, Reno, Laughlin, Lake Tahoe, Atlantic City, Biloxi, Baton Rouge, New Orleans, and Detroit offer the greatest number of job possibilities. Other employment settings include casino hotels in other areas of Nevada, Mississippi, New York, Louisiana, Colorado, Connecticut, Illinois, Arizona, and California.

Other regions hosting Indian gaming and land-based or riverboat gaming facilities offer additional opportunities. New casinos and casino hotels are constantly under construction. More casinos and casino hotels are also opening every year as areas legalize gambling.

Advancement Prospects

Executive Chefs working in this area can advance their careers by locating similar positions in larger or more prestigious facilities. This is often accomplished after the individual obtains experience and develops a professional reputation.

Education and Training

Recommended training for this position is attendance at a culinary school, institute, or academy. One of the most well known in the country is the Culinary Institute of America (CIA). Other training options include apprenticeships. The American Culinary Federation (ACF) as well as the Culinary Institute of America (CIA) offer apprenticeship programs. Other apprenticeships are available through hotel and restaurant chains.

Special Requirements

Depending on state requirements the individual in this position may be required to hold a valid health card from the local public health department.

Experience, Skills, and Personality Traits

Executive Chefs in casinos and casino hotels need a great deal of experience in restaurants. Prior experience as sous chefs, executive sous chefs, and/or executive chefs in other setting are helpful.

Individuals must extremely talented in culinary skills. They also need management and administrative skills. The ability to teach others is necessary.

Unions and Associations

Individuals interested in pursuing careers as Executive Chefs can obtain additional career information by contacting the American Culinary Federation (ACF), the International Association of Culinary Professionals, or a culinary academy or institute.

Tips for Entry

1. A hotel apprenticeship program in this field is an excellent way of obtaining training and experience.
2. The better your training and skills the more marketable you will be. Get the best training you possibly can.
3. You may have to "audition" for this type of job. The facility can see how you deal with situations in the kitchen.
4. Send your résumé and a short cover letter to the human resources departments of casinos and casino hotels to inquire about job openings.
5. Jobs may be advertised in the classified sections of newspapers in areas hosting gaming. Look under classifications such as "Chef," "Executive Chef," "Casino Hotels," and "Food and Beverage."
6. Many executive search firms and headhunters place people in these positions.
7. Contact an Executive Chef whose work you admire and inquire about apprenticeship possibilities.

RESTAURANT SOUS CHEF

Duties: Working under direction of executive chef; preparing dishes, sauces, and other recipes; assisting in supervision of kitchen staff.

Alternate Title(s): Sous Chef; Chef

Salary Range: $27,000 to $60,000+

Employment Prospects: Good

Advancement Prospects: Fair

Best Geographical Location(s) for Position: Las Vegas, Reno, Laughlin, Lake Tahoe, Atlantic City, Biloxi, Baton Rouge, New Orleans, and Detroit offer most opportunities; other regions with land-based, riverboat, or Indian gaming facilities offer additional opportunities.

Prerequisites:

Education or Training—Apprentice program or training at culinary institute or academy; see text.

Experience and Qualifications—Supervisory experience in culinary setting.

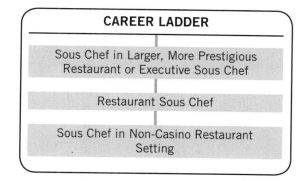

Special Skills and Personality Traits—Cooking skills; supervisory skills; organization; ability to follow style of executive chef; familiarity with variety of cuisines.

Special Requirements—Valid health card from local public health department may be required.

Position Description

Casinos and casino hotels have a variety of restaurants serving different types of food, some more domestic, others more international. The executive chef decides what recipes and dishes should be included on the menu in each casino hotel restaurant. Once this is determined, the executive chef develops recipe specifications. Sous Chefs are then trained in the preparation of each dish on the menu.

The Restaurant Sous Chef is responsible for cooking the recipes exactly as the casino hotel executive chef instructs. Variations or experimenting on the recipes must usually be approved by the executive chef.

The Sous Chef maintains the quality and style of food preparation in the kitchen. It is essential that the Sous Chef prepares recipes exactly as the executive chef has instructed so that dishes consistently taste the same no matter which chef cooks them.

The Sous Chef is responsible for assisting the executive chef in areas other than cooking. Responsibilities vary depending on the specific restaurant. For example, the Sous Chef may take inventory of food in the kitchen, order supplies, and accept and check deliveries.

Other duties of the Restaurant Sous Chef may include:

- Assisting in the training of apprentices and other kitchen workers
- Supervising kitchen staff

Salaries

Sous Chefs working in casinos and casino hotel restaurants are compensated in two ways. Some individuals are paid an hourly wage, others a weekly salary. Annual earnings range from $27,000 to $60,000 or more.

Factors affecting earnings include the geographic location, size, and prestige of the specific casino hotel and type of restaurant. Other variables include the experience, training, and responsibilities of the individual.

Employment Prospects

Employment opportunities are good for Sous Chefs. Qualified individuals can find employment in casino and casino hotel restaurants throughout the country and the world. Restaurants in gaming areas are often open 24 hours a day. Depending on the restaurant outlet, individuals work various shifts.

Las Vegas, Reno, Laughlin, Lake Tahoe, Atlantic City, Biloxi, Baton Rouge, New Orleans, and Detroit offer the greatest number of job possibilities. Other employment

settings include casinos and casino hotels in other areas of Nevada, Mississippi, New York, Louisiana, Colorado, Connecticut, Illinois, Arizona, and California.

Other regions hosting Indian gaming and land-based or riverboat gaming facilities offer additional opportunities. New casinos and casino hotels are constantly under construction. More casinos and casino hotels are opening every year as areas legalize gambling.

Advancement Prospects

Sous Chefs can climb the career ladder in a number of ways. They might locate a similar position in a larger or more prestigious casino hotel restaurant, resulting in increased responsibilities and earnings, or may be promoted to executive sous chef.

With experience, sous chefs can advance to executive chefs.

Education and Training

Training requirements for Sous Chefs vary, depending on the specific facility. Training is available at culinary schools, institutes, and academies throughout the country.

Some casino hotels require or prefer that Sous Chefs complete a training or apprentice program from one of the major culinary institutes such as the Culinary Institute of America (CIA). Other training options include apprenticeships with the American Culinary Federation (ACF). Apprenticeships may also be available through hotel and restaurant chains.

Special Requirements

Depending on the specific state individuals may be required to hold a valid health card from the local public health department.

Experience, Skills, and Personality Traits

Culinary experience is necessary to obtain a job as Sous Chef in a casino hotel restaurant. In many facilities, individuals must have experience as sous chef in other restaurants or hotels.

Supervisory experience as well as culinary expertise is also necessary for this job. A familiarity with a variety of cuisines in useful.

Unions and Associations

Individuals interested in pursuing careers as Sous Chefs can obtain additional career information by contacting the American Culinary Federation (ACF), the International Association of Culinary Professionals, or a culinary academy or institute.

Tips for Entry

1. Jobs may be advertised in the classified sections of newspapers in areas hosting gaming. Look under classifications such as "Chef," "Sous Chef," "Casino Hotels Opportunities," and "Food and Beverage,"
2. Send or fax your résumé with a short cover letter to the human resources director of casino hotels.
3. If you live in an area hosting casino hotels, stop by the human resources departments to inquire about openings.
4. The better your training, the more marketable you will be. Get the best training possible.
5. You may have to "audition" for this job. The facility can see how you deal with situations in the kitchen.
6. Contact an executive chef whose work you admire and inquire about apprenticeship possibilities.
7. Some headhunters and search firms specialize in placing individuals seeking these types of positions.

PASTRY CHEF

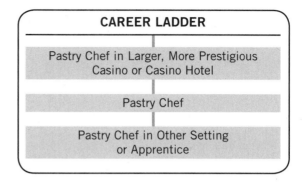
Position Description

Dessert is the grand finale of a meal. Many restaurants are remembered for their spectacular desserts and dessert specialties. The individual in charge of preparing desserts in a restaurant is called the Pastry Chef.

This individual has a number of responsibilities. He or she is expected to prepare all the desserts on the restaurant's menu. The Pastry Chef may handle this task alone or may have helpers, including pastry trainees. Depending on the size and structure of the hotel and the number of restaurants, the Pastry Chef may be responsible for preparing the desserts for all the restaurants on-site or just one.

While the name of the position implies that the individual makes pastries, he or she is responsible for making an array of desserts and components, including pies, cakes, tortes, tarts, custards, flans, ice cream, petit fours, strudels, fruit concoctions, cookies, confections, sauces, fillings, and frostings. The Pastry Chef working in this type of environment must know everything about both domestic desserts and those with an international flavor. A full working knowledge of sugar, pastillage, and chocolate is also required for full desserts and decorating.

The Pastry Chef makes desserts that are on the menu on a regular basis. It is essential that desserts not be stale or taste old. The Pastry Chef may also be responsible for creating dessert specials that use seasonal or local ingredients such as fruits or nuts or have holiday themes. The individual may also develop dessert specials low in calories or fat. Some Pastry Chefs are known for specialties they have created using chocolate.

The Pastry Chef also maintains a supply of certain basic dessert components such as puff pastry, meringues, genoise layers, and ice creams.

The Pastry Chef must create desserts that have a consistent taste, often using standardized recipes. If the Pastry Chef has assistants or trainees, he or she is responsible for suggesting methods and procedures to assure a consistent product.

The Pastry Chef is responsible for fashioning table and pastry decorations. These can include ornaments from sugar paste and icings. The individual must know how to properly use a cream bag, spatula, and other tools to decorate desserts.

The Pastry Chef may work varied hours. The individual usually bakes early at a time when the restaurant is closed and other cooks don't need the ovens.

After baking pastries and making any necessary sauces or fillings, the Pastry Chef assembles and decorates the desserts. Presentation of desserts is essential to the success of the Pastry Chef. In some restaurants the Pastry Chef decorates each plate for each dessert. In others, this task is left to others under the direction of the Pastry Chef.

Other responsibilities of the Pastry Chef may include:

- Determining what supplies are needed
- Ordering supplies
- Scheduling employees
- Training assistants

Salaries

Earnings for Pastry Chefs range from $27,000 to $75,000 or more depending on a number of factors. These include the size, type, prestige, and geographic location of the specific restaurant. Other variables include the training, responsibilities, and reputation of the individual.

Employment Prospects

While this is a competitive field, employment prospects are fair for skilled Pastry Chefs in casino and casino hotel restaurants. Individuals may work for one restaurant or be responsible for the desserts in all the hotel's eateries. Pastry Chefs may also find part-time opportunities.

Las Vegas, Reno, Laughlin, Lake Tahoe, Atlantic City, Biloxi, Baton Rouge, New Orleans, and Detroit offer the greatest number of job possibilities. Other employment settings include casinos and casino hotels in other areas of Nevada, Mississippi, New York, Louisiana, Colorado, Connecticut, Illinois, Arizona, and California.

Other regions hosting Indian gaming and land-based or riverboat gaming facilities offer additional opportunities. New casinos and casino hotels are constantly under construction. More casinos and casino hotels are also opening every year as areas legalize gambling.

Advancement Prospects

Pastry Chefs working in casino and hotel restaurants can climb the career ladder by obtaining experience and locating similar positions in larger, more prestigious facilities. Depending on training, the Pastry Chef may move to other food-related positions such as sous chef.

Some Pastry Chefs move out on their own and open up catering businesses or sell pastries to existing caterers, bakeries, and restaurants.

Education and Training

Education and training requirements vary. Pastry Chefs often are graduates of culinary schools. Others have completed apprenticeships in restaurants, bakeries, or with other pastry chefs. Some talented individuals have taken numerous cooking and baking classes or are self-taught in this art.

Whatever the training is, it is mandatory that the Pastry Chef has the knowledge to prepare all the basics. As noted previously, the individual must also have the ability to work in chocolate, sugar, and pastillage.

Special Requirements

Depending on the specific state individuals may be required to hold a valid health card from the local public health department.

Experience, Skills, and Personality Traits

Pastry Chefs should have a vast amount of experience working with various types of pastries, chocolates, fillings, and sauces. This experience can be obtained through a job in a bakery or small restaurant.

A certain amount of skill and artistry sets one Pastry Chef apart from others. Individuals must be creative and artistic in this line of work.

Unions and Associations

Additional career information regarding Pastry Chefs may be obtained by contacting the American Culinary Federation (ACF), the International Association of Culinary Professionals (IACP), and the National Restaurant Association (NRA).

Tips for Entry

1. Get experience by working with a skilled pastry chef as a trainee or apprentice.
2. Positions in this field are advertised in the newspaper classified section under headings such as "Pastry Chef," "Casino Hotels," "Casino Restaurants," "Food Service," and "Riverboat Casinos."
3. Join trade associations. They often offer educational opportunities as well as conferences and professional guidance.
4. In many situations you will have to prepare samples of your work.
5. Take classes and workshops in pastry making, chocolate, and desserts.
6. Create your own special dessert. It might give you an edge over other applicants.

BAKER

CAREER PROFILE

Duties: Preparing bread, rolls, and additional baked products for use in restaurants and food outlets in casino hotel.

Alternate Title(s): None

Salary Range: $25,000 to $45,000+

Employment Prospects: Fair

Advancement Prospects: Fair

Best Geographical Location(s) for Position: Las Vegas, Reno, Laughlin, Lake Tahoe, Atlantic City, Biloxi, Baton Rouge, New Orleans, and Detroit offer most opportunities; other regions with land-based, riverboat, or Indian gaming facilities offer additional opportunities.

Prerequisites:

Education or Training—High school diploma or equivalent; vocational trade school; apprentice program; see text.

Experience and Qualifications—Experience in food service or bakery.

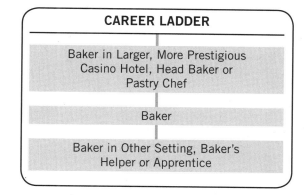

CAREER LADDER

Baker in Larger, More Prestigious Casino Hotel, Head Baker or Pastry Chef

Baker

Baker in Other Setting, Baker's Helper or Apprentice

Special Skills and Personality Traits—Baking skills; familiarity with variety of baking procedures and preparations; physical stamina.

Special Requirements—Valid health card from local public health department may be required.

Position Description

Casinos and casino hotels often have a great number of restaurants on their property. Bakers are responsible for preparing a variety of fresh bread and baked goods for these outlets on a daily basis.

Depending on the type of restaurants in the facility, Bakers make a wide array of baked goods. These can include rolls, bagels, croissants, muffins, biscuits, and scones. Various types of yeast breads might include corn, sourdough, rye, white, wheat, french, and pumpernickel. Some may be light and others dark and hearty.

The Baker is also responsible for preparing certain crossover items such as Danish pastries, sticky buns, sweet rolls, and other sweet breads. The individual may be required to bake quick breads prepared without yeast, as well as traditional breads. These might include specialties such as banana, lemon, orange, or nut breads or muffins. Bakers generally do not prepare desserts, since these are usually done by pastry chefs.

Bakers working in casino hotels usually prepare each bread product according to established recipe specifications. In this way, every product consistently tastes the same no matter which Baker prepares it.

When preparing baked goods, individuals must measure or weigh ingredients accurately before mixing and shaping. Yeast breads must be proofed so the bread can rise properly before baking the dough.

Other duties of Bakers in casino hotels may include:

• Specifying ingredients that need to be ordered
• Baking specialty breads at the request of the head baker, pastry chef, or executive chef

Salaries

Bakers working in casino hotels are usually paid an hourly wage ranging from $12.00 to $22.00 or more and may earn between $25,000 and $45,000 or more annually. In some settings, they might be compensated with a weekly salary instead.

Factors affecting earnings include the geographic location, size, and prestige of the specific casino hotel. Other variables include the experience, training, and responsibilities of the individual.

Employment Prospects

Employment prospects are fair for qualified individuals seeking to be Bakers. Restaurants in gaming areas are often open 24 hours a day. In order to keep fresh baked goods available, individuals may work various shifts.

Las Vegas, Reno, Laughlin, Lake Tahoe, Atlantic City, Biloxi, Baton Rouge, New Orleans, and Detroit offer the greatest number of job possibilities. Other employment settings include casinos and casino hotels in other areas of Nevada, Mississippi, New York, Louisiana, Colorado, Connecticut, Illinois, Arizona, and California.

Other regions hosting Indian gaming and land-based or riverboat gaming facilities offer additional opportunities. New casinos and casino hotels are constantly under construction. More casinos and casino hotels are also opening every year as areas legalize gambling.

Advancement Prospects

Bakers can advance their careers in a number of ways. With experience and training, some are promoted to head Bakers. Others find similar positions in larger or more prestigious casino hotels. This results in increased responsibilities and earnings. Bakers who wish to move into pastry baking should obtain additional training or education.

Education and Training

Casino hotels often prefer employees to have a high school diploma or the equivalent. Additional training may include courses or programs in professional bread baking offered at trade or vocational technical schools and community colleges. Other training is available at culinary schools, institutes, and academies throughout the country. Apprentice programs are also an excellent way to learn this trade.

Experience, Skills, and Personality Traits

Experience in the preparation of bread and baked goods is necessary. This may be obtained through apprenticeships or jobs in restaurants or bakeries. Some Bakers worked as baker's helpers or assistants prior to being full-fledged Bakers.

Individuals must be able to stand for extended periods of time.

Special Requirements

Depending on the specific state individuals may be required to hold a valid health card from the local public health department.

Unions and Skills

Depending on the location and specific casino or casino hotel, this may be a unionized position. In Atlantic City, for example, Bakers are represented by the Local 54 of the Hotel Employees and Restaurant Employees International Union.

Individuals interested in pursuing a career as Baker can obtain additional career information by contacting the human resources departments of casino hotels, the American Institute of Baking (AIB), and trade or vocational technical schools offering programs in bread and baked good production.

Tips for Entry

1. Visit the human resources departments of casino hotels to inquire about job openings.
2. Continue taking courses in baking a variety of baked goods. This will make you more marketable.
3. Contact a baker in a hotel or commercial bakery whose work you admire and inquire about apprenticeship possibilities.
4. Jobs may be advertised in the classified sections of newspapers in areas hosting gaming. Look under classifications such as "Baker," "Casino Hotels Opportunities," and "Food and Beverage."
5. Call casino hotels to get their job hotline numbers. Call often. They update job openings frequently. Contact each casino directly to get its job hotline phone number.
6. Don't forget to look for jobs online. Casino Web sites often offer possibilities.

GARDE-MANGER

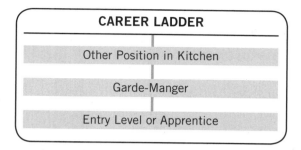

Position Description

Casinos often mean bright lights and excitement. Casino restaurants often showcase some of the same pizazz through their elaborate and creative presentations of food. The person responsible for preparing cold foods in an attractive manner is called the Garde-Manger. Sometimes the individual may be referred to as the Chef Garde-Manger.

This individual prepares a wide variety of cold foods, including fruits, vegetables, salads, aspics, pates, and canapes.

The Garde-Manger must prepare foods in a decorative manner. For example, the individual may mold egg, tuna, chicken, or shrimp salad into various shapes, or create crudités that resemble huge bouquets of flowers. He or she might also carve fruits into decorate bowls or style fruit into impressive-looking animals, vehicles, and vessels. These may then be filled with cut-up fruits, spreads, or vegetables.

A creative Garde-Manger Chef takes a simple platter of cold meats, cheeses, vegetables, or fruits and makes it an artistic masterpiece.

The Garde-Manger may prepare cold garnishes for plates, or large decorations out of cold foods for guest rooms. The elaborate ice carvings the Garde-Manger prepares are often the items many guests remember at buffets and in banquet rooms. The Garde-Manger must be able to carve and design different creations depending on the theme of the banquet or buffet.

Other responsibilities of the Garde-Manger may include:

- Preparing cold buffets in an attractive manner
- Making sure cold foods are prepared to minimize waste

Salaries

Garde-Mangers usually earn an hourly wage ranging from $7.00 to $16.00 or more and may earn $15,000 to $33,000 annually. Factors affecting earnings include the geographic location, size, and prestige of the casino or casino hotel, as well as the experience and responsibilities of the individual.

Employment Prospects

Employment prospects are good for Garde-Mangers seeking employment in casinos or casino hotels. Individuals may work full- or part-time in casino or casino hotel restaurants or their banquet facilities.

Las Vegas, Reno, Laughlin, Lake Tahoe, Atlantic City, Biloxi, Baton Rouge, New Orleans, and Detroit offer the greatest number of job possibilities. Other employment

settings include casino hotels in other areas of Nevada, Mississippi, New York, Louisiana, Colorado, Connecticut, Illinois, Arizona, and California.

Other regions hosting Indian gaming and land-based or riverboat gaming facilities offer additional opportunities. New casinos and casino hotels are constantly under construction. More casinos and casino hotels are also opening every year as areas legalize gambling.

Advancement Prospects

When training to work in the kitchen, the Garde-Manger is usually the position at which individuals start. From there, with experience and training, they can be promoted to other stations in the kitchen.

Education and Training

Educational requirements for Garde-Mangers vary. A high school diploma or the equivalent is usually preferred by most casinos and casino hotels. Facilities often assist those without the minimum education get a GED.

The Garde-Manger Chef may either obtain training in a vocational technical school or receive on-the-job training. Many casinos and casino hotels offer training and apprentice programs in which individuals learn various aspects of food preparation.

Special Requirements

Depending on the specific state, a valid health card from the local public health department may be required.

Experience, Skills, and Personality Traits

Garde-Mangers interested in working in casino hotel restaurants should have prior experience in food service.

Individuals should be creative and enjoy working around food. Physical stamina is necessary as Garde-Mangers often must stand for extended periods of time. Manual dexterity is also essential, as is the ability to work quickly under pressure.

Unions and Associations

Individuals interested in pursuing careers in this area can obtain additional information by contacting the Educational Foundation of the National Restaurant Association (EFNRA), the Council on Hotel, Restaurant and Institutional Education (CHRIE), the American Culinary Federation (ACF), and the International Association of Culinary Professionals (IACP).

Tips for Entry

1. Stop by the human resources departments of casino and casino hotels to inquire about job openings.
2. Look for new casinos under construction. Apply early.
3. Jobs are often advertised in the classified sections of newspapers in areas hosting gaming. Look under classifications such as "Restaurants," "Casino/Hotel Opportunities," "Garde-Manger," "Casino Hotel Restaurants," or "Food and Beverage."
4. Training programs are excellent ways to get experience in this field.
5. Don't forget to surf the net for job possibilities. Many casino Web sites list job openings.

CASINO OR CASINO HOTEL RESTAURANT MANAGER

Duties: Overseeing restaurant operation; training, supervising, and scheduling employees; setting service standards; dealing with customer service problems.

Alternate Title(s): Restaurant Outlet Manager

Salary Range: $25,000 to $75,000+

Employment Prospects: Good

Advancement Prospects: Fair

Best Geographical Locations(s) for Position: Las Vegas, Reno, Laughlin, Lake Tahoe, Atlantic City, Biloxi, Baton Rouge, New Orleans, and Detroit offer most opportunities; other regions with land-based, riverboat, or Indian gaming facilities offer additional opportunities.

Prerequisites:

Education or Training—Educational requirements vary; associate's or bachelor's degree in restaurant management preferred; see text.

Experience and Qualifications—Supervisory experience in restaurant outlets.

CAREER LADDER

Restaurant Manager in Larger, More Prestigious Casino/Casino Hotel Restaurant or Manager of Restaurant Operations

Casino or Casino Hotel Restaurant Manager

Assistant Restaurant Manager

Special Skills and Personality Traits—Supervisory skills; management skills; communication skills; business skills; organization.

Special Requirements—Minimum age requirements; valid health card from the local public health department may be necessary.

Position Description

Casinos and casino hotels host a variety of restaurant outlets. Each outlet has a Restaurant Manager responsible for an array of duties overseeing the restaurant operation.

The Restaurant Manager may be in charge of interviewing, hiring, and training restaurant employees. Often the original recruitment and interviewing is done by the casino or casino hotel human resources department. However, the Manager usually has a say in the hiring process. Restaurant personnel may include assistant managers, hosts, hostesses, waiters, waitresses, and bus people. Chefs are usually hired by the executive chef of the casino hotel.

The Restaurant Manager supervises employees and explains restaurant procedures, rules, and regulations. The individual also oversees the training of new employees.

The Restaurant Manager may be expected to keep track of invoices from suppliers for food, equipment, and services. He or she may be responsible for order-

ing supplies and scheduling repair calls for restaurant equipment. In some situations, these tasks may be handled by others.

The Restaurant Manager makes sure the restaurant and its employees comply with health and safety rules and regulations as well as with local liquor laws. Other important functions of the individual include maintaining food quality and assuring prompt, courteous service.

The Restaurant Manager handles customer complaints and problems. When dealing with these situations, the Manager must try to solve problems quickly and calmly.

Other responsibilities of the Restaurant Manager may include:

- Scheduling employees
- Counting cash and charge receipts at the end of the shift
- Balancing cash against sales receipts
- Meeting financial goals
- Evaluating performance of staff

Salaries

Annual earnings for Restaurant Managers in casinos and casino hotels range from $25,000 to $75,000 or more depending on a number of factors, including the geographic location, size, and prestige of the specific casino or casino hotel, as well as the restaurant itself.

Other variables include the experience, education, and responsibilities of the individual. Those working in more prestigious, full-service restaurants in larger casinos or casino hotels in the gambling capitals usually earn more than their counterparts in other areas.

Employment Prospects

Employment prospects are good for Restaurant Managers seeking employment in casinos and casino hotels. Depending on the facility, restaurants may have one Manager or a day Manager and a night Manager.

Restaurant Manager positions vary in different types of restaurant settings, including gourmet restaurants, full-service restaurants, buffet-style restaurants, specialty restaurants, family restaurants, ethnic food restaurants, and coffee shops.

A trend has emerged in many larger, luxury casinos, which import famous-name eateries in an effort to entice more patrons. For example, Mandalay Bay in Las Vegas features the famous Border Grill Restaurant. The Venetian Casino Resort features Emeril Lagasse's Delmonico Steak House. The MGM Grand showcases Wolfgang Puck's Cafe. Such restaurants offer many opportunities for employment and advancement.

Las Vegas, Reno, Laughlin, Lake Tahoe, Atlantic City, Biloxi, Baton Rouge, New Orleans, and Detroit offer the greatest number of job possibilities. Other employment settings include casino hotels in other areas of Nevada, Mississippi, New York, Louisiana, Colorado, Connecticut, Illinois, Arizona, and California.

Other regions hosting Indian gaming and land-based or riverboat gaming facilities offer additional opportunities. New casinos and casino hotels are constantly under construction. More casinos and casino hotels are also opening every year as areas legalize gambling.

Advancement Prospects

Restaurant Managers can advance their careers in a number of ways. Individuals may obtain experience and land jobs in larger or more prestigious restaurants or casinos, resulting in increased responsibilities and earnings. Depending on experience, education, and career aspirations, individuals may also be promoted to other administrative positions such as manager of restaurant operations, food and beverage manager, or assistant manager.

Education and Training

Educational requirements vary from job to job. Positions, especially in prestigious, full-service restaurants, often require either a two- or four-year degree in restaurant and food service management or a related field. In some cases, experience is accepted in lieu of education requirements.

Some facilities also offer extensive training programs in-which individuals learn every aspect of restaurant operations.

Special Requirements

Depending on the specific state, and the specific facility, individuals may be required to meet minimum age requirements. They may also be required to hold a valid health card from the local public health department.

Experience, Skills, and Personality Traits

Restaurant Managers in casinos and casino hotels should have at least two years supervisory experience in the food and beverage industry. Experience in gourmet or fine restaurant management may be required.

Restaurant Managers should be well-spoken, articulate people with good communication skills. Complete understanding of the operation of restaurants in essential.

The Educational Foundation of the National Restaurant Association (EFNRA) offers voluntary certification for individuals working in food service management. Those who complete classes, pass a written exam, and meet standards of work experience in the field can earn the designation of Foodservice Management Professional (FMP).

Unions and Associations

Individuals interested in pursuing careers in this field can obtain additional information by contacting the Educational Foundation of the National Restaurant Association (EFNRA) and the Council on Hotel, Restaurant and Institutional Education (CHRIE).

Tips for Entry

1. Training programs can offer excellent experience.
2. Send your résumé to the human resources departments of casinos and casino hotels.
3. Jobs are often advertised in the classifieds in areas hosting gaming. Look under "Restaurant Manager," "Restaurant Outlet Manager," "Casino Hotels," "Casino Hotel Restaurants," "Casinos," or "Food Service."
4. Casinos like to promote from within. Get your foot in the door and move up the career ladder.

MAITRE D'HOTEL

CAREER PROFILE

Duties: Managing dining room of fine restaurant; assisting manager in training and scheduling wait staff; handling customer service problems.

Alternate Title(s): Maitre d'

Salary Range: $30,000 to $78,000+

Employment Prospects: Fair

Advancement Prospects: Fair

Best Geographical Location(s) for Position: Las Vegas, Reno, Laughlin, Lake Tahoe, Atlantic City, Biloxi, Baton Rouge, New Orleans, and Detroit offer most opportunities; other regions with land-based, riverboat, or Indian gaming facilities offer additional opportunities.

Prerequisites:

Education or Training—Training requirements vary; see text.

Experience and Qualifications—Experience in dining room of fine restaurant is required.

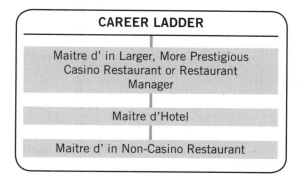

CAREER LADDER

Maitre d' in Larger, More Prestigious Casino Restaurant or Restaurant Manager

Maitre d'Hotel

Maitre d' in Non-Casino Restaurant

Special Skills and Personality Traits—Personable; supervisory skills; organized; communication skills; articulate; well-groomed.

Special Requirements—Minimum age requirement TAM card, health card from the local health department may be needed.

Position Description

When visiting a casino, in addition to gambling, many people look forward to dining in a nice restaurant with good food, service, and atmosphere. While casinos and casino hotels often offer a variety of restaurants, usually at least one is a fine dining establishment. While the manager is responsible for overseeing the entire restaurant operation, fine dining estalishments also may employ a Maitre d'Hotel. These individuals, often referred to as Maitre d's, are responsible for managing the front of the house in the restaurant.

The Maitre d', working under the supervision of the restaurant manager, assists in setting the standards and style for service in the dining room. The individual assists in the training of the wait staff as well as bus people, hosts, hostesses, and others who work in the dining room. The individual oversees and supervises these employees.

Fine restaurants usually have reservation books. The Maitre d' is responsible for keeping abreast of reservations to make sure there is enough staff scheduled during busy times. Because many casino restaurants have walk-ins, the individual also often forecasts business.

The Maitre d' greets customers and welcomes them to the dining establishment. The individual sometimes escorts patrons to tables, assisting the hosts or hostesses when they are busy with other guests. The Maitre d' tells patrons about specials and makes sure a wine steward or member of the wait staff is sent over in timely fashion.

The Maitre d' is responsible for arranging seating for large groups of guests. He or she accommodates any special seating requests. The Maitre d' may handle other special needs at the request of patrons, for example, champagne with an engagement ring in the glass for a couple about to become engaged or a birthday cake complete with candles and singing waiters.

The Maitre d' makes sure everything in the front of the house is in order, including making sure fresh flowers are in place, candles lit, napkins folded, and tables set.

The Maitre d' often walks around the dining room, stopping at tables to ask patrons if they need anything and making sure everyone is pleased with the service and the food. If they are any problems, the Maitre d' makes every effort possible to correct them to the guests' satisfaction.

When guests are done with their meal and ready to leave, the Maitre d' assists them with their coats and thanks them for visiting the establishment.

Other responsibilities of the Maitre d' may include:

- Acting in capacity of wine steward
- Recommending and serving wines to patrons
- Scheduling front of the house employees
- Evaluating the performance of front of the house staff

Salaries

Annual earning for Maitre d's in casinos and casino hotels range from $30,000 to $78,000 or more depending on a number of factors, including the geographic location, size, and prestige of the casino or casino hotel, as well as the specific restaurant. Other variables include the experience and responsibilities of the individual. Maitre d's may also receive tips from patrons.

Employment Prospects

Employment prospects are fair for Maitre d's seeking employment in casinos and casino hotel fine restaurants. Positions may be found in a variety of eateries, including gourmet restaurants, full-service restaurants, specialty restaurants, and ethnic restaurants.

Las Vegas, Reno, Laughlin, Lake Tahoe, Atlantic City, Biloxi, Baton Rouge, New Orleans, and Detroit offer the greatest number of job possibilities. Other employment settings include casinos and casino hotels in other areas of Nevada, Mississippi, New York, Louisiana, Colorado, Connecticut, Illinois, Arizona and California.

Other regions hosting Indian gaming and land-based or riverboat gaming facilities offer additional opportunities. New casinos and casino hotels are constantly under construction. More casinos and casino hotels are also opening every year as areas legalize gambling.

Advancement Prospects

Maitre d's can advance their careers in a number of ways. Individuals may obtain experience and locate similar jobs in larger or more prestigious restaurants, resulting in increased earnings.

Depending on experience, education, and career aspirations, some Maitre d's may also be promoted to positions such as restaurant managers.

Education and Training

Educational requirements for Maitre d's in casino and casino hotel restaurants vary from job to job. In many cases, experience is accepted in lieu of education requirements. Most facilities require applicants to hold a high school diploma or the equivalent.

Some casino hotel restaurants prefer that applicants complete courses in dining room management, wine service, and hospitality from two- or four-year colleges or vocational technical schools. Others accept on-the-job training. Many casinos and casino hotels offer training programs in which individuals learn various aspects of restaurant operations.

Experience, Skills, and Personality Traits

Maitre d's working in casinos and casino hotels should have experience working in a fine restaurant. Most start their careers as waitpersons. Many casino restaurants require prior experience as a Maitre d'.

Maitre d's should be neatly groomed individuals. They must be well-spoken and articulate with good communication skills. Individuals should enjoy being around others and providing good customer service. Understanding of restaurant "front of the house" operation is mandatory.

Special Requirements

Depending on the specific state and facility in which the individual works, he or she may need to meet minimum age requirements, hold a TAM (Techniques of Alcohol Management) card and a valid health card from the local public health department.

Unions and Associations

Individuals interested in pursuing a career in this area can obtain additional information by contacting the Educational Foundation of the National Restaurant Association (EFNRA) and the Council on Hotel, Restaurant and Institutional Education (CHRIE).

Tips for Entry

1. Visit the human resources departments of casinos and casino hotels to inquire about job openings.
2. Also fax or send your résumé and a short cover letter to human resources departments.
3. Stop by privately owned restaurants in casino facilities. These might also offer additional opportunities.
4. Jobs are often advertised in the classified sections of newspapers in areas hosting gaming. Look under classifications such as "Restaurants," "Maitre D," "Casino/Hotel Opportunities," "Food Service," "Fine Restaurant," "Casino Hotel Restaurants," or "Food and Beverage."
5. Training programs can offer excellent experience in this field.
6. Check out casino and casino hotel Web sites. Many list their job openings.

RESTAURANT HOST/HOSTESS

Duties: Welcoming patrons to restaurant; assigning tables to customers; escorting patrons to tables; providing menus.

Alternate Title(s): None

Salary Range: $15,000 to $35,000+

Employment Prospects: Good

Best Geographical Location(s) for Position: Las Vegas, Reno, Laughlin, Lake Tahoe, Atlantic City, Biloxi, Baton Rouge, New Orleans, and Detroit offer most opportunities; other regions with land-based, riverboat, or Indian gaming facilities offer additional opportunities.

Prerequisites:

Education or Training—Minimum of high school diploma or GED; no specific training requirements.

Experience and Qualifications—Experience working in service, food, or hospitality industry useful, but not always required.

CAREER LADDER

Restaurant Host/Hostess in Larger, More Prestigious Restaurant or Maitre d'Hotel, Dining Room Supervisor or Restaurant Manager

↑

Restaurant Host/Hostess

↑

Entry Level or Host/Hostess in Non-Casino Restaurant Setting

Special Skills and Personality Traits—Interpersonal skills; customer service skills; pleasant; organized.

Special Requirements—Minimum age requirements; TAM card and a valid health card from the local public health department may be required.

Position Description

Casinos and casino hotels usually have a number of restaurants, each with its own personality and flavor. The casino or casino hotel restaurant Host or Hostess is responsible for giving patrons their first impression of the restaurant. This individual greets and welcomes patrons. Functions include making sure that patrons have a pleasant and enjoyable meal and ensuring that service is prompt and courteous.

After the Host or Hostess greets patrons, the individual escorts them to their seats and provides menus. Sometimes the restaurant is busy and the Host or Hostess takes the name and number of people in the party and puts the information on a waiting list. The individual informs the people the approximate time it will take for a table to be ready. He or she may also direct the patrons to a lounge or other area to wait until their table is available.

Other functions of the Host or Hostess may include:

- Answering the restaurant telephone
- Scheduling dining reservations
- Handling complaints of dissatisfied patrons
- Organizing special services that may be required
- Acting as cashier

Salaries

Restaurant Hosts and Hostesses generally are paid an hourly wage ranging from approximately $7.00 to $12.00 per hour. In some dining establishments they receive tips. Individuals may have earnings of $15,000 to $35,000 or more depending on a number of factors, including the geographic location, size, and prestige of the specific casino or casino hotel. Other variables include the size, prestige, and type of restaurant, as well as if the person augments his or her income with tips.

Generally, Hosts or Hostesses working in fine restaurants have higher earnings than their counterparts working in other types of dining establishments.

Employment Prospects

Employment opportunities are abundant for restaurant Hosts and Hostesses. Individuals work various hours depending on the specific job. Casinos and casino hotels often feature a wide variety of restaurants, including fine dining restaurants, coffee shops, family-style restaurants, buffet-style restaurants, and ethnic eateries, among others.

Las Vegas, Reno, Laughlin, Lake Tahoe, Atlantic City, Biloxi, Baton Rouge, New Orleans, and Detroit offer the greatest number of job possibilities. Other employment

settings include casino hotels in other areas of Nevada, Mississippi, New York, Louisiana, Colorado, Connecticut, Illinois, Arizona, and California.

Other regions hosting Indian gaming and land-based or riverboat gaming facilities offer additional opportunities. New casinos and casino hotels are constantly under construction. More casinos and casino hotels are opening every year as areas legalize gambling.

Advancement Prospects

Restaurant Hosts and Hostesses can climb the career ladder by locating similar positions in better or more prestigious facilities. In larger establishments, they may also advance to supervisory jobs, including maitre d'hotel, dining room supervisor, or restaurant manager. Experience and/or additional training may be required.

Education and Training

Training requirements vary from job to job. Some positions do not require any type of prior training, while others provide on-the-job training.

Most restaurants in the casino and casino hotel industry prefer to hire high school graduates or those with the GED equivalent.

Experience, Skills, and Personality Traits

Experience requirements also vary. In some restaurants, this is an entry-level position. In others, prior experience in the hospitality, service, or food and beverage industries is required or preferred.

Hosts and Hostesses should be friendly, well-spoken people with a neat and clean appearance. Customer service skills are mandatory. Individuals should also be organized and have the ability to prioritize.

Unions and Associations

Individuals interested in pursuing a career as a Host or Hostess should contact the National Restaurant Association (NRA) for more information.

Special Requirements

Depending on the specific state and facility in which an individual works he or she may need to meet minimum age requirements, and also hold a TAM (Techniques of Alcohol Management) card and a valid health card from the local public health department.

Tips for Entry

1. Stop by human resources departments to inquire about job openings.
2. Check out openings in privately owned restaurants located in casino complexes.
3. Jobs are often advertised in the classified sections of newspapers in areas hosting gaming. Look under classifications such as "Host/Hostess," "Restaurant Host/Hostess," "Food Service," "Casino Restaurant," and "Casinos."
4. Jobs may also be listed on casino job hotlines. These are frequently updated messages listing jobs available. You can call each casino directly to get its job hotline phone number.
5. Surf the net. Many casino Web sites list their job openings.

SERVER

Duties: Taking patrons' orders; serving food and beverages; preparing check.

Alternate Title(s): Food Server; Waiter; Waitress

Salary Range: $12,000 to $18,000+ plus tips

Employment Prospects: Excellent

Advancement Prospects: Good

Best Geographical Location(s) for Position: Las Vegas, Reno, Laughlin, Lake Tahoe, Atlantic City, Biloxi, Baton Rouge, New Orleans, and Detroit offer most opportunities; other regions with land-based, riverboat, or Indian gaming facilities offer additional opportunities.

Prerequisites:

Education or Training—Minimum of high school diploma or GED; see text.

Experience and Qualifications—Prior experience waiting tables may be required for some positions.

Special Skills and Personality Traits—Good memory; math skills; pleasant; personable; customer service skills; ability to carry heavy trays.

CAREER LADDER

Dining Room Supervisor, Maitre d'Hotel, or Server in Larger, More Prestigious Eatery

Server

Server in Other Setting or Entry Level

Special Requirements—Health certificate may be required; may have minimum age requirements; may need TAM card, valid health card from the local public health department depending on specific state and restaurant.

Position Description

Servers are the food service workers who deal with customers in restaurants. They may also be referred to as Waiters or Waitresses. The service patrons receive when visiting restaurants often determines whether or not they will return.

Servers work in a variety of settings in casino and casino hotel restaurants—small, informal cafes or large, elegant restaurants. Whatever the setting, individuals are responsible for making the patron's gastronomic visit an enjoyable experience.

While specific duties are similar for all Servers, they are often performed differently, depending on the type of establishment in which the individual works. Those working in coffee shops in the hotel provide fast, efficient, and courteous service. However in the hotel's fine restaurants, the wait staff must be more attentive. Meals in these settings are served in a more leisurely manner, and servers offer more personal attention to patrons. Individuals working in these settings may, for example, recommend wines or explain how various items are prepared. They may also prepare certain dishes at tableside, such as salads or flaming desserts.

Servers take customers' orders and tell patrons about specials. When orders are ready, individuals bring the food and beverages from the kitchen and serve the customers. After the meal, Servers prepare an itemized check, manually or by computer.

Servers must be able to stand for long periods of time and carry heavy trays of food and dishes. Many people, however, enjoy such work as it affords individuals the opportunity to meet a large number of people, often on a flexible work schedule.

Usually larger or more prestigious fine restaurants employ special people to handle specific projects. Individuals working in smaller restaurants may handle more generalized tasks. In some settings Servers are required to perform duties associated with other food and beverage service jobs. These may include the following:

- Acting as a host or hostess
- Escorting patrons to tables
- Setting up and clearing tables
- Waiting on customers at counters
- Taking payment from customers

Salaries

Earnings for Servers in this industry vary tremendously. As a rule, earnings are a combination of hourly wages and tips from customers. Hourly earnings vary depending on the type of establishment in which the individual works.

Base wages range from approximately $5.50 to $8.50 or more per hour. With tips, Servers earn between $15 and $60 per hour or more. Tips generally average between 10 percent and 20 percent of a patron's check. Therefore, those working in expensive, fine restaurants usually earn more than their counterparts in other types of eateries.

Employment Prospects

There are unlimited opportunities for both full- and part-time employment. Servers work in a variety of settings, including coffee shops, casino hotel fine restaurants, on-site casino restaurants, ice-cream parlors, fast food eateries, family restaurants, and buffet-style restaurants.

Las Vegas, Reno, Laughlin, Lake Tahoe, Atlantic City, Biloxi, Baton Rouge, New Orleans, and Detroit offer the greatest number of job possibilities. Other employment settings include casino hotels in other areas of Nevada, Mississippi, New York, Louisiana, Colorado, Connecticut, Illinois, Arizona, and California.

Other regions hosting Indian gaming and land-based or riverboat gaming facilities offer additional opportunities. New casinos and casino hotels and constantly under construction. More casinos and casino hotels are opening every year as areas legalize gambling.

Advancement Prospects

Some individuals look on this position as a job, not a career. It offers immediate income and flexible hours. Others who enjoy the flexibility and the opportunity of meeting different people see it as a career choice. Opportunities for advancement in this career are often limited. Individuals may, however, increase earnings and tips by locating similar positions in better, more expensive restaurants. Some Servers advance to supervisory positions such as dining room supervisor or maitre d'hotel.

Education and Training

While there are usually no formal educational requirements, most food establishments in the gaming industry prefer applicants to have at least a high school diploma or GED.

Some restaurants provide on-the-job training so that Servers have the ability to wait on customers in a manner specified by the individual restaurant.

Experience, Skills, and Personality Traits

Experience as a Server is required by some fine restaurants, especially those with rigid table service standards. In others, there may be no experience requirement.

Individuals in this line of work should be pleasant and well spoken with a neat and clean appearance. They should enjoy dealing with others. The ability to carry heavy trays is often needed. A good memory is also useful, as are math skills.

Special Requirements

Many states require employees working in the food or beverage industry to provide a health certificate showing they are free of contagious diseases as well as a TAM (Techniques of Alcohol Management) card. Depending on the specific state and type of eatery, there may also be minimum age requirement.

Unions and Associations

Depending on the location and specific casino, this may or may not be a unionized position. For example, in unionized casinos and casino hotels in Las Vegas, Servers might be members of the Culinary Workers Local #225. In Atlantic City Servers are represented by the Local 54 Hotel Employees and Restaurant Employees International Union.

Additional career information may be obtained by contacting the National Restaurant Association (NRA) and the Council on Hotel, Restaurant and Institutional Education (CHRIE).

Tips for Entry

1. If you have no experience and are interested in working in a fine restaurant, find a short-term job as a Server in another type of eatery first to get experience.
2. Positions in this field are advertised in newspaper classified sections under headings such as "Waiter," "Waitress," "Food Server," Server," "Casino Hotels," "Casino Restaurants," "Food Service," and "Riverboat Cruises."
3. Stop by the employment office of a casino or casino hotel. There is often a great deal of turnover in these positions.
4. Check casino job hotlines. These are frequently updated messages listing jobs available. Call each casino directly to get its job hotline phone number.

NIGHTCLUB MANAGER

Duties: Managing the operations of a club.
Alternate Title(s): Club Manager
Salary Range: $25,000 to $75,000+
Employment Prospects: Fair
Advancement Prospects: Fair
Best Geographical Location(s) for Position: Las Vegas, Reno, Laughlin, Lake Tahoe, Atlantic City, Biloxi, Baton Rouge, New Orleans, and Detroit offer most opportunities; other regions with land-based, riverboat, or Indian gaming facilities offer additional opportunities.
Prerequisites:
Education or Training—Formal or informal on-the-job training.
Experience and Qualifications—Experience in casinos, clubs, or entertainment industry useful; knowledge of food and beverage industry, entertainment and music business.

CAREER LADDER

```
┌─────────────────────────────────────┐
│  Nightclub Manager in Larger, More   │
│  Prestigious Club or Showroom        │
└─────────────────────────────────────┘
              ↑
┌─────────────────────────────────────┐
│  Nightclub Manager                   │
└─────────────────────────────────────┘
              ↑
┌─────────────────────────────────────┐
│  Assistant Nightclub Manager         │
└─────────────────────────────────────┘
```

Special Skills and Personality Traits—Supervisory skills; business skills; interpersonal skills; aggressive; management skills; communication skills; organization.
Special Requirements—Minimum age requirements, TAM card, health card from local public health department.

Position Description

Casinos and casino hotels feature a variety of nightclubs for their patrons. Nightclub Managers are in charge of managing the operation of the club. They handle the day-to-day running of the establishment. Individuals have varied responsibilities within the scope of the job, depending on the type of establishment, its size, and structure.

Other sections of this book discuss hotel casino entertainment. In some cases the facility hosts big showrooms in addition to nightclubs. In other situations, the nightclub is the focus of the hotel's entertainment.

Many larger casino hotels host special attractions and a theme that surrounds every aspect of the property, including the nightclub. In many cases the theme determines the type of entertainment behind the club's success. A club might use live entertainment, employ DJs, or a combination of both.

The Nightclub Manager is in charge of determining what type of entertainment the club wants to use as well as what type of patrons the club wants to attract—people who prefer to drink, eat, dance, listen to music, see comedy shows, or just plain relax. Managers must often research other clubs in the area in order to decide the direction their clubs should take.

Responsibilities of the job include auditioning talent, such as comedians, bands, singers, musicians, and DJs. In some situations, the individual negotiates and signs contracts. In others, this function falls to someone else in the casino hotel.

The Nightclub Manager may also be in charge of hiring and training other key personnel, including bartenders, waitresses, waiters, hosts and hostesses, chefs, security guards, or lighting and sound people, sometimes in conjunction with other hotel departments.

The Nightclub Manager must see to it that all state and local alcohol laws are adhered to. Clubs can be closed down if there are infractions. Depending on the size and structure of the club, the Manager might also be responsible for the purchase and control of food and/or alcoholic beverages. In some clubs, the Manager oversees a food and beverage manager who handles this function.

During the day the Manager may be in charge of developing budgets, bookkeeping, checking receipts, and paying bills. The individual may also be responsible for determining the type of advertising campaign that will be most effective. In addition, he or she may implement advertising programs and develop special promotions. In some situations, the Nightclub Manager works with the hotel's marketing and advertising departments on these functions.

Many of the duties of the Nightclub Manager are handled at night when the club is open. Some of these duties include:

- Handling problems that crop up during the evening
- Dealing with customer complaints
- Totaling nightly receipts
- Putting nightly receipts in safe or making night deposit

Salaries

Earnings for Nightclub Managers range from $25,000 to $75,000 or more annually depending on the size, location, popularity, and type of club. Other factors include the experience and responsibilities of the individual.

Generally, the larger and more prestigious the casino hotel and club, the higher the earning potential of the Manager. Nightclub Managers in entertainment gaming capitals such as Las Vegas and Atlantic City usually earn more than their counterparts in gaming establishments in other parts of the country.

Employment Prospects

Employment prospects for Nightclub Managers in the gaming industry are fair. Employment settings range from very small clubs to large entertainment showrooms, depending on the type of facility. Individuals may be Managers of clubs specializing in a variety of types of entertainment, including piano bars, rock and roll, country music, jazz, blues, comedy, musical productions, show groups, or magic acts.

Las Vegas, Reno, Laughlin, Lake Tahoe, Atlantic City, Biloxi, Baton Rouge, New Orleans, and Detroit offer the greatest number of job possibilities. Other employment settings include casinos and casino hotels in other areas of Nevada, Mississippi, New York, Louisiana, Colorado, Connecticut, Illinois, Arizona, and California.

Other regions hosting Indian gaming and land-based or riverboat gaming facilities offer additional opportunities. New casinos and casino hotels are constantly under construction. More casinos and casino hotels are opening every year as areas legalize gambling.

Advancement Prospects

Nightclub Managers with experience can advance to similar jobs in larger, more prestigious facilities. This results in increased earnings and responsibilities. Nightclub Managers may climb the career ladder by starting at a smaller hotel nightclub, obtain experience, and

then be promoted to the Manager of a large showroom. Some Nightclub Managers strike out in their own and open up their own clubs.

Education and Training

There is no formal educational requirement for Nightclub Managers. Some facilities prefer or require training in food service or the hospitality industry. Others require that Managers participate in either formal or informal on-the-job training programs.

Special Requirements

Depending on the specific state, the individual may be required to meet minumum age requirements as well as hold a valid TAM (Techniques of Alcohol Management) card and a valid health card from the local public health department.

Experience, Skills, and Personality Traits

Experience requirements vary for Nightclub Managers. Some facilities prefer that a candidate have previously worked as an assistant manager in a club. Others may accept experience in various facets of business or the entertainment industry. Experience working in casino hotels in any capacity is helpful.

Individuals should have basic knowledge of the food and beverage and entertainment and/or music business. They should be cognizant of drawing up contracts, negotiating, and booking talent. The ability to supervise others is mandatory. Nightclub Managers must be able to handle a great many projects at the same time and still keep a cool head.

Unions and Associations

Additional information regarding careers in this area may be obtained by contacting the National Restaurant Association (NRA) or the human resources departments of casino hotels.

Tips For Entry

1. Job openings are often advertised in newspaper classified sections in areas hosting casino hotels. Look under headings such as "Nightclub Manager," "Club Manager," "Nightclub," "Manager," "Management," "Entertainment," "Hospitality," "Music Club Manager," "Comedy Club Manager," "Casino Club Manager," or "Hotel Club Manager."
2. If you do not live in a gaming area and are interested in working in this environment, obtain short-term subscriptions to newspapers in geographic areas you are considering.

3. Send your résumé and a short cover letter to the human resources departments of casino hotels, inquiring about openings. Ask that your résumé be kept on file.
4. Turnover is high in this field. You might start out working as a host or hostess in a club, learn the ropes, them move up the career ladder to become the Nightclub Manager.
5. Check out casino Web sites. Many list job openings online.

BARTENDER/FRONT OF HOUSE

CAREER PROFILE

Duties: Mixing and serving alcoholic and nonalcoholic drinks for patrons.

Alternate Title(s): None

Salary Range: $16,000 to $28,000+ plus tips

Employment Prospects: Excellent

Advancement Prospects: Fair

Best Geographical Location(s) for Position: Las Vegas, Reno, Laughlin, Lake Tahoe, Atlantic City, Biloxi, Baton Rouge, New Orleans, and Detroit offer most opportunities; other regions with land-based, riverboat, or Indian gaming facilities offer additional opportunities.

Prerequisites:

Education or Training—High School diploma or equivalent usually required; training at bartending school or vocational-technical school; see text.

Experience and Qualifications—Prior experience as bartender in club, bar, or restaurant.

CAREER LADDER

```
Bartender in Larger, More Prestigious
Casino or Casino Hotel or Assistant
Beverage Manager

        ↑

Bartender-Front of the House

        ↑

Bartender in Other Setting
```

Special Skills and Personality Traits—Interpersonal skills; customer service skills; drink mixing skills.

Special Requirements—Certification and state licensing may be required; minimum age requirements; TAM card, health card.

Position Description

Jobs in casinos and casino hotels are generally separated into front-of-the-house and back-of-the-house categories. The front of the house is the section of the hotel or casino that is accessible to the public. The back of the house is the section of the facility where employees work that is not accessible to the public.

Bartenders working in casinos and casino hotels can work either in the front of the house or the back of the house. Individuals working in the front of the house usually have more contact with patrons than their counterparts.

Bartenders in the front of the house may work in the hotel or casino bar, lounge restaurant, or banquet area. They are responsible for mixing and serving both alcoholic and nonalcoholic drinks for patrons.

Bartenders fill drink orders for customers sitting at the bar, as well as orders taken by waiters and waitresses from patrons seated in the restaurant, club, or bar.

Bartenders must know how to mix a great variety of drink recipes. They must have the ability to accomplish this quickly and accurately. Bartenders must also be able to mix drinks in the specific ways customers request. Many bartenders develop or concoct their own specialty drinks.

Successful Front-of-the-House Bartenders often socialize with patrons by listening to them and having light conversation. Bartenders are responsible for informing the beverage manager or assistant beverage manager of needed inventory of liquor, mixes, or other necessary bar supplies.

Other functions of the Front-of-the-House Bartender may include:

- Arranging bottles and glassware into attractive displays
- Serving snacks or food items to patrons seated at bar
- Collecting payments from patrons and operating the cash register
- Cleaning up the bar after patrons have left
- Monitoring liquor inventory

Salaries

Front-of-the-House Bartenders working in casinos and casino hotel facilities usually earn an hourly wage ranging from $7.00 to $14.00 or more plus tips and may make between $13,000 and $29,000 annually. Factors affecting earnings include the geographic location, size, type, and prestige of the specific casino, hotel, restaurant, bar, club, and/or lounge. Other variables may include the experience and duties of the individual, as well as his or her personality. There are some Bartenders who earn $18,000 and others who earn $80,000 or more with tips.

In unionized settings, the union may negotiate minimum earnings.

Employment Prospects

Employment opportunities are abundant for qualified Bartenders. Individuals may work in a variety of settings, including casino hotels, casino nightclubs, casino and casino hotel restaurants, and casino bars and lounges.

Las Vegas, Reno, Laughlin, Lake Tahoe, Atlantic City, Biloxi, Baton Rouge, New Orleans, and Detroit offer the greatest number of job possibilities. Other employment settings include casino hotels in other areas of Nevada, Mississippi, New York, Louisiana, Colorado, Connecticut, Illinois, Arizona, and California.

Other regions hosting Indian gaming and land-based or riverboat gaming facilities offer additional opportunities. New casinos and casino hotels are constantly under construction. More casinos and casino hotels are opening every year as areas legalize gambling.

Advancement Prospects

Bartenders working in the front of the house may advance their careers in a number of ways. Some individuals enjoy the social contact of bartending. These people may climb the career ladder by locating similar jobs in larger or more prestigious facilities. This usually results in increased earnings and tips.

Others advance their careers by becoming an assistant or full-fledged beverage manager, or bar, lounge, or nightclub manager. This career move often requires additional experience and/or training.

Education and Training

Training requirements vary from job to job. Most casinos and casino hotels prefer individuals to be high school graduates or have the equivalent. Experienced bartending may often be substituted for education. Facilities also require individuals to have some sort of formal training, accomplished by attending bartending schools, vo-tech schools, or academies. These schools often provide certification in bartending.

Special Requirements

Some casinos either require or prefer their Bartenders to be certified. This certification can be obtained through attending bartending school or other training.

Additionally, since Bartenders work around alcohol, there are also minimum age requirements. Depending on the specific state in which the casino is located, there may be other requirements Bartenders must fulfill. These may include state licensing, a health card from the local public health department, and an alcohol awareness card, which may also be referred to as a TAM card. TAM stands for Techniques of Alcohol Management.

Experience, Skills, and Personality Traits

Experience requirements, like training, vary. Most casino and casino hotel positions in this area prefer applicants to have prior bartending experience. Many casinos require individuals to be certified.

Bartenders should be friendly and well spoken with a neat and clean appearance. Customer service skills are mandatory. The ability to remember cocktail recipes as well as mix drinks quickly and accurately is essential.

Unions and Associations

Depending on the specific casino or casino hotel and its location, this may be a unionized position. In unionized situations in Las Vegas, for example, individuals may be members of the Bartenders & Beverage Local #165. In Atlantic City, Bartenders are represented by Local 54 of the Hotel Employees and Restaurants Employees International Union.

Individuals interested in pursuing a Bartender career can obtain additional information by contacting the National Restaurant Association (NRA), local bartending schools, or vo-tech schools offering courses and programs in bartending.

Tips for Entry

1. Bartending schools, especially those in areas hosting gaming and gaming hotels, often offer job placement possibilities.
2. Jobs may be advertised on casino job hotlines. These are frequently updated messages listing jobs available. Call each casino directly to get its job hotline phone number.
3. Stop by human resources departments to inquire about job openings.
4. Jobs are often advertised in the classified sections of newspapers in areas hosting gaming. Look under classifications such as "Bartenders," "Restaurant/Lounge Bartender," "Food and Beverage," "Front Of The House Jobs," and "Casino."

BARTENDER/BACK OF HOUSE

Duties: Mixing alcoholic and nonalcoholic beverages in service bars.

Alternate Title(s): None

Salary Range: $18,000 to $35,000+; may also share tips.

Employment Prospects: Good

Advancement Prospects: Fair

Best Geographical Location(s) for Position: Las Vegas, Reno, Laughlin, Lake Tahoe, Atlantic City, Biloxi, Baton Rouge, New Orleans, and Detroit offer most opportunities; other regions with land-based, riverboat, or Indian gaming facilities offer additional opportunities.

Prerequisites:

Education or Training—High school diploma or equivalent usually required; training at bartending school or vocational-technical school; see text.

CAREER LADDER

```
Front-of-the-House Bartender or
Assistant Beverage Manager

Bartender/Back of the House

Bartender in Other Setting
```

Experience and Qualifications—Prior experience as bartender in club, bar, or restaurants; certification and state licensing may be required.

Special Skills and Personality Traits—Drink mixing skills; organization; good memory.

Special Requirements—Certification may be required; state licensing; TAM card; health card; minimum age requirements.

Position Description

Most casinos and casino hotels employ Back-of-the-House Bartenders. The back of the house is the section of the facility where employees work that is not accessible to the public.

Bartenders working in casinos and casino hotels work either in the front of the house or the back of the house. The Bartender in the front of the house has contact with patrons. The individual working in the back of the house usually has no contact with patrons, but deals with waiters and waitresses bringing drink orders.

Bartenders in the back of the house usually work at the service bar in the hotel showroom, restaurant, club, or banquet area. They are responsible for mixing and preparing alcoholic and nonalcoholic drinks in service bars. Bartenders fill drink orders for customers seated at tables in the hotel's showroom, restaurant, or lounge.

As with Front-of-the-House Bartenders, those working the back of the house must know how to mix a great variety of drink recipes. They must have the ability to accomplish this quickly and accurately. Bartenders must also be able to mix drinks in the specific ways customers request.

Other functions of the Back-of-the-House Bartender may include:

- Informing beverage manager or assistant beverage manager of needed inventory of liquor, mixes, or other necessary bar supplies
- Monitoring liquor inventory

Salaries

Back-of-the-House Bartenders working in casinos and casino hotel facilities usually earn an hourly wage ranging from $8.50 to $17.00 or more. They often also share tips with cocktail servers, waiters, and waitresses. This may be done with a tip pool. The reason Back-of-the-House Bartenders may receive higher hourly earnings than their counterparts in the front of the house is that the ratio of tips is often different because it is shared.

Factors affecting earnings include the geographic location, size, type, and prestige of the specific casino, hotel, restaurant, or showroom. Other variables include the experience of the individual.

In unionized settings, the union may negotiate minimum earnings.

Employment Prospects

Employment opportunities are good for qualified Bartenders. Individuals work in a variety of settings, including casino hotels, casino nightclubs, casino showrooms, and casino and casino hotel restaurants.

Las Vegas, Reno, Laughlin, Lake Tahoe, Atlantic City, Biloxi, Baton Rouge, New Orleans, and Detroit offer the greatest number of job possibilities. Other employment settings include casino hotels in other areas of Nevada, Mississippi, New York, Louisiana, Colorado, Connecticut, Illinois, Arizona, and California.

Other regions hosting Indian gaming and land-based or riverboat gaming facilities offer additional opportunities. New casinos and casino hotels are constantly under construction. More casinos and casino hotels are opening every year as areas legalize gambling.

Advancement Prospects

Bartenders working in the back of the house may advance their careers in a number of ways. Some individuals want to earn more tips or want the socializing aspect of the job and move to a position in the front of the house. Others may climb the career ladder by locating similar jobs in larger or more prestigious facilities.

Some Bartenders advance their careers by becoming assistant beverage managers. This career move often requires additional experience and/or training.

Education and Training

Training requirements vary from job to job. Most facilities require individuals to be high school graduates or have the equivalent. They may accept bartending experience in lieu of education.

Some employers require that individuals be certified, accomplished through formal training in bartending at appropriate schools or academies.

Special Requirements

Some casinos either require or prefer their Bartenders to be certified. This certification can be obtained through attending bartending school or other training.

Additionally, since Bartenders work around alcohol, there are also minimum age requirements. Depending on the specific state in which the casino is located, there may be other requirements Bartenders must fulfill. These may include state licensing, a health card from the local public health department, and an alcohol awareness card, which may also be referred to as a TAM card. TAM stands for Techniques of Alcohol Management.

Experience, Skills, and Personality Traits

Experience requirements, like training vary. Most casinos and casino hotels prefer applicants with bartending experience. As noted previously, many casinos also require that individuals be certified.

Back-of-the-House Bartenders need the ability to remember a variety of cocktail recipes, as well as the ability to mix drinks quickly and accurately.

Unions and Associations

Depending on the specific casino or casino hotel and its location, this may be a unionized position. In unionized situations in Las Vegas, for example, individuals may be members of the Bartenders & Beverage Local #165. In Atlantic City, Bartenders are represented by Local 54 of the Hotel Employees and Restaurant Employees International Union.

Individuals interested in pursuing careers as Bartenders can obtain additional career information by contacting the National Restaurant Association (NRA), local bartending schools, or vo-tech schools offering courses and programs in bartending.

Tips for Entry

1. Bartending schools, especially those in areas hosting gaming and gaming hotels, often offer job placement possibilities.
2. Jobs are often advertised in the classified sections of newspapers in areas hosting gaming. Look under classifications such as "Bartenders," "Restaurant/Lounge Bartender," "Food and Beverage," "Back-Of-The-House Jobs," and "Casinos."
3. Stop by the human resources departments of casinos and casino hotels to inquire about job openings.
4. These jobs are often advertised on casino job hotlines, frequently updated messages listing jobs available. Call each casino directly to get its job hotline phone number.

COCKTAIL SERVER

CAREER PROFILE

Duties: Serving cocktails and nonalcoholic drinks to patrons.

Alternate Title(s): Cocktail Waitress; Cocktail Waiter

Salary Range: $15,000 to $19,000+ plus tips

Employment Prospects: Excellent

Advancement Prospects: Fair

Best Geographical Locations(s) for Position: Las Vegas, Reno, Laughlin, Lake Tahoe, Atlantic City, Biloxi, Baton Rouge, New Orleans, and Detroit offer most opportunities; other regions with land-based, riverboat, or Indian gaming facilities offer additional opportunities.

Prerequisites:

Education or Training—High school diploma or equivalent required or preferred; see text.

Experience and Qualifications—Prior experience working in food or beverage industry helpful, but not always required; state licensing may be required.

Special Skills and Personality Traits—Customer service skills; interpersonal skills; friendly.

Special Requirements—State licensing may be required; health card; TIPS or TAM certification.

CAREER LADDER

```
┌─────────────────────────────────────┐
│  Cocktail Server in Larger, More     │
│  Prestigious Casino/Casino Hotel or  │
│  Cocktail Server Coordinator         │
│  or Supervisor                       │
└─────────────────────────────────────┘
                  │
┌─────────────────────────────────────┐
│  Cocktail Server                     │
└─────────────────────────────────────┘
                  │
┌─────────────────────────────────────┐
│  Cocktail Server in Other Setting    │
│  or Entry Level                      │
└─────────────────────────────────────┘
```

Position Description

The main function of Cocktail Servers working in casinos and casino hotels is to serve alcoholic and nonalcoholic beverages to patrons. They may work in areas such as the showroom or clubs where patrons are seated. Individuals may also work in the casino area where customers are gambling.

Cocktail Servers take patrons' drink orders. They write down the drink order for each table or patron. Individuals then bring the order to the bar for a bartender to fill. Drinks are put on a tray, and the Cocktail Server brings them back and serves them to the customers.

Cocktail Servers ask patrons if they want refills. They also compute the bill when patrons are finished.

Cocktail Servers working in large showrooms are often assigned areas to work. They must take drink orders and fill them in crowded rooms. These individuals, however, may have the opportunity to see shows as they are working.

Cocktail Servers working in the gaming area are responsible for serving individuals who are gambling, some of whom may be high roller customers.

Other functions of Cocktail Servers may include:

- Keeping tables clear of used drink glasses
- Providing clean ashtrays
- Taking payments from patrons

Salaries

Cocktail Servers working in casinos and casino hotels earn an hourly wage ranging from minimum wage to $9.00 or more plus tips. They share tips in a tip pool with bartenders. Individuals may earn between $15,000 and $19,000 annually.

Factors affecting earnings include the geographic location, size, type, and prestige of the specific casino, hotel, restaurant, showroom, or lounge. Other factors include the personality and customer service skills of the server. Over the years, while not an everyday occurance there have reportedly been cases where servers were tipped not only large amounts of money but cars or even a house. One of the great things about working as a cocktail server in a casino is that when people are having a good time or have just won, they often tip more than they normally might in another situation.

In unionized settings, the union may negotiate minimum earnings.

Employment Prospects

Employment opportunities are excellent for Cocktail Servers interested in working in casinos and casino hotels. Individuals may work throughout the property, including the gaming floor, nightclubs, showrooms, restaurants, lounges, and bars.

Las Vegas, Reno, Laughlin, Lake Tahoe, Atlantic City, Biloxi, Baton Rouge, New Orleans, and Detroit offer the greatest number of job possibilities. Other employment settings include casino hotels in other areas of Nevada, Mississippi, New York, Louisiana, Colorado, Connecticut, Illinois, Arizona, and California.

Other regions hosting Indian gaming and land-based or riverboat gaming facilities offer additional opportunities. New casinos and casino hotels are constantly under construction. More casinos and casino hotels are opening every year as areas legalize gambling.

Advancement Prospects

Cocktail Servers may advance their careers in a number of ways. Those interested in staying Cocktail Servers may find similar positions in larger or more prestigious facilities, usually resulting in increased tip earning.

Others may climb the career ladder by being promoted to supervisory positions such as cocktail server coordinator or cocktail server supervisor. These career moves may require additional experience and/or training.

Education and Training

Many positions in casinos and casino hotels require individuals to be high school graduates or have the equivalent. They may take job experience in lieu of the educational requirement.

Training is not required for employment in this field. However, for those who are interested, these are academies and vocational technical schools offering training for Cocktail Servers.

Special Requirements

Depending on the specific state in which the casino where the Cocktail Server is working is located, there may be a number of special requirements. These include meeting the minimum age requirements of the specific state, getting a health card, and being licensed by a regulatory agency. Those working around alcohol will often also need to be certified in some manner in alcohol awareness such as TIPS (Techniques for Intervention Procedures). In Las Vegas, for example, individuals need to possess a TAM card. TAM stands for Techniques of Alcohol Management.

Experience, Skills, and Personality Traits

Prior experience as a Cocktail Server may or may not be required. Knowledge and understanding of beverage service is preferred.

Individuals should be personable people who enjoy interacting with others. They should be well spoken with a neat appearance. A good memory is helpful for remembering who ordered what drink.

Unions and Associations

Depending on the location and specific casino, this may or may not be a unionized position. For example, in unionized casinos and casino hotels in Las Vegas, Cocktail Servers might be members of the Culinary Workers Local #225. In Atlantic City, Cocktail Servers are represented by Local #54 Hotel Employees and Restaurant Employees International Union.

Individuals interested in pursuing a career as a Cocktail Server can obtain additional career information by contacting the National Restaurant Association (NRA) or vo-tech schools offering courses in this area.

Tips for Entry

1. Schools in areas with casinos and casino hotels offering programs for Cocktail Servers usually have job placement services.
2. Jobs are often advertised in the classified sections of newspapers in areas hosting gaming. Look under classifications such as "Cocktail Servers," "Restaurant/Lounge Cocktail Server," "Food and Beverage," "Casino Showroom," and "Casinos."
3. Check casino job hotlines, frequently updated messages listing jobs available. Call each casino directly to get its job hotline phone number.
4. Stop by the human resources departments of casinos and casino hotels to inquire about job openings.

CASINO AND CASINO HOTEL HUMAN RESOURCES DEPARTMENTS

DIRECTOR OF HUMAN RESOURCES

Duties: Directing operations of human resources department; supervising and monitoring department employees; developing and administering policies; recruitment; overseeing employee relations.

Alternate Title(s): Human Resources Director, H.R. Director

Salary Range: $35,000 to $125,000+

Employment Prospects: Fair

Advancement Prospects: Fair

Best Geographical Location(s) for Position: Las Vegas, Reno, Laughlin, Lake Tahoe, Atlantic City, Biloxi, Baton Rouge, New Orleans, and Detroit offer the greatest number of opportunities; other regions hosting Indian gaming and land-based or riverboat gaming facilities offer additional opportunities.

Prerequisites:

Education or Training—Minimum of bachelor's degree preferred; see text.

Experience and Qualifications—Five to 10 years' experience in human resources.

Special Skills and Personality Traits—Communication skills; interpersonal skills; management skills; knowledge of federal and state employment laws; writing skills; organized.

Position Description

Casinos and casino hotels employ large numbers of people. The department that handles employment is called the human resources department. In some facilities it may also be referred to as the personnel or employment department. The individual in charge of overseeing the department is called the Director of Human Resources.

This is a very important position. At one time or another, everyone who is hired must go through the human resources department. The individual directs the operation of the department. The Director is responsible for planning, organizing, and controlling everything that happens within the human resources department.

The Director of Human Resources develops, writes, and administers policies. These policies have a direct impact on the employees who are hired and the manner in which they are expected to work. They also have a great impact on the atmosphere and the way the casino or casino hotel functions.

The Director of Human Resources oversees several departments headed by other managers. Each of these departments specializes in a personnel activity. These may include employment, compensation, bene-

fits, training and development, employee relations, and employee licensing.

The Director is in charge of strategic planning as it relates to human resources. The individual may develop programs designed to enhance training, provide internship opportunities, and create career development within the property.

Other duties of the casino or casino hotel Director of Human Resources may include:

- Overseeing special projects and promotional events such as job fairs to stimulate recruitment of potential employees
- Building employee relations programs
- Developing and coordinating personnel programs

Salaries

The Director of Human Resources in casino and casino hotels earns between $35,000 and $125,000 or more annually. Factors affecting earnings include the geographic location, size, and prestige of the specific casino or casino hotel, as well as the education, experience, and responsibilities of the individual. Generally, those with the most education and experience working in larger facilities in the gambling capitals earn the highest salaries.

Employment Prospects

While employment opportunities are not plentiful, they are available for qualified individuals. Those seeking jobs in this area may have to relocate. As gaming moves into additional areas, there will be even more opportunities.

Las Vegas, Reno, Laughlin, Lake Tahoe, Atlantic City, Biloxi, Baton Rouge, New Orleans, and Detroit offer the greatest number of opportunities. Other regions hosting Indian gaming and land-based or riverboat gaming facilities offer additional opportunities.

Advancement Prospects

The Director of Human Resources may climb the career ladder in a number of ways. The individual may locate a similar position in a larger or more prestigious facility, resulting in increased responsibilities and earnings. He or she might also be promoted to a position such as vice president of human resources.

Education and Training

Generally, most casinos and casino hotels prefer that their Directors of Human Resources hold a minimum of a bachelor's degree. The best major is one earned in human resources. However, majors in other areas are often acceptable with work experience.

Additional courses, workshops, and seminars in human resources, labor relations, personnel, compensation, employee relations, gaming, and the hospitality industry are very helpful.

Experience, Skills, and Personality Traits

Five to 10 years' experience working in human resources and related areas is usually necessary for this position. Individuals often have worked in the human resources department in various positions. Many have been personnel directors or the Director of Human Resources in areas other than gaming. Experience working in human resources in the hospitality industry, hotels, or casinos is preferred in most instances.

Human Resources Directors should have supervisory and administrative skills. Writing and communication skills are also necessary. Individuals must have total knowledge of all federal and state employment laws.

Unions and Associations

Those interested in learning more about careers in this field should contact the Society for Human Resources Management (SHRM).

Tips for Entry

1. Get your foot in the door of a casino hotel. Most promote from within. If you have experience in human resources, see what positions are open and then move up the career ladder.
2. Jobs may be advertised in the classified sections of newspapers in areas hosting gaming. Look under classifications such as "Casino/Hotel Director of Human Resources," "Casino Human Resources Director," "Human Resources," or "Casino/Hotel Opportunities."
3. Openings are often advertised on the Internet. They may be located via the home pages of casino hotels. They may also be found doing a search of "Casino" or "Casino Hotel Job Opportunities."
4. Contact executive recruiters specializing in the gaming or hospitality industries.

HUMAN RESOURCES CLERK

Position Description

Casinos and casino hotels employ a great many people. Prior to becoming employed, each individual must be recruited, screened, and interviewed. The Human Resources Clerk has an array of duties depending on the specific job. The individual, who may also be called an interviewer or human resources coordinator, is responsible for greeting applicants upon arrival at the casino hotel for the initial interview.

The Human Resources Clerk schedules pre-employment job interviews with applicants. He or she is responsible for conducting pre-interviews with potential employees to determine their qualifications, as well as for seeing if they match those of job openings. The individual ascertains the skills, personality traits, education, and training of applicants. In this manner, the Human Resources Clerk can determine what other jobs the potential employee may be qualified for.

The Human Resources Clerk must also screen applicants. There may be a number of people for each job opening. The Clerk weeds out those who do not have the proper qualifications or might not fit into the casino hotel environment.

Other duties of the casino or casino hotel Human Resources Clerk may include:

- Making sure potential employees can meet necessary licensing requirements
- Assisting applicants with applications
- Checking references
- Handling administrative functions

Salaries

Human Resources Clerks earn between $10.00 and $16.00 or more per hour with annual earnings ranging between $21,000 to $34,000 or more. Factors affecting earnings include the geographic location, size, and prestige of the specific facility, as well as the experience, education, and responsibilities of the individual. Generally, those with the most education and experience working in larger casino hotels in the gambling capitals earn the highest salaries.

Employment Prospects

Employment prospects for Human Resources Clerks aspiring to work in casinos and casino hotels are good.

Las Vegas, Reno, Laughlin, Lake Tahoe, Atlantic City, Biloxi, Baton Rouge, New Orleans, and Detroit offer the greatest number of opportunities. Other regions hosting Indian gaming and land-based or riverboat gaming facilities offer additional opportunities.

Advancement Prospects

Individuals may climb the career ladder in a number of ways. Some people obtain experience and locate similar positions in larger or more prestigious facilities. This results in increased responsibilities and earnings. Others who have the proper education and training may eventually be promoted to different positions in the human resources department.

Education and Training

Casinos and casino hotels prefer, but may not always require, Human Resources Clerks to have a college degree. Good majors include human resources, liberal arts, public relations, marketing, communications, and hotel management. Experience working in human resources may be accepted in lieu of education.

Courses, workshops, and seminars in interviewing, recruiting, vocational counseling, and human resources will be useful.

Experience, Skills, and Personality Traits

Experience working in human resources, recruiting, or vocational counseling is usually required. Some individuals may have worked in public or private personnel offices or departments prior to being hired at the casino or casino hotel. Others may have moved up the ranks in the human resources department of the casino.

Knowledge and understanding of the gaming and hospitality industries is necessary. Individuals should be objective and articulate with good communication skills. The ability to make people comfortable is useful. Interviewing skills are essential.

Unions and Associations

Those interested in learning more about careers in human resources in casino hotels should contact the human resources departments of casinos and casino hotels.

Tips for Entry

1. Get your foot in the door of a casino or casino hotel human resources department. Start as a secretary or administrative assistant if there are no current openings as a Human Resources Clerk. Most casinos promote from within, and you can move up the career ladder.

2. Jobs may be advertised in the classified sections of newspapers in areas hosting gaming. Look under classifications such as "Casino/Gaming," "Human Resources," "Human Resources Clerk," "Interviewer," or "Casino/Gaming Opportunities."

3. Visit the human resources departments of casinos and inquire about job openings. You might also consider sending or faxing a résumé and a short cover letter.

4. Most casinos also have job hotlines, frequently updated messages listing jobs available. You can call each casino directly to obtain its job hotline phone number.

5. Openings are often advertised on the Internet. They may be located via the home pages of casino hotels. They may also be found by doing a search of casino, casino hotel, or gaming job opportunities.

6. Visit casino and casino hotel job fairs.

TRAINING MANAGER

CAREER PROFILE

Duties: Developing and facilitating classes, seminars, workshops, and other training programs for casino and casino hotel employees.

Alternate Title(s): Training and Development Manager

Salary Range: $28,000 to $58,000+

Employment Prospects: Fair

Advancement Prospects: Fair

Best Geographical Location(s) for Position: Las Vegas, Reno, Laughlin, Lake Tahoe, Atlantic City, Biloxi, Baton Rouge, New Orleans, and Detroit offer the greatest number of opportunities; other regions hosting Indian gaming and land-based or riverboat gaming facilities offer additional opportunities.

Prerequisites:

Education or Training—Educational requirements vary; see text.

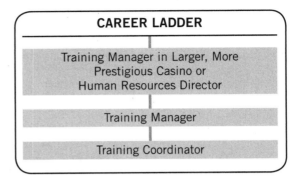

CAREER LADDER

Training Manager in Larger, More Prestigious Casino or Human Resources Director

Training Manager

Training Coordinator

Experience and Qualifications—Human resources or training background.

Special Skills and Personality Traits—Communication skills; interpersonal skills; writing skills; ability to speak in public; creative; organized.

Position Description

Casinos and casino hotels employ large staffs. Training Managers are employed by these facilities to develop programs for employees in a multitude of areas and a variety of subjects, depending on the needs of the specific casino or casino hotel. In some facilities, the individual may be called the training and development manager.

The Training Manager has a great deal of responsibility. The individual facilitates all classes personally or works with a staff. Staff members may include a training coordinator and other trainers to handle this task.

The Training Manager works with the director of human resources, who writes and administers policies. These policies have a direct impact on the way employees are expected to work. The human resources director may, at his or her discretion, ask the Training Manager to develop programs designed to enhance training within the property, as well as to provide internship opportunities.

The Training Manager develops and facilitates orientation programs for new employees. During orientation, employees learn the policies of the casino as well as any governmental regulations that may affect their job performance. The orientation program also explains to staff members how they are expected to act on the job.

The program also alerts employees to situations that are acceptable as well as unacceptable.

As customer service is mandatory to the success of casinos and casino hotels, it is essential that every employee treat every guest in a courteous and gracious manner. An important function of Training Managers in casinos is teaching employees about good customer service and how it should be provided to guests.

The Training Manager may offer classes in interactive management, also known as IM. These classes assist management in learning how to better communicate with their employees. Other subjects covered in this type of class often include acceptable methods for staff member discipline and how to speak to subordinates without coming across abruptly.

The Training Manager may design TIPS classes, which are offered to employees who work around alcohol, such as bartenders, cocktail servers, dealers, and floorpersons. TIPS classes teach these employees how to deal properly with customers who are intoxicated—the signs to look for in those who have had enough alcohol and how to stop serving patrons without causing a scene.

To those working in the casino area, Training Managers offer classes covering governmental regulations. For example, employees may need to learn how to fill in currency transaction reports (CTR). These are needed whenever customers win over $10,000 in a 24-hour period.

Other duties of the casino or casino hotel Training Manager may include:

- Creating and directing programs to teach department directors, managers, and supervisors methods of conducting training within their departments
- Teaching department directors, managers, and supervisors proper procedures for interview techniques and employment reviews
- Training employees in team building so that managers, supervisors, and subordinates all work together

Salaries

Training Managers in casinos and casino hotels earn between $28,000 and $58,000 or more annually. Factors affecting earnings include the geographic location, size, and prestige of the specific casino or casino hotel, as well as the education, experience, and responsibilities of the individual. Generally, those with the most education and experience working in larger facilities earn the highest salaries.

Employment Prospects

Employment prospects for Training Managers aspiring to work in casinos or casino hotels are fair. Most employment opportunities for Training Managers are located in areas hosting a large number of casinos. Las Vegas, Reno, Laughlin, Lake Tahoe, Atlantic City, Biloxi, Baton Rouge, New Orleans, and Detroit offer the greatest number of opportunities. Other regions hosting Indian gaming and land-based or riverboat gaming facilities offer additional opportunities.

As gaming moves into additional areas, there will be even more jobs.

Advancement Prospects

Training Managers working in casinos and casino hotels may advance their careers by locating similar positions in larger or more prestigious facilities. Individuals might also climb the career ladder by obtaining additional experience and training and becoming director of human resources. Some Training Managers strike out on their own and become Training Consultants.

Education and Training

Educational requirements vary from casino to casino for Training Managers. Some facilities require or pre-fer individuals to hold a bachelor's degree in human resources, communications, the hospitality industry, or a related field. Others may accept those with a high school diploma with a background and experience in training, human resources, and/or the hospitality industry.

Experience, Skills, and Personality Traits

As noted, experience in human resources, training, and the hospitality industry are needed. Training Managers usually have worked as training coordinators or trainers prior to their appointment.

This is a highly visible position. Almost everyone in the casino knows the Training Manager. The individual must have excellent interpersonal and employee relations skills. Training Managers must also have both verbal and written communication skills. The ability to speak effectively in front of groups of people is essential to this position.

Unions and Associations

Those interested in learning more about careers in this field should contact the American Society of Training and Development (ASTD).

Tips For Entry

1. Become either an active or affiliate member of ASTD. This may give you the edge over another applicant with the same qualifications.
2. Get your foot in the door of a casino hotel. Most promote from within. If you have experience in training, see if a position exists as a trainer. Get experience and climb the career ladder.
3. Openings are often advertised on the Internet. They may be located via the home pages of casino hotels. They may also be found doing a search of casino or casino hotel job opportunities.
4. Jobs may be advertised in the classified sections of newspapers in areas hosting gaming. Look under classifications such as "Casino/Hotel Director Training Manager," "Training and Development Manager," "Casino Training and Development Manager," "Casino/Hotel Opportunities," or "Human Resources."
5. You may be asked to conduct an impromptu training presentation as part of your interview process. Develop a sample program ahead of time and rehearse it before the interview.

COMPENSATION AND BENEFITS MANAGER

CAREER PROFILE

Duties: Overseeing and coordinating employee wage, salary, and benefits programs in casino or casino hotel; supervising compensation and benefits office employees.

Alternate Title(s): Benefits Manager; Compensation Manager

Salary Range: $32,000 to $65,000+

Employment Prospects: Fair

Advancement Prospects: Fair

Best Geographical Location(s) for Position: Las Vegas, Reno, Laughlin, Lake Tahoe, Atlantic City, Biloxi, Baton Rouge, New Orleans, and Detroit offer the greatest number of opportunities; other regions hosting Indian gaming and land-based or riverboat gaming facilities offer additional opportunities.

Prerequisites:

Education or Training—Educational requirements vary; see text.

CAREER LADDER

```
┌─────────────────────────────────────────────┐
│  Compensation and Benefits Manager           │
│  in Larger, More Prestigious Casino or        │
│  Director of Compensation and Benefits        │
├─────────────────────────────────────────────┤
│  Compensation and Benefits Manager            │
├─────────────────────────────────────────────┤
│  Benefits Coordinator                         │
└─────────────────────────────────────────────┘
```

Experience and Qualifications—Experience in human resources, benefits, or labor relations.

Special Skills and Personality Traits—Communication skills; interpersonal skills; computer skills; patience; familiarity with and understanding of compensation and benefits programs in the industry.

Position Description

Casinos, like many other large businesses, have many employees. In most casinos and casino hotels, employees receive a variety of benefits in addition to their compensation. The person in charge of overseeing and directing the various benefit plans and compensation packages of employees is called the Compensation and Benefits Manager. The individual has a variety of responsibilities.

The Compensation and Benefits Manager is in charge of overseeing the employees in the benefits and compensation office. These may include a benefits coordinator who works under the Compensation and Benefits Manager administering the health insurance and other benefit plans, compensation and benefits analysts, and benefit clerks.

The Compensation and Benefits Manager tracks employee evaluations often to determine employee raises. The Compensation and Benefits Manager may also determine raise amounts by the length of time employees are in service, the amount of training, grade levels, or promotions. Raise amounts usually must be placed within the policy set by management.

The Compensation and Benefits Manager is usually one of the checkpoints an employee must go through when hired by a casino or casino hotel. The Manager is in charge of discussing the type of compensation the employee will receive for the job. Depending on the specific job, the employee may be paid hourly or receive a set weekly salary. The Compensation and Benefits Manager may also explain to the employee whether he or she will be paid on a weekly or bi-weekly basis.

At this time, the Compensation and Benefits Manager also explains the benefits that are offered as part of the job. These may include, but are not limited to, health insurance, life insurance, pension plans, profit sharing, child care, educational reimbursement, paid holidays, and vacations.

The Compensation and Benefits Manager is responsible for answering any questions regarding compensation or benefits. The individual may refer employees to others working in the department for answers or assistance.

The Compensation and Benefits Manager gathers information regarding salaries, wages, and benefits offered within the industry, as well as in the area in which the casino or casino hotel is located. The individual uses this information to analyze the casino's programs and make recommendations for new programs.

Other duties of the casino or casino or casino hotel Compensation and Benefits Manager may include:

- Ensuring that employees meets the proper employment requirements
- Making sure accurate files are maintained on all employees, as well as the benefits and compensation they receive

Salaries

The Compensation and Benefits Manager in a casino or casino hotel earns between $32,000 and $65,000 or more annually. Factors affecting earnings include the geographic location, size, and prestige of the specific casino or casino hotel, as well as the education, experience, and responsibilities of the individual.

Individuals with a great deal of experience working with large numbers of employees in casino hotels earn the highest salaries.

Employment Prospects

Most casinos and casino hotels have Compensation and Benefits Managers. The greatest number of employment opportunities exist in areas hosting gaming with large numbers of casinos.

Las Vegas, Reno, Laughlin, Lake Tahoe, Atlantic City, Biloxi, Baton Rouge, New Orleans, and Detroit offer the greatest number of opportunities. Other regions hosting Indian gaming and land-based or riverboat gaming facilities offer additional opportunities. As gaming moves into additional areas, there will be even more jobs available.

Advancement Prospects

Casino and casino hotel Compensation and Benefits Managers may take a number of paths toward career advancement. Individuals may be promoted to the job of director of compensation and benefits in larger facilities where the position exists. Others may locate similar positions in larger facilities, resulting in increased responsibilities and earnings.

Compensation and Benefits Managers with experience in additional areas of human resources may also advance to positions such as the assistant director of human resources or, in some facilities, the director of the department.

Education and Training

Educational requirements vary for Compensation and Benefits Managers. College is often required or preferred with a degree in human resources, personnel management, labor relations, compensation and benefits, business management, or economics.

For those who have moved up the ranks in the compensation and benefits area, a high school diploma or its equivalent and experience may be acceptable.

Experience, Skills, and Personality Traits

Experience in human resources, personnel administration, labor relations, insurance administration, benefits, or compensation is necessary. As noted previously, some individuals have obtained experience by moving up the ranks. They began as benefit clerks or had prior experience as benefits coordinators.

Individuals must have knowledge and understanding of insurance programs, retirement plans, labor relations, and wage and benefit trends. Compensation and Benefit Managers should have excellent communication and interpersonal skills. Management, administrative, and supervisory skills are also needed.

Unions and Associations

Those interested in learning more about careers in this field should contact the International Foundation of Employee Benefit Plans (IFEBP) and the American Compensation Association (ACA).

Tips for Entry

1. Jobs may be advertised in the classified sections of newspapers in areas hosting gaming. Look under classifications such as "Casino/Hotel Opportunities," "Casino/Gaming," "Benefits and Compensation," or "Benefits and Compensation Manager."
2. Look for jobs in casinos and casino hotels on the Internet. They may be located via the home pages of casino hotels. They may also be found doing a search of casino or casino hotel job opportunities.
3. Visit the human resources departments of casinos and casino hotels to see what employment opportunities are available.
4. Fax or send your résumé to human resources departments.
5. Casinos often promote from within. Get your foot in the door and move up the ranks.

BENEFITS COORDINATOR

CAREER PROFILE

Duties: Handling casino's or casino hotel's employee benefits program; administering health insurance and pension plans; signing up employees to proper plans.

Alternate Title(s): None

Salary Range: $27,000 to $39,000+

Employment Prospects: Fair

Advancement Prospects: Fair

Best Geographical Location(s) for Position: Las Vegas, Reno, Laughlin, Lake Tahoe, Atlantic City, Biloxi, Baton Rouge, New Orleans, and Detroit offer the greatest number of opportunities; other regions hosting Indian gaming and land-based or riverboat gaming facilities offer additional opportunities.

Prerequisites:

Education or Training—Minimum of a high school diploma or equivalent and on-the-job training; see text.

CAREER LADDER

```
Compensation and Benefits Manager

Benefits Coordinator

Benefits Clerk
```

Experience and Qualifications—Experience working in human resources department preferred.

Special Skills and Personality Traits—Communication skills; interpersonal skills; computer skills; patience; familiarity and understanding of insurance programs and pension plans.

Position Description

Employees working in casinos and casino hotels receive a variety of benefits. While these vary in each facility, they often include health insurance, life insurance, pension plans, profit sharing, child care, educational reimbursement, paid holidays, and vacations.

The Benefits Coordinator works in the casino's employee benefits office. This is usually a subdivision of the human resources department. In some facilities, the Benefits Coordinator also handles the duties of the compensation coordinator or manager.

Great benefits are a major advantage to employees working in casinos. The Benefits Coordinator is responsible for making sure employees not only know what is offered and what they are entitled to, but understand how to take advantage of these benefits as well.

One of the major benefits of working in most casinos is health insurance. This may include a variety of plans, including major medical, dental, and vision. The Benefits Coordinator is in charge of explaining what each plan entails and helping employees determine which plan is best for them. The Benefits Coordinator administers the health insurance plan on behalf of the casino and its employees.

The individual signs up employees and assists them in participating in applicable plans. The Coordinator is also responsible for making insurance forms available and helping employees fill them in when necessary. As part of this function, the Benefits Coordinator acts as a liaison between the insurance company and the casino to ensure that employees receive reimbursement or other benefits.

The Benefits Coordinator is responsible for answering any questions from employees regarding their benefits. Individuals may have questions about their health insurance, pension plan, or other benefits provided to them.

The Benefits Coordinator gathers necessary information from employees for the records. The individual must maintain accurate files on all employees and the benefits they receive.

Other duties of the casino or casino hotel Benefits Coordinator may include:

- Administering pension and other retirement plans
- Explaining educational reimbursement policies
- Handling compensation responsibilities
- Making sure payments are made in a timely fashion to correct parties

Salaries

The Benefits Coordinator in a casino or casino hotel earns between $27,000 and $39,000 or more annually.

Factors affecting earnings include the geographic location, size, and prestige of the specific casino or casino hotel, as well as the education, experience, and responsibilities of the individual.

Experienced individuals handling the benefits of large numbers of employees earn the highest salaries. Earnings will also be at the higher end of the scale in facilities where the benefits coordinator also handles compensation responsibilities.

Employment Prospects

Employment prospects are fair for people seeking this position. Almost every casino and casino hotel has a Benefits Coordinator or someone who handles the responsibilities. The greatest number of employment opportunities for these individuals exist in areas hosting gaming with large numbers of casinos.

Las Vegas, Reno, Laughlin, Lake Tahoe, Atlantic City, Biloxi, Baton Rouge, New Orleans, and Detroit offer the greatest number of opportunities. Other regions hosting Indian gaming and land-based or riverboat gaming facilities offer additional opportunities.

As gaming moves into additional areas, there will be even more jobs available.

Advancement Prospects

There are a number of advancement paths for Benefits Coordinators. Some individuals obtain experience and locate similar positions in larger facilities. Others may be promoted to benefits and compensation managers or directors.

Benefits Coordinators aspiring to move out of the benefits area, but still desiring to work in human resources, may become a human resources generalist or a supervisor in other areas of the human resources department.

Education and Training

Educational requirements vary for Benefits Coordinators. A high school diploma or its equivalent is usually the minimum education required, along with on-the-job training.

A bachelor's degree may be preferred and is helpful in climbing the career ladder. Colleges and universities offer programs leading to degrees in compensation and benefits, personnel, and human resources.

Any courses, workshops, and seminars completed in insurance, profit sharing, or pension plan administration will be helpful.

Experience, Skills, and Personality Traits

Experience in human resources, personnel administration, insurance administration, benefits, or compensation is necessary. Many individuals obtain experience by working as a benefits clerk in the compensation and benefits office.

Understanding of insurance programs and pension plans is helpful. Benefits Coordinators need excellent communication and interpersonal skills. Patience is also essential so as to be able to explain hard-to-understand plans and benefits.

Unions and Associations

Those interested in learning more about careers in this field should contact the International Foundation of Employee Benefit Plans (IFEBP) and the American Compensation Association (ACA).

Tips for Entry

1. Most casinos promote from within. If you are interested in this career and don't have experience, see if positions are open as benefits clerks. Learn what you can and climb the career ladder.
2. Jobs may be advertised in the classified sections of newspapers in areas hosting gaming. Look under classifications such as "Casino/Hotel Opportunities," "Casino/Gaming," "Benefits Coordinator," or "Benefits Department."
3. Openings are often advertised on the Internet. They may be located via the home pages of casino hotels. They may also be found doing a search of casino or casino hotel job opportunities.
4. Stop by the human resources departments of casinos and casino hotels to see what employment opportunities are available.
5. Fax or send your résumé to the human resources departments.

EMPLOYEE RELATIONS MANAGER

Duties: Creating and planning employee events and functions; developing and editing employee publications; handling employee grievances.

Alternate Title(s): None

Salary Range: $45,000 to $80,000+

Employment Prospects: Fair

Advancement Prospects: Fair

Best Geographical Location(s) for Position: Las Vegas, Reno, Laughlin, Lake Tahoe, Atlantic City, Biloxi, Baton Rouge, New Orleans, and Detroit offer the greatest number of opportunities; other regions hosting Indian gaming and land-based or riverboat gaming facilities offer additional opportunities.

Prerequisites:

Education or Training—Minimum of a bachelor's degree; see text.

Experience and Qualifications—Experience in human resources.

CAREER LADDER

Employee Relations Manager in Larger, More Prestigious Casino or Casino Hotel or Personnel or Human Resources Director

Employee Relations Manager

Human Resources Clerk or Other Position in Human Resources

Special Skills and Personality Traits—Communication skills; organization; detail-oriented; interpersonal skills; knowledge of negotiation and arbitration.

Position Description

Casinos and casino hotels need a wide variety of employees in order to run efficiently. Some casinos have over 1,000 employees; larger ones may employ 2,500 people or more. The Employee Relations Manager usually works in the human resources department. The individual makes sure employees are kept abreast of what's happening within the casino. The Employee Relations Manager also helps keep employees satisfied with their jobs.

The Employee Relations Manager acts as a liaison between management and employees, bringing employee problems to the attention of management, and, conversely, explaining management policies to employees. In order to do this, the individual must meet with management to learn about new policies or changes in existing ones.

The Employee Relations Manager is responsible for handling staff communications. This may include developing and writing letters, memos, flyers, posters, and employee newsletters. In some settings, the Manager hands some of these duties on to an assistant. In this event, the individual is responsible for editing and checking the written communications.

Many feel that one of the plusses of working in a casino environment is that it is somewhat like an extended family. The Employee Relations Manager is responsible for the development and implementation of employee events. These activities not only boost morale, but help everyone relax while getting to know one another on a different basis. The Employee Relations Manager may develop functions such as picnics, parties, dances, and basketball or softball games.

The Employee Relations Manager may be responsible for working with union shop stewards. The individual must attend their meetings and relay information to management. In some cases, he or she works with other management people negotiating union requests.

Other duties of the Employee Relations Manager working in a casino or casino hotel may include:

- Conducting training seminars and workshops for employees
- Investigating and answering employee grievances
- Negotiating with employees regarding grievances
- Arranging events to recognize casino employees for long or outstanding service
- Supervising others in the department

Salaries

Employee Relations Managers earn salaries ranging from $45,000 to $80,000 annually. Factors affecting earnings include the geographic location, size, and prestige of the specific casino or casino hotel, as well as the education, experience, and responsibilities of the individual. Generally, those working in larger facilities who are responsible for greater numbers of employees earn higher salaries.

Employment Prospects

Employment prospects for Employee Relations Managers are fair. They generally can be found in mid-sized and larger facilities. In smaller properties, the director of human resources or personnel director may handle the functions of the Employee Relations Manager. Individuals usually work normal business hours. They may be required to work overtime or on weekends when emergencies arise, during negotiations, or when employee events are scheduled.

Advancement Prospects

Employee Relations Managers may advance their careers by locating similar positions in larger casinos. Individuals climb the career ladder by being promoted to human resources or personnel director. There are also Employee Relations Managers who go into public relations as well.

Education and Training

A bachelor's degree is usually required to become an Employee Relations Manager in a casino or casino hotel. Work experience may sometimes be accepted in lieu of formal education.

A broad educational background with courses in group dynamics, negotiation, arbitration, labor relations, human resources, personnel, public relations, marketing, communications, journalism, English, business, writing, and psychology will be useful.

Experience, Skills, and Personality Traits

Individuals interested in becoming Employee Relations Managers should have experience in the human resources field.

Employee Relations Managers should be personable people who genuinely like others. Individuals need good communication skills with the ability to speak articulately to groups of people. They must be able to write clearly and accurately.

Employee Relations Managers additionally must have good understanding of the attitudes of both employees and those in management. General knowledge of group dynamics, negotiations, and arbitration is also needed.

Unions and Associations

Those interested in learning more about careers as Employee Relations Managers may obtain information from the Society for Human Resources Management (SHRM) or the Public Relations Society of America (PRSA), as well as the human resources departments in casinos and casino hotels.

Tips for Entry

1. Visit the human resources departments of casinos and inquire about job openings. Send or fax a résumé and a short cover letter.
2. Many casinos have job hotline numbers. These offer current job opportunities available at the facility.
3. Openings are often advertised on the Internet. They may be located via the home pages of casino hotels. They may also be found by doing a search of "Casino," "Casino Hotel," or "Gaming Job Opportunities."
4. Jobs may be advertised in the classified sections of newspapers in areas hosting gaming. Look under classifications such as "Casino/Gaming Opportunities," "Employee Relations Manager," "Employee Relations," or "Casinos/Casino Hotels."

CASINO OR CASINO HOTEL PAYROLL CLERK

CAREER PROFILE

Duties: Ensuring that employees' paychecks are correct; calculating earnings and deductions; computing pay; maintaining backup files; researching payroll records.

Alternate Title(s): Payroll Specialist

Salary Range: $16,000 to $32,000+

Employment Prospects: Good

Advancement Prospects: Good

Best Geographical Location(s) for Position: Las Vegas, Reno, Laughlin, Lake Tahoe, Atlantic City, Biloxi, Baton Rouge, New Orleans, and Detroit offer the greatest number of opportunities; other regions hosting Indian gaming and land-based or riverboat gaming facilities offer additional opportunities.

Prerequisites:

Education or Training—High school diploma or equivalent.

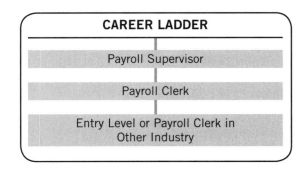

CAREER LADDER

Payroll Supervisor

Payroll Clerk

Entry Level or Payroll Clerk in Other Industry

Experience and Qualifications—Accounting or payroll background preferred, but not always required.

Special Skills and Personality Traits—Detail-oriented; organized; ability to work accurately with numbers; data-entry skills.

Position Description

Casinos and casino hotels employ large numbers of staff members. Payroll Clerks, also called payroll specialists, help ensure that employees' paychecks are correct. Specific responsibilities depend on the specific facility and the manner in which payroll is handled. Generally, Payroll Clerks are responsible for inputting data regarding employees' pay, as well as maintaining and researching these records.

Payroll Clerks are responsible for calculating the earnings of employees, including regular and overtime hours. Individuals must also calculate deductions such as income tax withholdings, social security, credit union payments, and insurance. This task may be accomplished by computers.

Hourly employees of the casino and casino hotel punch time cards. At the end of the pay period, Payroll Clerks are responsible for screening time cards to make sure there are no calculating, coding, or other types of errors. Pay is then computed by subtracting allotments such as retirement, federal and state taxes, and insurance from employees' gross earnings. When a computer performs these calculations, it alerts the Payroll Clerk

to problems or errors in data. The individual can then adjust the errors.

Payroll Clerks enter the correct data on checks, check stubs, and master payroll sheets, or more commonly on forms for computer preparation of checks. Individuals are also expected to prepare and distribute pay envelopes.

Payroll Clerks correct any problems in employees' checks or explain calculations. These may include adjusting monetary errors or incorrect amounts of vacation time.

Other responsibilities of Payroll Clerks working at casinos and casino hotels may include:

- Typing, checking, and filing wage information forms
- Keeping wage and fringe benefit information on employees
- Maintaining records of employee sick leave pay and nontaxable wages
- Performing additional clerical tasks

Salaries

Payroll Clerks working at casinos and casino hotels are paid on an hourly basis. Earnings range from $7.50 to

$15.00 per hour or more. Factors affecting earnings include the experience, level of training, and responsibilities of the individual, as well as the geographic location, size, and prestige of the specific casino or casino hotel.

Employment Prospects

Employment prospect are good for Payroll Clerks in casinos and casino hotels. All casinos and casino hotels employ Payroll Clerks. This is generally a day-shift position. Individuals can find employment on either a full-time or part-time basis.

Las Vegas, Reno, Laughlin, Lake Tahoe, Atlantic City, Biloxi, Baton Rouge, New Orleans, and Detroit offer the greatest number of opportunities. Other regions hosting Indian gaming and land-based or riverboat gaming facilities offer additional opportunities.

Advancement Prospects

Payroll Clerks can advance their careers by obtaining experience and advancing to positions such as payroll supervisors.

Education and Training

A high school diploma or the equivalent is the minimum required for this position in most casinos and casino hotels. While no specific training may be necessary, individuals must have the ability to use adding machines, calculators, computers, and word processors. Knowledge of office machinery use may be self-taught or learned in high school or business courses in vo-tech schools, community colleges, or adult education classes. Some casinos and casino hotels also offer on-the-job training.

Experience, Skills, and Personality Traits

In some facilities Payroll Clerk may be an entry-level job, while in others it may require a background in accounting or payroll.

Payroll Clerks must be detail-oriented, organized individuals who enjoy working with numbers. Accuracy as well as the ability to find and correct math errors is essential. Data-entry skills are mandatory.

Unions and Associations

Those interested in learning more about careers in this area should contact the human resources departments of casinos and casino hotels.

Tips for Entry

1. Jobs are often advertised in the classified sections of newspapers in areas hosting gaming. Look under classifications such as "Payroll Clerk," "Payroll Specialist," "Casinos," "Casino Hotels," "Payroll," or "Casino Opportunities."
2. Visit the human resources departments of casino and casino hotels to see if there are any job openings in this area.
3. Get experience working in the payroll department in any industry, even for a short time. This will make you more marketable when seeking a job in casinos.
4. Most casinos have job hotlines. These are frequently updated messages listing jobs available. You can call each casino directly to get its job hotline phone number.
5. Surf the net. In addition to popular job sites like www.monster.com and www.hotjobs.com most casinos have employment sections listing job openings on their Web sites.

CASINO HOTEL HEALTH CLUBS AND SPAS

SPA MANAGER

CAREER PROFILE

Duties: Overseeing the day to day operations of casino and casino hotel spa; assuring that guests have an overall positive experience; hiring, supervising, scheduling and motivating staff; overseeing business operations in spa; determining treatments offered.

Alternate Title(s): Spa Director

Salary Range: $35,000 to $75,000+

Employment Prospects: Fair

Advancement Prospects: Fair

Best Geographical Location(s) for Position: Positions located in areas hosting gaming; Las Vegas, Reno, Laughlin, Lake Tahoe, Atlantic City, Biloxi, Baton Rouge, New Orleans, Detroit, and Black Hawk offer the greatest number of opportunities; other regions with land-based riverboat or Indian gaming facilities offer additional opportunities.

Prerequisites:

Education or Training—Educational requirements vary; see text.

Experience—Experience working in spas and health clubs.

CAREER LADDER

```
Spa Manager for Larger, More Prestigious
Casino or Casino Hotel, or Spa Manager
in Other Industry

Casino or Casino Hotel Spa Manager

Assistant Spa Manager
```

Special Skills and Personality Traits—Supervisory skills; management skills; motivational; organization skills; communication skills; problem solving skills; understanding of gaming and hospitality industries; knowledge of various spa services.

Special Requirements—Certification in CPR necessary; Red Cross lifeguard certification may be required; other licenses and certifications may be necessary.

Position Description

Casinos and casino hotels today provide more than just a place to gamble and overnight accommodations for guests. Instead, many facilities strive to provide visitors with an exceptional experience by offering the ultimate in amenities such as fine dining, luxurious rooms, and lavish spas.

When planning a trip to a casino or casino hotel, in addition to gambling, many guests look forward to pampering themselves with a visit to one of these spas. Sometimes that spa visit might only last for an hour; in other situations, a guest may plan an entire day at the spa. No matter what the length of the visit, the experience guests have at the spa can often impact whether they come back to a property, or how much they end up spending on gambling during their visit.

For many years casino and casino hotel spas were part of the facility's health club or gyms. Today many casinos and casino hotels host new luxurious spas created as entities unto themselves. The individual responsible for overseeing the day-to-day activities of the casino and casino hotel spa is called the Spa Manager or spa director.

The casino or casino hotel Spa Manager is expected to set the tone for the facility. Within the scope of the job, the individual is expected to create a relaxing, warm, and inviting atmosphere where guests feel comfortable and pampered, and will want to come back.

The Spa Manager is ultimately in charge of every aspect of the spa. This includes the way it looks, the way it is run, the services it offers, and of course, the way employees treat each guest.

The Spa Manager is responsible for handling the business operation of the facility and is ultimately responsible for the bottom line. He or she must do everything possible to increase profits.

Depending on the specific spa and its structure, the facility may provide an array of pampering services and treatments for men and women including hairstyling, manicures, pedicures, facials, various types of massages, wraps, stress-reduction therapies, hot-stone restorative therapies, reflexology, craniosacral therapy, Watsu water therapy, and more. Some spas additionally offer weight management advice and exercise classes.

The spa may also offer pools, saunas, Jacuzzis, whirlpools, and more.

As part of the job, the Spa Manager must determine what types of services and treatments provide the most revenue for the facility as well as what services guests want. He or she will then find ways to direct resources toward providing those services. In order to do this, the Spa Manager must have a thorough understanding of the profit contributions each service and department within the spa provide.

A spa can be beautiful, lavish, extravagant, and provide all the finest services, but in the end, without good employees, the facility will ultimately be nothing. A big part of the job of the Spa Manager is making sure that doesn't happen. The Spa Manager is responsible for hiring people who are not only above the bar in their area of expertise, but also in customer service and people skills as well.

The manager is responsible for making sure that employees treat each guest with the utmost care while striving to ensure that each guest leaves the spa feeling better than when he or she came in.

The Spa Manager is expected to train and motivate all spa employees. This may be done either formally or informally. Training may cover areas ranging from spa policies, procedures, customer service, equipment usage, services, and employing low-key sales skills to sell services to spa guests.

The Spa Manager is responsible for scheduling employees so all shifts are covered. He or she may do this or delegate these duties to an assistant manager.

The individual often helps develop the direction in which the spa goes, including its culture, furnishings, decorations, amenities, and services.

Many spa facilities also host retail outlets, which sell casino or casino hotel or spa branded merchandise. Other facilities additionally host restaurants serving light or healthy food choices. The Spa Manager is responsible for staffing and overseeing these outlets as well.

While spa patrons at casino and casino hotel spas may be transient, many guests return to the same hotel to gamble on a regular basis. The Spa Manager is expected to make an effort to welcome guests back, often keeping track of the services each guest uses.

The Spa Manager may develop promotions and specials designed to attract these people back to the spa on their return trips. The individual may also develop promotions and specials designed to attract people who live in the local area as well. This is often done with the assistance of the marketing or advertising department.

The Spa Manager at a casino or casino hotel must be a presence in the facility. He or she is expected to meet and greet spa patrons, answer guest questions, and be sure they are pleased with the spa and its services. Being accessible to patrons is essential in this job.

At times, the Spa Manager may be called upon by a concierge or casino host to fit a casino guest in for a service or schedule a special spa service requested by a guest. The individual is expected to do his or her best to accommodate the guest. This may be especially important when dealing with high rollers.

The Spa Manager is ultimately responsible for everything that happens in the spa. If there is a problem, the individual must take care of it immediately to the patron's satisfaction. At times, this may mean comping the service for a guest. While customer service is important in every industry, those working in casinos and the hospitality industries feel it is especially important.

Additional responsibilities of the casino or casino hotel Spa Manager include:

- Implementing spa membership promotions
- Developing budgets
- Assuring that the spa is clean and safe
- Negotiating with vendors for products or services
- Reporting any accidents or incidents
- Handling patron complaints
- Building employee moral

Salaries

Salaries for Casino and Casino Hotel Spa Managers can range from approximately $35,000 to $75,000, and may run higher. Factors affecting earnings include the specific facility's type, prestige, size, and geographic location.

Other factors affecting earnings include the responsibilities, training, and experience of the individual. Generally, individuals with a great deal of experience working in larger and more prestigious spas in the gaming capitals will earn more than their counterparts in smaller facilities.

Employment Prospects

Employment prospects are fair for casino or casino hotel Spa Managers and getting better every year. While spas are not found in every casino hotel, they are becoming more and more popular.

Opportunities may be located in most of the larger or more prestigious casino hotels in Las Vegas, Reno, Laughlin, Lake Tahoe, and Atlantic City, as well as many of the smaller properties. Other opportunities may be located in Biloxi, Baton Rouge, New Orleans, Detroit, and Black Hawk, as well as in other regions hosting Indian gaming and land-based or riverboat gaming facilities.

Advancement Prospects

Advancement prospects are fair for casino and casino hotel Spa Managers. Individuals may climb the career ladder by finding similar positions in larger and more prestigious casino and casino hotel spas. In some cases, Spa Managers advance their careers by finding similar jobs in larger or more prestigious facilities outside the hospitality and gaming industries. Other individuals may strike out on their own and open their own spas.

Education and Training

Education and training requirements vary for Spa Manager depending on the specific job. Some spas just require their managers to hold a high school diploma, have a proven track record, and an appropriate amount of experience.

Others either require or prefer a college background or degree. Good choices for majors include business management, hospitality administration, physical education, or health sciences.

Recently, a number of colleges have also begun running spa management programs that usually include internship opportunities.

Classes, seminars, and workshops in business management, the hospitality industry, spa services, retail management, and fitness will be useful.

Special Requirements

Spa Managers may be required to be certified in CPR and other first-aid areas. If the spa has a pool, the Spa Manager may also be required to hold Red Cross lifeguard certification. Individuals who provide specific services such as massage therapy or may also be required to hold licenses or certifications.

Experience, Skills, and Personality Traits

Generally, the larger and more prestigious the casino and casino hotel spa, the more experience the Spa Manager will need. Most positions require applicants to have a background in management or administration. Prior work in a spa or health club will usually be required. Those aspiring to work in a large casino spa or casino hotel spa will generally need experience working in these kind of spas.

Spa Managers need to get along with a variety of people on different levels. The ability to make people feel comfortable is essential.

Individuals need to be organized and detail oriented. Administrative, management, and supervisory skills are necessary. Problem solving skills are critical. The ability to motivate employees to be the best they can be is also crucial.

An understanding of the hospitality industry is also needed. A full knowledge of spa services is necessary as well. The ability to speak a second language may also be helpful.

Unions and Associations

Individuals may be members of a number of different trade associations geared toward those working in the spa industry. These include the Day Spa Association (DSA), the Spa Association (SPAA), the Las Vegas Spa Association (LVSA), and the International Spa Association (ISPA). These groups bring together professionals in the industry and provide opportunities for network and professional support.

Tips for Entry

1. Get a job working in a local spa or health club in any capacity. This will look good on your résumé and give you experience working in health clubs.
2. Positions in this field are advertised in the newspaper classified section in areas hosting casinos. Look under the headings of "Spa Manager," "Spa Director," "Casino Hotels," "Cruise Ships Jobs," "Casino Jobs," "Spas," or under the name of a specific casino or casino hotel.
3. Jobs may also be located online. Check out the Web sites of casinos and casino hotels. Many post openings on their sites.
4. Don't forget to check traditional job sites such as www.monster.com and www.hotjobs.com as well as job sites specific to casinos, casino hotels, the hospitality industry, and spas.
5. Send your résumé to casino hotel human resources departments.
6. Casino job hotlines may advertise job openings in this area. These are frequently updated messages listing jobs available. You can call each casino directly to get its job hotline phone number.
7. Join professional associations. Many have networking opportunities as well as job listings.

HEALTH CLUB MANAGER

CAREER PROFILE

Duties: Hiring, training, supervising, and coordinating activities of staff; attending to day-to-day activities of health club.

Alternate Title(s): Spa Manager

Salary Range: $24,000 to $55,000+

Employment Prospects: Fair

Advancement Prospects: Fair

Best Geographical Location(s) for Position: Las Vegas, Reno, Laughlin, Lake Tahoe, Atlantic City, Biloxi, Baton Rouge, New Orleans, and Detroit offer the greatest number of opportunities; other regions hosting Indian gaming and land-based or riverboat gaming facilities offer additional opportunities.

Prerequisites:

Education or Training—Educational requirements vary; see text.

Experience and Qualifications—Experience in health club or spa management or administration

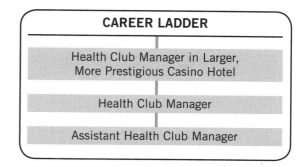

CAREER LADDER

Health Club Manager in Larger, More Prestigious Casino Hotel

Health Club Manager

Assistant Health Club Manager

preferred; knowledge of exercise and exercise equipment; certification may be required.

Special Skills and Personality Traits—Management skills; supervisory skills; detail-oriented; personable; communication skills; organized; physically fit; energetic.

Special Requirements—CPR training, Red Cross lifeguard certification, and/or Red Cross Water Safety Instructor certificate may be required.

Position Description

Many casino hotels host health clubs and spas as amenities for guests. Health Club Managers in casino hotels have a number of responsibilities. First and foremost, they attend to the day-to-day activities of the health club.

Most health club guests in casino hotels are transient. Many guests, however, return to the same hotel to gamble on a regular basis and therefore may become members of the hotel's health club as well. Hotels may also sell health club memberships to people who live in the local area. Entrance requirements to hotel health clubs vary. In some, individuals must just be a guest of the hotel. In others, the Health Club Manager sells memberships or charges entrance fees to patrons. The individual is responsible for keeping records of the club's clientele and any payments received.

The Health Club Manager may also be in charge of developing promotions to bring people into the club. The individual works on this responsibility with the hotel's advertising and marketing departments.

The Manager is expected to meet guests and make sure they are pleased with the club's services. The individual shows them around and tells them what services

are available. Being accessible to patrons is essential to this type of job.

Depending on the facility, health clubs offer pools, saunas, Jacuzzis, whirlpools, exercise classes, and a variety of exercise equipment. Some health clubs offer an array of other amenities, including facials and massages.

The Health Club Manager is an administrative position. The individual is in charge of hiring and firing personnel within the facility. The Manager also trains and supervises employees. Other staff members may include assistant managers, receptionists, exercise directors, aerobic instructors, lifeguards, masseurs, masseuses, and pool attendants. The Manager is in charge of assigning and scheduling workers to meet the needs of guests.

The Health Club Manager must be able to fully explain the operation and purpose of equipment within the club to both employees and clientele.

The Manager notifies health care personnel and hotel administration regarding any accidents within the club. He or she is also responsible for making sure reports are written and filed regarding accidents or mishaps.

The Health Club Manager is responsible for making sure that the club facility is kept in good order and run in a safe and efficient manner. If equipment breaks down, the individual must make sure it is either fixed or replaced. Facilities must be kept immaculate.

Other responsibilities of the Health Club Manager may include:

- Running exercise classes
- Filling in for staff members
- Handling customer complaints
- Solving any problems

Salaries

Earnings for Health Club Managers in casino hotels range from $24,000 to $55,000 or more depending on a number of variables, including the specific facility, type, size, and geographic location. Other factors affecting earnings include the responsibilities, training, and experience of the individual.

Employment Prospects

Health clubs and spas are not found in every casino hotel. They are, however, usually located in most of the larger or more prestigious casino hotels in Las Vegas, Reno, Laughlin, Lake Tahoe, and Atlantic City. Other opportunities may be located in Biloxi, Baton Rouge, New Orleans, and Detroit, as well as in other regions hosting Indian gaming and land-based or riverboat gaming facilities.

Advancement Prospects

Health Club Managers can advance their careers by locating similar positions in larger or more prestigious facilities. In some cases, individuals find jobs in health clubs outside of the hospitality industry. Some Health Club Managers climb the career ladder by opening up their own health club facility.

Education and Training

Education and training requirements vary depending on the specific job. Some facilities require their Managers to be college graduates. A degree in business, physical education, or a related field is preferred.

Hotels may hire individuals without college, however, if they possess work experience.

Special Requirements

Depending on the job, the Health Club Manager may be required to hold one or more certifications, including Red Cross lifeguard certification and/or the Red Cross Water Safety Instructor certification. Individuals generally also are required to have CPR training.

Experience, Skills, and Personality Traits

Individuals should have some background in management or administration. Prior work in a health club or spa is usually preferred.

Health Club Managers deal with a variety of people and circumstances on different levels. They should be organized and detail-oriented. Administrative, management, and supervisory skills are necessary. Problem-solving skills are mandatory.

Health Club Managers should be friendly people who enjoy working with others.

Unions and Associations

Additional career information for those aspiring to become Health Club Managers can be obtained by contacting the Aerobics and Fitness Association of America (AFAA) or IDEA Health and Fitness Association.

Tips for Entry

1. Get a job working in a local health club in any capacity. This will look good on your résumé and give you experience working in health clubs.
2. Positions in this field are advertised in the newspaper classified section in areas hosting casinos. Look under the headings of "Health Club Manager," "Casino Hotels," "Cruise Ships Jobs," Health Clubs," or "Hotel Spa."
3. Send your résumé to casino hotel human resources departments.
4. Casino job hotlines may advertise job openings in this area. These are frequently updated messages listing jobs available. You can call each casino directly to get its job hotline phone number.
5. Check out the home pages of casino hotels on the Internet. Many have employment opportunities listed on their Web site.

HEALTH CLUB INSTRUCTOR

CAREER PROFILE

Duties: Assisting in supervising health club guests; leading exercise and aerobics classes; instructing individuals in use of exercise equipment.

Alternate Title(s): Exercise Instructor; Aerobic Instructor

Salary Range: $15,000 to $30,000+

Employment Prospects: Good

Advancement Prospects: Fair

Best Geographical Location(s) for Position: Las Vegas, Reno, Laughlin, Lake Tahoe, Atlantic City, Biloxi, Baton Rouge, New Orleans, and Detroit offer the greatest number of opportunities; other regions hosting Indian gaming and land-based or riverboat gaming facilities offer additional opportunities.

Prerequisites:

Education or Training—Educational requirements vary; see text.

Experience and Qualifications—Knowledge of exercise and exercise equipment; certification may be required; see text.

CAREER LADDER

Health Club Instructor in Larger, More Prestigious Casino Hotel or Assistant Health Club Manager

Health Club Instructor

Health Club or Exercise Instructor in Different Setting

Special Skills and Personality Traits—Physically fit; energetic; personable; communication skills.

Special Requirements—CPR training, Red Cross lifeguard certification, and/or Red Cross Water Safety Instructor certificate may be required.

Position Description

Casino hotels usually host health clubs, gyms, and spas that offer guests pools, saunas, whirlpools, massages, beauty treatments, exercise classes, and an array of exercise equipment. They may also have employees to pamper guests, including hairstylists, manicurists, skin care specialists, and makeup artists.

The casino hotel Health Club Instructor has a wide array of responsibilities depending on the structure of the specific facility. The individual assists in the supervision of health club guests. When guests visit, Health Club Instructors welcome them, showing them the facilities and what services are offered.

Instructors may also be required to lead exercise classes. Individuals must understand how all the exercise equipment in the facility work and have the ability to illustrate to guests how to use them properly.

Instructors help the assistant manager and manager of the club when needed. They are responsible for reporting accidents to them, as well as for making out accident reports.

The Health Club Instructor may be required to perform minor first aid on guests. In emergencies, if qualified, individuals may have to perform CPR on guests in need. While Instructors are not usually hired to act as pool lifeguards, they may, on occasion, pinch hit.

Other responsibilities of the casino hotel Health Club Instructor may include:

- Reporting malfunctioning equipment to management
- Keeping club area neat and clean
- Explaining benefits of exercise equipment

Salaries

Casino hotel Health Club Instructors are usually paid an hourly wage. This can range from $7.00 to $15.00 or more per hour or about $15,000 to $30,000 annually. Factors affecting earnings include the experience, training, and responsibilities of the individual, as well as the geographic location, size, and prestige of the specific casino hotel.

Employment Prospects

Employment prospects for casino hotel Health Club Instructors are good. The greatest number of opportunities are located in large casino hotels hosting spas and health clubs. Las Vegas, Reno, Laughlin, Lake Tahoe, Atlantic City, Biloxi, Baton Rouge, New Orleans, and Detroit offer most opportunities. Other regions hosting Indian gaming and land-based or riverboat gaming facilities offer additional prospects.

Advancement Prospects

There are a number of different advancement opportunities for Health Club Instructors working in casino hotel spas and health clubs. Individuals may obtain experience and locate similar positions in larger or more prestigious facilities. Health Club Instructors may also be promoted to the position of assistant health club manager.

Education and Training

Educational requirements vary from job to job. Many casino hotels prefer or require that Health Club Instructors hold a college degree in physical education or a related field. Some colleges now offer degrees in exercise and fitness. Work experience will often be accepted by many facilities in lieu of education requirements. Some casino hotels may not require college, but may require training in exercise, aerobics, and related areas. Additional courses and seminars in aerobics techniques, exercise physiology, exercise biochemistry, and exercise science will also be helpful.

Special Requirements

Depending on the specific job of the individual and its responsibilities, he or she may be required to hold one or more certifications including the Red Cross lifeguard certification and/or the Red Cross Water Safety Instruc-tor certification. Health Club Instructors may also be required to have CPR training.

Experience, Skills, and Personality Traits

Experience requirements, like education and training requirements, vary. Some casino hotel health clubs require or prefer that individuals have experience working in other health clubs or spas.

Unions and Associations

Individuals interested in pursuing careers in health clubs can obtain additional information by contacting the American Red Cross, National Safety Council, or American Heart Association. They may also contact the Aerobics and Fitness Association of America (AFAA).

Tips for Entry

1. Jobs are often advertised in the classified sections of newspapers in areas hosting gaming. Look under classifications such as "Health Club Instructor," "Health Club," "Spa," "Casino Hotel Spa," or "Casino Hotel Health Club."

2. Obtain training and experience by contacting corporate headquarters of health and fitness clubs and gyms that are franchise operations. These groups often offer training programs and job placement.

3. Call casino job hotlines to see if jobs are open in this area. Job hotlines are frequently updated messages listing jobs available. You can call each casino directly to get its job hotline phone number.

4. Send your résumé and a short cover letter to the human resources departments of casinos and casino hotels, as well as to their corporate offices to inquire about job openings.

5. Look for new casinos being built. Apply early for the best positions.

CASINO AND CASINO HOTEL RETAIL SHOPS

RETAIL SUPERVISOR/STORE MANAGER

Duties: Providing day-to-day management of casino hotel shop; supervising and training sales associates; scheduling employees; providing accounting of sales; assisting customers; overseeing loss prevention.

Alternate Title(s): None

Salary Range: $19,000 to $42,000+

Employment Prospects: Excellent

Advancement Prospects: Good

Best Geographical Location(s) for Position: Las Vegas, Reno, Laughlin, Lake Tahoe, Atlantic City, Biloxi, Baton Rouge, New Orleans, and Detroit offer the greatest number of opportunities; other regions hosting Indian gaming and land-based or riverboat gaming facilities offer additional opportunities.

Prerequisites:

Education or Training—A minimum of a high school diploma or equivalent; some positions

CAREER LADDER

Store Manager in Larger, More Prestigious Store or Shop

Retail Supervisor/Store Manager

Assistant Store Manager

require college background or degree; on-the-job training.

Experience and Qualifications—Prior experience in retail store management or retailing.

Special Skills and Personality Traits—Supervisory skills; customer service skills; sales ability; communication skills; pleasant.

Position Description

Casinos and casino hotels like to keep customers on the property once they arrive. Management, therefore, tries to have as many amenities as possible on-site. These facilities have a wide array of restaurants for all tastes and pocketbooks. Many also host a variety of on-site retail shops.

The individual who provides the day-to-day management of the casino hotel shop is called the Store Manager or Retail Shop Supervisor.

Store Managers have a number of responsibilities. They establish and implement policies, goals, objectives, and procedures for the specific shop. This may be done in conjunction with other casino administrators.

Store Managers supervise the sales associates working in the store. As part of this function, they must train associates in all necessary areas. This includes writing sales slips, using the cash register, processing credit cards, and approving checks.

The Store Manager is responsible for scheduling employees. The individual must take into account the days and hours the store is expected to be busiest to make sure enough employees are on hand to adequately service customers.

Store Managers assign duties and oversee the activities of sales associates, including pricing and ticketing goods, placing them on display, and cleaning and organizing shelves, displays, and inventory in stockrooms.

In order for merchandise to sell, the Store Manager makes sure it is displayed in an attractive manner. Store Managers may handle this duty themselves or assign it to other employees.

The Store Manager is ultimately responsible for everything that occurs in the store. The Manager maintains customer satisfaction, sometimes working on the sales floor greeting and assisting customers with purchases.

Other duties of the casino or casino hotel Retail Store Manager may include:

- Developing and coordinating sales promotions
- Overseeing loss prevention
- Reviewing sales records and accounting for sales
- Keeping track of inventory
- Ordering merchandise

Salaries

Retail Store Managers working in casinos and casino hotels may either be paid a weekly salary, or be paid an hourly wage ranging between $9.00 and $20.00 per hour. They may also earn commissions on sales in addition to their hourly salary or bonuses for increases in sales.

Factors affecting earnings include the geographic location, size, and prestige of the casino or casino hotel, as well as the specific type of shop. Other variables include the experience and responsibilities of the individual.

There are some individuals who earn an annual salary of approximately $19,000 and others who earn approximately $42,000 or more.

Employment Prospects

Employment prospects are excellent for qualified individuals aspiring to be Retail Store Managers in casinos and casino hotels. Most facilities have one or more shops. Individuals work various shifts, including daytime and swing shift. Casinos that are open 24 hours a day may require a Supervisor or Manager to work the graveyard shift.

Employment opportunities depend on the type of shops in the casino—sundry shops, boutiques, souvenir shops, gift shops, floral shops, candy stores, and jewelry stores.

Many of the new multimillion-dollar casino hotels also have large upscale shopping areas filled with exclusive stores.

Advancement Prospects

With experience and/or additional training, Store Managers working in casinos or casino hotels may be promoted to management positions in larger or more prestigious stores in the facility.

Education and Training

Casinos and casino hotels generally prefer Store Managers to have a high school diploma or the equivalent. Many facilities assist individuals who do not have this education in obtaining a GED. Work experience is often accepted in lieu of education.

While there is not usually any formal training requirement for this position, any training individuals have received in buying, retailing, or store management will be useful. Many Store Managers have moved up the career ladder by starting as sales associates and learning as they go.

Experience, Skills, and Personality Traits

This is not an entry-level position. Experience in retail sales and management is usually required.

Store Managers must have supervisory and administrative skills. They should be personable people with good customer service skills. Sales ability and merchandising skills are necessary.

Unions and Associations

Those interested in learning more about careers in retailing can obtain information from the National Retail Federation (NRF).

Tips for Entry

1. Visit the human resources departments of casinos and casino hotels to learn about job openings.
2. Check with stores directly to see if they have openings, then fill out applications.
3. Jobs are often advertised in the classified sections of newspapers in areas hosting gaming. Look under classifications such as "Casinos/ Gaming," "Casinos/Hotels," "Retail Opportunities," "Casino Shop Manager," or "Casino Hotel Shops."
4. Most casinos have job hotlines. These are frequently updated messages listing jobs available. You can call each casino directly to get its job hotline phone number.

SALES ASSOCIATE—RETAIL

CAREER PROFILE

Duties: Working in casino hotel shops; assisting customers; selling merchandise; handling cashier duties.

Alternate Title(s): Sales Clerk

Salary Range: $15,000 to $25,000+

Employment Prospects: Excellent

Advancement Prospects: Good

Best Geographical Location(s) for Position: Las Vegas, Reno, Laughlin, Lake Tahoe, Atlantic City, Biloxi, Baton Rouge, New Orleans, and Detroit offer the greatest number of opportunities; other regions hosting Indian gaming and land-based or riverboat gaming facilities offer additional opportunities.

Prerequisites:

Education or Training—High school diploma or equivalent; on-the-job training.

Experience and Qualifications—Sales experience helpful, but not always required.

Special Skills and Personality Traits—Customer service skills; sales ability; communication skills; pleasant; money-handling skills.

Position Description

Casinos and casino hotels are often like small cities. In addition to the gaming area and hotel, there are restaurants, spas, and shops. Depending on the specific casino, there may be a variety of retail establishments. These can include newspaper and sundry shops, souvenir stores, kiosks, clothing stores, boutiques, and gift shops.

Every store and shop in the casino needs Sales Associates, also referred to as sales clerks.

Sales Associates assist customers. They must determine what each customer's needs are. Customer service is extremely important in this job. Sales Associates must make every person who comes into the retail establishment feel comfortable, whether they just are browsing or want to buy.

Sales Associates must know the stock in their store and be able to answer questions regarding merchandise. Individuals offer suggestions to customers regarding purchase possibilities.

Once patrons decide what they want to purchase, Sales Associates are responsible for taking payment. Individuals must know how to ring up purchases and make correct change if people are paying with cash. They must also know the proper procedure for accepting checks, charging items to guest's rooms, or processing credit card charges.

Sales Associates stock, price, and ticket merchandise. They are responsible for putting merchandise out in displays. Sales Associates also are expected to clean and organize shelves, as well as keep the shop neat and orderly.

Other duties of the casino or casino hotel shop Sales Associate include:

- Handling loss prevention
- Accounting for sales
- Putting out and displaying merchandise

Salaries

Sales Associates working in casinos and casino hotels earn between $7.00 and $12.00 per hour or more or about $15,000 to $25,000 per year. Factors affecting earnings include the geographic location, size, and prestige of the casino or casino hotel, as well as the specific type of shop. Other variables include the experience and responsibilities of the individual. In some stores Sales Associates earn a commission in addition to the hourly wage.

Employment Prospects

Employment prospects are excellent for Sales Associates in casinos and casino hotels. Most facilities have one or more shops. Individuals work in various shifts, including daytime and swing shift. In casinos that are open 24 hours a day, shops also need employees for the graveyard shift.

Advancement Prospects

With experience and/or additional training, Sales Clerks may be promoted to supervisory retail positions, including assistant manager or manager.

Education and Training

Most casinos and casino hotels prefer Sales Associates to have a high school diploma or the equivalent. Many facilities assist individuals who do not have this education in obtaining a GED.

On-the-job training in handling customers with sales, as well as using the cash register and credit card machines, is usually provided.

Experience, Skills, and Personality Traits

In some establishments entry-level positions may be open. Many facilities, however, prefer that individuals have some type of retail sales experience.

Sales Associates must be courteous and pleasant. Customer service skills, sales ability, and money-handling skills are essential.

Unions and Associations

Those interested in learning more about careers as Sales Associates can obtain information from the National Retail Merchants Association (NRMA).

Tips for Entry

1. While retail experience is not always needed, it is usually preferred. Remember to include any prior retail experience on your job application or résumé.

2. Jobs are often advertised in the classified sections of newspapers in areas hosting gaming. Look under classifications such as "Casinos/Gaming," "Casinos/Hotels," "Retail Opportunities," "Sales Associates," "Sales Clerks," or "Casino Hotel Shops."

3. Most casinos have job hotlines. These are frequently updated messages listing jobs available. You can either call each casino directly to obtain its job hotline phone number or obtain a copy of "Casino Job Hotline Phone Number Directory." The address is in the resource section of this book.

4. Stop by the human resources departments of casinos and casino hotels to learn about job openings.

CASINO AND CASINO HOTEL SUPPORT PERSONNEL

EXECUTIVE SECRETARY

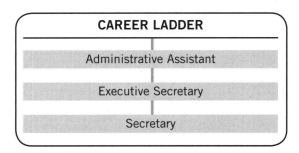

Position Description

Casinos and casino hotels have many executives, many of whom have executive secretaries. Executive Secretaries are responsible for many of the duties of general office secretaries. However, they often have additional responsibilities.

Executive Secretaries type a wide array of correspondence and reports. While general office secretaries just type this correspondence, Executive Secretaries are often responsible for composing some of it. For example, the individual may answer letters for the executive or compose memos on his or her behalf. These will usually be approved by the executive.

The Executive Secretary is responsible for necessary computer software programs. The Executive Secretary often takes and transcribes dictation from a transcription machine or directly from the executive.

The Executive Secretary oversees other secretaries and clerks in the office. The individual instructs these employees to photocopy documents, file, collate papers and reports, send faxes, and input information into the computer.

The Executive Secretary is often privy to confidential conversations and information that must remain within the office. To maintain confidentiality, the Exec-

utive Secretary may be required to handle personally certain files that contain this type of information.

Other duties of the Executive Secretary working in a casino or casino hotel may include:

- Returning phone calls for the executive
- Scheduling appointments for meetings
- Screening calls and visitors
- Taking notes at meetings

Salaries

Executive Secretaries working in casinos and casino hotels earn between $10.00 and $20.00 or more per hour. Some Executive Secretaries are paid a yearly salary ranging from $23,000 to $42,000 plus instead of an hourly wage.

Factors affecting earnings include the geographic location, size, and prestige of the specific facility, as well as the experience, education, and responsibilities of the individual.

Employment Prospects

Employment prospects for casino and casino hotel Executive Secretaries are good. Individuals may work for executives of the hotel or casino in various areas, including but not limited to casino management, marketing, legal affairs, hotel management, casino operations, and public relations.

Las Vegas, Reno, Laughlin, Lake Tahoe, Atlantic City, Biloxi, Baton Rouge, New Orleans, and Detroit offer the greatest number of opportunities. Other regions hosting Indian gaming and land-based or riverboat gaming facilities offer additional opportunities.

Advancement Prospects

Executive Secretaries often advance their careers by becoming administrative assistants to casino or casino hotel executives. In some instances, with additional training, Executive Secretaries may also move into other areas of casino employment.

Education and Training

Casinos and casino hotels usually require Executive Secretaries to hold a minimum of a high school diploma or the equivalent. Secretarial school or secretarial courses are useful. Individuals aspiring to advance their career may need a college background or degree.

Experience, Skills, and Personality Traits

Executive Secretaries working in casinos and casino hotels must have at least two or three years of prior office experience. Individuals must be well-groomed and articulate with excellent communication skills. Understanding of the workings of the specific casino or hotel department is useful.

Executive Secretaries should accurately type between 65 and 80 words a minute accurately. Word processing and computer skills are necessary. The abilities to take dictation is usually required.

Individuals need interpersonal skills and a pleasant phone manner. Good judgment is essential. The ability to keep office matters confidential is mandatory.

Unions and Associations

Those interested in learning more about careers as Executive Secretaries should contact the human resources departments of casinos and casino hotels. Individuals may also contact the International Association of Administrative Professionals (IAAP) for additional information.

Tips for Entry

1. Check the job hotlines of casinos and casino hotels to see what openings are available. Call each casino directly to get its job hotline phone number.
2. Jobs may be advertised in the classified sections of newspapers in areas hosting gaming. Look under classifications such as "Casino/Gaming," "Executive Secretary," or "Casino Opportunities."
3. Visit the human resources departments of casinos to inquire about job openings. Send or fax a résumé and a short cover letter to the director of human resources.
4. Make sure you are up to date on software by taking courses. This will make you more marketable.
5. Casinos like to promote from within. Get your foot in the door and move up to this position.

SECRETARY/VARIOUS DEPARTMENTS

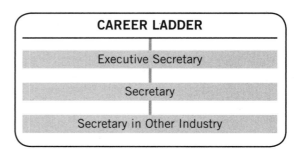

Position Description

The gaming industry, like many other industries, requires secretaries. These people help casino and hotel departments and offices run smoothly. Secretaries handle a wide array of clerical duties. They type a variety of correspondence, envelopes, and reports. Specific typing responsibilities depend on the department in which the individual is working. Typing is done on a word processor or computer. Individuals might additionally be required to use various computer software programs necessary to the department.

A Secretary might be required to take and transcribe dictation, as well as to take shorthand. The Secretary must photocopy documents, file, maintain files, collate reports, sort mail, answer phones, and send faxes.

Secretaries working in various gaming departments may handle additional duties. For example, the Secretary working in the slot office may assist in coordinating small slot tournaments. A great many duties of Secretaries working in the casino area depend on the specific department in which the individual works.

Other duties of the Secretary working in a casino or casino hotel may include:

- Answering letters and other correspondence
- Returning phone calls
- Making appointments for meetings
- Screening calls and visitors

Salaries

Secretaries working in casinos and casino hotels earn between $7.00 and $12.00 per hour or more or about $15,000 to $25,000 annually.

Factors affecting earnings include the geographic location, size, and prestige of the specific facility, as well as the experience, education, and responsibilities of the individual.

Employment Prospects

Employment prospects for casino and casino hotel Secretaries are excellent. Individuals may be employed in any department of the hotel or casino, including human resources, marketing, public relations, or administration.

Las Vegas, Reno, Laughlin, Lake Tahoe, Atlantic City, Biloxi, Baton Rouge, New Orleans, and Detroit offer the greatest number of opportunities. Other regions hosting Indian gaming and land-based or riverboat gaming facilities offer additional opportunities.

Advancement Prospects

One of the advantages about working as a Secretary in a casino or casino hotel is that promotion is usually done from within. Secretaries who want to remain in administrative work may move up to executive secretaries or administrative assistants.

Those who want to move out of secretarial work may obtain training and locate positions in other departments in either the administrative area, the casino, or hotel.

Education and Training

Casinos and casino hotels usually require that Secretaries and executive secretaries have a high school diploma or the equivalent. Secretarial courses as well as those in computers and various software packages are helpful.

Experience, Skills, and Personality Traits

Experience working in an office is preferred. Secretaries should accurately type between 55 and 65 words per minute. Word processing and computer skills are usually necessary. The ability to take dictation is often required or preferred.

Individuals should have interpersonal skills with a pleasant telephone manner. Good judgment is also needed.

Unions and Associations

Those interested in learning more about careers as Secretaries should contact the human resources departments of casinos and casino hotels. Individuals may also write to the International Association of Administrative Professionals (IAAP) for additional information.

Tips for Entry

1. Jobs may be advertised in the classified sections of newspapers in areas hosting gaming. Look under classifications such as "Casino/Gaming," "Secretary," or "Casino Opportunities-Secretarial."

2. This is a good job to get your foot in the door of a casino or casino hotel. Learn what you can and work hard. You will have a good chance of moving up the career ladder.

3. Stop by the human resources departments of casinos and inquire about job openings. Send or fax a résumé and a short cover letter.

4. Most casinos also have job hotlines that tell about current job openings. You can call each casino directly to get its job hotline phone number.

CASINO AND CASINO HOTEL WEB SITES

WEBMASTER

HTML and other programming languages; graphic and layout skills; knowledge of gaming and hospitality industries; good verbal and written communications skills.

Special Requirements—Voluntary certification available.

Position Description

Most companies today have a presence on the World Wide Web. Casinos and casino hotels are no exception. Web sites are an important part of the way casinos and casino hotels promote and market themselves and their services.

The Webmaster is the individual in charge of creating, putting together, and maintaining the Web site. The casino or casino hotel Webmaster has many responsibilities.

Depending on the situation, he or she may work alone or may assign tasks to assistants, content producers, copywriters, graphic artists, etc. Generally, this is the case for Webmasters responsible for large casino Web sites.

One of the first things the Webmaster must do is find a host for the site. In order for a casino or casino hotel (or any company) to have a Web site, it must rent a space or location on the Web. This may be done by obtaining a host. The casino or casino hotel pays the host for the right to place its site online on the host's space. In some instances, the casino and the host are one and the same.

In order for individuals to be able to locate the casino or casino hotel's Web site, it must have a Web address. This is called the domain name. If the casino is a new one, the Webmaster may need to work with the casino management to develop a Web address that people can remember and that is available. Most often the Web address is the casino or casino hotel's name.

The Webmaster's duties depend to a great extent on the size and structure of the casino and casino hotel, and the importance it puts on the Web site. Duties also will be dependent on whether the Web site has already been set up or whether it needs to be revamped.

The Webmaster is expected to determine the direction the casino or casino hotel wants the Web site to take and the goals of the Web site. Does the management just want to maintain a Web presence? Do they want people to be able to make reservations and book rooms online? Do they want to sell branded merchandise? Do they want people to be able to join a loyalty program online? Will there be separate sites for the casino and the casino hotel? Does the casino want to sell advertising to other companies to increase revenue? Once the

Webmaster understands what the casino management wants, he or she can get to work.

The Webmaster may be responsible for developing and creating the casino's Web site on the World Wide Web. He or she must design the site so that it is exciting and easy to navigate and use. The Webmaster must be sure that each Web page on the site opens easily and quickly. If they do not, people will often leave the site and surf to another location.

The Webmaster will develop the site, adding photos of the casino, the hotel, animations or other graphics, and possibly sound. In creating the site, the Webmaster must manipulate images to the proper size and format. If this is not done correctly, an image may either be too large, slowing down the loading of a Web page, or too small, making it difficult to see clearly. In many cases, the casino may already have a site, but needs or wants to have it revamped and redesigned.

The Webmaster develops the site's search function so that people can search for something specific on the site quickly and easily. He or she may program pop-up windows, features, reservation systems, shopping carts, secure payment systems, the ability to see videos of action at the casino, and a variety of other functions. The Webmaster may also build in technology so the casino management can find out how long people stay on a specific Web page, which part of the site is most popular, and how many hits the site gets.

Developing and designing the Web site is just one part of the job of the Webmaster. He or she is additionally responsible for the continued management and maintenance of the site. In order to keep a Web site fresh and timely, the Webmaster may change the homepage and update other parts of the site frequently—sometimes the site content changes daily. This might occur, for example, as hotel room rates change, specials are added, entertainment changes, or individuals win large jackpots. The Webmaster must make changes and remove out-of-date content.

Web sites are created in special languages so they can be displayed on the Internet. Text, for example, is coded in a language called HTML, or hypertext markup language. Other languages may be used as well. The Webmaster must know how to format the special languages. Part of the job of the Webmaster is to monitor the site on a continuing basis. Every time new content or a link is added, the individual or one of his or her assistants must be sure everything on the site is working and all links are accurate.

The casino and casino hotel Webmaster is expected to make sure that the site is user-friendly. When there are problems with the site, the individual is responsible for handling them. This may include responding to inquiries from browsers having problems with the site.

Additional responsibilities of the casino and casino hotel Webmaster might include:

- Dealing with security issues
- Repairing software bugs
- Testing links to assure they are working properly
- Handling problems with the site

Salaries

Earnings for casino and casino hotel Webmasters can vary greatly ranging from approximately $33,000 to $86,000. Factors affecting earnings include the size, prestige, and location of the casino or casino hotel as well as the size and importance to the casino of its Web site.

Other factors affecting earnings include the responsibilities, professional reputation, and experience of the individual. Webmasters who are responsible for handling more than one Web site, such as those in charge of a corporate family of casino and casino hotel Web sites, will generally earn more than their counterparts who are only responsible for one site.

Employment Prospects

Employment prospects are good for casino and casino hotel Webmasters. While some casinos and casino hotels have just one Webmaster, larger casinos and casino hotels often have more than one individual in this position. Individuals may find employment in large or small casinos and casino hotels, bingo halls, poker rooms, and racinos.

As a result of the nature of the job, some employers may allow their Webmasters to telecommute all or part of the time. Individuals may also find part-time or consulting positions.

Advancement Prospects

Advancement prospects for casino and casino hotel Webmasters are fair and getting better every day. Talented individuals may advance to positions handling the Web sites for larger and more prestigious casinos and casino hotels. This will result in increased responsibilities and earnings.

Others may advance their careers by becoming senior Webmasters for large gaming companies with more than one casino resulting in the responsibility of a number of sites. Some Webmasters decide to strike out on their own and open consulting firms.

Education and Training

Education and training requirements vary for casino and casino hotel Webmasters. Some positions may require a formal education such as a bachelor's degree with a major in computer science or information processing. Others may not have formal educational requirements as long as individuals can demonstrate competence.

Some Webmasters are self-taught. Some have taken classes. Others have college backgrounds or degrees in computers, programming, languages, graphics, Web authoring, and the Internet.

However it is learned, Webmasters must know HTML. It is also necessary to know other programming languages, such as ColdFusion, Perl, and Active Server Pages. Knowing how to integrate databases is a plus.

It is essential that Webmasters update their skills by self-study and/or classes, seminars, and workshops to keep up with changes in technology.

Special Requirements

Voluntary Certified Web Professional (CWP) certification is available from various industry organizations. This certification demonstrates that individuals have attained professional status in their field.

Experience, Skills, and Personality Traits

Experience requirements depend, to a great extent, on the size and prestige of the specific casino or casino hotel. Those seeking positions with large, prestigious casinos and casino hotels will generally be required to have a minimum of two to three years experience as either a Webmaster or in Web application development or administration. Larger, more prestigious casinos and casino hotels will also want their Webmasters to have a proven track record and experience.

Creativity is essential to the success of Webmasters. Individuals should also have excellent written and verbal communication skills. A total knowledge and understanding of computer technology is vital. An understanding of the gaming industry is also useful.

Unions and Associations

Individuals interested in learning more about careers in the field may obtain additional information by contacting the Internet Professional Association (IProA), the International Webmasters Association (IWA), and the World Organization of Webmasters (WOW).

Tips for Entry

1. Positions may be located in the classified section of newspapers in areas hosting gaming. Look under headings such as "Webmaster," "Casinos," "Web Careers," and so on. In some situations, casinos and casino hotels may also take out box ads in the classified section advertising many different jobs.

2. Many casinos and casino hotels have job openings posted on their Web sites. Look for sections such as "Employment," "Jobs," or "Work for Us."

3. Don't forget other online searches. Check out traditional job sites such as www.monster.com and www.hotjobs.com. You might also want to check out some of the career sites dedicated to the gaming industry, or even Internet jobs.

4. Get experience by volunteering to put Web sites together for not-for-profit organizations or civic groups. Don't forget to add your name as the creator and Webmaster.

5. If you are still in school, look for internships. These will give you on-the-job training, experience, and the opportunity to make important contacts. Contact casino human resource departments to see what they offer.

6. Send your résumé and a short cover letter to the human resource department of casinos and casino hotels for which you might be interested in working. You never know when an opening might exist.

WEB SITE CONTENT PRODUCER

Position Description

Web sites give casinos and casino hotels a presence on the Web. This is essential for all businesses, but especially important to casinos and casino hotels, which have the potential to attract visitors from not only across the country but around the world.

Many people surf the net checking out various Web sites in order to help them decide what casino to visit and in which hotel to stay. It is helpful for casinos and casino hotels to have people surfing the net not only to visit their Web site once, but to keep them visiting in hopes of enticing them to visit the actual casino or casino hotel.

In order to make Web sites interesting so that potential guests will want to keep coming back to the site, many casinos and casino hotels employ Web Site Content Producers.

The main function of the Web Site Content Producer is to create and develop interesting and unique content for the casino's site. In this position, individuals are responsible for conceptualizing, developing and maintaining content so that the site will attract and retain visitors. In an attempt to engage visitors to keep them on the site longer and to return, the Web Site Content Producer may use a variety of techniques. In addition to developing interesting stories and articles for the Web site, the individual may develop e-mail text, videos, and photos for inclusion. The individual may additionally develop blogs and podcasts in an effort to develop interest in the casino and casino hotel. These techniques help get visitors involved. This in turn often leads to the opportunity to solicit positive reviews or user comments.

Individuals in this position are responsible for researching and writing engaging stories and articles in a variety of areas and categories. Their job is a sort of combination of a print journalist and editor.

Depending on the size, structure, and extent of a casino and casino hotel's Web site, there may be more than one content producer. One may handle events and promotions, another may handle news, and yet another may be responsible for writing business stories about the casino and casino hotel. It all depends on how comprehensive the casino wants its site to be.

Casinos hosting large sites or the sites of more than one casino and casino hotel may have a senior or executive Web Site Content Producer. He or she may then be responsible for overseeing the work of the other content producers.

Casino and casino hotel Web Site Content Producers are often responsible for overseeing staff copywriters and graphic artists. Some content producers are also responsible for finding and retaining freelancers to write articles on specific subjects or specific areas.

A content producer in charge of the entire casino site may, for example, find writers to do stories covering various areas of the gaming industry, including pieces on winning strategies, restaurants, entertainment, or even careers in casinos. Once he or she gets the stories, the content producer is responsible for editing them and giving them to the webmaster to put online.

Casino and casino hotel Web Site Content Producers may also develop pieces on various subjects. Depending on the specific area the Content Producer is responsible for, he or she may be expected to develop and maintain relationships with local news media as well as community, tourism, commerce, and related organizations. These relationships are helpful in creating unique, interesting, and appealing content.

The individual may be responsible for interviewing people such as casino and casino hotel visitors, jackpot winners, corporate executives, or other employees. He or she may also be expected to arrange for photos, and obtain other information to make the online stories interesting.

One of the exciting things about the Internet is that it can be interactive. With this in mind, the content producer may develop surveys and questionnaires or other pieces to involve those visiting the site.

In some instances, the interactive part of the site may be related to promotions, events or entertainment happenings at the casino and casino hotel. For example, the casino may be hosting the final concert of a megastar in its theater, or there might be a huge progressive jackpot that is expected to be won within the next few days. Web site visitors may be asked to give their opinions or thoughts, and within minutes their words can help generate excitement.

The casino and casino hotel Web Site Content Producer is often responsible for finding pictures, animation, and other graphics to make the content more appealing. He or she may employ the services of graphic artists, photographers, or others to accomplish this task. The individual may work with the webmaster to find images that are appropriate and will look good but not affect the ease of opening the site.

In order to keep the site fresh, casino and casino hotel Web Site Content Producers may be responsible for daily updates. In situations where a casino or a casino hotel is owned by a large gaming company, the Web Site Content Producer may be responsible for developing content for the Web sites of more than one casino or casino hotel.

Other duties of casino and casino hotel Web Site Content Producers include:

- Staying up-to-date with casino and casino hotel events
- Responding to inquiries from people who visit the site
- Finding the best way to present information and graphics
- Handling webcams and chats
- Working with the Web site marketing manager in handling online contests and promotions
- Monitoring blogs and user comments to insure appropriate content

Salaries
Annual earnings for casino and casino hotel Web Site Content Producers can range from approximately $27,000 to $75,000 annually, and may be higher. Variables include the location, size, and prestige of the casino or casino hotel. Another important factor affecting earnings is whether the individual is responsible for one or more sites. Other variables influencing earnings include the responsibilities, experience, and professional reputation of the individual.

Employment Prospects
Employment prospects are fair for casino and casino hotel Web Site Content Producers and are getting better every day. Individuals may work for casinos and casino hotels of various sizes, as well as for racinos, poker rooms, riverboat casinos, bingo halls, and other Indian gaming facilities.

One of the neat things about being a Web Site Content Producer is that due to the nature of the job, some employers may allow individuals to telecommute all or part of the time. Individuals may also find part-time or consulting positions.

Advancement Prospects
Casino and casino hotel Web Site Content Producers may advance their careers in a number of ways. The most common method of advancement is locating a similar position at a larger, more prestigious casino or

casino hotel resulting in increased responsibilities and earnings. Individuals working in a specific area of Web site content producing may be promoted to an executive content producer. Some casino and casino hotel Web Site Content Producers find similar positions in other industries.

Education and Training

Education and training requirements vary for casino and casino hotel Web Site Content Producers. Most employers today prefer or require people in this position have at minimum a four-year college degree. Good choices for majors include journalism, communications, English, public relations, marketing, or liberal arts.

Courses, workshops, and seminars in public relations, writing, promotion, and journalism, or in the gaming and hospitality industries, will be helpful in honing skills and making new contacts.

While it may not be required, individuals who know HTML (a programming language) may have a leg up on other candidates.

Experience, Skills, and Personality Traits

Experience requirements depend to a great extent on the size and prestige of the specific casino or casino hotel as well as the importance it places on its Web site. Smaller casinos may not require their Web Site Content Producers to have a great deal of experience, as long as they demonstrate competency. Content producers for larger, more prestigious casinos and casino hotels that put a lot of importance on their Web sites will generally seek out individuals who have a proven track record. Many of these employers will want an individual with a minimum of three or four years experience creating, editing, and managing Web content.

Writing and editing experience will be useful, no matter what the capacity. The ideal candidate will be innovative, organized, and creative, with great communications skills and Internet savvy. An excellent command of the English language is needed for this type of position. An understanding of the gaming and hospitality industries is also helpful.

Web Site Content Producers should have the ability to multitask and work under pressure without getting flustered. People skills are mandatory in this position.

Unions and Associations

Individuals interested in learning more about careers in the field may obtain additional information by contacting the Internet Professional Association (IProA).

Tips for Entry

1. Positions may be located in the classified section of newspapers. Look under headings such as "Casino Web Site Content Producer," "Web Site Content Manager," "Casino Careers," "Casino Hotel Jobs", "Casinos," "Web Sites," and "Web Careers." Also look for ads under specific casino and casino hotel names.

2. Many casinos and casino hotels advertise their openings on their Web sites. Look for the section of the Web site entitled "Employment Opportunities," "Work for Us," or "Jobs."

3. This is the perfect type of job to seek online. Start with some of the more popular job sites such as www.hotjobs.com and www.monster.com and go from there.

4. Jobs openings may also be located on career sites specific to the casino and hospitality industries.

5. Get as much experience writing as you can. If you are still in school, get involved in your school newspaper and/or Web site.

6. Consider a part-time job for a local newspaper to get some writing experience and to build up your contacts.

7. Look for internships at casinos and casino hotels. These will give you on-the-job training, experience, and the opportunity to make important contacts. Contact the human resource department of casinos and casino hotels to see what they offer.

8. Send your résumé and a short cover letter to casinos and casino hotels for which you are interested in working. You can never tell when an opening exists.

WEB SITE MARKETING DIRECTOR

Duties: Develop and implement marketing plans and campaigns for casino or casino hotel Web site; handle day-to-day Web site marketing functions; plan and implement special promotions; oversee Web site advertising and public relations programs.

Alternate Title(s): Marketing Manager; Online Marketing Director; Online Director of Marketing

Salary Range: $35,000 to $73,000+

Employment Prospects: Fair

Advancement Prospects: Fair

Best Geographical Location(s) for Position: Positions located in areas hosting gaming; Las Vegas, Reno, Laughlin, Lake Tahoe, Atlantic City, Biloxi, Baton Rouge, New Orleans, Detroit, and Black Hawk offer most opportunities; other regions with land-based riverboat or Indian gaming facilities offer additional opportunities.

Prerequisites:

Education or Training—Bachelor's degree usually required or preferred.

CAREER LADDER

Web Site Marketing Director for Larger, More Prestigious Casino and Casino Hotel or Web Site Marketing Director for Other Industry or Casino and Casino Hotel Marketing Director

Casino and Casino Hotel Web Site Marketing Director

Assistant Web Site Marketing Director or Marketing Director in Other Industry

Experience—Marketing experience; experience handling Web site marketing.

Special Skills and Personality Traits—Creativity; good verbal and written communication skills; promotion skills; marketing skills; Internet savvy; understanding of casino and hospitality industries.

Position Description

Before the Internet, if people had questions about a casino or casino hotel, they might call up the facility, send away for brochures, or talk to friends, family, or colleagues in search of finding the information they wanted. Conversely, when casinos or casino hotels wanted to get the word out about their facility or about specials or promotions they were having, they had to rely on advertising, brochures, and word of mouth.

The Internet has changed the way most of us live our lives. When we need information, most of us today look it up on the Web. When we want to do research, we research on the Web. Information that might have taken days to locate can be found almost instantly with the click of a mouse.

The Internet has also changed the way companies throughout the world do business. Casinos and casino hotels are no exception.

People looking to book hotel reservations or get information about a casino or casino hotel often now look to the Internet. As a result, most casinos and casino hotels now not only *have* a Web presence, they

need it to compete and market their facilities effectively. Individuals responsible for handling the marketing of these sites are called Web Site Marketing Directors.

Responsibilities of individuals in this position will vary depending on the specific casino and casino hotel as well as its size, structure, and popularity. As with traditional businesses, a Web site must market its presence. The Web Site Marketing Director is expected to develop the concepts and campaigns that determine how the site will be marketed and how people will be attracted. He or she is responsible for determining the most effective techniques and programs to market the site and its contents and then find ways to implement them.

As part of the job, the Web Site Marketing Director plans and coordinates the site's marketing goals and objectives. How will people know the Web site is online? How will they know the Web address? How will they find it? Who is the site being marketed to? What will bring them there?

Web Site Marketing Directors may use traditional marketing techniques or may come up with new innovative methods and techniques to promote and market the casino or casino hotel Web site. For a very creative Web Site Marketing Director, the sky can be the limit on marketing activities. The Web Site Marketing Director is expected to find creative ways to get the Web address known so that when people think of the specific casino or casino hotel, they can easily find it on the Web. This might be done through promotions, advertising, or public relations.

The Web Site Marketing Director must be sure that the company's Web address, or URL, is added to all television commercials, print advertisements, brochures, billboards, stationery, products, and branded merchandise. This is important to get the casino's or casino hotel's name and Web address in the public eye as often as possible.

The casino and casino hotel Web Site Marketing Director will often use various forms of e-mail marketing and e-mail blasts to get people to visit the site. The individual must additionally find ways to track visitors to the site so he or she knows what areas of the Web site people are visiting, how long they are staying, and what brought them there.

The marketing director may work with the company's public relations department to send out press releases or develop ways to attract media attention that will hopefully help garner the attention of the general public. Once again, the more places the public sees the Web address, the more likely they are to remember it and visit it to see what's happening on the site.

In some cases, the marketing director may decide it is advantageous to advertise his or her company's Web site on other Web sites. This is often done with banner ads, which are advertisements where an individual on the Web just clicks on the banner and is taken to the site of the advertiser. The individual, may, for example, advertise the casino or casino hotel on a local newspaper's Web site or on a travel Web site.

The Web Site Marketing Director is expected to perform research in order to obtain information about visitors to the site. He or she may do this by preparing questionnaires or surveys placed strategically on the site. In order to entice people to answer questionnaires as well as to attract new visitors to the site, the marketing director may offer gifts, discounts to shows, rooms, or restaurants in the facility, or entry into sweepstakes.

The marketing director may work with either internal or external promotion companies developing these contests, sweepstakes, and other promotions that can be entered online. This gives people an extra incentive to go to the company's Web site. The more people who visit the Web site, the more "hits" the site gets. This is important not only to increase traffic, but because many companies also charge other companies to put their online advertisements on their site.

The Web Site Marketing Director may be expected to develop and execute an online customer acquisition plan. This may be accomplished in a number of ways ranging from simply asking people to join online to working with the player development department to come up with special Web site promotions for individuals with casino loyalty cards.

Many casino and casino hotel Web Site Marketing Directors also find that sweepstakes are an excellent way to build mailing lists. When people enter sweepstakes they generally are asked to provide their name, address, phone number, age, and e-mail address. In many cases, with the enticement of possibly winning a prize, people are also often enticed to give additional information, such as what type of casino games they enjoy, how much they usually spend on a gambling visit, what comps they prefer, and other demographics data.

This information is useful to the marketing director for a variety of reasons. It can help target what potential casino guests want. It can also help build information for e-mail lists, which in turn can be used to inform people about site changes, hotel rates, tournaments, new casino games, large winners, news, promotions, etc.

Casino and casino hotel Web Site Marketing Directors who come up with innovative and creative ideas often get the attention of the media who are composing articles or television or radio pieces. If the marketing director is lucky, these media pieces can generate literally hundreds of thousands of Web site hits. These hits then may turn into hotel and casino guests who have the potential of bringing in hundreds of thousands of dollars.

Depending on the size and structure of the specific casino or casino hotel, the Web Site Marketing Director may be responsible to the company's general marketing director or vice president of marketing, or may handle all the responsibilities of the companies traditional and online marketing.

In some cases, the casino and casino hotel Web Site Marketing Director is responsible for handling the marketing activities of all of the Web sites a casino corporation may own in its brand.

Other responsibilities of the casino or the casino hotel Web Site Marketing Director include:

- Developing and executing affiliate programs
- Tracking and measuring online advertising programs
- Developing and managing budgets for Web site marketing

Salaries

Earnings of casino and casino hotel Web Site Marketing Directors can range from approximately $35,000 to $73,000, or even more, annually. A number of factors affect earnings, including the size, popularity, and prestige of the specific casino or casino hotel as well as the experience and responsibilities of the individual.

Casino and casino hotel Web Site Marketing Directors who are responsible for more than one site will generally earn more than their counterparts who handle the marketing activities of only one site.

Employment Prospects

Employment prospects are fair for casino and casino hotel Web Site Marketing Directors. As mentioned earlier, almost every casino and casino hotel employs Web sites, meaning that most require people to handle their marketing activities.

It should be noted that in some situations, the duties of the Web Site Marketing Director may be outsourced.

Jobs for casino and casino hotel Web Site Marketing Directors may be located throughout the country in areas hosting casinos. These include among others Las Vegas, Reno, Laughlin, Lake Tahoe, Atlantic City, Biloxi, New Orleans, Detroit, and Black Hawk. Individuals working for large gaming corporations may be required to work in the corporate office. Some employers may allow the Web Site Marketing Directors to telecommute.

Advancement Prospects

Advancement prospects for casino and casino hotel Web Site Marketing Directors are fair. Individuals may climb the career ladder in a number of ways. Some may find similar positions with larger or more prestigious casinos or casino hotels. Other individuals may become the marketing directors for the entire casino or casino hotel company, or even the vice president of marketing. Others gain advancement by finding similar positions in other industries.

Education and Training

Casino and casino hotel Web Site Marketing Directors generally are required to hold at minimum a four-year college degree. Good choices for majors include marketing, public relations, advertising, journalism, liberal arts, English, communications, or business. Classes, seminars, and workshops in marketing, promotion, Web marketing, casino marketing, publicity, and public relations will be helpful in honing skills and making important contacts.

Experience, Skills, and Personality Traits

Experience requirements for casino and casino hotel Web Site Marketing Directors vary depending on the specific position. Generally, larger, more prestigious casino and casino hotels will require their Web Site Marketing Directors to have more experience than smaller casinos and casino hotels.

Casino and casino hotel Web Site Marketing Directors need to have the same skills as traditional marketing directors coupled with an understanding of Web marketing. Individuals should be creative, innovative, ambitious, articulate, and highly motivated. Excellent written and verbal communications skills are essential.

A knowledge of publicity, promotion, public relations, advertising, and market research techniques are necessary. The ability to multitask, handling many details at one time without getting flustered and stressed, is needed.

An understanding of the casino, gaming, and hospitality industries is helpful.

Unions and Associations

Casino and casino hotel Web Site Marketing Directors may belong to a number of trade associations including the Web Marketing Association (WMA), the American Marketing Association (AMA), the Marketing Research Association (MRA), and the Public Relations Society of America (PRSA). These organization provide professional support to members and often offer networking opportunities.

Tips for Entry

1. Positions are often advertised in the classified section of newspapers in areas hosting casinos. Look under headings such as "Marketing," "Marketing Director," "Marketing Manager," "Web Site Marketing," "Web Site Marketing Director," "Casinos," or "Casino Web Site Marketing Director."
2. Positions may also be located online. Start off by checking out some of the more popular career sites such as www.monster.com and www.hotjobs.com as well as career sites specific to the casino and hospitality industries.

3. Don't forget to check out casino and casino hotel Web sites. Many post their openings.
4. Search firms, head hunters, and recruiters specific to the casino, gaming, and hospitality industries might also have job openings.
5. Look for seminars, workshops, and courses in marketing, promotion, public relations, publicity, Web marketing, and the gaming industry. These are good opportunities to help you hone skills as well as to make valuable contacts.

APPENDIXES

APPENDIX I
GAMING ACADEMIES AND DEALER SCHOOLS

The following is a listing of gaming academies and dealer schools. Before enrolling in any school with which you are not familiar, check the school's reputation and credentials with the local Better Business Bureau and/or the specific state's licensing organization.

Gaming academies and dealer schools are located in many areas that feature gaming. Some are affiliated with local vocational technical schools, universities, or community colleges. Others are privately owned. Many casinos have their own training schools.

New gaming academies open as more areas legalize gaming. Casino human resources departments may know of additional schools or training facilities.

The author does not endorse any one school or gaming academy and provides the list only as a means to get you started.

ARIZONA

Arizona ABC Bartending & Casino School
5024 South Ash Avenue
Suite 109
Tempe, AZ 85282
Phone: (480) 777-2333
http://www.casinodealercollege.com

Casino World Dealing Academy
701 West Deer Valley Road
Phoenix, AZ 85027
Phone: (623) 879-0777
http://www.casinodealing.net

Mojave Community College
1971 Jagerson Avenue
Kingman, AZ 86401
Phone: (602) 757-4331
http://www.mohave.edu

CALIFORNIA

Academy of International Bartending and Casino Dealing
8340 Vickers Street
San Diego, CA 92111
Phone: (858) 560-6499
http://www.cardsandcocktails.com

Casino by Fitz Dealer School
825 Main Street
El Segundo, CA 90245
Phone: (310) 640-9708

Casino Career Center
28780 Old Town Front Street
Temecula, CA 92590
Phone: (951) 506-3119
http://www.school4dealers.com

The Casino College—Los Angeles
3470 Wilshire Boulevard
Los Angeles, CA 90010
Phone: (213) 380-9400
http://www.losangelescasinoschool.com

The Casino College—Sacramento
9529 Folsom Boulevard
East Sacramento, CA 95827
Phone: (916) 366-3500
http://www.ideal21.com

Casino Dealer School
22790 Alessandro Boulevard
Moreno Valley, CA 92553
Phone: (951) 653-0330
http://www.casinodealerschool.com

Casino Training Center
4838 North Blackstone Avenue
Fresno, CA 93726
Phone: (559) 224-1389
http://www.casinotraining.biz

Custom Casino Academy
12662 Hoover Street
Garden Grove, CA 92841
Phone: (714) 263-5241
http://www.customcasinoacademy.com

Dealer's Choice Professional School of Gaming
28900 Old Town Front Street
Temecula, CA 92590
Phone: (951) 699-1066
http://www.adealerschoice.net

Jack Black Casino Dealer School
13054 East Valley Boulevard
La Puente, CA 91746
Phone: (626) 968-3121
http://www.jackblackonline.com

Jack Black Casino Dealer School
323 West Valley Boulevard
Rialto, CA 92376
Phone: (909) 877-5678
http://www.jackblackonline.com

Mt. View National Bartenders School & Casino College
1398 West El Camino Real
Mountain View, CA 94040
Phone: (650) 968-9933
http://www.casinoandbarschool.
com

National Bartenders and Casino Dealers
904 West San Marcos Boulevard
San Marcos, CA 92069
Phone: (619) 591-4300

North County Dealer School
260 Crest Street
Escondido, CA 92025
Phone: (760) 432-9622
http://casinodealingschool.com

San Diego Dealer School
12328 1/2 Woodside Avenue
Lakeside, CA 92114
Phone: (619) 390-2931
http://www.SanDiegoDealerSchool.
com

San Francisco National Bartenders School & Casino College
870 Market Street
Suite 828
San Francisco, CA 94102
Phone: (415) 677-9777
http://www.casinoandbarschool.
com

South Bay Casino Dealers School
15665 South Hawthorne Boulevard
Lawndale, CA 90260
Phone: (310) 675-9499

COLORADO

American Bartenders & Casino Dealers School
1050 South Wadsworth Boulevard
Lakewood, CO 80214
Phone: (303) 937-6229
http://www.pcidealerschool.com

FLORIDA

Academy of Professional Poker Dealers
3095 South Military Trail
Lake Worth, FL 33463
Phone: (561) 965-5454

Casino Careers Institute
956 East Cypress Creek Road
Oakland Park, FL 33334
Phone: (561) 596-2188
http://www.floridacasinocareers.
com

Casino Dealer's Academy
7603 Davie Road Extension
Hollywood, FL 33024
Phone: (954) 432-8799
http://www.casinodealersacademy.
com

Casino Training Academy
Port of Miami
Terminal No. 1
1265 South America Way
Miami, FL 33132
Phone: (305) 371-3325

International Casino Institute
4401 Stirling Road
Hollywood, FL 33314
Phone: (954) 587-3325

National Bartender, Casino Games and Hospitality School
2502 2nd Street
Suite 201
Fort Myers, FL 33901
Phone: (239) 334-6300
http://www.bartenderdealer.com

National Bartenders, Casino Games and Hospitality School
28200 Old 41 Road
Suite 203
Bonita Springs, FL 34135
Phone: (239) 949-8665
http://www.bartenderdealer.com

Pinnacle Gaming Institute
6561 Stirling Road
Davie, FL 33024
Phone: (954) 966-5056
http://www.pgidice.com

Professional Dealer and Player School
1233 Lane Avenue South
Suite 17
Jacksonville, Florida 32205
Phone: (904) 317-6537
http://www.professionaldealerschol.
com

Real Deal Poker Academy
10387 Gandy Boulevard
St. Petersburg, FL 33702
Phone: (727) 576-9480
http://www.realdealpokeracademy.
com

INDIANA

Majestic Star Casino
1 Buffington Harbor Drive
Gary, IN 46406
Phone: (219) 977-9999
http://www.majesticstarcasino.com

LOUISIANA

Academy of Casino Dealing
2327 Veterans Boulevard
Kenner, LA 70062
Phone: (504) 467-8210

Crescent City School of Gaming & Bartending
209 North Broad Street
New Orleans, LA 70119
Phone: (504) 822-3362
http://www.dealingschool.com

Jefferson College
P.O. Box 1040
10 Westbank Expressway
Gretna, LA 70054
Phone: (504) 362-5787
http://www.gretnacareercollege.
com

MICHIGAN

Casinos Wild Inc.
20318 Van Born Road
Dearborn Heights, MI 48125
Phone: (313) 274-2850
http://www.casinoswild.com

MISSISSIPPI

Casino College of Mississippi
P.O. Box 718
Tunica Resorts, MS 38664
Phone: (662) 363-3300
http://www.casinocollege.net

Crescent City School of Gaming & Bartending
2981 Grand Casino Parkway South Extension
Tunica Resorts, MS 38664
Phone: (662) 363-9999
http://www.dealingschool.com

Crescent City School of Gaming & Bartending
1306 29th Avenue
Gulfport, MS 39501
Phone: (228) 822-2444
http://www.crescentschools.com

EZ Learn Casino Training
13180 Highway 67
Biloxi, MS 39532
Phone: (228) 396-2103

Virginia College at Biloxi
920 Cedar Lake Road
Biloxi, MS 39532
Phone: (228) 546-9100
http://www.vccasinocareers.com

NEVADA

LAS VEGAS

A+ Institute of Gaming
940 East Sahara Avenue
Las Vegas, NV 89104
Phone: (702) 650-0002

American School of Dealing
9620 South Las Vegas Boulevard
Las Vegas, NV 89123

Phone: (702) 270-2052
http://www.americanschoolofdealing.com

Casino Gaming School of Nevada
900 East Karen Avenue
Las Vegas, NV 89109
Phone: (702) 893-1788
E-mail: Info@Learn2deal.com
http://www.learntodeal.com

Community College of Southern Nevada
3200 East Cheyenne Avenue
North Las Vegas, NV 89117
Phone: (702) 651-4533
http://www.csn.edu

Crescent School of Gaming & Bartending
4180 South Sandhill Road
Las Vegas, NV 89121
Phone: (702) 458-9910
http://www.dealingschool.com

Dealers Training Center
3330 East Tropicana Avenue
Las Vegas, NV 89121
Phone: (702) 547-1171

Las Vegas Gaming & Technical Schools Inc.
1771 East Flamingo Road
Las Vegas, NY 89119
Phone: (702) 450-3167

Las Vegas School of Dealing
3850 South Valley View Boulevard
Las Vegas, NV 89103
Phone: (702) 368-1717

Let's Make a Dealer
4265 South Arville Street
Las Vegas, NV 89103
Phone: (702) 456-3325
http://www.letsmakeadealer.com

National Academy for Casino Dealers
557 East Sahara Avenue
Las Vegas, NV 89104
Phone: (702) 735-4884

PCI Dealers School
920 South Valley View Boulevard
Las Vegas, NV 89107
Phone: (702) 877-4724
http://www.pcidealerschool.com

The Poker Academy
4640 East Flamingo Road
Las Vegas, NV
Phone: (702) 45-POKER

UNLV International Gaming Institute
4505 Maryland Parkway
Box 456037
Las Vegas, NV 89154
Phone: (702) 895-3412
http://igi.unlv.edu

Vegas Career Schools
3333 South Maryland Parkway
Las Vegas, NV 89169
Phone: (702) 792-6299

RENO

Academy of Casino Careers
200 West Second Street
Reno, NV 89501
Phone: (775) 324-1169

CT Dealer School
130b East Plumb Lane
Park Lane Mall
Reno, NV 89502
Phone: (775) 287-5159

Reno Tahoe Job Training Academy
3702 South Virginia Street
Reno, NV 89502
Phone: (775) 329-5665
http://renodealingschool.com

University of Nevada, Reno
Institute for the Study of Gambling and Commercial Gaming
1664 North Virginia Street
Reno, NV 89557
Phone: (775) 784-1110
http://www.unr.edu

NEW HAMPSHIRE

Ace of Hearts Dealer Training School
50 Valley Hill Road
Pelham, NH 03076
Phone: (603) 821-1017
http://acehearts.net

NEW JERSEY

Atlantic Cape Community College's Casino Career Institute
1535 Bacharach Boulevard
Atlantic City, NJ 08401
Phone: (609) 343-4848
http://www.atlantic.edu

Boardwalk and Marina Casino Dealers School
1923 Bacharach Boulevard
Atlantic City, NJ 08401
Phone: (609) 344-1986

Professional Dealers School
20 Old Turnpike
Pleasantville, NJ 08233
Phone: (609) 272-0760
http://www.pdsonline.biz

NEW MEXICO

Casino Dealer School
5500 San Mateo Boulevard, NE
Albuquerque, NM 87109
Phone: (505) 830-2696
http://www.casinodealerschool.net

Mountain Gaming Academy
910 Carrizo Canyon Road
Mescalero, NM 88340
Phone: (505) 464-2082

West Side Gaming
2218 Southern Boulevard
Rio Rancho, NM 87124
Phone: (505) 994-0973

NEW YORK

Casino Career Training Center
1685 Elmwood Avenue
Buffalo, NY 14207
Phone: (716) 874-4700

Casino Dealing School of Rochester
4072 West Henrietta Road
Rochester, NY 14623
Phone: (585) 334-2121

OREGON

Area 52 Dealing School
P.O. Box 1354
Coos Bay, OR 97420
Phone: (541) 217-1493
http://chipandachain.net

WASHINGTON

Ace in the Hole Casino Dealer School
2118 Broadway
Everett, WA 98201
Phone: (360) 395-8055
http://www.casinodealerschool101.com

Blackjack Academy
15505 1st Avenue South
Burien, WA 98148
Phone: (206) 790-5018
http://www.blackjackacademy.netfirms.com

Casino Dealers School
807 Grand Boulevard
Vancouver, WA 98661
Phone: (360) 906-1579

Pacific Casino Training
19011 Woodinville-Snohomish Road NE
Suite 240
Woodinville, WA 98072
Phone: (425) 398-1020
http://www.pacificcasinotraining.com

Seattle Gaming Academy
115 North 85th Street
Seattle, WA 98103
Phone: (206) 781-8700

Vancouver Casino Dealer School
707 Grand Boulevard
Vancouver, WA 98661
Phone: (360) 906-1579

Vegas Gaming School
7140 Beacon Avenue South
Seattle, WA 98118
Phone: (206) 779-3838

CANADA

Casino Training Academy
215 Red River Road
Thunder Bay, ON P7B 1A5
Phone: (807) 346-0779
http://www.casinotrainingacademy.ca

Casino Dealer Internship Program
Westactive Community College
322 Water Street
Vancouver, BC V6B 1B6
Phone: (604) 696-9322
http://www.westactive.com

Fine Art Casino Dealer School
#4 - 2979 Pandosy Street
Kelowna, BC V1Y 1W1
Phone: (250) 717-6511
http://www.fineart.ca

Winning Touch Casino Gaming School
4685 Queen Street
Niagara Falls, ON L2E 2L9
Phone: (905) 357-7333

APPENDIX II
DEGREE PROGRAMS

A. COLLEGES AND UNIVERSITIES OFFERING MAJORS IN HOSPITALITY ADMINISTRATION AND MANAGEMENT

Casinos and casino hotels often accept experience in lieu of formal college education. However, many facilities maintain that a college background gives an applicant an edge in marketability and advancement prospects, as well as providing useful experiences not otherwise available.

The following is a selected list of four-year schools granting degrees with majors in hospitality administration and management. They are grouped by state.

More colleges are granting degrees in this discipline every year. Check out college guides in the reference section of libraries or guidance counseling centers for additional schools offering degrees in this field.

ALABAMA

Tuskegee University
102 Old Administration Building
Tuskegee, AL 36088
Phone: (334) 727-8500
E-mail: admissions@tuskegee.edu
http://www.tuskegee.edu

ARKANSAS

Arkansas Tech University
1605 Coliseum Drive
Russellville, AR 72801
Phone: (479) 968-0343
Fax: (479) 964-0522
E-mail: tech.enroll@atu.edu
http://www.atu.edu

Philander Smith College
812 West 13th Street
Little Rock, AR 72202
Phone: (501) 370-5310
Fax: (501) 370-5225
E-mail: admissions@philander.edu
http://www.philander.edu

University of Arkansas
232 Silas H. Hunt Hall
Fayetteville, AR 72701
Phone: (479) 575-5346

Fax: (479) 575-7515
E-mail: uofa@uark.edu
http://www.uark.edu

ARIZONA

Arizona Western College
P.O. Box 929
Yuma, AZ 85366
Phone: (928) 317-7600
Fax: (928) 344-7712
http://www.azwestern.edu

Cochise College
901 North Columbo Avenue
Sierra Vista, AZ 85635
Phone: (520) 515-5412
Fax: (520) 515-4006
E-mail: quickd@cochise.edu
http://www.cochise.edu

CALIFORNIA

National University
11255 North Torrey Pines Road
La Jolla, CA 92037
Phone: (800) 628-8648
Fax: (858) 541-7792
E-mail: dgiovann@nu.edu
http://www.nu.edu

San Diego State University
5500 Campanile Drive
San Diego, CA 92182
Phone: (619) 594-6336
E-mail: admissions@sdsu.edu
http://www.sdsu.edu

San Francisco State University
1600 Holloway Avenue
San Francisco, CA 94132
Phone: (415) 338-1113
Fax: (415) 338-7196
E-mail: ugadmit@sfsu.edu
http://www.sfsu.edu

San Jose State University
One Washington Square
San Jose, CA 95192
Phone: (408) 283-7500
Fax: (408) 924-2050
E-mail: contact@sjsu.edu
http://www.sjsu.edu

TUI University
5336 Plaza Drive, 3rd Floor
Cypress, CA 90630
Phone: (714) 816-0366
Fax: (714) 827-7407
E-mail: registration@tuiu.edu
http://www.tuiu.edu

COLORADO

Mesa State College
1100 North Avenue
Grand Junction, CO 81501
Phone: (970) 248-1802
Fax: (970) 248-1973
E-mail: admissions@mesastate.edu
http://www.mesastate.edu

Metropolitan State College of Denver
P.O. Box 173362
Denver, CO 80217
Phone: (303) 556-2615
http://www.mscd.edu

University of Denver
2197 South University Boulevard
Denver, CO 80208
Phone: (800) 525-9495
Fax: (303) 871-3301
E-mail: admission@du.edu
http://admission.du.edu/admissions

CONNECTICUT

University of New Haven
Bayer Hall
300 Boston Post Road
West Haven, CT 06516
Phone: (203) 932-7318
Fax: (203) 931-6093
http://www.newhaven.edu

DELAWARE

Delaware State University
1200 North DuPont Highway
Dover, DE 19901
Phone: (302) 857-6351
Fax: (302) 857-6908
E-mail: admissions@desu.edu
http://www.desu.edu

DISTRICT OF COLUMBIA

University of the District of Columbia
4200 Connecticut Avenue NW
Washington, DC 20008
Phone: (202) 274-6110
Fax: (202) 274-5553
http://www.udc.edu

FLORIDA

Florida Atlantic University
777 Glades Road
P.O. Box 3091
Boca Raton, FL 33431
Phone: (561) 297-3040
Fax: (561) 297-2758
E-mail: ugadmissions@fau.edu
http://www.fau.edu

Florida International University
University Park
11200 South West 8th Street
Miami, FL 33199
Phone: (305) 348-3675
Fax: (305) 348-3648
http://www.fiu.edu

Saint Leo University
P.O. Box 6665
Saint Leo, FL 33574
Phone: (352) 588-8283
Fax: (352) 588-8257
E-mail: admission@saintleo.edu
http://www.saintleo.edu

University of Central Florida
P.O. Box 160111
Orlando, FL 32816
Phone: (407) 823-3000
E-mail: admission@mail.ucf.edu
http://www.ucf.edu

University of West Florida
11000 University Parkway
Pensacola, FL 32514
Phone: (850) 474-2230
E-mail: admissions@uwf.edu
http://uwf.edu

IDAHO

Lewis-Clark State College
500 8th Avenue
Lewiston, ID 83501
Phone: (208) 792-2210
Fax: (208) 792-2876
E-mail: admissions@lcsc.edu
http://www.lcsc.edu

INDIANA

Ball State University
2000 West University Avenue
Muncie, IN 47306
Phone: (765) 285-8300
E-mail: askus@bsu.edu
http://cms.bsu.edu

Indiana University–Purdue University Fort Wayne
2101 East Coliseum Boulevard
Fort Wayne, IN 46805
Phone: (260) 481-6812
Fax: (260) 481-6880
E-mail: ask@ipfw.edu
http://www.ipfw.edu

Tri-State University
1 University Avenue
Angola, IN 46703
Phone: (260) 665-4100
E-mail: admit@tristate.edu
http://www.tristate.edu

ILLINOIS

Kendall College
900 N. North Branch Street
Chicago, IL 60622
Phone: (312) 752-2020
Fax: (312) 752-2021
E-mail: admissions@kendall.edu
http://www.kendall.edu

Lexington College
310 South Peoria Street
Chicago, IL 60607
Phone: (312) 226-6294
Fax: (312) 226-6405
E-mail: admissions@
    lexingtoncollege.edu
http://lexingtoncollege.edu

Lincoln College—Normal
715 West Raab Road
Normal, IL 61761
Phone: (309) 452-0500
E-mail: ncadmissionsinfo@
    lincolncollege.edu
http://www.lincolncollege.edu/
    normal

Midstate College
411 West Northmoor Road
Peoria, IL 61614
Phone: (309) 692-4092
Fax: (309) 692-3893
E-mail: midstate@midstate.edu
http://www.midstate.edu

Roosevelt University
Chicago Campus
430 South Michigan Avenue
Chicago, IL 60605
Phone: (877) APPLY-RU
Fax: (312) 341-4316
E-mail: applyRU@roosevelt.edu
http://www.roosevelt.edu

University of Illinois at
   Urbana–Champaign
901 West Illinois Street
Urbana, IL 61801
Phone: (217) 333-0302
Fax: (217) 244-4614
E-mail: ugradadmissions@uiuc.edu
http://www.uiuc.edu

IOWA

Kaplan University–Davenport
1801 East Kimberly Road
Suite 1
Davenport, IA 52807
Phone: (563) 355-3500
http://www.kaplancollegeia.com

KENTUCKY

University of Kentucky
100 W. D. Funkhouser Building
Lexington, KY 40506
Phone: (859) 257-2000
E-mail: admissio@uky.edu
http://www.uky.edu

Western Kentucky University
1906 College Heights Boulevard
Bowling Green, KY 42101
Phone: (270) 745-2551
Fax: (270) 745-6133
E-mail: admission@wku.edu
http://www.wku.edu

LOUISIANA

Northwestern State University
   of Louisiana
Natchitoches, LA 71497
Phone: (318) 357-4503
Fax: (318) 357-5567
E-mail: recruiting@nsula.edu
http://www.nsula.edu

University of New Orleans
2000 Lakeshore Drive
New Orleans, LA 70148
Phone: (504) 280-6595
Fax: (504) 280-5522
http://www.uno.edu

MAINE

Husson College
One College Circle
Bangor, ME 04401
Phone: (207) 941-7100
Fax: (207) 941-7935
E-mail: admit@husson.edu
http://www.husson.edu

MARYLAND

Morgan State University
Cold Spring Lane and Hillen Road
Baltimore, MD 21251
Phone: (443) 885-3000
http://www.morgan.edu

Sojourner-Douglass College
200 North Central Avenue
Baltimore, MD 21202
Phone: (800) 732-2630
http://sdc.edu

MASSACHUSETTS

Becker College
61 Sever Street
Worcester, MA 01609
Phone: (508) 791-9241
Fax: (508) 890-1500
E-mail: admissions@beckercollege.
   edu
http://www.beckercollege.edu

Boston University
121 Bay State Road
Boston, MA 02215
Phone: (617) 353-2300
E-mail: admissions@bu.edu
http://www.bu.edu/admissions

Endicott College
376 Hale Street
Beverly, MA 01915
Phone: (978) 921-1000

Fax: (978) 232-2520
E-mail: admissio@endicott.edu
http://www.endicott.edu

University of Massachusetts
   Amherst
37 Mather Drive
Amherst, MA 01003
Phone: (413) 545-0222
Fax: (413) 545-4312
http://www.umass.edu

MICHIGAN

Baker College of Flint
1050 West Bristol Road
Flint, MI 48507
Phone: (810) 766-4008
Fax: (810) 766-4049
http://www.baker.edu

Baker College of Owosso
1020 South Washington Street
Owosso, MI 48867
Phone: (989) 729-3350
Fax: (517) 729-3359
E-mail: mike.konopacke@baker.edu
http://www.baker.edu

Central Michigan University
Mt. Pleasant, MI 48859
Phone: (989) 774-3076
E-mail: cmuadmit@cmich.edu
http://www.cmich.edu

Concordia University
4090 Geddes Road
Ann Arbor, MI 48105
Phone: (734) 995-7450
Fax: (734) 995-4610
E-mail: admissions@cuaa.edu
http://www.cuaa.edu

Eastern Michigan University
400 Pierce Hall
Ypsilanti, MI 48197
Phone: (734) 487-3060
Fax: (734) 487-1484
E-mail: admissions@emich.edu
http://www.emich.edu

Ferris State University
1201 South State Street

Big Rapids, MI 49307
Phone: (231) 591-2000
Fax: (231) 591-3944
E-mail: admissions@ferris.edu
http://www.ferris.edu

Madonna University
36600 Schoolcraft Road
Livonia, MI 48150
Phone: (734) 432-5317
Fax: (734) 432-5393
E-mail: muinfo@madonna.edu
http://www.madonna.edu

Michigan State University
250 Administration Building
East Lansing, MI 48824
Phone: (517) 355-8332
Fax: (517) 353-1647
E-mail: admis@msu.edu
http://www.msu.edu

Northern Michigan University
1401 Presque Isle Avenue
Marquette, MI 49855
Phone: (906) 227-2650
Fax: (906) 227-1747
E-mail: admiss@nmu.edu
http://www.nmu.edu

MINNESOTA

The Art Institutes International Minnesota
15 South 9th Street
Minneapolis, MN 55402
Phone: (612) 332-3361
Fax: (612) 332-3934
http://www.artinstitutes.edu/minneapolis

National American University
1500 West Highway 36
Roseville, MN 55113
Phone: (651) 644-1265
http://www.national.edu

University of Minnesota, Crookston
2900 University Avenue
Crookston, MN 56716
Phone: (218) 281-8569
Fax: (218) 281-8575

E-mail: info@UMCrookston.edu
http://www.crk.umn.edu

MISSOURI

Missouri State University
901 South National Avenue
Springfield, MO 65804
Phone: (417) 836-5517
Fax: (417) 836-6334
E-mail: info@missouristate.edu
http://www.missouristate.edu

NEBRASKA

University of Nebraska—Lincoln
313 North 13th Street
Lincoln, NE 68588
Phone: (402) 472-2023
Fax: (402) 472-0670
E-mail: admissions@unl.edu
http://www.unl.edu

Kaplan University–Lincoln
1821 K Street
P.O. Box 82826
Lincoln, NE 68501
Phone: (402) 474-5315
http://www.hamiltonlincoln.com

NEVADA

University of Nevada, Las Vegas
Box 451021
4505 Maryland Parkway
Las Vegas, NV 89154
Phone: (702) 774-UNLV
Fax: (702) 774-8008
http://www.unlv.edu

University of Nevada, Reno
1664 North Virginia Street
Reno, NV 89557
Phone: (775) 784-4700
E-mail: asknevada@unr.edu
http://www.unr.edu

NEW HAMPSHIRE

Southern New Hampshire University
2500 North River Road

Manchester, NH 03106
Phone: (603) 645-9611
Fax: (603) 645-9693
http://www.snhu.edu

University of New Hampshire
4 Garrison Avenue
Durham, NH 03824
Phone: (603) 862-1360
Fax: (603) 862-0077
http://www.unh.edu/admissions

NEW JERSEY

Montclair State University
1 Normal Avenue
Montclair, NJ 07043
Phone: (973) 655-4444
E-mail: undergraduate.admissions@montclair.edu
http://www.montclair.edu

The Richard Stockton College of New Jersey
P.O. Box 195
Pomona, NJ 08240
Phone: (609) 652-4261
Fax: (609) 626-5541
E-mail: admissions@stockton.edu
http://www.stockton.edu

NEW MEXICO

National American University
4775 Indian School, NE
Albuquerque, NM 87110
Phone: (505) 265-7517
Fax: (505) 265-7542
http://www.national.edu

NEW YORK

Buffalo State College—State University of New York
1300 Elmwood Avenue
Buffalo, NY 14222
Phone: (716) 878-4017
Fax: (716) 878-6100
E-mail: admissions@buffalostate.edu
http://www.buffalostate.edu

Globe Institute of Technology
291 Broadway
New York, NY 10007
Phone: (212) 349-4330
E-mail: admissions@globe.edu
http://www.globe.edu

Monroe College–Bronx Campus
2501 Jerome Avenue
Bronx, NY 10468
Phone: (718) 933-6700
E-mail: ejerome@monroecollege.edu
http://www.monroecollege.edu

Monroe College–New Rochelle
434 Main Street
New Rochelle, NY 10801
Phone: (914) 654-3200
E-mail lscora@monroecollege.edu
http://www.monroecollege.edu

New York City College of Technology of the City University of New York
300 Jay Street
Brooklyn, NY 11201
Phone: (718) 260-5500
E-mail: achaconis@citytech.cuny.edu
http://www.citytech.cuny.edu
New York University

22 Washington Square North
New York, NY 10011
Phone: (212) 998-4500
http://admissions.nyu.edu

Paul Smith's College
P.O. Box 265
Paul Smiths, New York 12970
Phone: (518) 327-6227
Fax: (518) 327-6016
E-mail: admiss@paulsmiths.edu
http://www.paulsmiths.edu

Rochester Institute of Technology
Director of Undergraduate Admissions
60 Lomb Memorial Drive
Rochester, NY 14623

Phone: (585) 475-6631
Fax: (585) 475-7424
E-mail: admissions@rit.edu
http://www.rit.edu

St. John's University
8000 Utopia Parkway
Queens, NY 11439
Phone: (718) 990-2000
Fax: (718) 990-2160
E-mail: admhelp@stjohns.edu
http://www.stjohns.edu

State University of New York College of Agriculture and Technology at Morrisville
P.O. Box 901
Morrisville, NY 13408
Phone: (800) 258-0111
Fax: (315) 684-6427
E-mail: admissions@morrisville.edu
http://www.morrisville.edu

NORTH CAROLINA

Appalachian State University
ASU Box 32004
Boone, NC 28608
Phone: (828) 262-2120
http://www.appstate.edu

East Carolina University
Whichard Building 106
Greenville, NC 26858
Phone: (252) 328-6640
http://www.ecu.edu

North Carolina Central University
P.O. Box 19717
Durham, NC 27707
Phone: (919) 530-6298
Fax: (919) 530-7625
E-mail: admissions@nccu.edu
http://www.nccu.edu

University of North Carolina at Greensboro
1400 Spring Garden Street
P.O. Box 26170
Greensboro, NC 27402
Phone: (336) 334-5243

Fax: (336) 334-4180
E-mail: undergrad_admissions@uncg.edu
http://www.uncg.edu

Western Carolina University
Cullowhee, NC 28723
Phone: (828) 227-7317
Fax: (828) 227-7319
E-mail: admission@wcu.edu
http://www.wcu.edu

NORTH DAKOTA

North Dakota State University
P.O. Box 5454
Fargo, ND 58105
Phone: (701) 231-8643
E-mail: ndsu.admission@ndsu.edu
http://www.ndsu.edu

OHIO

Bowling Green State University
110 McFall Center
Bowling Green, OH 43403
Phone: (419) 372-BGSU
Fax: (419) 372-6955
E-mail: choosebgsu@bgsu.edu
http://www.bgsu.edu

Ohio State University
154 West 12th Avenue
Columbus, OH 43210
Phone: (614) 292-3980
Fax: (614) 292-4818
E-mail: professional@osu.edu
http://www.osu.edu

Ohio State University at Lima
4240 Campus Drive
Lima, OH 45804
Phone: (419) 995-8434
Fax: (419) 995-8483
E-mail: admissions@lima.ohio-state.edu
http://www.lima.osu.edu

Youngstown State University
One University Plaza
Youngstown, OH 44555
Phone: (330) 941-2000
Fax: (330) 941-3674

E-mail: enroll@ysu.edu
http://www.ysu.edu

PENNSYLVANIA

Indiana University of Pennsylvania
1011 South Drive
Indiana, PA 15705
Phone: (724) 357-2230
Fax: (724) 357-6281
E-mail: admissions-inquiry@iup.edu
http://www.iup.edu/admissions

Marywood University
2300 Adams Avenue
Scranton, PA 18509
Phone: (570) 348-6234
Fax: (570) 961-4763
E-mail: yourfuture@marywood.edu
http://www.mymarywood.com

Mercyhurst College Admissions
501 East 38th Street
Erie, PA 16546
Phone: (814) 824-2202
E-mail: admissions@mercyhurst.edu
http://admissions.mercyhurst.edu

Pennsylvania College of Technology
One College Avenue
Williamsport, PA 17701
Phone: (570) 327-4761
E-mail: PCTinfo@pct.edu
http://www.pct.edu/peter4

Robert Morris University
6001 University Boulevard
Moon Township, PA 15108
Phone: (800) 762-0097
http://www.rmu.edu

Seton Hill University
Box 991
One Seton Hill Drive
Greensburg, PA 15601
Phone: (800) 826-6234
Fax: (724) 830-1294
E-mail: admit@setonhill.edu
http://www.setonhill.edu

Temple University
1801 North Broad Street
Philadelphia, PA 19122
Phone: (215) 204-7200
E-mail: tuadm@temple.edu
http://www.temple.edu/undergrad

East Stroudsburg University of Pennsylvania
200 Prospect Street
East Stroudsburg, PA 18301
Phone: (570) 422-3542
Fax: (570) 422-3933
E-mail: undergrads@po-box.esu.edu
http://www.esu.edu

RHODE ISLAND

Johnson & Wales University
8 Abbott Park Place
Providence, RI 02903
Phone: (401) 598-1000
Fax: (401) 598-4901
E-mail: jwu@admissions.jwu.edu
http://www.jwu.edu

SOUTH CAROLINA

Bob Jones University
1700 Wade Hampton Boulevard
Greenville, SC 29614
Phone: (864) 242-5100
Fax: (800) 232-9258
E-mail: admissions@bju.edu
http://www.bju.edu

College of Charleston
66 George Street
Charleston, SC 29424
Phone: (843) 953-5670
Fax: (843) 953-6322
E-mail: admissions@cofc.edu
http://www.cofc.edu

University of South Carolina
Undergraduate Admissions
902 Sumter Street Access/Lieber College
Columbia, SC 29208
Phone: (803) 777-7700
E-mail: admissions-ugrad@sc.edu
http://www.sc.edu/admissions

University of South Carolina Beaufort
1 University Boulevard
Bluffton, SC 29909
Phone: (843) 208-8112
Fax: (843) 208-8015
E-mail: mrwilli5@gwm.sc.edu
http://www.sc.edu/beaufort

TENNESSEE

University of Memphis
101 John Wilder Tower
Memphis, TN 38152
Phone: (901) 678-2169
http://www.memphis.edu

TEXAS

Stephen F. Austin State University
P.O. Box 13051, SFA Station
Nacogdoches, TX 75962
Phone: (936) 468-2504
E-mail: admissions@sfasu.edu
http://www.gosfa.com

University of North Texas
Box 311277
Denton, TX 76203
Phone: (940) 565-3190
Fax: (940) 565-2408
E-mail: undergradadm@unt.edu
http://www.unt.edu

UTAH

Utah Valley State College
800 West University Parkway
Orem, UT 84058
Phone: (801) 863-8460
Fax: (801) 225-4677
E-mail: info@uvsc.edu
http://www.uvsc.edu

VERMONT

Champlain College
163 South Willard Street
Burlington, VT 05401
Phone: (802) 860-2727
Fax: (802) 860-2767
E-mail: admission@champlain.edu
http://www.champlain.edu

Johnson State College
337 College Hill
Johnson, VT 05656
Phone: (802) 635-1219
Fax: (802) 635-1230
E-mail: jscadmissions@jsc.vsc.edu
http://www.jsc.edu

VIRGINIA

James Madison University
481 Bluestone Drive
Harrisonburg, VA 22807
Phone: (540) 568-5681
Fax: (540) 568-3332
E-mail: admissions@jmu.edu
http://www.jmu.edu

Stratford University
13576 Minnieville Road
Woodbridge, VA 22192
Phone: (703) 897-1982
E-mail: admissions@stratford.edu
http://www.stratford.edu

WASHINGTON

Washington State University
P.O. Box 641067
Pullman, WA 99164
Phone: (509) 335-5586
Fax: (509) 335-4902
E-mail: admiss2@wsu.edu
http://www.wsu.edu

WEST VIRGINIA

**American Public University
System**
322-C West Washington Street
Charles Town, WV 25414
Phone: (877) 777-9081
Fax: (304) 724-3788
E-mail: info@apus.edu
http://www.apus.edu

Concord University
1000 Vermillion Street
Athens, WV 24712

Phone: (304) 384-5248
Fax: (304) 384-9044
E-mail: admissions@concord.edu
http://www.concord.edu

**Mountain State University
Information Center**
Box 9003
Beckley, WV 25802
Phone: (304) 929-4636
http://www.mountainstate.edu

WISCONSIN

University of Wisconsin–Stout
712 South Broadway Street
Menomonie, WI 54751
Phone: (715) 232-2639
Fax: (715) 232-2639
E-mail: admissions@uwstout.edu
http://www.uwstout.edu

B. COLLEGES AND UNIVERSITIES OFFERING MAJORS IN HOTEL AND RESTAURANT ADMINISTRATION

While casinos and casino hotels often accept experience in lieu of formal college education, many feel that a college background gives an applicant an edge in marketability and advancement prospects as well as providing valuable experience not otherwise available.

The following is a selected listing of four-year schools granting degrees with majors in hotel and restaurant administration. They are grouped by state.

Check out college guides in the reference section of libraries or guidance counseling centers for additional schools offering degrees in this field.

ALABAMA

Auburn University
202 Mary Martin Hall
Auburn, AL 36849
Phone: (334) 844-6446
E-mail: admissions@auburn.edu
http://www.auburn.edu

ARIZONA

Northern Arizona University
Office of Undergraduate
    Admissions
Box 4084

Flagstaff, AZ 86011
Phone: (928) 523-5511
E-mail: undergraduate.
    admissions@nau.edu
http://home.nau.edu

ARKANSAS

**University of Arkansas at Pine
Bluff**
Mail Slot 4981
1200 North University Drive
Pine Bluff, AR 71611
Phone: (870) 575-8487
http://www.uapb.edu

CALIFORNIA

**Alliant International
University**
10455 Pomerado Road
San Diego, CA 92131
Phone: (858) 635-4772
http://www.alliant.edu

**California State Polytechnic
University, Pomona**
3801 West Temple Avenue
Pomona, CA 91768
Phone: (909) 869-3210
http://www.csupomona.edu

California State University, Long Beach
1250 Bellflower Boulevard
Long Beach, CA 90840
Phone: (562) 985-4641
http://www.csulb.edu

University of San Francisco
2130 Fulton Street
San Francisco, CA 94117
Phone: (415) 422-6563
Fax: (415) 422-2217
E-mail: admission@usfca.edu
http://www.usfca.edu

COLORADO
Colorado State University
1062 Campus Delivery
Fort Collins, CO 80523
Phone: (970) 491-6909
Fax: (970) 491-7799
E-mail: admissions@colostate.edu
http://www.colostate.edu

National American University
5125 North Academy Boulevard
Colorado Springs, CO 80918
Phone: (719) 277-0588
Fax: (719) 277-0589
E-mail: csadmissions@national.edu
http://www.national.edu

University of Denver
2197 South University Boulevard
Denver, CO 80208
Phone: (303) 871-2036
E-mail: admission@du.edu
http://www.du.edu/admission

CONNECTICUT
University of New Haven
300 Boston Post Road
West Haven, CT 06516
Phone: (203) 932-7319
E-mail: adminfo@newhaven.edu
http://www.newhaven.edu

DELAWARE
University of Delaware
116 Hullihen Hall
Newark, DE 19716

Phone: (302) 831-8123
Fax: (302) 831-6905
E-mail: admissions@udel.edu
http://www.udel.edu

FLORIDA
Ave Maria University
5050 Ave Maria Boulevard
Ave Maria, FL 34142
Phone: (239) 280-2556
Fax: (239) 280-2559
http://www.avemaria.edu

Bethune-Cookman University
640 Dr. Mary McLeod Bethune
    Boulevard
Daytona Beach, FL
Phone: (386) 481-2600
Fax: (386) 481-2601
E-mail: admissions@cookman.edu
http://www.bethune.cookman.edu

Florida Metropolitan University–Pompano Beach Campus
225 North Federal Highway
Fort Lauderdale, FL 33304
Phone: (954) 783-7339
Fax: (954) 783-7964

Florida Southern College
111 Lake Hollingsworth Drive
Lakeland, FL 3380
Phone: (800) 274-4131
E-mail: fscadm@flsouthern.edu
http://www.flsouthern.edu

Johnson & Wales University
1701 Northeast 127th Street
North Miami, FL 33181
Phone: (305) 892-7002
Fax: (305) 892-7020
E-mail: admissions.mia@jwu.edu
http://www.jwu.edu

Northwood University, Florida Campus
2600 North Military Trail
West Palm Beach, FL 33409
Phone: (561) 478-5500
E-mail: fladmit@northwood.edu
http://www.northwood.edu

Schiller International University
300 East Bay Drive
Largo, FL 33770
Phone: (866) 748-4338
Fax: (727) 734-0359
E-mail: admissions@schiller.edu
http://www.schiller.edu

St. Thomas University
16401 Northwest 37th Avenue
Miami Gardens, FL 33054
Phone: (305) 628-6546
Fax: (305)-628-6591
E-mail: signup@stu.edu
http://www.stu.edu

Webber International University
1201 North Scenic Highway
P.O. Box 96
Babson Park, FL 33827
Phone: (863) 638-2910
E-mail: admissions@webber.edu
http://www.webber.edu

GEORGIA
Georgia Southern University
GSU P.O. Box 8024
Statesboro, GA 30460
Phone: (912) 681-5391
Fax: (912) 486-7240
E-mail: admissions@
    georgiasouthern.edu
http://www.georgiasouthern.edu

HAWAII
Brigham Young University–Hawaii
55-220 Kulanui Street
Oahu, HI 96762
Phone: (808) 293-3731
Fax: (808) 293-3741
E-mail: admissions@byuh.edu
http://www.byuh.edu

ILLINOIS
Aurora University
347 South Gladstone Avenue
Aurora, IL 60506

Phone: (630) 844-5533
E-mail: admission@aurora.edu
http://www.aurora.edu

KENDALL COLLEGE

Office of Admissions
900 N. North Branch Street
Chicago, IL 60622
Phone: (312) 752-2020
Fax: (312) 752-2021
E-mail: admissions@kendall.edu
http://www.kendall.edu

INDIANA

Purdue University
475 Stadium Mall Drive
Schleman Mall
West Lafayette, IN 47907
Phone: (765) 494-1776
Fax: (765) 494-0544
E-mail: admissions@purdue.edu
http://www.purdue.edu

IOWA

**Iowa State University of Science
and Technology**
100 Alumni Hall
Ames, IA 50011
Phone: (515) 294-5836
Fax: (515) 294-2592
E-mail: admissions@iastate.edu
http://www.iastate.edu

KANSAS

Kansas State University
119 Anderson Hall
Manhattan, KS 66506
Phone: (785) 532-6250
Fax: (785) 532-6393
E-mail: kstate@ksu.edu
http://www.ksu.edu

KENTUCKY

Sullivan University
3101 Bardstown Road
Louisville, KY 40205
Phone: (502) 456-6505
http://www.sullivan.edu

Asbury College
1 Macklem Drive
Wilmore, KY 40390
Phone: (859) 858-3511
Fax: (859) 858-3921
http://www.asbury.edu

LOUISIANA

Grambling State University
P.O. Drawer 1165
100 Main Street
Grambling, LA 71245
Phone: (318) 274-6183
E-mail: mossa@gram.edu
http://www.gram.edu

MAINE

Thomas College
180 West River Road
Waterville, ME 04901
Phone: (207) 859-1101
Fax: (207) 859-1114
E-mail: admiss@thomas.edu
http://www.thomas.edu

University of Maine at Machias
9 O'Brien Avenue
Machias, Maine 04654
Phone: (207) 255-1318
Fax: (207) 255-1363
E-mail: ummadmissions@maine.edu
http://www.umm.maine.edu

MARYLAND

Morgan State University
Cold Spring Lane and Hillen Road
Baltimore, MD 21251
Phone: (443) 885-3000
http://www.morgan.edu

**University of Maryland Eastern
Shore**
1 Backbone Road
Princess Anne, MD 21853
Phone: (410) 651-8410
http://www.umes.edu

MASSACHUSETTS

Becker College
61 Sever Street
Worcester, MA 01609

Phone: (508) 791-9241
E-mail: admissions@beckercollege.
 edu
http://www.beckercollege.edu

Boston University
121 Bay State Road
Boston, MA 02215
Phone: (617) 353-2300
E-mail: admissions@bu.edu
http://www.bu.edu/admissions

Lasell College
1844 Commonwealth Avenue
Newton, MA 02466
Phone: (617) 243-2225
Fax: (617) 243-2380
E-mail: info@lasell.edu
http://www.lasell.edu

Mount Ida College
777 Dedham Street
Newton, MA 02459
Phone: (617) 928-4553
Fax: 617-928-4507
E-mail: admissions@mountida.edu
http://www.mountida.edu

Assumption College
500 Salisbury Street
P.O. Box 15005
Worcester, MA 01609
Phone: (508) 767-7285
E-mail: admiss@assumption.edu
http://www.assumption.edu

MICHIGAN

Baker College of Muskegon
1903 Marquette Avenue
Muskegon, MI 49442
Phone: (231) 777-5207
Fax: (231) 777-5201
E-mail: kathy.jacobson@baker.edu
http://www.baker.edu

Baker College of Owosso
1020 South Washington Street
Owosso, MI 48867
Phone: (989)729-3350
Fax: (517) 729-3359
E-mail: mike.konopacke@baker.edu
http://www.baker.edu

Baker College of Port Huron
3403 Lapeer Road
Port Huron, MI 48060
Phone: (810) 985-7000
Fax: (810) 985-7066
E-mail: kenny_d@porthuron.baker.edu
http://www.porthuron.baker.edu

Central Michigan University
Mt. Pleasant, MI 48859
Phone: (989) 774-3076
Fax: (989) 774-7267
E-mail: cmuadmit@cmich.edu
http://www.cmich.edu

Ferris State University
1201 South State Street
Big Rapids, MI 49307
Phone: (231) 591-2000
Fax: (231) 591-3944
E-mail: admissions@ferris.edu
http://www.ferris.edu

Grand Valley State University
1 Campus Drive
Allendale, MI 49401
Phone: (616) 331-2025
E-mail: admissions@gvsu.edu
http://www.gvsu.edu

Michigan State University
250 Administration Building
East Lansing, MI 48824
Phone: (517) 355-8332
Fax: (517) 353-1647
E-mail: admis@msu.edu
http://www.msu.edu

MINNESOTA

Southwest Minnesota State University
1501 State Street
Marshall, MN 56258
Phone: (507) 537-6286
Fax: (507) 537-7145
E-mail: shearerr@southwestmsu.edu
http://www.southwestmsu.edu

MISSISSIPPI

University of Southern Mississippi
118 College Drive

Hattiesburg, MS 39406
Phone: (601) 266-5000
Fax: (601) 266-5148
E-mail: admissions@usm.edu
http://www.usm.edu

MISSOURI

University of Central Missouri
1400 Ward Edwards
Warrensburg, MO 64093
Phone: (660) 543-4170
Fax: (660) 543-8517
E-mail: admit@ucmo.edu
http://www.ucmo.edu

University of Missouri–Columbia
230 Jesse Hall
Columbia, MO 65211
Phone: (573) 882-7786
Fax: (573) 882-7887
E-mail: mu4u@missouri.edu
http://www.missiouri.edu

NEVADA

Sierra Nevada College
999 Tahoe Boulevard
Incline Village, NV 89451
Phone: (866) 412-4636
E-mail: admissions@sierranevada.edu
http://www.sierranevada.edu

University of Nevada, Las Vegas
Box 451021
4505 Maryland Parkway
Las Vegas, NV 89154
Phone: (702) 895-3011
Fax: (702) 774-8008
http://www.unlv.edu

NEW HAMPSHIRE

University of New Hampshire
4 Garrison Avenue
Durham, NH 03824
Phone: (603) 862-1360
Fax: (603) 862-0077
http://www.unh.edu/admissions

NEW JERSEY

Fairleigh Dickinson University
1000 River Road

Teaneck, NJ 07666
Phone: (800) 338-8803
E-mail: globaleducation@fdu.edu
http://www.fdu.edu

NEW MEXICO

National American University
4775 Indian School Road Northeast
Albuquerque, NM 87110
Phone: (505) 265-7517
Fax: (505) 265-7542
http://www.national.edu

NEW YORK

Buffalo State College–State University of New York
1300 Elmwood Avenue
Buffalo, NY 14222
Phone: (716) 878-4017
Fax: (716) 878-6100
E-mail: admissions@buffalostate.edu
http://www.buffalostate.edu

Cornell University
410 Thurston Avenue
Ithaca, NY 14850
Phone: (607) 255-5241
E-mail: admissions@cornell.edu
http://admissions.cornell.edu

Keuka College
Keuka Park, NY 14478
Phone: (315) 279-5254
Fax: (315) 279-5386
E-mail: admissions@mail.keuka.edu
http://www.keuka.edu

New York City College of Technology of the City University of New York
300 Jay Street
Brooklyn, NY 11201
Phone: (718) 260-5500
E-mail: achaconis@citytech.cuny.edu
http://www.citytech.cuny.edu

New York Institute of Technology
P.O. Box 8000

Old Westbury, NY 11568
Phone: (516) 686-1083
Fax: (516) 686-7613
E-mail: admissions@nyit.edu
http://www.nyit.edu

New York University
22 Washington Square North
New York, NY 10011
Phone: (212) 998-4500
http://admissions.nyu.edu

Niagara University
630 Bailo Hall
Niagara University, NY 14109
Phone: (716) 286-8700
Fax: (716) 286-8710
E-mail: admissions@niagara.edu
http://www.niagara.edu

Pace University
1 Pace Plaza
New York, NY 10038
Phone: (800) 874-7223
E-mail: infoctr@pace.edu
http://www.pace.edu

Paul Smith's College
P.O. Box 265
Paul Smiths, NY 12970
Phone: (518) 327-6227
Fax: (518) 327-6016
E-mail: admiss@paulsmiths.edu
http://www.paulsmiths.edu

State University of New York at Plattsburgh
101 Broad Street
Plattsburgh, NY 12901
Phone: (518) 564-2040
Fax: (518) 564-2045
E-mail: admissions@plattsburgh.edu
http://www.plattsburgh.edu

State University of New York College of Agriculture and Technology at Cobleskill
State Route 7
Cobleskill, NY 12043
Phone: (518) 255-5525
Fax: (518) 255-6769
E-mail: admissions@cobleskill.edu
http://www.cobleskill.edu

St. John's University
8000 Utopia Parkway
Queens, NY 11439
Phone: (718) 990-2000
Fax: (718) 990-2160
E-mail: admhelp@stjohns.edu
http://www.stjohns.edu

NORTH CAROLINA

East Carolina University
Whichard Building 106
Greenville, NC 27858
Phone: (252) 328-6640
http://www.ecu.edu

North Carolina Wesleyan College
3400 North Wesleyan Boulevard
Rocky Mount, NC 27804
Phone: (252) 985-5200
Fax: (252) 985-5295
E-mail: adm@ncwc.edu
http://www.ncwc.edu

OHIO

Ashland University
401 College Avenue
Ashland, OH 44805
Phone: (419) 289-5052
Fax: (419) 289-5999
E-mail: enrollme@ashland.edu
http://www.exploreashland.com

The University of Akron
277 East Buchtel Avenue
Akron, OH 44325
Phone: (330) 972-6427
Fax: (330) 972-7022
E-mail: admissions@uakron.edu
http://www.uakron.edu

The University of Findlay
1000 North Main Street
Findlay, OH 45840
Phone: (419) 434-4732
E-mail: admissions@findlay.edu
http://www.findlay.edu

OKLAHOMA

Langston University
P.O. Box 728

Langston, OK 73120
Phone: (405) 466-2984
Fax: (405) 466-3391
http://www.lunet.edu

Oklahoma State University
219 Student Union
Stillwater, OK 74078
Phone: (405) 744-5358
Fax: (405) 744-7092
E-mail: admissions@okstate.edu
http://www.okstate.edu

University of Central Oklahoma
100 North University Drive
Box 151
Edmond, OK 73034
Phone: (405) 974-2338
Fax: (405) 341-4964
E-mail: admituco@ucok.edu
http://www.ucok.edu

OREGON

Southern Oregon University
1250 Siskiyou Boulevard
Ashland, OR 97520
Phone: (541) 552-6411
E-mail: admissions@sou.edu
http://www.sou.edu

PENNSYLVANIA

Cheyney University of Pennsylvania
1837 University Circle
P.O. Box 200
Cheyney, PA 19319
Phone: (610) 399-2275
Fax: (610) 399-2099
E-mail: admissions@cheyney.edu
http://www.cheyney.edu

Keystone College
1 College Green
La Plume, PA 18440
Phone: (570) 945-8111
E-mail: admissions@keystone.edu
http://www.keystone.edu

Widener University
1 University Place

Chester, PA 19013
Phone: (610) 499-4126
E-mail: admissions.office@widener.edu
http://www.widener.edu

RHODE ISLAND

Johnson & Wales University
8 Abbott Park Place
Providence, RI 02903
Phone: (401) 598-1000
Fax: (401) 598-4901
E-mail: jwu@admissions.jwu.edu
http://www.jwu.edu

SOUTH DAKOTA

South Dakota State University
P.O. Box 2201
Brookings, SD 57007
Phone: (605) 688-4121
Fax: (605) 688-6891
E-mail: sdsu.admissions@sdstate.edu
http://www.sdstate.edu

TENNESSEE

University of Central Oklahoma
100 North University Drive
Edmond, OK 73034
Phone: (405) 974-2338
Fax: (405) 341-4964
E-mail: admituco@ucok.edu
http://www.ucok.edu

TEXAS

Austin College
900 North Grand Avenue
Sherman, TX 75090
Phone: (903) 813-3000
Fax: (903) 813-3198
E-mail: admission@austincollege.edu
http://www.austincollege.edu

Texas A&M University–Kingsville
Campus Box 105

Kingsville, TX 78363
Phone: (361) 593-2811
http://www.tamuk.edu

Texas Tech University
Box 45005
Lubbock, TX 79409
Phone: (806) 742-1480
Fax: (806) 742-0062
E-mail: admissions@ttu.edu
http://www.ttu.edu

University of Houston
Office of Admissions
122 East Cullen Building
Houston, TX 77204
Phone: (713) 743-1010
http://www.uh.edu/admissions

Wiley College
711 Wiley Avenue
Marshall, TX 75670
Phone: (903) 927-3222
Fax: (903) 923-8878
E-mail: ajones@wileyc.edu
http://www.wileyc.edu

VERMONT

Champlain College
163 South Willard Street
Burlington, VT 05401
Phone: (802) 860-2727
Fax: (802) 860-2767
E-mail: admission@champlain.edu
http://www.champlain.edu

VIRGINIA

Hampton University
Hampton, VA 23668
Phone: (757) 727-5495
Fax: (757) 727-5095
E-mail: barbara.inman@hamptonu.edu
http://www.hamptonu.edu

Stratford University
7777 Leesburg Pike
Falls Church, VA 22043
Phone: (703) 821-8570
Fax: (703) 734-5339
E-mail: admissions@stratford.edu
http://www.stratford.edu

Virginia Polytechnic Institute and State University
201 Burruss Hall
Blacksburg, VA 24061
Phone: (540) 231-6267
Fax: (540) 231-3242
E-mail: vtadmiss@vt.edu
http://www.vt.edu

WASHINGTON, D.C.

Howard University
2400 Sixth Street, NW
Washington, DC 20059
Phone: (202) 806-2700
http://www.howard.edu

WEST VIRGINIA

Bluefield State College
219 Rock Street
Bluefield, WV 24701
Phone: (304) 327-4067
Fax: (304) 325-7747
E-mail: bscadmit@bluefieldstate.edu
http://www.bluefielstate.edu

Concord University
1000 Vermillion Street
Athens, WV 24712
Phone: (304) 384-5248
Fax: (304) 384-9044
E-mail: admissions@concord.edu
http://www.concord.edu

West Virginia State University
Campus Box 197
P.O. Box 1000
Institute, WV 25112
Phone: (304) 766-3032
Fax: (304) 766-4158
E-mail: admissions@wvstateu.edu
http://www.wvstateu.edu

APPENDIX III
TRADE ASSOCIATIONS, UNIONS, AND OTHER ORGANIZATIONS

The following is a listing of trade and professional associations, unions, and organizations discussed in this book. There are also a number of other associations listed that might be of use to you.

The names, addresses, phone numbers, fax numbers, Web addresses, and e-mail addresses are included so that you can get in touch with any of the associations or unions for information.

Many of the organizations have branch offices located throughout the country. Organization headquarters can get you the phone number and address of the closest local branch.

Advertising Club of New York (ACNY)
235 Park Avenue South
New York, NY 10003
Phone: (212) 533-8080
Fax: (212) 533-1929
E-mail: gina@theadvertisingclub.org
http://www.theadvertisingclub.org

Advertising Production Club of New York
276 Bowery
New York, NY 10012
Phone: (212) 334-2018
Fax: (212) 431-5786
E-mail: admin@apc-ny.org
http://www.apc-ny.org

Advertising Research Foundation (ARF)
432 Park Avenue South
New York, NY 10016
Phone: (212) 751-5656
Fax: (212) 319-5265
E-mail: info@thearf.org
http://www.thearf.org

Advertising Women of New York (AWNY)
25 West 45th Street
New York, NY 10036
Phone: (212) 221-7969
Fax: (212) 221-8296
E-mail: awny@awny.org
http://www.awny.org

Aerobics and Fitness Association of America (AFAA)
15250 Ventura Boulevard
Sherman Oaks, CA 91403
Phone: (877) 968-7263
Fax: (818) 990-5468
E-mail: contactafaa@afaa.com
http://www.afaa.com

American Advertising Federation (AAF)
1101 Vermont Avenue NW
Washington, DC 20005
Phone: (202) 898-0089
Fax: (202) 898-0159
E-mail: aaf@aaf.org
http://www.aaf.org

American Association for Adult & Continuing Education
10111 Martin Luther King, Jr. Highway
Bowie, MD 20720
Phone: (301) 459-6261
Fax: (301) 459-6241
E-mail: aaace10@aol.com
http://www.aaace.org

American Association of Advertising Agencies (AAAA)
405 Lexington Avenue
New York, NY 10174
Phone: (212) 682-2500
Fax: (212) 682-8391
E-mail: barbara@aaaa.org
http://www.aaaa.org

American Bartenders' Association (ABA)
20925 Watertown Road
Waukesha, WI 53186
Phone: (800) 935-3232
Fax: (813) 752-2768
E-mail: info@americanbartenders.org
http://www.americanbartenders.org

American Culinary Federation (ACF)
180 Center Place Way
St. Augustine, FL 32095
Phone: (904) 824-4468
Fax: (904) 825-4758
E-mail: acf@acfchefs.net
http://www.acfchefs.org

American Federation of Musicians of the United States and Canada (AFM)
1501 Broadway
New York, NY 10036
Phone: (212) 869-1330
Fax: (212) 764-6134
E-mail: presoffice@afm.org
http://www.afm.org

American Gaming Association (AGA)
1299 Pennsylvania Avenue, NW

Washington, DC 20004
Phone: (202) 552-2675
Fax: (202) 552-2676
E-mail: info@americangaming.org
http://www.americangaming.org

American Hotel & Lodging Association (AH&LA)
1201 New York Avenue, NW
Washington, DC 20005
Phone: (202) 289-3100
Fax: (202) 289-3199
E-mail: infoctr@ahlaonline.org
http://www.ahma.com

American Institute of Baking (AIB)
1213 Bakers Way
P.O. Box 3999
Manhattan, KS 66505
Phone: (785) 537-4750
Fax: (785) 537-1493
E-mail: info@aibonline.org
http://www.aibonline.org

American Institute of Certified Public Accountants (AICPA)
1211 Avenue of the Americas
New York, NY 10036
Phone: (212) 596-6200
Fax: (212) 596-6213
E-mail: center@aicpa.org
http://www.aicpa.org

American Institute of Food and Wine (AIFW)
213-37 39th Avenue
Box 216
Bayside, NY 11361
Phone: (800) 274-2493
Fax: (718) 522-0204
E-mail: info@aiwf.org
http://www.aiwf.org

American Institute of Graphic Arts (AIGA)
164 Fifth Avenue
New York, NY 10010
Phone: (212) 807-1990
Fax: (212) 807-1799
E-mail: comments@aiga.org
http://www.aiga.org

American Marketing Association (AMA)
311 South Wacker Drive
Chicago, IL 60606
Phone: (312) 542-9000
Fax: (312) 542-9001
http://www.marketingpower.com

American Occupational Therapy Association (AOTA)
4720 Montgomery Lane
P.O. Box 31220
Bethesda, MD 20824
Phone: (301) 652-2682
Fax: (301) 652-7711
http://www.aota.org

American Red Cross National Headquarters (ARC)
P.O. Box 37243
Washington, DC 20013
Phone: (202) 303-4498
E-mail: info@usa.redcross.org
http://www.redcross.org

American Society for Training and Development (ASTD)
1640 King Street
P.O. Box 1443
Alexandria, VA 22313
Phone: (703)683-8100
Fax: (703)683-8103
E-mail: publications@astd.org
http://www.astd.org

American Society of Heating, Refrigerating and Air-Conditioning Engineers (ASHRAE)
1791 Tullie Circle, NE
Atlanta, GA 30329
Phone: (404) 636-8400
Fax: (404) 321-5478
http://www.ashrae.org

American Society of Travel Agents (ASTA)
1101 King Street
Alexandria, VA 22314
Phone: (703) 739-2782
Fax: (703) 684-8319
E-mail: askasta@astahq.com
http://www.astanet.com

Arizona Indian Gaming Association (AIGA)
2214 North Central Avenue
Phoenix, AZ 85004
Phone: (602) 307-1570
Fax: (602) 307-1568
http://www.azindiangaming.org

Art Directors Club (ADC)
106 West 29th Street
New York, NY 10001
Phone: (212) 643-1440
Fax: (212) 643-4266
E-mail: info@adcglobal.org
http://www.adcglobal.org

Association for Business Communication (ABC)
P.O. Box 6143
Nacogdoches, TX 75962
Phone: (936) 468-6280
Fax: (936) 468-6281
E-mail: abcjohnson@sfasu.edu
http://www.businesscommunication.org

Association for Women in Communications
3337 Duke Street
Alexandria, VA 22314
Phone: (703) 370-7436
Fax: (703) 370-7437
E-mail: info@womcom.org
http://www.womcom.org

Association of Gaming Equipment Manufacturers (AGEM)
Phone: (702) 812-6932
http://www.agem.org

Australasian Gaming Machine Manufacturers Association (AGMMA)
P.O. Box 420
Spit Junction
Mosman, New South Wales 2088
Australia
Phone: +61 2 99600125
Fax: +61 2 99600124
E-mail: info@agmma.com
http://www.agmma.com

Bartenders & Beverage Local #165
4825 West Nevso Drive
Las Vegas, NV 89103
Phone: (702) 384-7774
Fax: (702) 384-6213
http://www.herelocal165.org

British Casino Association (BCA)
38, Grosvenor Gardens
London SW1W 0EB
United Kingdom
Phone: +44 20 7730 1055
Fax: +44 20 7730 1050
E-mail: enquiries@
   britishcasinoassociation.org.uk
http://www.britishcasinoassociation.
   org.uk

California Nations Indian Gaming Association (CNIGA)
1415 L Street
Sacramento, CA 95814
Phone: (916) 448-8706
Fax: (916) 448-8758
http://www.cniga.com

Career College Association (CCA)
10 G Street NE
Washington, DC 20002
Phone: (202) 336-6700
Fax: (202) 336-6828
E-mail: cca@career.org
http://www.career.org

Casino Chip and Gaming Token Collectors Club (CCCC)
c/o Ralph Myers, Membership
   Officer
P.O. Box 35769
Las Vegas, NV 89133
Phone: (877) 4CC-GTCC
E-mail: membership@ccgtcc.com
http://www.ccgtcc.com

Casino Customer Care
P.O. Box 711
Monticello, NY 12701
Phone: (845) 794-7312

Casino Management Association (CMA)
P.O. Box 14610
Detroit, MI 48214
Phone: (313) 965-9038
Fax: (313) 961-1651

Casino Operators' Association of the UK (COA)
c/o Philip Lowther, General
   Secretary
15 Livesey Street
Sheffield S6 2BL
United Kingdom
Phone: +44 0114 281 6209
Fax: +44 0114 281 6199
E-mail: coa.generalsecretary@
   tiscali.co.uk
http://www.casinooperatorsassocia
   tion.org.uk

Colorado Gaming Association (CGA)
225 East 16th Avenue
Suite 260
Denver, CO 80203
Phone: (303) 237-5480
Fax: (303) 805-4475
E-mail: melrose53@prodigy.net
http://www.coloradogaming.com

Computer and Communications Industry Association (CCIA)
666 11th Street, NW
Washington, DC 20001
Phone: (202) 783-0070
Fax: (202) 783-0534
E-mail: ccia@ccianet.org
http://www.ccianet.org

Communications Workers of America (CWA)
501 3rd Street, NW
Washington, DC 20001
Phone: (202) 434-1100
Fax: (202) 434-1279
E-mail: cwaweb@cwa-union.org
http://www.cwa-union.org

Council on Hotel, Restaurant and Institutional Education
International Council on Hotel,
   Restaurant & Institutional
   Education

2810 North Parham Road
Richmond, VA 23294
Phone: (804) 346-4800
Fax: (804) 346-5009
E-mail: webmaster@chrie.org
http://www.chrie.org

Culinary Workers Local #226
1630 South Commerce Street
Las Vegas, NV 89102
Phone: (702) 385-2131
Fax: (702) 384-0845
E-mail: info@culinaryunion226.org

Direct Marketing Association Inc.
1120 Avenue of the Americas
New York, NY 10036
Phone: (212) 768-7277
Fax: (212) 302-6714
E-mail: customerservice@the-dma.
   org
http://www.the-dma.org

Educational Institute of the American Hotel & Lodging Association
800 North Magnolia Avenue
Orlando, FL 32803
Phone: (407) 999-8100
Fax: (407) 236-7848
E-mail: info@ei-ahla.org
http://www.ei-ahla.org

Educational Foundation of the National Restaurant Association
175 West Jackson Boulevard
Chicago, IL 60604
Phone: (312) 715-1010
Fax: (312) 583-9841
E-mail: info@nraef.org
http://www.nraef.org

European Gaming and Amusement Federation (EUROMAT)
Chaussee de Wavre 214 D
B-1050 Brussels
Belgium
Phone: +32 2 6261993
Fax: +32 2 6269501
E-mail: secretariat@euromat.org
http://www.euromat.org

Gaming Standards Association (GSA)
39355 California Street
Fremont, CA 94538
Phone: (510) 774-4007
Fax: (510) 608-5917
E-mail: info@gamingstandards.com
http://www.gamingstandards.com

Graphic Artists Guild (GAG)
90 John Street
New York, NY 10038
Phone: (212) 791-3400
Fax: (212) 791-0333
E-mail: admin@gag.org
http://www.gag.org

Hotel Brokers International (HBI)
1420 North West Vivion Road
Kansas City, MO 64118
Phone: (816) 505-4315
Fax: (816) 505-4319
E-mail: info@
    hotelbrokersinternational.com
http://www.
    hotelbrokersinternational.com

Hotel Sales and Marketing Association International (HSMAI)
1760 Old Meadow Road
McLean, VA 22102
Phone: (703) 506-3280
Fax: (703) 506-3266
E-mail: info@hsmai.org
http://www.hsmai.org

IDEA Health and Fitness Association
10455 Pacific Center Court
San Diego, CA 92121
Phone: (858) 535-8979
Fax: (858) 535-8234
E-mail: contact@ideafit.com
http://www.ideafit.com

Institute for Certification of Computing Professionals
2350 East Devon Avenue
Des Plaines, IL 60018
Phone: (847) 299-4227
Fax: (847) 299-4280

E-mail: office@iccp.org
http://www.iccp.org

Institute of Certified Travel Agents (ICTA)
148 Linden Street
Wellesley, MA 02482
Phone: (781) 237-0280
Fax: (781) 237-3860
E-mail: info@thetravelinstitute.
    com
http://www.thetravelinstitute.com

Institute of Internal Auditors (IIA)
247 Maitland Avenue
Altamonte Springs, FL 32701
Phone: (407)937-1100
Fax: (407)937-1101
E-mail: iia@theiia.org
http://www.theiia.org

Interactive Gaming Council (IGC)
175-2906 West Broadway
Vancouver, BC V6K 2G8
Canada
Phone: (604) 732-3833
Fax: (604) 732-3866
E-mail: executive.director@
    igcouncil.org
http://www.igcouncil.org

Interactive Gaming, Gambling and Betting Association (IGGBA)
Regency House
1-4 Warwick Street
London W1B 5LT
United Kingdom
Phone: +44 207 4794040
E-mail: chawkswood@rga.eu.com
http://www.argo.org.uk

International Alliance of Theatrical Stage Employees (IATSE)
1430 Broadway
New York, NY 10018
Phone: (212) 730-1770
Fax: (212) 730-7809
E-mail: organizing@iatse-intl.org
http://www.iatse-intl.org

International Association of Administrative Professionals (IAAP)
10502 NW Ambassador Drive
P.O. Box 20404
Kansas City, MO 64195
Phone: (816) 891-6600
Fax: (816) 891-9118
E-mail: rstroud@iaap-hq.org
http://www.iaap-hq.org

International Association of Business Communicators (IABC)
1 Hallidie Plaza
San Francisco, CA 94102
Phone: (415) 544-4700
Fax: (415) 544-4747
E-mail: service_centre@iabc.com
http://www.iabc.com

International Association for Computer Information Systems (IACIS)
c/o Dr. G. Daryl Nord, Managing Director
2200 College of Business
Oklahoma State University
Stillwater, OK 74078
Phone: (405) 744-8632
Fax: (405) 744-5180
E-mail: dnord@okstate.edu
http://www.iacis.org

International Association of Culinary Professionals (IACP)
304 West Liberty Street
Louisville, KY 40202
Phone: (502) 581-9786
Fax: (502) 589-3602
E-mail: iacp@hqtrs.com
http://www.iacp.com

International Brotherhood of Electrical Workers (IBEW)
900 Seventh Street, NW
Washington, DC 20001
Phone: (202) 833-7000
Fax: (202) 728-7676
E-mail: journal@ibew.org
http://www.ibew.org

International Executive Housekeepers Association (IEHA)
1001 Eastwind Drive
Westerville, OH 43081
Phone: (614) 895-7166
Fax: (614) 895-1248
E-mail: excel@ieha.org
http://www.ieha.org

International Foundation of Employee Benefit Plans (IFEBP)
18700 West Bluemound Road
P.O. Box 69
Brookfield, WI 53008
Phone: (262) 786-6710
Fax: (262) 786-8670
E-mail: ebinfo@ifebp.org,
    research@ifebp.org
http://www.ifebp.org

International Gaming, Inc.
25 Johnson Avenue
P.O. Box 73
Thornhill, ON L3T 3N1
Canada
Phone: (905) 731-5457
Fax: (905) 731-5457
E-mail: kusyszyn@yorku.ca

International Gaming Institute
Stan Fulton Building
4505 Maryland Parkway
Box 456037
Las Vegas, NV 89154
Phone: (702) 895-3903
Fax: (702) 895-1135
E-mail: epolivka@ccmail.nevada.edu

International Simulation and Gaming Association (ISAGA)
c/o John F. Lobuts
George Washington University

School of Business and Public Management
Monroe Hall
Washington, DC 20052
Phone: (202) 994-6918
Fax: (202) 994-4930
E-mail: lobuts@gwu.edu
http://www.isaga.info

Iowa Gaming Association (IGA)
4401 Westown Parkway
Three Fountains Complex
West Des Moines, IA 50266
Phone: (515) 267-9200
Fax: (515) 267-9300
E-mail: wese@iowagaming.org
http://www.iowagaming.org

Mail Advertising Service Association International (MASAI)
1421 Prince Street
Alexandria, VA 22314
Phone: (703) 836-9200
Fax: (703) 548-8204
E-mail: mfsa-mail@mfsanet.org
http://www.mfsanet.org

Marketing Research Association (MRA)
110 National Drive
Glastonbury, CT 06033
Phone: (860) 682-1000
Fax: (860) 682-1010
E-mail: email@mra-net.org
http://www.mra-net.org

Missouri Gaming Association
E-mail: contact@missouricasinos.org
http://www.missouricasinos.org

Missouri Riverboat Gaming Association
6609 Clayton Road
St. Louis, MO 63117
Phone: (314) 721-7704

Montana Gaming Group
c/o Rhonda Carpenter
3208 2nd Avenue
Great Falls, MT 59405
E-mail: info@
    montanagaminggroup.com
http://www.montanagaminggroup.
    com

National Association of Personnel Services (NAPS)
131 Prominence Lane
Suite 130
Dawsonville, GA 30534

Phone: (706) 531-0060
Fax: (866) 739-4750
E-mail: conrad.taylor@recruitinglife.
    com
http://www.recruitinglife.com

National Cosmetology Association (NCA)
401 North Michigan Avenue
Chicago, IL 60611
Phone: (312) 527-6765
Fax: (312) 464-6118
E-mail: nca1@ncacares.org
http://www.ncacares.org

National Indian Gaming Association (NIGA)
224 Second Street, SE
Washington, DC 20003
Phone: (202) 546-7711
Fax: (202) 546-1755
E-mail: estevens@indiangaming.org
http://www.indiangaming.org

National Indian Gaming Commission
1441 L Street, NW
Washington, DC 20005
Phone: (202) 632-7003
Fax: (202) 632-7066
E-mail: info@nigc.gov
http://www.nigc.gov

National Restaurant Association (NRA)
1200 17th Street, NW
Washington, DC 20036
Phone: (202) 331-5900
Fax: (202) 331-2429
http://www.restaurant.org

National Restaurant Association Educational Foundation (NRAEF)
175 West Jackson Boulevard
Chicago, IL 60604
Phone: (312) 715-1010
E-mail: info@nraef.org
http://www.nraef.org

National Retail Federation (NRF)
325 Seventh Street, NW

Washington, DC 20004
Phone: (202)783-7971
Fax: (202)737-2849
E-mail: bookInquiries@nrf.com
http://www.nrf.com

National Safety Council (NSC)
1121 Spring Lake Drive
Itasca, IL 60143
Phone: (630) 285-1121
Fax: (630) 285-1315
E-mail: info@nsc.org
http://www.nsc.org

National Society of Accountants (NSA)
1010 North Fairfax Street
Alexandria, VA 22314
Phone: (703) 549-6400
Fax: (703) 549-2984
E-mail: members@nsacct.org
http://www.nsacct.org

National Society of Professional Engineers (NSPE)
1420 King Street
Alexandria, VA 22314
Phone: (703) 684-2800
Fax: (703) 836-4875
E-mail: memserv@nspe.org
http://www.nspe.org

North American Gaming Regulators Association (NAGRA)
1000 Westgate Drive
St. Paul, MN 55114
Phone: (651) 203-7244
Fax: (651) 290-2266
E-mail: info@nagra.org
http://www.nagra.org

North American Simulation and Gaming Association (NASAGA)
P.O. Box 78636
Indianapolis, IN 46278
Phone: (317) 387-1424
Fax: (317) 387-1921
E-mail: info@nasaga.org
http://www.nasaga.org

One Club for Art and Copy (advertising and design)
21 East 26th Street
New York, NY 10010
Phone: (212) 979-1900
Fax: (212) 979-5006
E-mail: membership@oneclub.org
http://www.oneclub.org

Passenger Vessel Association (PVA)
901 North Pitt Street
Alexandria, VA 22314
Phone: (703) 518-5005
Fax: (703) 518-5151
E-mail: pvainfo@passengervessel.com
http://www.passengervessel.com

Promotion Marketing Association of America (PMAA)
257 Park Avenue
New York, NY 10010
Phone: (212) 420-1100
Fax: (212) 533-7622
E-mail: pma@pmalink.org
http://www.pmalink.org

Public Relations Society of America (PRSA)
33 Maiden Lane
New York, NY 10038
Phone: (212) 460-1400
Fax: (212) 995-0757
E-mail: exec@prsa.org
http://www.prsa.org

Refrigeration Service Engineers Society (RSES)
1666 Rand Road
Des Plaines, IL 60016
Phone: (847) 297-6464
Fax: (847) 297-5038
E-mail: general@rses.org
http://www.rses.org

Sales and Marketing Executive International (SMEI)
P.O. Box 1390
Sumas, WA 98295
Phone: (312) 893-0751
Fax: (604) 855-0165
http://www.smei.org

Society for Technical Communications (STC)
901 North Stuart Street
Arlington, VA 22203
Phone: (703) 522-4114
Fax: (703) 522-2075
E-mail: stc@stc.org
http://www.stc.org/

Society of Actuaries (SOA)
475 North Martingale Road
Schaumburg, IL 60173
Phone: (847) 706-3500
Fax: (847) 706-3599
E-mail: pfiglewicz@soa.org
http://www.soa.org

Society of Human Resources Management (SHRM)
1800 Duke Street
Alexandria, VA 22314
Phone: (703) 548-3440
Fax: (703) 535-6490
E-mail: forum@shrm.org
http://www.shrm.org

Society of Illustrators (SI)
128 East 63rd Street
New York, NY 10021
Phone: (212) 838-2560
Fax: (212) 838-2561
E-mail: info@societyillustrators.org
http://www.societyillustrators.org

Society of Wine Educators (SWE)
1212 New York Avenue, NW
Washington, DC 20005
Phone: (202) 347-5677
Fax: (202) 347-5667
E-mail: vintage@erols.com
http://www.societyofwineeducators.org

Society of Women Engineers (SWE)
230 East Ohio Street
Chicago, IL 60611
Phone: (312) 596-5223
Fax: (312) 596-5252
E-mail: hq@swe.org
http://www.swe.org

Southern Nevada Hotel
Concierge Association
http://www.snhca.com/home

Teamsters Local 995
(represents people working
in the hotel casino industry
and professional groups in
Las Vegas)
300 Shadow Lane
Las Vegas, NV 89106
Phone: (702) 385-0995
http://teamsters995.com

United Food and Commercial
Workers International
Union (UPCW)
1775 K Street, NW
Washington, DC 20006

Phone: (202) 223-3111
Fax: (202) 466-1562
E-mail: press@ufcw.org
http://www.ufcw.org

United Scenic Artists (USA)
29 West 38th Street
New York, NY 10018
Phone: (212) 581-0300
Fax: (212) 977-2011
E-mail: usamail@usa829.org
http://www.usa829.org

United States Department of
Labor (USDL)
200 Constitution Avenue, NW
Washington, DC 20210
Phone: (866) 4USA-DOL
http://www.dol.gov

United States Office of
Personnel Management and
the Veterans Administration
1900 E Street, NW
Washington, DC 20415
Phone: (202) 606-1800
http://www.opm.gov/veterans/html/
vetsinfo.asp

Veterans Administration
http://www.va.gov

World at Work
14040 North Northsight Boulevard
Scottsdale, AZ 85260
Phone: (877) 951-9191
http://www.worldatwork.org

APPENDIX IV
DIRECTORY OF AMERICAN CASINOS

The following is a directory of American casinos. It includes those that are land-based, floating, and docked riverboats, daily gaming cruises sailing territorial waters, and Indian gaming facilities.

Names, addresses, phone numbers, and Web addresses are included. Casinos are listed alphabetically by state. In states where there are a large number of cities or locations hosting casinos, they have been separated within the state by metropolitan area.

ARIZONA

Apache Gold Casino
P.O. Box 1210
San Carlos, AZ 85550
Phone: (928) 475-7800
http://www.apachegoldcasinoresort.com

Blue Water Casino
11300 Resort Drive
Parker, AZ 85344
Phone: (928) 669-7777
http://www.bluewaterfun.com

Bucky's Casino & Resort
530 East Merritt Street
Prescott, AZ 86301
Phone: (928) 776-1666
http://www.buckyscasino.com

Casino Arizona 101 & Indian Bend
9700 East Indian Bend
Scottsdale, AZ 85256
Phone: (480) 850-7777
http://www.casinoaz.com

Casino Arizona 101 & McKellips
524 North 92nd Street
Scottsdale, AZ 85256
Phone: (480) 850-7777
http://www.casinoaz.com

Casino Del Sol
5655 West Valencia Boulevard
Tucson, AZ 85757
Phone: (520) 883-1700
http://www.casinodelsol.com

Casino of the Sun
7406 South Camino De Oeste
Tucson, AZ 85757
Phone: (520) 883-1700
http://www.casinosun.com

Cliff Castle Casino & Hotel Lodge
555 Middle Verde Road
Camp Verde, AZ 86322
Phone: (928) 567-7999
http://www.cliffcastle.net

Cocopah Casino & Bingo
15136 South Avenue B
Somerton, AZ 85350
Phone: (928) 726-8066
http://www.cocopahresort.com

Desert Diamond Casino
1100 West Pima Mine Road
Sahuarita, AZ 85629
Phone: (520) 294-7777
http://www.desertdiamondcasino.com

Desert Diamond Casino–Nogales
7350 South Nogales Highway
Tucson, AZ 85706
Phone: (520) 294-7777
http://www.desertdiamondcasino.com

Fort McDowell Casino
P.O. Box 18359
Fountain Hills, AZ 85269
Phone: (602) 837-1424
http://www.fortmcdowellcasino.com

Gila River Casino–Lone Butte
1200 South 56th Street
Chandler, AZ 85226
Phone: (520) 796-7777
http://www.wingilariver.com

Gila River Casino–Vee Quiva
6443 North Komatke Lane
Laveen, AZ 85339
Phone: (520) 796-7777
http://www.wingilariver.com

Gila River Casino–Wild Horse
5512 West Wild Horse Pass
Chandler, AZ 85226
Phone: (520) 796-7727
http://www.wingilariver.com

Golden Hasan Casino
P.O. Box 10
Ajo, AZ 85321
Phone: (520) 362-2746
http://www.desertdiamondcasino.com

Harrah's Ak-Chin Casino Resort
15406 Maricopa Road
Maricopa, AZ 85239
Phone: (480) 802-5000
http://www.harrahs.com

Hon-Dah Resort Casino
777 Highway 260
Pinetop, AZ 85935

Phone: (928) 369-0299
http://www.hon-dah.com

Mazatzal Casino
P.O. Box 1820
Highway 87
Payson, AZ 85547
Phone: (928) 474-6044
http://www.777play.com

Mojave Crossing Casino
101 Aztec Road
Fort Mojave, AZ 86426
Phone: (928) 330-2555

Paradise Casino Arizona
450 Quechan Drive
Yuma, AZ 85364
Phone: (760) 572-7777
http://www.paradise-casinos.com

Spirit Mountain Casino
8555 South Highway 95
Mountain Valley, AZ 86440
Phone: (928) 346-2000

Yavapai Casino
1501 East Highway 69
Prescott, AZ 86301
Phone: (928) 445-5767
http://www.buckyscasino.com

ARKANSAS

Oaklawn Jockey Club
2705 Central Avenue
Hot Springs, AR 71902
Phone: (302) 674-4600
http://www.oaklawn.com

Southland Park Gaming & Racing
1550 North Ingram Boulevard
West Memphis, AR 72301
Phone: (870) 735-3670
http://www.southlandgreyhound.com

CALIFORNIA

Agua Caliente Casino
32-250 Bob Hope Drive
Ranco Mirage, CA 92270

Phone: (760) 321-2000
http://www.hotwatercasino.com

Augustine Casino
84001 Avenue 54
Coachella, CA 92236
Phone: (760) 391-9500
http://www.augustinecasino.com

Barona Valley Ranch Resort and Casino
1932 Wildcat Canyon Road
Lakeside, CA 92040
Phone: (619) 443-2300
http://www.barona.com

Bear River Casino
11 Bear Paws Way
Loleta, CA 95551
Phone: (707) 733-9644
http://www.bearrivercasino.com

Black Bart Casino
100 KWI Place
Willits, CA 95490
Phone: (707) 459-7330

Black Oak Casino
19400 Tuolumne Road North
Tuolumne, CA 94379
Phone: (209) 928-9300
http://www.blackoakcasino.com

Blue Lake Casino
777 Casino Way
Blue Lake, CA 95525
Phone: (707) 668-9770
http://www.bluelakecasino.com

Cache Creek Indian Bingo & Casino
14455 Highway 16
Brooks, CA 95606
Phone: (530) 796-3118
http://www.cachecreek.com

Cahuilla Creek Casino
52702 Highway 371
Anza, CA 92539
Phone: (951)763-1200
http://www.thefriendliestcasino.com

Casino Pauma
777 Pauma Revervation Raod
Pauma Valley, CA 92061
Phone: (760) 742-2177
http://www.casinopauma.com

Cherae Heights Casino
P.O. Box 635
Trinidad, CA 95570
Phone: (707) 677-3611
http://www.cheraeheightscasino.com

Chicken Ranch Bingo
1629 Chicken Ranch Road
Jamestown, CA 95327
Phone: (209) 984-3000

Chukchansi Gold Resort & Casino
711 Lucky Lane
Coarsegold, CA 93614
Phone: (559) 692-5200
http://www.chukchansigold.com

Chumash Casino Resort
3400 East Highway 246
Santa Ynez, CA 93460
Phone: (800) 248-6274
http://www.chumashcasino.com

Colusa Casino Resort & Bingo
3770 Highway 45
Colusa, CA 95932
Phone: (530) 458-8844
http://www.colusacasino.com

Coyote Valley Shodakai Casino
7751 North State Street
Redwood Valley, CA 95470
Phone: (707) 485-0700
http://www.coyotevalleycasino.com

Desert Rose Casino
901 County Road 56
Alturas, CA 96101
Phone: (530) 233-3141

Diamond Mountain Casino
900 Skyline Drive
Susanville, CA 96130
Phone: (530) 252-1100
http://www.diamondmountaincasino.com

Eagle Mountain Casino
P.O. Box 1659
Porterville, California 93258
Phone: (559) 788-6220
http://www.eaglemtncasino.com

Elk Valley Casino
2500 Rowland Hill Road
Crescent City, CA 95531
Phone: (707) 464-1020
http://www.elkvalleycasino.com

Fantasy Springs Casino
82-245 Indio Springs Drive
Indio, CA 92203
Phone: (760) 342-5000
http://www.fantasyspringsresort.com

Feather Falls Casino
3 Alverda Drive
Oroville, CA 95966
Phone: (530) 533-3885
http://www.featherfallscasino.com

Gold Country Casino
3030 Olive Highway
Oroville, CA 95966
Phone: (530) 538-4560
http://www.goldcountrycasino.com

Golden Acorn Casino and Travel Center
1800 Golden Acorn Way
Campo, CA 91906
Phone: (619) 938-6000
http://www.goldenacorncasino.com

Harrah's Rincon Casino & Resort
33750 Valley Center Road
Valley Center, CA 92082
Phone: (760) 751-3100
http://www.harrahs.com

Havasu Landing Resort & Casino
5 Main Street
Havasu Lake, CA 92363
Phone: (760) 858-4593
http://www.havasulanding.com

Hopland Sho-Ka-Wah Casino
13101 Nakomis Road

Hopland, CA 95449
Phone: (707) 744-1395
http://www.shokawah.com

Jackson Rancheria Casino & Hotel
12222 New York Ranch Road
Jackson, CA 95642
Phone: (209) 223-1677
http://www.jacksoncasino.com

Konocti Vista Casino Resort & Marina
2755 Mission Rancheria Road
Lakeport, CA 95453
Phone: (707) 262-1900
http://www.kvcasino.com

La Posta Casino
777 Crestwood Road
Boulevard, CA 91905
Phone: (619) 824-4100
http://www.lapostacasino.com

Lucky Bear Casino
P.O. Box 729
Hoopa, CA 95546
Phone: (530) 625-5198
http://luckybearcasinoandhotel.com

Lucky 7 Casino
350 North Indian Road
Smith River, CA 95567
Phone: (707) 487-7777
http://www.lucky7casino.com

Mono Wind Casino
37302 Rancheria Lane
Auberry, CA 93602
Phone: (559) 855-4350
http://www.monowind.com

Morongo Casino
49750 Seminole Drive
Cabazon, CA 92230
Phone: (951) 849-3080
http://www.morongocasinoresort.com

Paiute Palace Casino
2742 North Sierra Highway
Bishop, CA 93514

Phone: (760) 873-4150
http://www.paiutepalace.com

Pala Casino Spa and Resort
11154 Highway 76
Pala, CA 92059
Phone: (760) 510-5100
http://www.palacasino.com

Palace Indian Gaming Center
17225 Jersey Avenue
Lemoore, CA 93245
Phone: (559) 924-7751
http://www.thepalace.net

Paradise Casino
450 Quechan Drive
Fort Yuma, CA 92283
Phone: (760) 572-7777
http://www.paradise-casinos.com

Pechanga Resort and Casino
45000 Pechanga Parkway
Temecula, CA 92592
Phone: (951) 693-1819
http://www.pechanga.com

Pit River Casino
20265 Tamarack Avenue
Burney, CA 96013
Phone: (530) 335-2334
http://www.pitrivercasino.com

Red Earth Casino
3089 North Niver Road
Salton City, CA 92274
Phone: (760) 395-1800

Red Fox Casino & Bingo
200 Cahto Drive
Laytonville, CA 95454
Phone: (707) 984-6800

River Rock Casino
3250 Highway 128 East
Geyserville, CA 95441
Phone: (707) 857-2777
http://www.riverrockcasino.com

Robinson Rancheria Resort & Casino
1545 East Highway 20
Nice, CA 95464

Phone: (707) 275-9000
http://www.robinsonrancheria.biz

Rolling Hills Casino
2655 Barham Avenue
Corning, CA 96021
Phone: (530) 528-3500
http://www.rollinghillscasino.com

San Manuel Indian Bingo & Casino
5795 North Victoria Avenue
Highland, CA 92346
Phone: (909) 864-5050
http://www.sanmanuel.com

Santa Ysabel Resort and Casino
25575 Highway 79
Ysabel, CA 92070
Phone: (760) 782-0909
http://www.
    santaysabelresortandcasino.com

Soboba Casino
23333 Soboba Road
San Jacinto, CA 92583
Phone: (909) 654-2993
http://ww.soboba.net

Spa Resort Casino
140 North Indian Canyon Drive
Palm Springs, CA 92262
Phone: (760) 323-5865
http://www.sparesortcasino.com

Spotlight 29 Casino
46200 Harrison Place
Coachella, CA 92236
Phone: (760) 775-5566
http://www.spotlight29.com

Sycuan Resort & Casino
5469 Casino Way
El Cajon, CA 92019
Phone: (619) 445-6002
http://www.sycuan.com

Table Mountain Casino & Bingo
8184 Table Mountain Road
Friant, CA 93626
Phone: (559) 822-2485

Thunder Valley Casino
1200 Athens Avenue
Lincoln, CA 95648
Phone: (916) 408-777
http://www.thundervalleyresort.
    com

Twin Pine Casino
22223 Highway 29 at Rancheria
    Road
Middletown, CA 94561
Phone: (707) 987-0197
http://www.twinpine.com

COLORADO

BLACK HAWK

Ameristar Black Hawk
111 Richman Street
Black Hawk, CO 80422
Phone: (720) 946-4000
http://www.ameristar.com/
    blackhawk

Black Hawk Station
141 Gregory Street
Black Hawk, CO 80422
Phone: (303) 582-5582

Bull Durham Saloon & Casino
110 Main Street
Black Hawk, CO 80422
Phone: (303) 582-0810
http://www.bulldurhamcasino.com

Bullwhackers Casino
101 Gregory Street
Black Hawk, CO 80422
Phone: (303) 271-2500
http://www.bullwhackers.com

Canyon Casino
31 Main Street
Black Hawk, CO 80422
Phone: (303) 777-1111
http://www.canyoncasino.com

Colorado Central Station
340 Main Street
Black Hawk, CO 80422
Phone: (303) 582-3000
http://www.coloradocentralstation.
    com

Fitzgeralds Casino
101 Main Street
Black Hawk, CO 80422
Phone: (303) 582-6162
http://www.fitzgeraldsbh.com

Gilpin Hotel Casino
111 Main Street
Black Hawk, CO 80422
Phone: (303) 582-1133
http://www.thegilpincasino.com

Golden Gates Casino
261 Main Street
Black Hawk, CO 80422
Phone: (303) 582-1650
http://www.themardigrascasino.
    com

Eureka! Casino
211 Gregory Street
Black Hawk, CO 80422
Phone: (303) 582-1040

Isle of Capri Casino–Black Hawk
401 Main Street
Black Hawk, CO 80422
Phone: (303) 998-7777
http://www.isleofcapricasino.com

The Lodge Casino at Black Hawk
240 Main Street
Black Hawk, CO 80422
Phone: (303) 582-1771
http://www.thelodgecasino.com

Mardi Gras Casino
333 Main Street
Black Hawk, CO 80422
Phone: (303) 582-5600
http://www.themardigrascasino.
    com

Red Dolly Casino
530 Gregory Street
Black Hawk, CO 80422
Phone: (303) 582-1100
http://reddollycasino.net

Riviera Black Hawk Casino
444 Main Street

Black Hawk, CO 80422
Phone: (303) 582-1000
http://www.rivierablackhawk.com

Silver Hawk
100 Chase Street
Black Hawk, CO 80422
Phone: (303) 271-2500
http://www.bullwhackers.com

Wild Card Saloon & Casion
112 Main Street
Black Hawk, CO 80422
Phone: (303) 582-3412

CENTRAL CITY

Century Casino & Hotel
102 Main Street
Central City, CO 80427
Phone: (303) 582-5050
http://www.centurycasinos.com

Doc Holiday Casino
1010 Main Street
Central City, CO 80427
Phone: (303) 582-1400

Dostal Alley Saloon & Gaming Emporium
1 Dostal Alley
Central City, CO 80427
Phone: (303) 582-1610

Famous Bonanza/Easy Street
107 Main Street
Central City, CO 80427
Phone: (303) 582-5914
http://www.famousbonanza.com

Fortune Valley Hotel & Casino
321 Gregory Street
Central City, CO 80427
Phone: (303) 582-0800
http://www.fortunevalleycasino.com

CRIPPLE CREEK

Black Diamond Casino
425 East Bennett Avenue
Cripple Creek, CO 80813
Phone: (719) 689-2898

Brass Ass Casino
264 East Bennett Avenue

Cripple Creek, CO 80813
Phone: (719) 689-2104
http://www.triplecrowncasinos.com

Bronco Billy's Casino
233 East Bennett Avenue
Cripple Creek, CO 80813
Phone: (719) 689-2142
http://www.broncobillycasino.com

Colorado Grande Gaming Parlor
300 East Bennett Avenue
Cripple Creek, CO 80813
Phone: (719) 689-3517
http://www.coloradogrande.com

Creeker's Casino
274 East Bennett Avenue
Cripple Creek, CO 80813
Phone: (719) 689-3239
http://www.creekerscasino.com

Double Eagle Hotel & Casino
442 East Bennett Avenue
Cripple Creek, CO 80813
Phone: (719) 689-5000
http://www.decasino.com

Gold Rush Hotel & Casino
209 East Bennett Avenue
Cripple Creek, CO 80813
Phone: (719) 689-2646
http://www.grushcasino.com

Imperial Hotel & Casino
123 North Third Street
Cripple Creek, CO 80813
Phone: (719) 689-2922
http://www.imperialcasinohotel.com

Johnny Nolon's Casino
301 East Bennett Avenue
Cripple Creek, CO 80813
Phone: (719) 689-2080
http://www.johnnynolons.com

J. P. McGill's Hotel & Casino
232 East Bennett Avenue
Cripple Creek, CO 80813
Phone: (719) 689-2446
http://www.triplecrowncasinos.com

Midnight Rose Hotel & Casino
256 East Bennett Avenue

Cripple Creek, CO 80813
Phone: (719) 689-2864
http://www.triplecrowncasinos.com

Uncle Sam's Casino
251 East Bennett Avenue
Cripple Creek, CO 80813
Phone: (719) 689-2222
http://www.grushcasino.com

Wild Horse Casino
353 Myers Avenue
Cripple Creek, CO 80813
Phone: (719) 687-7777
http://www.thewildhorsecasino.com

Womack/Legens Hotel & Casino
200-220 East Bennett Avenue
Cripple Creek, CO 80813
Phone: (719) 689-0333
http://www.womackscasino.com

IGNACIO

Sky Ute Casino and Lodge
14826 Highway 172 North
Ignacio, CO 81137
Phone: (970) 563-3000
http://www.skyutecasino.com

TOWAOC

Ute Mountain Casino & RV Park
3 Weeminuche Drive
P.O. Drawer V
Towaoc, CO 81334
Phone: (970) 565-8800
http://www.utemountaincasino.com

CONNECTICUT

Foxwoods Resort Casino
Route 2
Mashantucket, CT 06338
Phone: (860) 312-3000
http://www.foxwoods.com

MGM Grand at Foxwoods
240 MGM Grand Drive
P.O. Box 3777
Mashantucket, CT 06338
Phone: (866) 436-9562
http://www.mgmatfoxwoods.com

Mohegan Sun Casino
1 Mohegan Sun Boulevard
Uncasville, CT 06382
http://www.mohegansun.com

DELAWARE

Delaware Park Racetrack & Slots
777 Delaware Park Boulevard
Wilmington, DE 19804
Phone: (302) 994-2521
http://www.delpark.com

Dover Downs Slots
1131 North DuPont Highway
Dover, DE 19901
Phone: (302) 674-4600
http://www.doverdowns.com

Midway Slots & Simulcast
Delaware State Fairgrounds
U.S. 13 South
Harrington, DE 19952
Phone: (302) 398-4920
http://www.midwayslots.com

FLORIDA

CAPE CANAVERAL AREA

Sterling Casino Lines
Terminal B
Cape Canaveral, FL 32920
Phone: (321) 783-2212
http://www.sterlingcasinoslines.com

SunCruz Casino–Port Canaveral
610 Glen Cheek Drive
Cape Canaveral, FL 32920
Phone: (321) 799-3511
http://www.suncruzcasino.com

CLEWISTON

Big Cypress Casino
30013 Josie Billie Highway
Clewiston, FL 33440
Phone: (863) 983-7245

DAYTONA

SunCruz Casino–Daytona
4880 Front Street

Ponce Inlet, FL 32127
Phone: (386) 322-9600
http://www.suncruzcasino.com

FORT LAUDERDALE

SeaEscape
3045 North Federal Highway
Fort Lauderdale, FL 33306
Phone: (954) 453-2200
http://www.seaescape.com

FORT MYERS BEACH

Big "M" Casino
450 Harbor Court
Fort Myers Beach, FL 33931
Phone: (239) 765-7529
http://www.bigcasino.com

HOLLYWOOD

Hollywood Seminole Gaming
41 North State Road 7
Hollywood, FL 33021
Phone: (954) 961-3220
http://ww.seminolehollywoodcasino.com

Seminole Hard Rock Hotel & Casino–Hollywood
1 Seminole Way
Hollywood, FL 33314
Phone: (954) 237-7625
http://www.seminolehardrockhollywood.com

IMMOKALEE

Seminole Casino Immokalee
506 South First Street
Immokalee, FL 33934
Phone: (941) 658-1313
http://www.theseminolecasino.com

JACKSONVILLE

SunCruz Casino–Jacksonville
4378 Ocean Street
Mayport, FL 32233
Phone: (904) 249-9300
http://www.suncruzcasino.com

KEY LARGO

SunCruz Casino–Key Largo
99701 Oversees Highway
Key Largo, FL 33037
Phone: (305) 451-0000
http://www.suncruzcasino.com

MADEIRA BEACH

Treasure Island Casino Cruz
150 John's Pass Boardwalk Place
Madeira Beach, FL 3370
Phone: (727) 399-9465
http://www.treasureislandcasinocruz.com

MIAMI AND MIAMI BEACH

Aquasino South Beach
390 Alton Road
Suite B
Miami Beach, FL 33139
Phone: (305) 532-0021
http://www.aquasinosouthbeach.com

Horizon's Edge Casino Cruises
200 North Biscayne Boulevard
Miami, FL 33131
Phone: (305) 523-2270
http://www.horizonsedge.com

Miccosukee Resort and Gaming
500 South West 177th Avenue
Miami, FL 33194
Phone: (305) 222-4600
http://www.miccosukee.com

OKEECHOBEE

Brighton Seminole Bingo and Casino
17735 Reservation Road
Okeechobee, FL 34974
Phone: (863) 467-9998
http://www.seminolecasinobrighton.com

PALM BEACH

Palm Beach Princess
One East 11th Street
Riviera Beach, FL 33404

Phone: (561) 845-2101
http://www.pbcasino.com

SunCruz Casino–Palm Beach
One East 11th Street
Riviera Beach, FL 33404
Phone: (561) 842-1889
http://www.suncruzcasino.com

PORT RICHEY

SunCruz Casino–Port Richey
7917 Bayview Street
Port Richey, FL 34668
Phone: (727) 848-3423
http://www.portricheycasino.com

ST. PETERSBURG

Casino Royale
151 107th Avenue
Suite F
Treasure Island, FL 33706
Phone: (727) 360-5900
http://www.casinoroyale21.com

Seminole Casino Coconut Creek
5550 Northwest 40th Street
Coconut Creek, FL 33073
Phone: (954) 977-6700
http://www.seminolecoconutcreek.
com

TAMPA

Seminole Hard Rock Hotel & Casino–Tampa
5223 North Orient Road
Tampa, FL 33610
Phone: (813) 627-7623
http://www.hardrockhotelcasino
tampa.com

GEORGIA

Emerald Princess II Casino
1 Gisco Point Drive
Brunswick, GA 31523
Phone: (912) 265-3558

Diamond Casino
8010 U.S. Highway 90 East
Wilmington Island

Savannah, GA 31410
Phone: (912) 897-3005
http://www.
diamondcasinosavannah.com

IDAHO

Bannock Peak Casino
1707 West Country Road
Pocatello, ID 83204
Phone: (208) 235-1308
http://www.sho-ban.com

Clearwater River Casino
17500 Nez Perce Road
Lewiston, ID 83501
Phone: (208) 746-5733
http://www.crcasino.com

Coeur D'Alene Casino Resort Hotel
U.S. Highway 95
P.O. Box 236
Worley, ID 83876
Phone: (208) 686-5106
http://www.cdacasino.com

Fort Hall Casino
P.O. Box 868
Hall, ID 83203
Phone: (208) 237-8778
http://www.forthallcasino.com

It'Se-Ye-Ye Casino
419 Third Street
Kamish, ID 83536
Phone: (208) 935-7860
http://www.crcasino.com

Kootenai River Inn Casino and Spa
Kootenai River Plaza
Bonners Ferry, ID 83805
Phone: (208) 267-8511
http://www.kootenairiverinn.com

ILLINOIS

Argosy's Empress Casino
2300 Empress Drive
Joliet, IL 60436
Phone: (815) 744-9400
http://www.argosycasinos.com

Casino Queen
200 South Front Street
East Saint Louis, IL 62201
Phone: (618) 874-5000
http://www.casinoqueen.com

Grand Victoria Casino
250 South Grove Avenue
Elgin, IL 60120
Phone: (847) 468-7000
http://www.grandvictoriacasino.
com

Harrah's Joliet
150 North Joliet Street
Joliet, IL 60432
Phone: (815) 740-7800
http://www.harrahs.com

Harrah's Metropolis
100 East Front Street
Metropolis, IL 62960
Phone: (618) 524-2628
http://www.harrahs.com

Hollywood Casino–Aurora
1 New York Street Bridge
Aurora, IL 60506
Phone: (630) 801-7000
http://www.hollywoodcasinoaurora.
com

Jumer's Casino Rock Island
1735 First Avenue
Rock Island, IL 61201
Phone: (309) 793-4200
http://www.jumerscri.com

Par-A-Dice Hotel Casino
21 Blackjack Boulevard
East Peoria, IL 61611
Phone: (309) 698-7711
http://www.par-a-dice.com

INDIANA

Argosy Casino & Hotel– Lawrenceburg
777 Argosy Parkway
Lawrenceburg, IN 47025
Phone: (812) 539-8000
http://www.argosy.com/cincinatti

Belterra Casino Resort and Spa
777 Belterra Drive
Belterra, IN 47020
Phone: (812) 427-4008
http://www.belterracasino.com

Blue Chip Casino & Hotel
2 Easy Street
Michigan City, IN 46360
Phone: (219) 879-7711
Web site: www.bluechip-casino.com

Casino Aztar
421 Northwest Riverside Drive
Evansville, IN 47708
Phone: (812) 433-4000
http://www.casinoaztar.com

French Lick Springs Resort & Casino
8670 West State Road 56
French Lick, IN 47432
Phone: (812) 936-9300
http://www.frenchlick.com

Grand Victoria Casino & Resort
600 Grand Victoria Drive
Rising Sun, IN 47040
Phone: (812) 438-1234
http://www.grandvictoria.com

Hoosier Park
4500 Dan Patch Circle
Anderson, IN 46013
Phone: (765) 642-7223
http://www.hoosierpark.com

Horseshoe Casino Hammond
777 Casino Center Drive
Hammond, IN 46320
Phone: (219) 473-7000
http://www.horseshoe.com/

Horseshoe Southern Indiana
11999 Avenue of the Emperors
Elizabeth, IN 47117
Phone: (812) 969-6000
http://www.horseshoe.coin

Indiana Downs
4200 North Michigan Road
Shelbyville, IN 46176
Phone: (317) 421-0000
http://www.indianadowns.com

Majestic Star Casinos & Hotel
1 Buffington Harbor Drive
Gary, IN 46406
Phone: (219) 977-7777
http://www.majesticstar.com

Resorts East Chicago
777 Resorts Boulevard
East Chicago, IN 46312
Phone: (219) 378-3000
http://www.resortseastchicago.com

IOWA

Argosy Casino–Sioux City
100 Larsen Park Road
Sioux City, IA 51101
Phone: (712) 294-5600
http://www.argosy.com/siouxcity

Ameristar Casino Council Bluffs
2200 River Road
Council Bluffs, IA 51501
Phone: (712) 328-8888
http://www.ameristarcasinos.com

Casino Omaha
1 Blackbird Bend Boulevard
Onawa, IA 51040
Phone: (712) 423-3700

Catfish Bend Casino–Burlington
3001 Wine Gard Avenue
Burlington, IA 52601
Phone: (319) 753-2946
http://www.catfishbendcasino.com

Catfish Bend Casino–Fort Madison
902 Riverview Drive
Fort Madison, IA 52627
Phone: (319) 372-2946
http://www.catfishbendcasino.com

Diamond Jo Casino Dubuque
400 East Third Street
Dubuque, IA 52001
Phone: (563) 690-2100
http://www.dimondjo.com

Diamond Jo Casino Worth
777 Diamond Jo Lane
Northwood, IA 50459
Phone: (641) 323-7777
http://www.diamonjo.com/worth

Harrah's Council Bluffs
One Harrah's Boulevard
Council Bluffs, IA 51501
Phone: (712) 329-6000
http://www.harrahs.com

Isle of Capri Casino–Bettendorf
1821 State Street
Bettendorf, IA 52722
Phone: (563) 359-7280
http://www.isleofcapricasino.com

Isle of Capri Casino–Marquette
100 Anti Monopoly Street
Marquette, IA 52158
Phone: (563) 873-3531
http://www.isleofcapricasino.com

Isle of Capri Casino–Waterloo
777 Isle of Capri Boulevard
Waterloo, IA 52701
Phone: (319) 833-4753
http://www.theislewaterloo.com

Meskwaki Bingo Casino Hotel
1504 305th Street
Tama, IA 52339
Phone: (641) 484-2108
http://www.meskwaki.com

Mississippi Belle II
311 Riverview Drive
Clinton, IA 52733
Phone: (563) 243-9000
http://www.belle2casino.com

Rhythm City Casino
101 West River Drive
Davenport, IA 52801
Phone: (319) 328-8000
http://www.rhythmcitycasino.com

Riverside Casino
3184 Highway 22
Riverside, IA 52327
Phone: (319) 648-1234
http://www.riversideresortand
  casino.com

Terrible's Lakeside Casino
777 Casino Drive
Osceola, IA 50213
Phone: (641) 342-9511
http://www.terribleslakeside.com

Wild Rose Casino & Resort
777 Main Street
Emmetsburg, IA 50536
Phone: (712) 852-3400
http://www.wildroseresorts.com

Winna Vegas Casino
1500 330th Street
Sloan, IA 51055
Phone: (712) 428-9466
http://www.winnavegas.biz

KANSAS

Casino Jackpot Drive
777 Jackpot Drive
White Cloud, KS 66094
Phone: (785) 595-3430

Golden Eagle Casino
1121 Goldfinch Road
Horton, KS 66439
Phone: (785) 486-6601
http://www.goldeneaglecasino.com

Harrah's Prairie Band Casino and Hotel
12305 150th Road
Mayetta, KS 66509
Phone: (785) 966-7777
http://www.pbpgaming.com

Sac & Fox Casino
1322 U.S. Highway 75
Powhattan, KS 66527
Phone: (785) 467-8000
http://www.sacandfoxcasino.com

LOUISIANA

Amelia Belle Casino
500 Lake Palourde Road
Amelia, LA 70340
Phone: (985) 384-6044
http://www.ameliabellecasino.com

Belle of Baton Rouge
103 France Street
Baton Rouge, LA 70802
Phone: (225) 378-6000
http://www.belleofbatonrouge.com

Boomtown Casino & Hotel Bossier City
300 Riverside Drive
Bossier City, LA 71171
Phone: (318) 746-0711
http://www.boomtownbossier.com

Boomtown Casino New Orleans
4132 Peters Road
Harvey, LA 70058
Phone: (504) 366-7711
http://www.boomtownneworleans.com

Coushatta Casino Resort
777 Coushatta Drive
Kinder, LA 70648
Phone: (318) 738-7300
http://www.coushattacasinoresort.com

Cypress Bayou Casino
P.O. Box 519
Charenton, LA 70523
Phone: (318) 923-7284
http://www.cypressbayou.com

Eldorado Casino Shreveport
451 Clyde Fant Parkway
Shreveport, LA 71101
Phone: (318) 220-0981
http://www.eldoradoshreveport.com

Harrah's New Orleans
Canal at the River
New Orleans, LA 70130
Phone: (504) 533-6000
http://www.harrahs.com

Hollywood Casino–Baton Rouge
1717 River Road North
Baton Rouge, LA 70802
Phone: (225) 381-7777
http://www.casinorouge.com

Horseshoe Casino Hotel– Bossier City
711 Horseshoe Boulevard
Bossier City, LA 71111
Phone: (318) 742-0711
http://www.horseshoe.com

DiamondJacks Casino–Bossier City
711 Isle of Capri Boulevard
Bossier City, LA 71111
Phone: (318) 678-7777
http:// www.diamondjacks.com

Isle of Capri–Lake Charles
100 Westlake Avenue
Westlake, LA 70669
Phone: (337) 430-0711
http://www.isleofcapricasino.com

L'Auberge du Lac Hotel & Casino
3202 Nelson Road
Lake Charles, LA 70601
Phone: (337) 475-2900
http://www.ldlcasino.com

Paragon Casino Resort
711 Paragon Place
Marksville, LA 71351
Phone: (318) 253-1946
http://www.paragoncasionresort.com

Sam's Town Hotel & Casino– Shreveport
315 Clyde Fant Parkway
Shreveport, LA 71101
Phone: (318) 424-7777
http://www.samstownshreveport.com

Treasure Chest Casino
5050 Williams Boulevard
Kenner, LA 70065
Phone: (504) 443-8000
http://www.treasurechest.com

MAINE

Hollywood Slots at Bangor
427 Main Street
Bangor, ME 04402

Phone: (207) 262-6146
http://www.hollywoodslotsatbangor.
   com

MASSACHUSETTS

Horizon's Edge Casino Cruise
76 Marine Boulevard
Lynne, MA 01905
Phone: (781) 581-7733
http://www.horizonsedge.com

MICHIGAN

Bay Mills Resort & Casino
11386 Lakeshore Drive
Brimley, MI 49715
Phone: (906) 248-3715
http://www.4baymills.com

Four Winds Casino
11111 Wilson Road
New Buffalo, MI 49117
Phone: (269) 926-4500
http://www.fourwindscasino.com

Greektown Casino
555 East Lafayette Boulevard
Detroit, MI 48226
Phone: (313) 223-2999
http://www.greektowncasino.com

Island Resort & Casino
W399 Highway 2
Harris, MI 49845
Phone: (906) 466-2941
http://www.islandresortandcasino.
   com

Kewadin Casino–Christmas
N7761 Candy Cane Lane
Munising, MI 49862
Phone: (906) 387-5475
http://www.kewadin.com

Kewardin Casino–Hessel
3 Mile Road
Box 789
Hessel, MI 49745
Phone: (906) 484-2903
http://www.kewadin.com

Kewardin Casino–Manistique
U.S. 2 East, Route 1
Box 1533D

Manistique, MI 39854
Phone: (906) 341-5510
http://www.kewadin.com

**Kewadin Casino Hotel–Sault
   Ste. Marie**
2186 Shunk Road
Sault Ste. Marie, MI 49783
Phone: (906) 632-0530
http://www.kewadin.com

Kewadin Casino–St. Ignace
3039 Mackinaw Trail
St. Ignace, MI 49781
Phone: (906) 643-7071
http://www.kewadin.com

Kings Club Casino
12140 West Lakeshore Drive
Brimley, MI 49715
Phone: (906) 248-3700
http://www.4baymills.com

Lac Vieux Desert Casino
N 5384 U.S. 45 North
Watersmeet, MI 49969
Phone: (906) 358-4226
http://www.lacvieuxdesert.com

Leelanau Sands Casino
2521 Northwest Bay Shore Drive
Sutton's Bay, MI 49682
Phone: (231) 271-4104
http://www.casino2win.com

Little River Casino
2700 Orchard Drive
Manistee, MI 49660
Phone: (231) 723-1535
http://www.littlerivercasinos.com

MGM Grand Detroit Casino
1777 Third Street
Detroit, MI 48226
Phone: (313) 393-7777
http://www.mgmgranddetroit.
   com

Motor City Casino
2901 Grand River Avenue
Detroit, MI 48201
Phone: (313) 237-7711
http://www.motorcitycasino.com

Ojibwa Casino–Baraga
797 Michigan Avenue
Baraga, MI 49908
Phone: (906) 353-6333
http://www.ojibwacasino.com

Ojibwa Casino–Marquette
105 Acre Trail
Marquette, MI 49855
Phone: (906) 249-4200
http://www.ojibwacasino.com

Soaring Eagle Casino & Resort
6800 East Soaring Eagle Boulevard
Mount Pleasant, MI 48858
Phone: (517) 775-5777
http://www.soaringeaglecasino.com

Turtle Creek Casino
7741 M-72 East
Williamsburg, MI 49690
Phone: (231) 534-8888
http://www.casino2win.com

MINNESOTA

Black Bear Casino & Hotel
1785 Highway 210
Carlton, MN 55718
Phone: (218)878-2327
http://www.blackbearcasinohotel.
   com

Fond-du-Luth Casino
129 East Superior Street
Duluth, MN 55802
Phone: (218) 722-0280
http://www.fondduluthcasino.com

Fortune Bay Resort and Casino
1430 Bois Forte Road
Tower, MN 55790
Phone: (218) 753-6400
http://www.fortunebay.com

Grand Casino Hinckley
777 Lady Luck Drive
Hinckley, MN 55037
Phone: (320) 384-7777
http://www.grandcasinosmn.com

Grand Casino Mille Lacs
777 Grand Avenue

Onamia, MN 56359
Phone: (320) 532-7777
http://www.grandcasinosmn.com

Grand Portage Lodge & Casino
P.O. Box 233
Grand Portage, MN 55605
Phone: (218) 475-2401
http://www.grandportage.com

Jackpot Junction Casino Hotel
P.O. Box 420
Morton, MN 56270
Phone: (507) 644-3000
http://www.jackpotjunction.com

Little Six Casino
2354 Sioux Trail Northwest
Prior Lake, MN 55372
Phone: (952) 445-9000
http://www.littlesixcasino.com

Mystic Lake Casino Hotel
2400 Mystic Lake Boulevard
Prior Lake, MN 55372
Phone: (952) 445-9000
http://www.mysticlake.com

Northern Lights Casino
6800 Y Frontage Road Northwest
Walker, MN 56484
Phone: (218) 547-2744
http://www.northernlightscasino.com

Palace Casino Hotel
6280 Upper Cass Frontage Road Northwest
Cass Lake, MN 56633
Phone: (218) 335-7000
http://www.palacecasinohotel.com

Prarie's Edge Casino Resort
5616 Prarie's Edge Lane
Granite Falls, MN 56241
Phone: (320) 564-2121
http://www.prairiesedgecasino.com

Seven Clans Casino Red Lake
Highway 1 East
Red Lake, MN 56671
Phone: (218) 679-2500
http://www.sevenclanscasino.com

Seven Clans Casino Thief River Falls
Route 3, Box 168A
Thief River Falls, MN 56701
Phone: (218) 681-4062
http://www.sevenclanscasino.com

Seven Clans Casino Warroad
1012 East Lake Street
Warroad, MN 56763
Phone: (218) 386-3381
http://www.sevenclanscasino.com

Shooting Star Casino Hotel
777 Casino Boulevard
Mahnomen, MN 56557
Phone: (218) 935-2701
http://www.starcasino.com

Treasure Island Resort Casino
5734 Sturgeon Lake Road
Red Wing, MN 55066
Phone: (651) 388-6300
http://www.treasureislandcasino.com

White Oak Casino
45830 U.S. Highway 2
Deer River, MN 56636
Phone: (218) 246-9600
http://www.whiteoakcasino.com

MISSISSIPPI

BAY ST. LOUIS

Hollywood Casino Bay St. Louis
711 Hollywood Boulevard
Bay St. Louis, MS 39520
Phone: (228) 467-9527

Silver Slipper Casino
5000 South Beach Boulevard
Bay St. Louis, MS 39520
Phone: (228) 396-5943
http://www.silverslipper-ms.com

BILOXI

Beau Rivage
875 Beach Boulevard
Biloxi, MS 39530
Phone: (228) 386-7111
http://www.beaurivageresort.com

Boomtown Casino–Biloxi
676 Bayview Avenue
Biloxi, MS 39530
Phone: (228) 435-7000
http://www.boomtownbiloxi.com

Grand Casino Resort Biloxi
265 Beach Boulevard
Biloxi, MS 39530
Phone: (228) 436-2946
http://www.grandbiloxi.com

Hard Rock Hotel and Casino–Biloxi
777 Beach Boulevard
Biloxi, MS 39530
Phone: (228) 374-7625
http://www.hardrockbiloxi.com

IP Hotel and Casino
850 Bayview Avenue
Biloxi, MS 39530
Phone: (228) 436-3000
http://www.ipbiloxi.com

Isle of Capri Casino & Hotel–Biloxi
151 Beach Boulevard
Biloxi, MS 39530
Phone: (228) 436-4753
http://www.isleofcapricasino.com/Biloxi

Palace Casino Resort
158 Howard Avenue
Biloxi, MS 39530
Phone: (228) 432-8888
http://www.palacecasinoresort.com

Treasure Bay Casino and Hotel
1980 Beach Boulevard
Biloxi, MS 39531
Phone: (228) 385-6000
http://www.treasurebay.com

GREENVILLE

Bayou Caddy's Jubilee Casino
242 South Walnut Street
Greenville, MS 38701
Phone: (662) 335-1111

Lighthouse Point Casino
199 North Lakefront Road

Greenville, MS 38701
Phone: (662) 334-7711
http://www.lighthouse-casino.com

GULFPORT

Island View Casino Resort
3300 West Beach Boulevard
Gulfport, MS 39501
Phone: (228) 314-2100
http://www.islandviewcasino.com

LULA

Isle of Capri Casino & Hotel–Lula
777 Isle of Capri Parkway
Lula, MS 38644
Phone: (662) 363-4600
http://www.isleofcapricasino.com

NATCHEZ

Isle of Capri Casino & Hotel–Natchez
53 Silver Street
Natchez, MS 39120
Phone: (601) 445-0605
http://www.isleofcapricasino.com

PHILADELPHIA

Pearl River Resort
Highway 16 West
Philadelphia, MS 39350
Phone: (601) 650-1234
http://www.pearlriverresort.com

TUNICA

Bally's Tunica
1450 Bally's Boulevard
Tunica Resorts, MS 38664
Phone: (662) 357-1500
http://www.ballystunica.com

Fitzgeralds Casino/Hotel
711 Lucky Lane
Robinsonville, MS 38664
Phone: (662) 363-5825
http://www.fitzgeraldstunica.com

Gold Strike Casino Resort
100 Casino Center Drive
Robinsonville, MS 38664

Phone: (662) 357-1111
http://www.goldstrikemississippi.com

Grand Casino Tunica
13615 Old Highway 61 North
Robinsonville, MS 38664
Phone: (662) 363-2788
http://www.grandtunica.com

Hollywood Casino Tunica
1150 Casino Strip Resorts Boulevard
Robinsonville, MS 38664
Phone: (662) 357-7700
http://www.hollywoodtunica.com

Horseshoe Casino & Hotel
1021 Casino Center Drive
Robinsonville, MS 38664
Phone: (662) 357-5500
http://www.horseshoe.com

Resorts Tunica
1100 Casino Strip Boulevard
Robinsonville, MS 38664
Phone: (662) 363-7777
http://www.resortstunica.com

Sam's Town Tunica
1477 Casino Strip Boulevard
Robinsonville, MS 38664
Phone: (662) 363-0711
http://www.samstowntunica.com

Sheraton Casino & Hotel
1107 Casino Center Drive
Robinsonville, MS 38664
Phone: (662) 363-4900
http://www.harrahs.com

VICKSBURG

Ameristar Casino Hotel–Vicksburg
4146 Washington Street
Vicksburg, MS 39180
Phone: (601) 638-1000
http://www.ameristarcasinos.com

DiamondJacks Casino–Vicksburg
3990 Washington Street
Vicksburg, MS 39180

Phone: (601) 636-5700
http://www.diamondjacks.com

Horizon Casino Hotel
1310 Mulberry Street
Vicksburg, MS 39180
Phone: (601) 636-3423
http://www.horizonvicksburg.com

Rainbow Hotel Casino
1380 Warrenton Road
Vicksburg, MS 39182
Phone: (601) 636-7575
http://www.rainbowcasino.com

MISSOURI

BOONVILLE

Isle of Capri Casino–Boonville
100 Isle of Capri Boulevard
Boonville, MO 65233
Phone: (660) 882-1200
http://www.isleofcapricasino.com

CARUTHERSVILLE

Casino Aztar
777 East Third Street
Caruthersville, MO 63830
Phone: (573) 333-6000
http://www.casinoaztarmo.com

KANSAS CITY

Ameristar Casino Hotel–Kansas City
3200 North Ameristar Drive
Kansas City, MO 64161
Phone: (816) 414-7000
http://www.ameristarcasinos.com/kc

Argosy Casino
777 Northwest Argosy Parkway
Riverside, MO 64150
Phone: (816) 746-3100
http://www.argosy.com/kansascity

Harrah's North Kansas City
One Riverboat Drive
North Kansas City, MO 64116
Phone: (816) 472-7777
http://www.harrahs.com

Isle of Capri Casino–Kansas City
1800 East Front Street
Kansas City, MO 64120
Phone: (816) 855-7777
http://www.isleofcapricasino.com

LA GRANGE

Terrible's Mark Twain Casino
104 Pierce Street
La Grange, MO 63348
Phone: (573) 655-4770
http://www.terriblesmarktwain.com

ST. JOSEPH

Terrible's St. Jo Frontier Casino
77 Francis Street
St. Joseph, MO 64501
Phone: (816) 279-5514
http://www.terriblesstjofrontier.com

ST. LOUIS

Ameristar Casino St. Charles
P.O. Box 720
St. Charles, MO 63302
Phone: (314) 949-4300
http://www.ameristarcasinos.com/
stcharles

Harrah's St. Louis
777 Casino Center Drive
Maryland Heights, MO 63043
Phone: (314) 770-8100
http://www.harrahs.com

Lumiere Place Casino Resort
727 North First Street
St. Louis, MO 63102
Phone: (314) 450-5000
http://www.lumiereplace.com

President Casino–St. Louis
800 North First Street
St. Louis, MO 63102
Phone: (314) 622-3000
http://www.presidentcasino.com

MONTANA

Charging Horse Casino
P.O. Box 1259

Lame Deer, MT 59043
Phone: (406) 477-6677

Discovery Lodge Casino
1 Tree Lane
Cut Bank, MT 59427
Phone: (406) 873-2885

Four C's Cafe & Casino
Rocky Boy Route, Box 544
Box Elder, MT 59521
Phone: (406) 395-4863

Glacier Peaks Casino
209 North Piegan Street
Browning, MT 59417
Phone: (406) 338-2274
http://www.glaciercash.com

KwaTaqNuk Resort
49708 Highway 93 East
Polson, MT 59860
Phone: (406) 883-3636
http://www.kwataqnuk.com

Little Big Horn Casino
P.O. Box 580
Crow Agency, MT 59022
Phone: (406) 638-4000

Silver Wolf Casino
Highway 25 East
P.O. Box 726
Wolf Point, MT 59201
Phone: (406) 653-3475

NEVADA

AMARGOSA VALLEY

Longstreet Hotel Casino RV Resort
Route 373, HCR 70
Amargosa Valley, NV 89020
Phone: (775) 372-1777
http://www.longstreetcasino.com

BEATTY

Stagecoach Hotel & Casino
P.O. Box 836
Beatty, NV 89003
Phone: (775) 553-2419

BOULDER CITY

Hacienda Hotel & Casino
U.S. Highway 93
Boulder City, NV 89005
Phone: (702) 293-5000
http://www.haciendaonline.com

CARSON CITY

Carson Nugget
507 North Carson Street
Carson City, NV 89701
Phone: (775) 882-1626
http://www.ccnugget.com

Carson Station Hotel Casino
900 South Carson Street
Carson City, NV 89702
Phone: (775) 883-0900
http www.carsonstation.com

Casino Fandango
3800 South Carson Street
Carson City, NV 89005
Phone: (775) 885-7000
http://www.casinofandango.com

Gold Dust West
2171 Highway 50
East Carson City, NV 89701
Phone: (775) 885-9000
http://www.gdwcasino.com

ELKO

Commercial Casino
345 Fourth Street
Elko, NV 89801
Phone: (775) 738-2111
http://www.commercialcasino.
com

Red Lion Inn & Casino
2065 Idaho Street
Elko, NV 89801
Phone: (775) 738-2111
http://www.redlioncasino.com

Stockmen's Hotel & Casino
340 Commercial Street
Elko, NV 89801
Phone: (775)738-5141
http://www.stockmenscasinos.com

ELY

Hotel Nevada & Gambling Hall
501 Aultman Street
Ely, NV 89301
Phone: (775) 289-6665
http://www.hotelnevada.com

FALLON

Bonanza Inn & Casino
855 West Williams Avenue
Fallon, NV 89406
Phone: (775) 423-6031

Stockman's Casino
1560 West Williams Avenue
Fallon, NV 89406
Phone: (775) 423-2117
http://www.stockmanscasino.com

GARDNERVILLE

Sharkey's Nugget
1440 Highway 395 North
Gardnerville, NV 89410
Phone: (775) 782-3133

Topaz Lodge & Casino
1979 Highway 395 South
Gardnerville, NV 89410
Phone: (775) 266-3338
http://www.topazlodge.com

HENDERSON

Eldorado Casin
140 Water Street
Henderson, NV 89105
Phone: (702) 564-1811
http://www.eldoradocasino.com

Fiesta Henderson Casino Hotel
777 West Lake Mead Drive
Henderson, NV 89015
Phone: (702) 558-7000
http://www.fiestacasino.com

Green Valley Ranch Resort
2300 Paseo Verde Drive
Henderson, NV 89102
Phone: (702) 617-7777
http://www.greenvalleyrachresort.
    com

Jokers Wild
920 North Boulder Highway
Henderson, NV 89105
Phone: (702) 564-8100
http://www.jokerswildcasino.com

Sunset Station Hotel and Casino
1301 West Sunset Road
Henderson, NV 89014
Phone: (702) 547-7777
http://www.sunsetstation.com

INDIAN SPRINGS

Indian Springs Casino
372 Tonopah Highway
Indian Springs, NV 89108
Phone: (702) 879-3456
http://www.dirtymore.com

JACKPOT

Barton's Club 93
P.O. Box 523
Jackpot, NV 89825
Phone: (775) 755-2341
http://www.bartonsclub93.com

Cactus Pete's Resort Casino
1385 Highway 93
Jackpot, NV 89825
Phone: (775) 755-2321
http://www.ameristarcasinos.com

Horseshu Hotel & Casino
1385 Highway 93
Jackpot, NV 89825
Phone: (702) 755-7777
http://www.ameristarcasinos.com

JEAN

Gold Strike Hotel & Gambling Hall
1 Main Street
P.O. Box 19278
Jean, NV 89019
Phone: (702) 477-5000
http://www.stopatjean.com

LAKE TAHOE

Bill's Casino
U.S. Highway 50

Stateline, NV 89449
Phone: (775) 588-6611
http://www.harrahs.com

Cal-Neva Resort Spa & Casino
2 Stateline Road
Crystal Bay, NV 89402
Phone: (775) 832-4000
http://www.calnevaresort.com

Crystal Bay Club Casino
14 State Route 28
Crystal Bay, NV 89402
Phone: (775) 833-6333
http://www.crystalbaycasino.com

Harrah's Lake Tahoe
18 Highway 50
P.O. Box 8
Lake Tahoe, NV 89449
Phone: (775)588-6611
http://www.harrahs.com

Harveys Resort Hotel/Casino–Lake Tahoe
18 Highway 50
Lake Tahoe, NV 89449
Phone: (775) 588-2411
http://www.harveys.com

Hyatt Regency Lake Tahoe
Resort & Casino
P.O. Box 3239
Incline Village, NV 89450
Phone: (775) 832-1234
http://www.laketahoehyatt.com

Lake Tahoe Horizon
50 Highway 50
P.O. Box C
Lake Tahoe, NV 89449
Phone: (775) 588-6211
http://www.horizoncasino.com

Lakeside Inn and Casino
Highway 50 at Kingsbury Grade
Stateline, NV 89449
Phone: (775) 588-7777
http://www.lakesideinn.com

Montbleu Resort Casino & Spa
55 Highway 50
Stateline, NV 89449

Phone: (775) 588-3515
http://www.montbluresort.com

Tahoe Biltmore Lodge & Casino
#5 Highway 28
P.O. Box 115
Crystal Bay, NV 89042
Phone: (775) 831-0660
http://www.tahoebiltmore.com

LAS VEGAS

Arizona Charlie's Hotel & Casino
740 South Decatur Boulevard
Las Vegas, NV 89107
Phone: (702) 255-5200
http://www.azcharlies.com

Bally's Las Vegas
3635 Las Vegas Boulevard South
Las Vegas, NV 89109
Phone: (702) 739-4111
http://www.ballyslv.com

Bellagio
3600 Las Vegas Boulevard South
Las Vegas, NV 89109
Phone: (702) 693-7111
http://www.bellagioresort.com

Bill's Gambling Hall & Saloon
3595 Las Vegas Boulevard South
Las Vegas, NV 89109
Phone: (702) 737-2000
http://www.billslasvegas.com

Binion's Gambling Hall and Hotel
128 East Fremont Street
Las Vegas, NV 89101
Phone: (702) 382-1600
http://www.binions.com

Boulder Station Hotel & Casino
4111 Boulder Highway
Las Vegas, NV 89121
Phone: (702) 432-7777
http://www.stationcasinos.com

Caesars Palace
3570 Las Vegas Boulevard South
Las Vegas, NV 89109
Phone: (702) 731-7110
http://www.caesars.com

California Hotel & Casino
12 Ogden Avenue
Las Vegas, NV 89101
Phone: (702) 385-1222
http://www.thecal.com

Casino Royale & Hotel
3411 Las Vegas Boulevard South
Las Vegas, NV 89109
Phone: (702) 737-3500
http://www.casinoroyalhotel.com

Circus Circus Hotel & Casino
2880 Las Vegas Boulevard South
Las Vegas, NV 89109
Phone: (702) 734-0410
http://www.circuscircus.com

El Cortez Hotel & Casino
600 East Fremont Street
Las Vegas, NV 89101
Phone: (702) 385-5200
http://www.elcortezhotelcasino.com

Ellis Island Casino
4178 Koval Lane
Las Vegas, NV 89109
Phone: (702) 734-8638
http://www.ellisislandcasino.com

Excalibur Hotel and Casino
3850 Las Vegas Boulevard South
Las Vegas, NV 89109
Phone: (702) 597-7777
http://www.excaliburcasino.com

Fitzgeralds Casino & Holiday Inn
301 Fremont Street
Las Vegas, NV 89101
Phone: (702) 388-2400
http://www.fitzgeralds.com

Flamingo Hilton Las Vegas
3555 Las Vegas Boulevard South
Las Vegas, NV 89109
Phone: (702) 733-3111
http://www.hilton.com

Four Queens Hotel and Casino
202 Fremont Street
Las Vegas, NV 89101
Phone: (702) 385-4011
http://www.fourqueens.com

Fremont Hotel & Casino
200 East Fremont Street
Las Vegas, NV 89101
Phone: (702) 385-3232
http://www.fremontcasino.com

Gold Coast Casino & Hotel
4000 West Flamingo Road
Las Vegas, NV 89103
Phone: (702) 367-7111
http://www.goldcoastcasino.com

Golden Gate Hotel & Casino
1 Fremont Street
Las Vegas, NV 89101
Phone: (702) 385-1906
http://www.goldengatecasino.com

The Golden Nugget
129 East Fremont Street
Las Vegas, NV 89101
Phone: (702) 385-7111
http://www.goldennugget.com

Hard Rock Hotel & Casino
4455 Paradise Road
Las Vegas, NV 89109
Phone: (702) 693-5000
http://www.hardrockhotel.com

Harrah's Las Vegas
3475 Las Vegas Boulevard South
Las Vegas, NV 89109
Phone: (702) 369-5000
http://www.harrahslv.com

Hooters Casino Hotel
115 East Tropicana Avenue
Las Vegas, NV 89109
Phone: (702) 739-9000
http://www.hooterscasinohotel.com

Imperial Palace Hotel & Casino
3535 Las Vegas Boulevard South
Las Vegas, NV 89109
Phone: (702) 731-3311
http://www.imperialpalace.com

Lady Luck Casino Hotel
206 North Third Street
Las Vegas, NV 89101
Phone: (702) 477-3000
http://www.ladylucklv.com

Las Vegas Auto and Truck Plaza
8050 South Industrial Road
Las Vegas, NV 89118
Phone: (702) 361-1176

Las Vegas Hilton
3000 Paradise Road
Las Vegas, NV 89109
Phone: (702) 732-5111
http://www.hilton.com

Longhorn Casino
5288 Boulder Highway
Las Vegas, NV 89122
Phone: (702) 435-9170

Luxor Las Vegas
3900 Las Vegas Boulevard South
Las Vegas, NV 89119
Phone: (702) 262-4000
http://www.luxor.com

Main Street Station Hotel & Casino
200 North Main Street
Las Vegas, NV 89101
Phone: (702) 387-1896
http://www.mainstreetcasino.com

Mandalay Bay
3950 Las Vegas Boulevard South
Las Vegas, NV 89109
Phone: (702) 632-7777
http://www.mandalaybay.com

MGM Grand Hotel Casino
3799 Las Vegas Boulevard South
Las Vegas, NV 89109
Phone: (702) 891-1111
http://www.mgmgrand.com

The Mirage
3400 Las Vegas Boulevard South
Las Vegas, NV 89109
Phone: (702) 791-7111
http//www.mirage.com

Monte Carlo Resort & Casino
3770 Las Vegas Boulevard South
Las Vegas, NV 89109
Phone: (702) 730-7777
http://www.monte-carlo.com

Nevada Palace Hotel & Casino
5255 Boulder Highway
Las Vegas, NV 89122
Phone: (702) 458-8810
http://www.nvpalace.com

New York-New York Hotel & Casino
3790 Las Vegas Boulevard South
Las Vegas, NV 89109
Phone: (702) 740-6969
http://www.nynyhotelcasino.com

The Orleans Hotel & Casino
4500 West Tropicana Avenue
Las Vegas, NV 89103
Phone: (702) 365-7111
http://www.orleanscasino.com

O'Shea's Casino
3555 Las Vegas Boulevard South
Las Vegas, NV 89109
Phone: (702) 697-2667

Palace Station Hotel & Casino
2411 West Sahara Avenue
Las Vegas, NV 89102
Phone: (702) 367-2411
http://www.stationcasinos.com

The Palms
4321 Flamingo Road
Las Vegas, NV 89103
Phone: (702) 942-7777
http://www.thepalmslasvegas.com

Paris Casino Resort
3655 Las Vegas Boulevard South
Las Vegas, NV 89109
Phone: (702) 967-4401
http://www.parislasvegas.com

Planet Hollywood
3667 Las Vegas Boulevard South
Las Vegas, NV 89109
Phone: (702) 785-5555
http://www.planethollywoodresort.com

Plaza Hotel & Casino
1 Main Street
Las Vegas, NV 89101
Phone: (702) 386-2110
http://www.plazahotelcasino.com

Rampart Casino
221 North Rampart Boulevard
Las Vegas, NV 89128
Phone: (702) 507-5900
http://www.rampartcasino.com

Red Rock Resort Spa Casino
10973 West Charleston Boulevard
Las Vegas, NV 89135
Phone: (702) 797-777
http://www.redrockstaton.com

Rio Suites Hotel & Casino
3700 West Flamingo Road
Las Vegas, NV 89103
Phone: (702) 252-7777
http://www.playrio.com

Riviera Hotel & Casino
2901 Las Vegas Boulevard South
Las Vegas, NV 89109
Phone: (702) 734-5110
http://www.theriviera.com

Sahara Hotel & Casino
2535 Las Vegas Boulevard South
Las Vegas, NV 89109
Phone: (702) 737-2111
http://www.saharavegas.com

Sam's Town Hotel & Gambling Hall
5111 Boulder Highway
Las Vegas, NV 89122
Phone: (702) 456-7777
http://www.samstownlvnv.com

Santa Fe Station Hotel & Casino
4949 North Rancho Drive
Las Vegas, NV 89130
Phone: (702) 658-4900
http://www.santafestationlasvegas.com

Silver Saddle Saloon
2501 East Charleston Boulevard

Las Vegas, NV 89104
Phone: (702) 474-2900

Silverton Hotel Casino & RV Resort
3333 Blue Diamond Road
Las Vegas, NV 89139
Phone: (702) 263-7777
http://www.silvertoncasino.com

Slots-A-Fun Casino
2890 Las Vegas Boulevard South
Las Vegas, NV 89109
Phone: (702) 794-3814

South Point Hotel and Casino
9777 Las Vegas Boulevard South
Las Vegas, NV 89123
Phone: (702) 796-7111
http://www.southpointcasino.com

Stratosphere Hotel & Casino
2000 Las Vegas Boulevard South
LasVegas, NV 89117
Phone: (702) 383-7777
http://www.stratospherehotel.com

Suncoast Hotel and Casino
9000 Alta Drive
Las Vegas, NV 89145
Phone: (702) 616-7111
http://www.suncoastcasino.com

Terrible's Hotel and Casino
4100 Paradise Road
Las Vegas, NV 89156
Phone: (702) 733-7000
http://www.terriblescasinos.com

Treasure Island
3300 Las Vegas Boulevard South
Las Vegas, NV 89109
Phone: (702) 849-7111
http://www.treasureislandlasvegas.com

Tropicana Resort & Casino
380 Las Vegas Boulevard South
Las Vegas, NV 89109
Phone: (702) 739-2222
http://www.tropicanalv.com

Tuscany Suite & Casino
255 East Flamingo Road

Las Vegas, NV 89109
Phone: (702) 893-8933
http://www.tuscanylasvegas.com

Vegas Club Hotel & Casino
18 East Fremont Street
Las Vegas, NV 89101
Phone: (702) 385-1664
http://www.vegasclubcasino.net

The Venetian Resort Hotel Casino
3355 Las Vegas Boulevard South
Las Vegas, NV 89109
Phone: (702) 733-5000
http://www.venetian.com

Western Hotel & Casino
899 East Fremont Street
Las Vegas, NV 89101
Phone: (702) 384-4620
http://www.westernhotelcasino.com

Westin Causuarina Hotel & Casino
160 East Flamingo Road
Las Vegas, NV 89109
Phone: (702) 836-5900
http://www.starwoodhotels.com

Wild Wild West Casino
3330 West Tropicana Avenue
Las Vegas, NV 89103
Phone: (702) 736-8988

Wynn Las Vegas
3145 Las Vegas Boulevard South
Las Vegas, NV 89109
Phone: (702) 770-70000
http://www.wynnlasvegas.com

LAUGHLIN

Aquarius Casino Resort
1900 South Casino Drive
Laughlin, NV 89029
Phone: (702) 298-5111
http://www.aquariuscasinoresort.com

Avi Resort & Casino
1000 Aha Macav Parkway
Laughlin, NV 89039

Phone: (702) 535-555
http://www.avicasino.com

Colorado Belle Hotel & Casino
2100 South Casino Drive
Laughlin, NV 89029
Phone: (702) 298-4000
http://www.coloradobelle.com

Don Laughlin's Riverside Resort Hotel and Casino
1650 South Casino Drive
Laughlin, NV 89029
Phone: (702) 298-2535
http://www.riversideresort.net

Edgewater Hotel Casino
2020 South Casino Drive
Laughlin, NV 89029
Phone: (702) 298-2453
http://www.edgewater-casino.com

Golden Nugget Laughlin
2300 South Casino Drive
Laughlin, NV 89029
Phone: (702) 298-7111
http://www.gnlaughlin.com

Harrah's Laughlin Casino & Hotel
2900 South Casino Drive
Laughlin, NV 89029
Phone: (702) 298-4600
http://www.harrahs.com

Pioneer Hotel & Gambling Hall
2200 South Casino Drive
Laughlin, NV 89029
Phone: (702) 298-2442
http://www.pioneerlaughlin.com

Ramada Express Hotel & Casino
2121 South Casino Drive
Laughlin, NV 89029
Phone: (702) 298-4200
http://www.ramadaexpress.com

River Palms Resort & Casino
2700 South Casino Drive
Laughlin, NV 89029
Phone: (702) 298-2242
http://www.river-palms.com

LOVELOCK

Sturgeon's Casino
1420 Cornell Avenue
Lovelock, NV 89419
Phone: (775) 273-2971

MCDERMITT

Say When Casino
P.O. Box 375
McDermitt, NV 89421
Phone: (775) 532-8515
http://www.saywhencasino.com

MESQUITE

Casablanca Resort & Casino
P.O. Box 2727
Mesquite, NV 89024
Phone: (702) 346-7259
http://www.casablancaresort.com

Eureka Casino & Hotel
275 Mesa Boulevard
Mesquite, NV 89024
Phone: (702) 346-4600
http://www.eurekamesquite.com

Oasis Resort Hotel & Casino
P.O. Box 360
Mesquite, NV 89024
Phone: (702) 346-5232
http://www.oasisresort.com

Virgin River Hotel–Casino
100 Pioneer Boulevard
Mesquite, NV 89027
Phone: (702) 346-7777
http://www.virginriver.com

MINDEN

Carson Valley Inn
1627 Highway 395 North
Minden, NV 89423
Phone: (775) 782-9711
http://www.cvinn.com

NORTH LAS VEGAS

Barcelona Hotel & Casino
5011 East Craig Road
North Las Vegas, NV 89115
Phone: (702) 644-6300
http://www.barcelonalasvegas.com

Bighorn Casino
3016 East Lake Mead Boulevard
North
North Las Vegas, NV 89030
Phone: (702) 642-1940

Cannery Hotel & Casino
2121 East Craig Road
North Las Vegas, NV 89030
Phone: (702) 507-5700
http://www.cannerycasinos.com

Fiesta Casino Hotel
2400 North Rancho Drive
North Las Vegas, NV 89130
Phone: (702) 631-7000
http://www.fiestacasino.com

Jerry's Nugget
1821 Las Vegas Boulevard North
North Las Vegas, NV 89030
Phone: (702) 399-3000
http://www.jerrysnugget.com

Opera House Saloon and Casino
2542 Las Vegas Boulevard North
North Las Vegas, NV 89030
Phone: (702) 649-8801

The Poker Palace
2757 Las Vegas Boulevard North
North Las Vegas, NV 89030
Phone: (702) 649-3799

Silver Nugget
2140 Las Vegas Boulevard North
North Las Vegas, NV 89030
Phone: (702) 399-1111
http://www.silvernuggetcasino.
com

Speedway Casino
3227 Civic Center Drive
North Las Vegas, NV 89030
Phone: (702) 399-3297
http://www.speedwaycasino.com

Texas Station
2101 Texas Star Lane
North Las Vegas, NV 89102
Phone: (702) 631-1000
http://www.texasstation.com

Wildfire Casino
1901 North Rancho Drive
North Las Vegas, NV 89106
Phone: (702) 648-3801
http://www.wildfirecasinolasvegas.
com

PAHRUMP

Pahrump Nugget Hotel & Gambling Hall
681 South Highway 160
Pahrump, NV 89048
Phone: (775) 751-6500
http://www.pahrumpnugget.com

Saddle West Hotel, Casino and RV Park
1220 South Highway 160
Pahrump, NV 89048
Phone: (775) 727-111
http://www.saddlewest.com

Terrible's Lakeside Casino & RV Park
5870 South Homestead Road
Pahrump, NV 89048
Phone: (775) 751-7770
http://www.terribleslakesidecasino
rvpark.com

Terrible's Town Casino
771 Frontage Road
Pahrump, NV 89048
Phone: (775) 751-7777
http://www.terriblestownpahrump.
com

PRIMM

Buffalo Bill's Resort & Casino
31900 Las Vegas Boulevard South
Primm, NV 89019
Phone: (702) 382-1212
http://www.primmvalleyresorts.
com

Primm Valley Resort & Casino
31900 Las Vegas Boulevard South
Primm, NV 89019
Phone: (702) 382-1212
http://www.primadonna.com

Whiskey Pete's Hotel & Casino
100 West Primm Boulevard

Primm, NV 89019
Phone: (702) 382-1212
http://www.primadonna.com

Atlantis Casino Resort
3800 South Virginia Street
Reno, NV 89502
Phone: (775) 825-4700
http://www.atlantiscasino.com

Bonanza Casino
4720 North Virginia Street
Reno, NV 89503
Phone: (775) 323-2724
http://www.bonanzacasino.com

Bordertown Casino RV Resort
19575 Highway 395 North
Reno, NV 89506
Phone: (775) 972-1309
http://www.bordertowncasinorv.
com

**Circus Circus Hotel Casino–
Reno**
500 North Sierra Street
Reno, NV 89503
Phone: (775) 329-0711
http://www.circusreno.com

**Club Cal-Neva/Virginian Hotel
and Casino**
38 East Second Street
Reno, NV 89505
Phone: (775) 323-1046
http://www.clubcalneva.com

Diamond Casino at Holiday Inn
1010 East 6th Street
Reno, NV 89512
Phone: (775) 786-5151

Eldorado Hotel and Casino
345 North Virginia Street
Reno, NV 89501
Phone: (775) 786-5700
http://www.eldoradoreno.com

Fitzgeralds Casino Hotel–Reno
255 North Virginia Street
Reno, NV 89504

Phone: (775) 785-3300
http://www.fitzgeraldsreno.com

Grand Sierra Resort & Casino
2500 East 2nd Street
Reno, NV 89595
Phone: (775) 789-2000
http://www.grandsierraresort.com

Harrah's Reno Casino Hotel
219 North Center Street
Reno, NV 89501
Phone: (775) 786-3232
http://www.harrahs.com

Peppermill Hotel Casino–Reno
2707 South Virginia Street
Reno, NV 89502
Phone: (775) 826-2121
http://www.peppermillcasino.com

Sands Regency Hotel Casino
345 North Arlington Avenue
Reno, NV 89501
Phone: (775) 348-2200
http://www.sandsregency.com

Siena Hotel Spa Casino
1 South Lake Street
Reno, NV 89501
Phone: (775) 337-6260
http://www.sienareno.com

Silver Legacy Resort Casino
407 North Virginia Street
Reno, NV 89501
Phone: (775) 329-4777
http://www.silverlegacy.com

Searchlight Nugget Casino
100 North Highway 95
Searchlight, NV 89046
Phone: (702) 297-1201

Alamo Travel Center
1959 East Greg Street
Sparks, NV 89431
Phone: (775) 355-8888
http://www.thealamo.com

Baldini's Sports Casino
865 South Rock Boulevard
Sparks, NV 89431
Phone: (775) 358-0116
http://www.baldinissportscasino.com

John Ascuaga's Nugget
1100 Nugget Avenue
Sparks, NV 89431
Phone: (775) 356-3300
http://www.janugget.com

Rail City Casino
2121 Victorian Avenue
Sparks, NV 89431
Phone: (775) 359-9440
http://www.railcity.com

Silver Club Hotel Casino
1040 Victorian Avenue
Sparks, NV 89432
Phone: (775) 358-4771
http://www.silverclub.com

Western Village Inn & Casino
815 Nichols Boulevard
Sparks, NV 89432
Phone: (775) 331-1069

Tonopah
Station House
P.O. Box 1351
Tonopah, NV 89049
Phone: (775) 482-9777

Boomtown Hotel and Casino
P.O. Box 399
Verdi, NV 89439
Phone: (775) 345-6000
http://www.boomtowncasinos.com

Four Way Bar and Casino
U.S. 93 and Interstate 80
Wells, NV 89835
Phone: (775) 752-3344

Montego Bay Casino Resort
100 Wendover Boulevard

West Wendover, NV 89883
Phone: (775) 664-9100
http://www.montegobaywendover.
com

Peppermill Inn & Casino
680 Wendover Boulevard
West Wendover, NV 89883
Phone: (775) 664-2255
http://www.peppermillwendover.com

Rainbow Hotel & Casino
1045 Wendover Boulevard
West Wendover, NV 89883
Phone: (775) 664-4000
http://www.rainbowwendover.com

Red Garter Hotel & Casino
P.O. Box 2399
West Wendover, NV 89883
Phone: (775) 664-3315
http://www.redgartercasino.com

**Wendover Nugget Hotel &
Casino**
101 Wendover Boulevard
West Wendover, NV 89883
Phone: (775) 664-2221
http://www.wendovernugget.com

**Model T Casino Hotel & RV
Park**
1130 West Winnemucca Boulevard
Winnemucca, NV 89446
Phone: (775) 623-2588
http://www.modelt.com

Red Lion Inn and Casino
741 Winnemucca Boulevard
Winnemucca, NV 89445
Phone: (775) 623-2565
http://www.redlionwin.com

Winners Hotel Casino
185 West Winnemucca Boulevard
Winnemucca, NV 89445
Phone: (775) 623-2511
http://www.winnerscasino.com

Casino West
11 North Main Street

Yerington, NV 89447
Phone: (775) 463-2481

NEW JERSEY

Ceasars Atlantic City
2100 Pacific Avenue
Atlantic City, NJ 08401
Phone: (609) 348-4411
http:www.caesars.com

Harrah's Casino Hotel
777 Harrah's Boulevard
Atlantic City, NJ 08401
Phone: (609) 441-5000
http://www.harrahs.com

Resorts Atlantic City
1133 Boardwalk
Atlantic City, NJ 08401
Phone: (609) 344-6000
http://www.resortsac.com

Showboat Casino Hotel
801 Boardwalk
Atlantic City, NJ 08401
Phone: (609) 343-4000
http://www.harrahs.com

Tropicana Casino Resort
Brighton Avenue and Boardwalk
Atlantic City, NJ 08401
Phone: (609) 340-4000
http://www.tropicana.net

Trump Marina Hotel Casino
Huron Avenue and Brigantine
Boulevard
Atlantic City, NJ 08401
Phone: (609) 441-2000
http://www.trumpmarina.com

Trump Plaza Hotel and Casino
Boardwalk at Mississippi Avenue
Atlantic City, NJ 08401
Phone: (609) 441-6000
http://www.trumpplaza.com

Trump Taj Mahal Casino Resort
1000 Boardwalk at Virginia Avenue
Atlantic City, NJ 08401
Phone: (609) 449-1000
http://www.trumptaj.com

NEW MEXICO

Apache Nugget Casino
P.O. Box 650
Dulce, NM 87528
Phone: (505) 759-3777
http://www.apachenugget.com

**Best Western Jicarilla Inn and
Casino**
U.S. Highway 64
Dulce, NM 87529
Phone: (505) 759-3663
http://www.bestwesternnewmexico.
com

Big Rock Casino Bowl
419 North Riverside Drive
Espanola, NM 87532
Phone: (505) 747-3100
http://www.bigrockcasino.com

Camel Rock Casino
17486-A Highway 84/285
Santa Fe, NM 87501
Phone: (505) 984-8414
http://www.camelrockcasino.com

Casino Apache Travel Center
25845 U.S. Highway 70
Ruidoso, NM 88340
Phone: (505) 464-7777

Casino Express
14500 Casino Avenue
Albuquerque, NM 87120
Phone: (505) 552-7777

Cities of Gold Casino Hotel
10 B Cities of Gold Road
Santa Fe, NM 87501
Phone: (505) 455-3313
http://www.citiesofgold.com

**Dancing Eagle Casino and RV
Park**
Interstate 40
Exit 8
Casa Blanca, NM 87007
Phone: (505) 552-1111
http://www.dancingeaglecasino.
com

Inn of the Mountain Gods Resort and Casino
277 Carrizo Canyon Road
Mescalero, NM 88340
Phone: (505) 464-7777
http://www.innofthemountaingods.com

Isleta Gaming Palace
11000 Broadway Southeast
Albuquerque, NM 87022
Phone: (505) 724-3800
http://www.isletacasinoresort.com

Ohkay Casino
P.O. Box 1270
San Juan Pueblo, NM 87566
Phone: (505) 747-1668

Palace West Casino
State Road 45
Albuquerque, NM 87105
Phone: (505) 869-4102
http://www.isletaeagle.com

Route 66 Casino
14500 Central Avenue
Albuquerque, NM 87105
Phone: (505) 352-7866
http://www.rt66casino.com

Sandia Resort and Casino
30 Rainbow Road Northeast
Albuquerque, NM 87184
Phone: (505) 796-7500
http://www.sandiacasino.com

San Felipe Casino Hollywood
25 Hagen Road
Algodones, NM 87001
Phone: (505) 867-6700
http://www.sanfelipecasino.com

Santa Ana Star Casino
54 Jeme Dam Canyon Road
Bernalilo, NM 87004
Phone: (505) 867-0000
http://www.santaanastar.com

Sky City Casino
P.O. Box 519
San Fidell, NM 87049
Phone: (505) 552-6017
http://www.skycitycasino.com

SunRay Park and Casino
39 Road 5568
Farmington, NM 87401
Phone: (505) 566-1200
Fax: (505) 326-4292
http://www.sunraygaming.com

Taos Mountain Casino
P.O. Box 1477
Taos, NM 87571
Phone: (505) 758-4460
http://www.taosmountaincasino.com

Zia Park Race Track and Black Gold Casino
3901 West Miller Drive
Hobbs, NM 88240
Phone: (505) 492-7000
http://www.blackgoldcasino.net

NEW YORK

Akwesasne Mohawk Casino
Route 37, Box 670
Hogansburg, NY 13655
Phone: (518) 358-2222
http://www.mohawkcasino.com

Empire City at Yonkers Raceway
810 Yonkers Avenue
Yonkers, NY 10704
Phone: (914) 968-4200
http://www.yonkersraceway.com

Fairgrounds Gaming and Raceway
5600 McKinley Parkway
Hamburg Fairgrounds
Hamburg, NY 14075
Phone: (716) 649-1280
http://www.buffaloraceway.com

Finger Lakes Gaming and Racetrack
5887 Route 96
Farmington, NY 14425
Phone: (585) 924-3232
http://www.fingerlakesgaming.com

Lakeside Gaming–Seneca Falls
2552 State Route 89
Seneca Falls, NY 13148
Phone: (315) 568-0994

Lakeside Gaming–Union Springs
271 Cayuga Street
Union Springs, NY 13160
Phone: (315) 889-5416

Mohawk Bingo Palace
202 State Route 37
Hogansburg, NY 13655
http://www.mohawkpalace.com

Monticello Gaming and Raceway
204 Route 17B
Monticello, NY 12701
Phone: (845) 794-4100
http://www.monticelloraceway.com

Saratoga Gaming and Raceway
342 Jefferson Street
Saratoga Springs, NY 12866
Phone: (518) 584-2110
http://www.saratogaraceway.com

Seneca Allegany Casino and Hotel
777 Seneca Allegany Boulevard
Salamanca, NY 14779
Phone: (716) 945-9300
http://www.senecaalleganycasino.com

Seneca Buffalo Creek Casino
1 Fulton Street
Buffalo, NY 14204
Phone: (716) 853-7576
http://www.senecagamingcorp.com/sbcc

Seneca Gaming–Irving
11099 Route 5
Irving, NY 14081
Phone: (716) 549-6356
http://www.senecagames.com

Seneca Gaming–Salamanca
768 Broad Street
Salamanca, NY 14779

Phone: (716) 945-4080
http://www.senecagames.com

Seneca Niagara Casino
310 Fourth Street
Niagara Falls, NY 14303
Phone: (716) 299-1100
http://www.senecaniagaracasino.com

Tioga Downs
2184 West River Road
Nichols, NY 13812
Phone: (888) 946-8464
http://www.tiogadowns.com

Turning Stone Casino Resort
5218 Patrick Road
Verona, NY 13478
Phone: (315) 361-7711
http://www.turningstone.com

Vernon Downs
4229 Stuhlman Road
Vernon, NY 13476
Phone: (315) 829-2201
http://www.vernondowns.com

NORTH CAROLINA

Harrah's Cherokee Casino
P.O. Box 1959
Cherokee, NC 28719
Phone: (828) 497-7777
http://www.harrahs.com

NORTH DAKOTA

Dakota Magic Casino
16849 102nd Street Southeast
Hankinson, ND 58041
Phone: (701) 634-3000
http://www.dakotamagic.com

Four Bears Casino & Lodge
202 Frontage Road
New Town, ND 58763
Phone: (701) 627-4018
http://www.4bearscasino.com

Prairie Knights Casino and Lodge
7932 Highway 24
Fort Yates, ND 58538

Phone: (701) 854-7777
http://www.prairieknights.com

Sky Dancer Hotel & Casino
Highway 5 West
Belcourt, ND 58316
Phone: (701) 244-2400
http://www.skydancercasino.com

Spirit Lake Casino & Resort
7889 Highway 57
Spirit Lake, ND 58370
Phone: (701) 766-4747
http://www.spiritlakecasino.com

Turtle Mountain Chippewa Casino
P.O. Box 1449
Highway 5 West
Belcourt, ND 58316
Phone: (701) 477-3281

OKLAHOMA

Ada Gaming Center
1500 North Country Club Road
Ada, OK 74820
Phone: (580) 436-3740
http://www.chickasaw.net

Ada Travel Plaza
201 Latta Road
Ada, OK 74820
Phone: (580) 310-0900
http://www.chickasaw.net

Baby Grand Casino
4901 South Highway Drive
McLoud, OK 7485I
Phone: (405) 964-7263

Black Gold Casino
288 Mulberry Lane
Wilson, OK 73463
Phone: (580) 668-9248
http://www.chickasaw.net

Blue Star Gaming and Casino
30 White Eagle Drive
Ponca City, OK 74601
Phone: (580) 765-0040

Bristow Indian Bingo
121 West Lincoln

Bristow, OK 74010
Phone: (918) 367-9168

Buffalo Run Casino
1000 Buffalo Run Boulevard
Miami, OK 74354
Phone: (918) 542-7140
http://www.buffalorun.com

Cash Springs Gaining Center
West First and Muskogee Streets
Sulphur, OK 73086
Phone: (580) 622-2156

Checotah Indian Community Bingo
830 North Broadway
Checotah, OK 74426
Phone: (918) 473-5200

Cherokee Casino and Resort
19105 East Timbercrest Circle
Catoosa, OK 74015
Phone: (918) 384-7800
http://www. cherokeecasino.com

Cherokee Casino–Ft. Gibson
U.S. Highway 62
Ft. Gibson, OK 74338
Phone: (918) 478-9526
http://www.cherokeecasino.com

Cherokee Casino–Roland
Interstate 40 and Highway 64
Roland, OK 74954
Phone: (918) 427-7491
http://www.cherokeecasino.com

Cherokee Casino–Sallisaw
1621 West Ruth Avenue
Sallisaw, OK 74955
Phone: (918) 774-1600
http://www.cherokeecasino.com

Cherokee Casino–Siloam
7300 West U.S. Highway 412
West Siloam Springs, OK 74338
Phone: (918) 422-6301
http://www.cherokeecasino.com

Cherokee Casino–Tahlequah
16489 Highway 62
Tahlequah, OK 74464

Phone: (918) 207-3600
http://www.cherokeecasino.com

Chisholm Trail Casino
7807 North Highway 81
Duncan, OK 73533
Phone: (580) 255-1668
http://www.chickasaw.net

Choctaw Casino–Broken Bow
1790 South Park Drive
Broken Bow, OK 74728
Phone: (580) 584-5450
http://choctawcasinos.com

Choctaw Casino–Durant
3735 Choctaw Road
Durant, OK 74701
Phone: (580) 920-0160
http://www.choctawcasinos.com

Choctaw Casino–Grant
Route 1, Box 17-1
Grant, OK 74748
Phone: (580) 326-8397
http://www.choctawcasinos.com

Choctaw Casino–Idabel
1425 Southeast Washington
Idabel, OK 74745
Phone: (580) 286-5710
http://www.choctawcasinos.com

Choctaw Casino–McAlester
1638 South George Nigh
   Expressway
McAlester, OK 74501
Phone: (918) 423-8161
http://www.choctawcasinos.com

Choctaw Casino–Pocolo
3400 Service Road
Pocola, OK 74902
Phone: (918) 436-7761
http://www.choctawcasinos.com

Choctaw Casino–Stringtown
895 North Highway 69
Stringtown, OK 74569
Phone: (580) 346-7862
http://www.choctawcasinos.com

Cimarron Casino
821 West Freeman Avenue

Perkins, OK 74059
Phone: (405) 547-5352
http://www.iowanation.org

Comanche Nation Casino
402 South East Interstate Drive
Lawton, OK 73502
Phone: (580) 354-2000
http://www.comanchenationcasino.
   com

Comanche Red River Casino
Highway 36 and Highway 70
Devol, OK 73531
Phone: (580) 299-3378
http://vvww.
   comancheredrivercasino.com

Comanche Spur
9047 US Highway 62
Eldon, Oklahoma 73538
Phone: (580) 492-5502
http://www.comanchespur.com

Comanche Star Casino
Rt 3 and Hwy 53
Walters, OK 73572
Phone: (580) 875-2092
http://www.comanchenation.com/
   starcasino.html

Creek Nation Casino–Eufaula
806 Forest Avenue
Eufaula, OK 74432
Phone: (918) 689-9191

Creek Nation Casino–
   Muscogee
3420 West Peak Boulevard
Muskogee, OK 74403
Phone: (918) 683-1825
http://www.muscogee-casino.com

Creek Nation Casino–Okemah
1100 South Woodie Guthrie
Okemah, OK 74859
Phone: (918) 623-0051
http://www.creeknationcasino.com

Creek Nation Casino–
   Okmulgee
1901 North Wood Drive
Okmulgee, OK 74447

Phone: (918) 756-8400
http://www.cncokmulgee.com

Creek Nation Casino–Tulsa
1616 East 81st Street
Tulsa, OK 74137
Phone: (918) 299-8518
http://www.creeknationcasino.com

Creek Nation Travel Plaza
Highway 75 and 56 Loop
Okmulgee, OK 74447
Phone: (918) 752-9500

Duck Creek Casino
10085 Ferguson Road
Beggs, OK 74421
Phone: (918) 267-3468

Feather Warrior Casino
1407 South Clarence Nash
   Boulevard
Watonga, OK 73772
Phone: (580) 623-7333

Fire Lake Entertainment
   Center
1601 South Gordon Cooper Drive
Shawnee, OK 74801
Phone: (405) 273-2242
http://www.potawatomi.org

Fire Lake Grand Casino
777 Grand Casino Boulevard
Shawnee, OK 74851
Phone: (405) 964-7263
http://www.firelakegrand.com

Fort Sill Apache Casino
2315 East Gore Boulevard
Lawton, OK 73502
Phone: (580) 248-5905

Golden Pony Casino
Hwy. 1-40, Exit 227
Clearview Road
Okemah, OK 74859
Phone: (918) 623-2620
http://www.goldenponycasino.com

Gold Mountain Casino
1410 Sam Noble Parkway
Ardmore, OK73401

Phone: (580) 223-3301
http://www.chickasaw.net

Gold River Bingo and Casino
Highway 281
Anadarko, OK 73005
Phone: (405) 247-6979
http://www.goldriverok.com

Goldsby Gaming Center
1038 West Sycamore Road
Norman, OK 73072
Phone: (405) 329-5447
http://www.chickasaw.net

Grand Lake Casino
24701 South 655th Road
Grove, OK 74344
Phone: (918) 786-8528

High Winds Casino
61475 East 100 Road
Miami, OK 74354
Phone: (918) 541-9463

Kaw Southwind Casino
5640 North LaCann Drive
Newkirk, OK 74647
Phone: (580) 362-2578
http://www.southwindcasino.com

Keetoowah Casino
2450 South Muskogee
Tahlequah, OK 74464
Phone: (918) 456-6131

Lucky Star Casino–Concho
7777 North Highway 81
Concho, OK 73022
Phone: (405) 262-7612
http://www.luckystarcasino.org

Lucky Turtle Casino
64499 East Highway 60
Wyandotte, OK 74370
Phone: (918) 678-3767

Madill Gaming Center
902 South First Street
Madill, OK 73446
Phone: (580) 795-7301

Marlow Gaming Center
Route 3

Marlow, OK 73055
Phone: (580) 255-1668
http://www.chickasaw.net

Miami Tribe Entertainment
202 South 8 Tribes Trail
Miami, OK 74354
Phone: (918) 542-8670

Million Dollar Elm Casino– Sand Springs
301 Blackjack Drive
Sand Springs, OK 74063
Phone: (918) 699-7519
http://www.milliondollarelm.com

Million Dollar Elm Casino– Bartlesville
222 Alien Road
Bartlesville, OK 74003
Phone: (918) 335-7519
http://www.milliondollarelm.com

Million Dollar Elm Casino– Hominy
Highway 99
Hominy, OK 74035
Phone: (918) 885-2990
http://vvww.milliondollarelm.com

Million Dollar Elm Casino– Pawhuska
201 Northwest 15th Street (at Highway 99)
Pawhuska, OK 74056
Phone: (918) 287-1072
http://www.milliondollarelm.com

Million Dollar Elm Casino– Tulsa
951 West 36th Street North
Tulsa, OK 74127
Phone: (918) 699-7740
http://www.milliondollarelm.com

Mystic Winds Casino
12052 Highway 99
Seminole, OK 74868
Phone: (405) 382-3218

Native Lights Casino
12375 North Highway 77
Newkirk, OK 74647

Phone: (580) 448-3100
http://www.nativelightscasino.com

Newcastle Gaming Center
2457 Highway 62 Service Road
Newcastle, OK 73065
Phone: (405) 387-6013
http://www.chickasaw.net

Pawnee Trading Post Casino
1291 Agency Road
Pawnee, OK 74058
Phone: (918) 762-4466
http://www.tradingpostcasino.com

Peoria Gaming Center
8520 South Highway 69A
Miami, OK 74354
Phone: (918) 540-0303

Riverwind Casino
1544 West State Highway 9
Norman, OK 73072
Phone: (405) 364-7171
http://www.riverwindcasino.con

Sac and Fox Casino
42008 Westech Road
Shawnee, OK 74804
Phone: (405) 275-4700
http://www.sandfcasino.com

Seven Clans Paradise Casino
7500 Highway 177
Red Rock, OK 74651
Phone: (580) 723-4005

Silver Buffalo Casino
620 East Colorado Drive
Anadarko, OK 73005
Phone: (405) 247-5471
http://www.silverbuffalocasino.com

The Stables Casino
530 H Street Southeast
Miami, OK 74354
Phone: (918) 542-7884
http://www.the-stables.com

Texoma Gaming Center
1795 Highway 70 East
Kingston, OK 73439
Phone: (580) 564-6000
http://www.chickasaw.net

Thackerville Travel Plaza
Interstate 35, Exit 1
Thackerville, OK 73459
Phone: (580) 276-4706
http://www.chickasaw.net

Thunderbird Casino
15700 East State Highway 9
Norman, OK 73026
Phone: (405) 360-9270

Tonkawa Casino
1000 Alien Drive
Tonkawa, OK 74653
Phone: (580) 628-2624
http://www.tonkawacasino.com

Treasure Valley Gaming Center
1-35, Exit 55 (Highway 7)
Davis, OK 73030
Phone: (580) 369-2895
http://ww.chickasaw.net

Washita Gaming Center
P.O. Box 307
Paoli, OK 73074
Phone: (405) 484-7777
http://www.chickasaw.net

Wilson Travel Plaza
354 Route 1
Wilson, OK 73463
Phone: (580) 668-9248
http://www.chickasaw.net

WinStar Casino
Interstate 35, Exit 1
Thackerville, OK 73459
Phone: (580) 276-4229
http://www.winstarcasinos.com

Wyandotte Nation Casino
1 Jackpot Place
Wyandotte, OK 74370
Phone: (918) 678-4946
http://www.winstarcasinos.com

OREGON

Kah-Nee-Ta High Desert Resort & Casino
6823 Highway 8
Warm Springs, OR 97761

Phone: (541) 553-1112
http://www.kahneeta.com

Kla-Mo-Ya Casino
34333 Highway 97 North
Chiloquin, OR 97624
Phone: (541) 783 7529
http://www.klamoyacasino.com

The Mill Resort & Casino
3201 Tremont Avenue
North Bend, OR 97459
Phone: (541) 756-8800
http://www.themillcasino.com

Old Camp Casino
2205 West Monroe Street
Burns, OR 97720
Phone: (541) 573-1500
http://www.oldcampcasino.com

Seven Feathers Hotel & Casino Resort
146 Chief Miwaleta Lane
Canyonville, OR 97417
Phone: (541) 839-1111
http://www.sevenfeathers.com

Spirit Mountain Casino
P.O. Box 39
Grand Ronde, OR 97343
Phone: (503) 879-2350
http://www.spirit-mountain.com

Three Rivers Casino
1845 US Highway 126
Florence, OR 97439
Phone: (541) 997-7529
http://www.threeriverscasino.com

Wild Horse Gaming Resort
72777 Highway 331
Pendleton, OR 97801
Phone: (541) 278-2274
http://www.wildhorseresort.com

PENNSYLVANIA

Harrah's Chester Casino & Racetrack
35 East 5th Street
Chester, PA 19013

Phone: (484) 490-2207
http://www.harrahs.com

Hollywood Casino at Penn National
720 Bow Creek Road
Grantville, PA 17028
Phone: (717) 469-2211
http://www.pennnational.com

The Meadows
P.O. Box 499
Meadow Lands, PA 15347
Phone: (724) 225-9300
http://www.meadowsgaming.com

Mohegan Sun at Pocono Downs
1280 Highway 315
Wilkes-Barre, PA 18702
Phone: (570) 831-2100
http://www.poconodowns.com

Mount Airy Resort & Casino
44 Woodland Road
Mount Pocono, PA 18344
Phone: (570) 243-4800
http://www.mtairyresort.com

Philadelphia Park Casino and Racetrack
3001 Street Road
Bensalem, PA 19020
Phone: (215) 639-9000
http://www.philadelphiapark.com

Presque Isle Downs & Casino
8199 Perry Highway
Erie, PA 16509
http://www.presqueisledowns.com

RHODE ISLAND

Newport Grand
150 Admiral Kalbfus Road
Newport, RI 02840
Phone: (401) 849-5000
http://www.newportgrand.com

Twin River
1600 Louisquisset Pike
Lincoln, RI 02865
http://www.twinriver.com

SOUTH CAROLINA

Discover Casino Cruises
4491 Waterfront Avenue
Little River, SC 29566
Phone: (843) 249-9811
http://www.diamondcasinocruises.
com

**SunCruz Casino–Myrtle
Beach**
99705 Mineola Avenue
Little River, SC 29566
Phone: (843) 280-2933
http://www.suncruzcasino.com

SOUTH DAKOTA

DEADWOOD

B. B. Cody's
681 Main Street
Deadwood, SD 57732
Phone: (605) 578-3430

Best Western Hickok House
137 Charles Street
Deadwood, SD 57732
Phone: (605) 578-1611
http://www.bestwestern.com

Bourbon Street
667 Main Street
Deadwood, SD 57732
Phone: (605) 578-1297

**Buffalo Bodega Gaming
Complex**
658 Main Street
Deadwood, SD 57732
Phone: (605) 578-9993

Bullock Hotel
633 Main Street
Deadwood, SD 57732
Phone: (605) 578-1745

Cadillac Jack's Gaming Resort
360 Main Street
Deadwood, SD 57732
Phone: (605) 578-1500
http://www.cadillacjacksgaming.
com

Celebrity Hotel & Casino
629 Main Street
Deadwood, SD 57732
Phone: (605) 578-1909
http://www.celebritycasinos.com

**Deadwood Dick's Saloon &
Nickel Dick's**
51 Sherman Street
Deadwood, SD 57732
Phone: (605) 578-3224
http://www.deadwooddicks.com

Deadwood Gulch Resort
304 Cliff Street
Deadwood, SD 57732
Phone: (605) 578-1294
http://www.deadwoodgulch.com

Deadwood Gulch Saloon
560 Main Street
Deadwood, SD 57732
Phone: (605) 578-1207

First Gold Hotel & Gaming
270 Main Street
Deadwood, SD 57732
Phone: (605) 578-977
http://www.firstgold.com

Four Aces
531 Main Street
Deadwood, SD 57732
Phone: (605) 578-2323
http://www.fouracesdeadwood.com

Goldberg's
670 Main Street
Deadwood, SD 57732
Phone: (605) 578-1515

Gold Country Inn
801 Main Street
Deadwood, SD 57732
Phone: (605) 578-2393

**Gold Dust Gaming &
Entertainment Complex**
688 Main Street
Deadwood, SD 57732
Phone: (605) 578-2100

Gulches of Fun
225 Club Street
Deadwood, SD 57732
Phone: (605) 578-7550

Hickok's Saloon
685 Main Street
Deadwood, SD 57732
Phone: (605) 578-2222

**Lucky 8 Gaming Hall/Super8
Motel**
196 Cliff Street
Deadwood, SD 57732
Phone: (605) 575-2535
http://www.deadwoodsuper8.com

Midnight Star
677 Main Street
Deadwood, SD 57732
Phone: (605) 578-1555
http://www.themidnightstar.com

**Mineral Palace Hotel &
Gaming Complex**
601 Main Street
Deadwood, SD 57732
Phone: (605) 578-2036
http://www.mineralpalace.com

Miss Kitty's Gaming Emporium
647 Main Street
Deadwood, SD 57732
Phone: (605) 578-1811
http://www.historicbullock.com/
kitty

Mustang Sally's
634 Main Street
Deadwood, SD 57732
Phone: (605) 578-2025

Old Style Saloon #10
657 Main Street
Deadwood, SD 57732
Phone: (605) 578-3346
http://www.saloon10.com

Oyster Bay Fairmont Hotel
628 Main Street
Deadwood, SD 57732
Phone: (605) 578-2205

Silverado Franklin Historic Hotel and Gaming Complex
709 Main Street
Deadwood, SD 57732
Phone: (605) 578-3670
http://www.silveradocasino.com

Tin Lizzie Gaming
555 Main Street
Deadwood, SD 57732
Phone: (605) 578-1715
http://www.tinlizzie.com

Wild Bill Bar and Gambling Hall
608 Main Street
Deadwood, SD 57732
Phone: (605) 578-2177

Wild West Winners Casino
622 Main Street
Deadwood, SD 57732
Phone: (605) 578-1100

Wooden Nickel
9 Lee Street
Deadwood, SD 57732
Phone: (605) 578-1952

OTHER SOUTH DAKOTA AREAS

Dakota Connection
RR 1, Box 177-B
Sisseton, SD 57602
Phone: (605) 698-4273
http://www.dakotanationgaming.com

Dakota Sioux Casino
16415 Sioux Conifer Road
Watertown, SD 57201
Phone: (605) 882-2051
http://www.dakotanationgaming.com

Fort Randall Casino
East Highway 46
Pickstown, SD 57357
Phone: (605) 487-7871
http://www.fortrandall.com

Golden Buffalo Casino
P.O. Box 204

Lower Brule, SD 57548
Phone: (605) 473-5577

Grand River Casino
P.O. Box 639
Mobridge, SD 57601
Phone: (605) 845-7104
http://www.grandrivercasino.com

Lode Star Casino
P.O. Box 140
Fort Thompson, SD 57339
Phone: (605) 245-6000
http://www.lodestarcasino.com

Prarie Wind Casino
HC 49, Box 10
Pine Ridge, SD 57770
Phone: (605) 533-6300
http://www.prariewindcasino.com

Rosebud Casino
P.O. Box 21
Mission, SD 57555
Phone: (605) 378-3800
http://www.rosebudcasino.com

Royal River Casino & Bingo
607 South Veterans Street
Flandreau, SD 57028
Phone: (605) 977-3746
http://www.royalrivercasino.com

TEXAS

Kickapoo Lucky Eagle Casino
Lucky Eagle Drive
Eagle Pass, TX 78852
Phone: (830) 758-1995
http://www.
    kickapooluckyeaglecasino.com

Texas Treasure Casino Cruises
1401 West Wheeler Avenue
Arizona Pass, TX 78336
Phone: (361) 758-4444
http://www.txtreasure.com

WASHINGTON

Chewelah Casino
2555 Smith Road
Chewelah, WA 99109

Phone: (509) 935-6167
http://www.chewelahcasino.com

Coulee Dam Casino
515 Birch Street
Coulee Dam, WA 99155
Phone: (509) 633-0766
http://www.colvillecasinos.com

Emerald Queen Hotel and Casino
5700 Pacific Highway East
Fife, WA 98424
Phone: (206) 594-7777
http://www.emeraldqueen.com

Emerald Queen Casino at I-5
2024 East 29th Street
Tacoma, WA 98404
Phone: (206) 383-1572
http://www.emeraldqueen.com

Little Creek Casino
91 West Highway 108
Shelton, WA 98584
Phone: (360) 427-7711

Lucky Dog Casino
19330 North Highway 101
Shelton, WA 98584
Phone: (360) 877-5656
http://www.theluckydogcasino.com

Lucky Eagle Casino
12888 188th Road SW
Rochester, WA 98579
Phone: (360) 273-2000
http://www.luckyeagle.com

Mill Bay Casino
455 East Wapato Lake Road
Manson, WA 98871
Phone: (509) 687-2102
http://www.colvillecasinos.com

Muckleshoot Indian Casino
2402 Auburn Way South
Auburn, WA 98002
Phone: (206) 804-4444
http://www.muckleshootcasino.com

Nooksack River Casino
5048 Mt. Baker Highway

Deming, WA 98244
Phone: (360) 592-5472
http://www.nooksackcasino.com

Northern Lights Casino
12885 Casino Drive
Anacortes, WA 98221
Phone: (360) 293-2691
http://www.swinomishcasino.com

Northern Quest Casino
North 100 Hayford Road
Airway Heights, WA 99001
Phone: (509) 242-7000
http://www.northernquest.com

Okanogan Bingo Casino
41 Appleway Road
Okanogan, WA 98840
Phone: (509) 422-4646
http://www.colvillecasinos.com

The Point Casino
7989 Salish Lane Northeast
Kingston, WA 98346
Phone: (360) 297-0070
http://www.pointnopointcasino.
   com

**Quil Ceda Creek Nightclub and
   Casino**
6410 33rd Avenue Northeast
Tulalip, WA 98271
Phone: (360) 551-1111
http://www.quilcedacreekcasino.
   coin

**Quinault Beach Resort and
   Casino**
78 Route 115
Ocean Shores, WA 98569
Phone: (360) 289-9466
http://www.quinaultbeachresort.
   com

Red Wind Casino
12919 Yelm Highway
Olympia, WA 98513
Phone: (360) 412-5000
http://www.redwingcasino.net

7 Cedars Casino
27056 Highway 101

Sequim, WA 98382
Phone: (360) 683-7777
http://www.7cedarscasino.com

Shoalwater Casino
4112 Highway 105
Tokeland, WA 98590
Phone: (360) 267-2046

Silver Reef Hotel and Casino
4876 Haxton Way
Ferndale, WA 98248
Phone: (360) 383-0777
http:::/www.silverreefcasino.com

Skagit Valley Casino
590 Dark Lane
Bow, WA 98232
Phone: (360) 724-7777
http://www.theskagit.com

**Suquamish Clearwater Casino
   Resort**
15347 Suquamish Way Northeast
Suquamish, WA 98392
Phone: (360) 598-8700
http://www.clearwatercasino.com

Tulalip Casino
6410 33rd Avenue Northeast
Marysville, WA 98271
Phone: (360) 651-111
http://www.tulalipcasino.com

Two Rivers Casino and Resort
6828-B Highway 25 South
Davenport, WA 99122
Phone: (509) 772-4000
http://www.tworiverscasinoand
   resort.com

Yakama Nation Legends Casino
580 Fort Road
Toppenish, WA 98948
Phone: (509) 865-8800
http://www.yakamalegends.com

WEST VIRGINIA

Charles Town Races
P.O. Box 551
Charles Town, WV 25414

Phone: (304) 723-7001
http://www.ctownraces.com

**Mountaineer Park and Gaming
   Resort**
State Route 2
Chester, WV 26034
Phone: (304) 387-2400
http://www.mtrgaming.com

**Tri-State Greyhound Park &
   Video Lottery**
1 Greyhound Lane
Cross Lanes, WV 25356
Phone: (304) 776-1000
http://www.tristateracetack.com

**Wheeling Downs Race Track &
   Gaming Center**
1 South Stone Street
Wheeling, WV 26003
Phone: (304) 232-5050
http://www.www.wheelingdowns.
   com

WISCONSIN

Bad River Lodge and Casino
U.S. Highway 2
P.O. Box 11
Odanah, WI 54861
Phone: (715) 682-6102
http://www.badriver.com

DeJope Gaming
4002 Evan Acres Road
Madison, WI 53718
Phone: (608) 223-9575
http://www.dejope.com

Ho Chunk Casino
S3214A Highway 12
Baraboo, WI 53913
Phone: (608) 223-9576
http:// www.ho-chunk.com

**Hole in the Wall Casino and
   Hotel**
P.O. Box 98 Highway 35 & 77
 Danbury, WI 54830
Phone: (715) 656-3444
http://www.holeinthewallcasino.
   com

Isle Vista Casino
Highway 13 North
Box 1167
Bayfield, WI 58414
Phone: (715) 779-3712

Lake of the Torches Resort Casino
510 Old Abe Road
Lac du Flambeau, WI 54538
Phone: (715) 588-7070
http://www.lakeofthetorches.com

LCO Casino, Lodge and Convention Center
13767 West Country Road B
Hayward, WI 54843
Phone: (715) 634-5643
http://www.lcocasino.com

Majestic Pines Bingo and Casino
W9010 Highway 54 East
Black River Falls, WI 54615
Phone: (715) 284-9098
http://www.mpcwin.com

Menominee Casino, Bingo and Hotel
P.O. Box 760
Highway 47 & 55
Keshena, WI 54135
Phone: (715) 799-3600
http://www.menomineecasino
    resort.com

Mohican North Star Casino
W12180A Country Road A
Bowler, WI 54416
Phone: (715) 787-3110
http://www.mohicannorth.com

Mole Lake Regency Casino
Highway 55
Mole Lake, WI 54520
Phone: (715) 478-5290
http://www.molelake.com

Oneida Bingo and Casino
2020 Airport Drive
Green Bay, WI 54313
Phone: (920) 494-4500
http://www.oneidabingoandcasino.
    com

Potawatomi Bingo Casino
1721 West Canal Street
Milwaukee, WI 53233
Phone: (414) 645-6888
http://www.paysbig.com

Potawatomi Bingo/Northern Lights Casino
P.O. Box 140
Highway 32
Carter, WI 54566
Phone: (715) 473-2021
https://www.cartercasino.com

Rainbow Casino and Bingo
949 Country Road G

Nekoosa, WI 54457
Phone: (715) 886-4560
http://www.rbcwin.com

St. Croix Casino and Hotel
777 U.S. Highway 8
Turtle Lake, WI 54889
Phone: (715) 986-4777
http://www.stcroixcasino.com

Whitetail Crossing Casino
27867 Highway 21
Tomah, WI 54660
Phone: (608) 372-3721

WYOMING

Little Wind Casino
690 Blue Sky Highway
Ethete, WY 82520
Phone: (307) 335-8703

Wind River Casino
10369 Highway 789
Riverton, WY 82501
Phone: (307) 856-3964
http://www.windrivercasino.com

APPENDIX V
DIRECTORY OF CANADIAN CASINOS

The following is a directory of selected Canadian casinos. Due to space limitations, this list is not inclusive. Names, addresses, phone numbers, and Web addresses are included when available. Casinos are separated by province and city.

ALBERTA

CALGARY

Cash Casino
4140 Blackfoot Trail Southeast
Calgary, AB T2G 4E6
Phone: (403) 287-1635
http://www.cashcasino.ca

Casino Calgary
1420 Meridian Road Northeast
Calgary, AB T2A 2N9
Phone: (403) 248-9467
http://www.casinoabs.com

Deerfoot Inn and Casino
11500 35 Street Southeast
Calgary, AB T2Z 3W4
Phone: (877) 236-5225
http://www.deerfootinn.com

Elbow River Casino
218 18th Avenue Southeast
Calgary, AB T2G 1L1
Phone: (403) 289-8880
http://www.elbowrivercasino.com

Grey Eagle Casino and Bingo
3777 Grey Eagle Drive
Calgary, AB T3E 3X8
Phone: (403) 385-3777
http://www.greyeaglecasino.ca

Silver Dollar Casino
1010 42nd Avenue Southeast
Calgary, AB T2G 1Z4
Phone: (403) 243-3000
http://www.silverdollarcalgary.com

Stampede Casino
421 12th Avenue South East
Calgary, AB T2G 2W1
Phone: (403) 514-0900
http:// www.stampedecasino.com

Camrose
Camrose Resort and Casino
3201 48 Avenue
Camrose, AB T4V 0K9
Phone: (780) 679-0904
http://www.camroseresortcasino.com

EDMONTON

Baccarat Casino Address
10128 104th Avenue Northwest
Edmonton, AB T5J 4Y8
Phone: (780) 413-3178

Casino Edmonton
7055 Argyll Road
Edmonton, AB T6C 4A5
Phone: (780) 463-9467
http://www.casinoabs.com

Casino Yellowhead
12464 153rd Street
Edmonton, AB T5V 1S5
Phone: (780) 424-9467
http://www.casinoabs.com

Century City and Hotel
13103 Fort Road
Edmonton, AB T6C 4A5
Phone: (780) 643-4000
http://www.cnty.com/casinos/
edmonton

Palace Casino
West Edmonton Mall
2710, 8882 170 Street
Edmonton, AB T5T 4J2
Phone: (780) 444-2112
http://www.palacecasino.com

ENOCH

River Cree Resort and Casino
Whitemud Drive and Winterburn Road
Enoch, AB T7X 3Y3
Phone: (780) 484-2121
http://rivercreeresort.com

FORT MCMURRAY

Boomtown Casino
9825 Hardin Street
Fort McMurray, AB T9H 4G9
Phone: 780-790-9739
http://www.

GRANDE PRAIRIE

Great Northern Casino
10910 107 Avenue
Grande Prairie, AB T8V 7R2
Phone: (780) 539-454
http://www.greatnortherncasino.net

LETHBRIDGE

Casino Lethbridge
3756 2nd Avenue South
Lethbridge, AB T1J 4Y9
Phone: (403) 381-9467
http://www.casinoabs.com

MEDICINE HAT

Casino by Vanshaw
1051 Ross Glen Drive Southeast
Medicine Hat, AB T1B 3Z4
Phone: (403) 504-4586
http://www.medhatlodge.com

MORLEY

Stoney Nakoda Resort and Casino
Highway 40 and Highway 1
Morley, AB T0L 1N0
Phone: (403) 881-2830
http://www.stoneynakodaresort.com

RED DEER

Cash Casino-Red Door
6350 67 Street
Red Deer, AB T4P 3L7
Phone: (403) 346-3339
http://www.cashcasino.ca

Jackpot Casino
4590 47th Avenue
Red Deer, AB T4N 6P8
Phone: (403) 342-5825

ST. ALBERT

Gold Dust Casino
24 Boudreau Road
St. Albert, AB T8N 6K3
Phone: (780) 460-8092
http://www.golddustcasino.ca

WHITECOURT

Eagle River Casino
Highway 43 and Highway 32 North
Whitecourt, AB T7S 1P7
Phone: (780) 779-2727
http://www.eaglerivercasino.ca

BRITISH COLUMBIA

ABBOTSFORD

Playtime Gaming Abbotsford
30835 Peardonville Road
Abbotsford, BC V2A 4N9
Phone: (604) 854-6522

BURNABY

Burnaby Villa Casino
4320 Dominion Street
Burnaby, BC V5G 4M7
Phone: (604) 436-2211

COQUITLAM

Boulevard Casino
2080 United Boulevard
Coquitlam, BC V3K 6W3
Phone: (604) 523-6888
http://www.blvdcasino.com

CRANBROOK

Casino of the Rockies
7777 Mission Road
Cranbrook, BC V1C 7E5
Phone: (250) 417-2772
http://www.steugene.ca/casino

KAMLOOPS

Lake City Casino Kamloops
540 Victoria Steet
Kamloops, BC V1Y 1P6
Phone: (250) 372-3336
http://www.lakecitycasinos.com

KELOWNA

Lake City Casino Kelwna
1300 Water Street
Kelowna, BC V1Y 9P3
Phone: (250) 860-9467
http://www.lakecitycasinos.com/kelowna/index.html

LANGLEY CITY

Cascades Casino
20393 Fraser Highway
Langley City, BC V3A 7N2
Phone: (604) 530-2211
http://www.cascadescasino.ca

NANAIMO

Great Canadian Casino–Nanaimo
620 Terminal Avenue
Nanaimo, BC V9R 5E2
Phone: (250) 753-3033
http://www.greatcanadiancasinos.com/nanaimo

NEW WESTMINSTER

Royal City Star Riverboat Casino
788 Quayside Drive
New Westminster, BC V3M 6Z6

Phone: (604) 519-3660
http://www.royaltowers.com/royalcitystarcasino.htm

Starlight Casino
350 Gifford Street
New Westminster, BC V3M 7A3
Phone: (604) 777-2946
http://www.starlightcasino.ca

PENTICTON

Lake City Casino Penticton
21 Lakeshore Drive West
Penticton, BC V2A 7M5
Phone: (250) 487-1280
http://www.lakecitycasinos.com/penticton/index.html

PRINCE GEORGE

Treasure Cove Casino
2003 Highway 97 South
Prince George, BC V2N 7A3
Phone: (250) 561-2421
http://www.treasurecovecasino.com

QUESNEL

Billy Barker Casino Resort
308 McLean Street
Quesnel, BC V2J 2N9
Phone: (250) 992-5533
http://www.billybarkercasino.com

RICHMOND

River Rock Casino
8811 River Road
Richmond, BC V6X 3P8
Phone: (604) 273-1895
http://www.riverrock.com

VANCOUVER

Edgewater Casino
750 Pacific Boulevard South
Plaza of Nations
Vancouver, BC V6B 5E7
Phone: (604) 687-3343
http://www.edgewatercasino.ca

VICTORIA

Great Canadian Casino–Royal
1708 Island Highway
Victoria, BC V9B 1H8

Phone: (250) 391-0311
http://www.greatcanadiancasinos.com/viewroyal

MANITOBA

GINEW

Roseau River First Nation Community Hall
Highway 75
Ginew, MB R0A 2R0
Phone: (204) 427-2193

SCANTERBURY

South Beach Casino
One Ocean Drive
Scanterbury, MB R0E 1W0
Phone: (877) 77-LUCKY
http://www.southbeachcasino.ca

THE PAS

Aseneskak Casino
Highway 10 Opaskwayak
The Pas, MB R0B 2J0
Phone: (204) 627-2250
http://www.bestlittlecasino.ca

WINNEPEG

Club Regent Casino
1425 Regent Avenue West
Winnipeg, MB R2C 3B2
Phone: (204) 957-2700
http://www.casinosofwinnipeg.com

McPhillips Street Station Casino
484 McPhillips Street
Winnipeg, MB R3G 3H3
Phone: (204) 957-3900
http://www.casinosofwinnipeg.com

NEW BRUNSWICK

FREDERICTON

Fredricton Raceway
Smythe and Saunders Streets
Fredericton, NB E3B 4Y9
Phone: (506) 458-9819

ST. JOHN

Exhibition Park Raceway
McAllister Drive

Saint John, NB E2L 3V1
Phone: (506) 636-6934
http://www.eprraceway.com

NEWFOUNDLAND AND LABRADOR

GOULDS

St. John's Raceway
Lakeview Drive
Goulds, NL A1S 1G7
Phone: (709) 745-6550

NOVA SCOTIA

DARTMOUTH

Dartmouth Spotsplex Bingo
110 Wyse Road
Dartmouth, NS B3A 1M2
Phone: (902) 464-2600
http:// www.dartmouthsportsplex.com

HALIFAX

Casino Nova Scotia–Halifax
1983 Upper Water Street
Halifax, NS B3J 3Y5
Phone: (902) 425-7777
http://www.casinonovascotia.com

SYDNEY

Casino Nova Scotia–Sydney
525 George Street
Sydney, NS B1P 1K5
Phone: (902) 563-7776
http://www.casinonovascotia.com

ONTARIO

BRANTFORD

OLG Casino Brantford
40 Icomm Drive
Brantford, ON N3S 7S9
Phone: (519) 752-5004
http://corporate.olgc.ca/charity/brantford.jsp

Gananoque

Thousand Islands Charity Casino
380 Highway 2
Gananoque, ON K7G 2V4

Phone: (613) 382-6800
http://www.corporate.olgc.ca/charity/thousand.jsp

NIAGRA FALLS

Casino Niagra
5705 Falls Avenue
Niagara Falls, ON L2E 6T3
Phone: (905) 374-3598
http://www.casinoniagara.com

Fallsview Casino Resort
6380 Fallsview Boulevard
Niagara Falls, ON L2G 7X5
Phone: (905) 374-3598
http://www.fallsviewcasinoresort.com

PORT PERRY

Great Blue Heron Casino
21777 Island Road
Port Perry, ON L9L 1B6
Phone: (905) 985-4888
http:// www.greatblueheroncasino.com

RAMA

Casino Rama
5899 Rama Road
Rama, ON L0K 1T0
Phone: (705) 329-3325
http://www.casinorama.com

THUNDER BAY

OLG Casino Thunder Bay
50 South Cumberland Street
Thunder Bay, ON P7B 5L4
Phone: (807) 683-1935

WINDSOR

Caesars Windsor
377 Riverside Drive East
Windsor, ON N9A 7G7
Phone: (519) 258-7878
http://www.casinowindsor.com

QUEBEC

GATINEAU

Casino du Lac Leamy
1 Casino Boulevard

Gatineau, QC J8Y 6W3
Phone: (819) 772-2100
http://www.casino-du-lac-leamy.com

LA MALBAIE

Casino de Charlevoix
183 Rue Richelieu
La Malbaie, QC G5A 1X8
Phone: (418) 665-5300
http://www.casino-de-charlevoix.com

MONTREAL

Casino de Montreal
183 Rue Richelieu
La Malbaie, QC G5A 1X8
Phone: (418) 665-5300
http://www.casino-de-charlevoix.com

QUEBEC CITY

Ludoplex Québec
250G, boulevard Wilfrid-Hamel

ExpoCité
Quebec City, QC G1L 5A7
Phone: (877) 700-5836
http://www.ludoplex-quebec.com

SASKATCHEWAN

MOOSE JAW

Casino Moose Jaw
21 Fairford Street East
Moose Jaw, SK S6H Canada
Phone: (306) 694-3888
http://www.casinomoosejaw.com

NORTH BATTLEFORD

Gold Eagle Casino
11902 Railway Avenue
North Battleford, SK S9A 3K7
  Canada
Phone: (306) 446-3833
 http://www.siga.sk.ca/gold_eagle/
  index.html

PRINCE ALBERT

Northern Lights Casino
44 Marquis Road West
Prince Albert, SK S6V 7Y5
Phone: (306) 764-4777
http://www.siga.sk.ca

REGINA

Casino Regina
1880 Saskatchewan Drive
Regina, SK S4P 0B2
Phone: (306) 565-3000
http://www.casinoregina.com

SASKATOON

Dakota Dunes Casino
Highway 219
Saskatoon, SK S7N 4K4
Phone: (306) 667-6400
http://www.dakotadunes.ca

APPENDIX VI
DIRECTORY OF CRUISE LINES

The following is a selected listing of cruise lines featuring cruises with onboard casinos. Contact the human resources department of each line to inquire about openings and opportunities. While you will have the opportunity to travel in this type of position, don't forget that when working in casinos on cruise ships you will be away from home for extended periods of time.

American Canadian Caribbean Line
461 Water Street
P.O. Box 368
Warren, RI 02885
Phone: (401) 247-0955
Fax: (401) 247-2350
E-mail: info@accl-smallships.com
http://www.accl-smallships.com

Carnival Cruise Lines
3655 Northwest 87th Avenue
Miami, FL 33178
Phone: (305) 599-2600
Fax: (305) 406-4700
http://www.carnival.com

Celebrity Cruise Lines
1080 Caribbean Way
Miami, FL 33132
Phone: (305) 262-6677
Fax: (305) 267-3505
E-mail: contact@celebritycruises.com
http://www.celebritycruises.com

Costa Cruise Lines
200 South Park Road
Hollywood, FL 33021
Phone: (954) 266-5600
E-mail: communication@us.costa.it
http://www.costacruise.com

Crystal Cruise Lines
2049 Century Park East
Los Angeles, CA 90067
Phone: (888) 722-0021
http://www.crystalcruises.com

Cunard Lines
6100 Blue Lagoon Drive
Miami, FL 33126
Phone: (305) 463-3000
Fax: (305) 463-3010
E-mail: info@cunard.com
http://www.cunardline.com

Holland America Line
300 Elliott Avenue West
Seattle, WA 98119
Phone: (206) 281-3535
Fax: (206) 281-7110
http://www.hollandamerica.com

Norwegian Cruise Line
7665 Corporation Center Drive
Miami, FL 33126
Phone: (305) 436-4000
Fax: (305) 436-4120
http://www.ncl.com

Princess Cruise Lines
24844 Avenue Rockefeller
Santa Clarita, CA 91355
Phone: (661) 753-0000
http://www.princess.com

Regent Seven Seas Cruise Line
1000 Corporate Drive
Fort Lauderdale, FL 33334
Phone: (310) 312-3368
http://www.regent-seven-seas-cruises-discount.com

Royal Caribbean Cruise Line
1050 Caribbean Way
Miami, FL 33132
Phone: (305) 539-6000
http://www.royalcaribbean.com

APPENDIX VII
GAMING CONFERENCES AND EXPOS

Conferences and expos are a great way to learn about new trends in the gaming industry as well as to attend seminars and to network. This is a listing of some of the more prominent conferences and expos.

Use this list as a beginning. To find additional conferences, contact industry trade associations.

Bingoworld Conference & Expo
BNP Media Gaming Group
505 East Capovilla Avenue, Suite 102
Las Vegas, NV 89119
Phone: (718) 432-8529
http://www.bingoexpo.com
Held each March in Las Vegas and produced by BNP Media, the world's largest bingo conference and tradeshow offers exhibits, seminars, and networking opportunities. It includes Bingo Mexico & Americas, a specialized look at bingo in Latin America.

Casino Marketing Conference
BNP Media Gaming Group
505 East Capovilla Avenue, Suite 102
Las Vegas, NV 89119
Phone: (718) 432-8529
http://www.casinomarketing2008.com
Held each July in Las Vegas and jointly produced by BNP Media and Raving Consulting Company, this is a hard-hitting, senior-level conference that addresses marketing challenges across all facets of the gaming industry. It includes in-depth seminars, exhibits, and networking opportunities.

East Coast Gaming Congress
http://www.eastcoastgaming
   congress.com
Atlantic City conference for the gaming industry of the eastern states.

Florida Gaming Summit
BNP Media Gaming Group
505 East Capovilla Avenue, Suite 102
Las Vegas, NV 89119
Phone: (718) 432-8529
http://www.floridagamingsummit.com
Held each October in Florida and jointly produced by BNP Media and Spectrum Gaming Group, this regional conference offers in-depth seminars, exhibits and networking.

Gaming Technology Summit
BNP Media Gaming Group
505 East Capovilla Avenue, Suite 102
Las Vegas, NV 89119
Phone: (718) 432-8529.
http://www.gametechsummit.com
Held each May in Las Vegas and jointly produced by BNP Media and WhiteSand Consulting, this unique conference and tradeshow provides hands-on technology updates, insights, and strategies for the gaming professional. It features numerous in-depth seminars, exhibits, and networking opportunities.

Global Gaming Expo (G2E)
Phone: (888) 314-1378
E-mail: info@globalgamingexpo.com
http://www.globalgamingexpo.com
Held annually each November in Las Vegas, the Global Gaming Expo (also known as G2E) is the largest gaming tradeshow and conference in the world. The expo is organized by the American Gaming Association and Reed Expositions. It provides industry professionals, gaming executives, and buyers for the gaming industry the opportunity to meet, network, and do business. The expo offers a full conference track as well as exhibits on the trade show floor.

New York Gaming Summit
BNP Media Gaming Group
505 East Capovilla Avenue, Suite 102
Las Vegas, NV 89119
Phone: (718) 432-8529
http://www.nysummit.com
Held each June in New York and produced by BNP Media, this regional conference offers in-depth seminars, exhibits and networking opportunities for those interested in the New York and Northeast gaming markets.

Southern Gaming Summit
BNP Media Gaming Group
505 East Capovilla Avenue, Suite 102
Las Vegas, NV 89119
Phone: (718) 432-8529
http://www.sgsummit.com

Held each May in Biloxi, MS, and produced by BNP Media in association with the Mississippi Casino Operators Association, Southern Gaming Summit is the largest commercial gaming show outside of Las Vegas. It offers a large exhibit hall, in-depth seminars, and plenty of networking opportunities.

APPENDIX VIII
SEMINARS AND WORKSHOPS

The following is a listing of associations and companies that offer workshops, seminars, and courses. This is by no means a compete listing. Many associations, schools, agencies, and companies offer other seminars and workshops. Because subject matter changes frequently, many of the organizations running these workshops and seminars did not wish to have their programs listed.

This listing is for your information. It is offered to help you find programs of interest. The author does not endorse any specific program and is not responsible for subject content.

The Advertising Research Foundation
432 Park Avenue South
New York, NY 10016
Phone: (212) 751-5656
http://www.thearf.org
The Advertising Research Foundation conducts a number of conferences and seminars throughout the year on advertising and marketing research.

American Management Association
http://www.american-management-association.org
The American Management Association offers seminars in a wide variety of areas of training ranging from office skills to executive management.

Casino Customer Care Seminars
Shelly Field Organization
Booking and Public Relations Office
P.O. Box 711
Monticello, NY 12701
Phone: (845) 794-7312
http://www.shellyfield.com
Customer service is essential in the gaming industry. Casino Customer Care Seminars offer a variety of training programs to casinos for their employees to the hospitality and casino industry.

Direct Management Association (DMA)
1120 Avenue of the Americas
New York, NY 10036
Phone: (212) 768-7277
Fax: (212) 302-6714
http://www.the-dma.org
The Direct Marketing Association (DMA) offers educational programs, seminars, and workshops in direct marketing.

Global Gaming Expo Training & Development Institute
http://www.globalgamingexpo.com
The Global Gaming Expo Training & Development Institute provides seminar tracks for middle management in the gaming industry. Held in conjunction with the Global Gaming Expo, the seminar is held annually in Las Vegas.

Institute for the Study of Gambling and Commercial Gaming
University of Nevada, Reno
Reno, NV 89557
Phone: (775) 784-1477
http://www.unr.edu/gaming/edp.asp
The Institute for the Study of Gambling and Commercial Gaming offers an executive leadership program for professionals working in the gaming industry.

Morowitz Gaming Advisors
248 South New York Road
Galloway, NJ 08205
Phone: (609) 652-6472
E-mail: info@MorowitzGaming.com
Morowitz Gaming Advisors offer a variety of programs of interest to those in the gaming industry, including a gaming management executive series.

National Indian Gaming Association (NIGA)
224 Second Street, SE
Washington, DC 20003
Phone: (202) 546-7711
Fax: (202) 546-1755
E-mail: info@indiangaming.org
http://www.indiangaming.org
The National Indian Gaming Association offers a variety of seminars and programs throughout the year in an array of training areas. They also host the National Indian Gaming Association Seminar Institute which

offers an array of certificate programs in gaming management, hospitality management, and becoming a certified gaming commissioner among others. In addition, the NIGA offers on-site programs in various areas of the gaming industry.

Shelly Field Motivational Programs and Seminars

SFO Booking Office
P.O. Box 711
Monticello, NY 12701
Phone: (845) 794-7312
http://www.shellyfield.com

Shelly Field offers a variety of motivational programs, seminars, and keynote presentations to casinos, conventions, and corporations throughout the country in areas including careers, human resources, employee recruitment and retention, customer service, motivation, empowerment, humor in the workplace, stress management, and gaming.

Stress Busters: Beating the Stress in Your Work and Your Life Seminars and Keynote Presentations

SFO Booking Office
P.O. Box 711
Monticello, NY 12701

Phone: (845) 794-7312
http://www.shellyfield.com

Stress is a fact of life and a key issue in today's work environment, and casinos are no exception. Stressed employees are never the casino's best employees. Managing stress on a daily basis is a big step toward managing overall stress. Stress Busters seminars offer programs, workshops, and keynote presentations to casinos, conventions, and corporations throughout the country on busting the stress out of life and work.

Public Relations Society of America (PRSA)

33 Maiden Lane
New York, NY 10038
Phone: (212) 460-1400
Fax: (212) 995-0757

The Public Relations Society of America offers seminars, conferences, and workshops in an array of public relations–oriented subjects.

UNLV International Gaming Institute

The UNLV International Gaming Institute is one of the most recognized gaming schools in the world. It offers a wide array of casino management seminars, certificate programs, and lecture series in all facets of the gaming industry.

APPENDIX IX
GAMING INDUSTRY WEB SITES

The Internet hosts a wealth of information on gaming, casinos, and industry news. The following is a selected listing of Web sites related to the gaming industry. Use this list as a beginning. There are many more sites on the World Wide Web to explore.

Alberta Gaming Research Institute
http://www.abgaminginstitute.ualberta.ca
Links to research on Canadian gaming.

American Gaming Association
http://www.americangaming.org
Trade association for the gaming industry.

Atlantic City Casino Gambling & Casino Guide
http://www.atlanticcitynj.com/visitors_casino.asp
Information on Atlantic City.

Canadian Gaming News
http://www.canadiangaming.com
News about Canadian gaming.

Casino Center
http://www.casinocenter.com
Information on casinos, gaming, and publications.

Casino City
http://www.casinocity.com
Casino directory and other casino information.

Casino Journal
http://www.casinojournal.com
Industry periodical online.

Casinoman.net
http://www.casinoman.net
Information on online gambling and gambling in general.

Casinonet
http://www.casinonet.com
Info on online casinos.

Casino Vendors
http://www.casinovendors.com
Information on vendors for casino products.

Center for Gaming Research– UNLV
http://gaming.unlv.edu
Gambling resources and informaiton.

Christiansen Capital Advisors
http://www.cca-i.com
Iinformation on gaming industry.

Colorado Casinos
http://www.coloradocasinos.net
Info on casinos and casino hotels in Colorado.

Detroit News Casino Guide
http://info.detnews.com/casino/casinodirectory.cfm
Information on casinos in the Detroit area.

Gambling Treatment & Research Center
http://www.gamblingtreatment.net
Information on gambling treatment and research from the University of Connecticut Health Center.

Global Gaming Expo
http://www.globalgamingexpo.com
Largest gaming industry expo.

IGT
https://www.igt.com
Gaming machine manufacturer Web site.

Indian Gaming
http://www.indiangaming.com

International Gaming & Wagering Business
http://www.igwb.com
Gaming industry publication.

LasVegas.com
http://www.lasvegas.com
Everything about Las Vegas.

Las Vegas Review Journal
http://www.lvrj.com
Las Vegas newspaper.

Michigan Gaming
http://www.michigangaming.com
Information on gaming in the state of Michigan.

Michigan Gaming Control Board
http://www.michigan.gov/mgcb
Licenses and regulates casinos in the state.

OG Paper
http://www.ogpaper.com
Gambling and entertainment news.

Pechanga.net
http://www.pechanga.net
Indian gaming news.

Rolling Good Times
http://www.rgtonline.com
Gambling news.

Shellyfield.com
http://www.shellyfield.com
Information on careers, stress
  management, and training
  programs in the gaming industry.

The Casino Net
http://www.thecasinonet.com
Gaming information.

Urbino Net
http://urbino.net
Gaming news.

APPENDIX X
CAREER AND JOB WEB SITES

The Internet is a premier resource for information, no matter what you need. Surfing the net can help you locate almost anything you want from information to services and everything in between.

Throughout the appendices of this book, whenever possible, Web site addresses have been included to help you find information quicker. This listing contains an assortment of career and job oriented Web sites. Some are geared specifically to the casino and hospitality industries, while others are more general.

Use this list as a start. More sites are emerging every day. This listing is for your information. The author is not responsible for any site content. Inclusion or exclusion in this listing does not imply any one site is endorsed or recommended over another by the author.

American Casino and Entertainment Properties, LLC
https://www.hrapply.com/stratosphere/Setup.app

Binions Gambling Hall Employment
http://www.binions.com/employment/index.html

The Borgata–Atlantic City
http://www.borgatajobs.com

Boyd Gaming Careers
http://www.boydgaming.com/careers

Careerbuilder.com
http://www.careerbuilder.com

Career Voyages
http://www.careervoyages.gov

Casino Association of Indiana
http://www.casinoassociation.org

Casino Careers Online
http://www.casinocareers.com

Casino Executive Search
http://www.casinoexecsearch.com

Casino Jobs Blog
http://www.casinodealercollege.com/casino_jobs

CasinoStaff.com
http://www.casinostaff.com

Foxwoods Resort Casino Careers
http://www.foxwoods.jobs

GamblingJobs.com
http://www.gamblingjobs.com

Gecko Hospitality
http://www.geckohospitality.com

Hard Rock Las Vegas
http://www.hardrockhotel.com/employment.cfm

Harrah's Employment
http://www.harrahs.com/harrahs-corporate/careers-home.html

Hoteljobs.com
http://www.hoteljobs.com

HotJobs.com
http://www.hotjobs.com

Indeed.com
http://www.indeed.com

LasVegasCasinojobs.com
http://www.lvcasinojobs.com

Majestic Star Casinos
http://vegas.fitzgeralds.com

MGM Grand–Foxwoods Employment
http://www.mgmatfoxwoods.com/AboutUs/Employment.aspx

MGM Mirage Careers
http://www.mgmmiragecareers.com

Mohegan Sun Employment
http://mohegansun.com/employment

Monster.com
http://www.monster.com

Norwegian Cruise Lines
http://www.ncl.com/nclweb/cruiser/cmsPages.html?pageId=JoinOurTeam

Palms Las Vegas Casino Resort Employment
http://www.palms.com/employment.php

Plaza Hotel Casino Careers
http://www.plazahotelcasino.com/careers.php

Planet Hollywood
http://www.planethollywoodresort.com/ftr_careers.php

Recruiting Nevada
http://www.recruitingnevada.com

Resorts International Careers
https://www.hrapply.com/resorts/
setup.app

**Sahara Casino Hotel
Employment**
http://www.saharavegas.com/
employment

ShellyField.com Casino Careers
http://shellyfield.com/casinocareers.
htm

Silverton Casino Hotel Jobs
https://www.jobflash.com/websub/
user/reg.jsp?company_id=260

Station Casinos Careers
http://www.stationcasinos.com/
corp/careers

**Tropicana Casino–Atlantic City
Careers**
http://www.tropicana.net/
employment

Tropicana Casino–Las Vegas
http://www.tropicanalv.com

Trump Casinos–Atlantic City
http://www.trumpemployment.com

**Tuscany Suites and Casino
Employment**
http://www.tuscanylv.com/index.
php?pid=CAREERS

**Venetian Resort and Casino
Employment**
http://www.venetian.com/Pages.
aspx?id=680

APPENDIX XI
RECUITERS, SEARCH FIRMS, AND HEADHUNTERS

The following is a selected listing of recruiters, search firms, and headhunters that specialize in the gaming, hospitality and restaurant industries. Space restrictions limit listing every company and firm.

This listing is for your information. Use it as a start. The author is not responsible for any site content. Inclu-sion or exclusion in this listing does not imply any one company is endorsed or recommended over another by the author.

Boutique Search Firm
3916 Sepulveda Boulevard
Culver City, CA 90230
Phone: (310) 398-9320
Fax: (310) 398-9541
http://www.boutiquesearchfirm.com

Bristol Associates
5757 West Century Boulevard
Suite 628
Los Angeles, CA 90045
Phone: (310) 670-0525
Fax: (310) 670-4075
http://www.bristolassoc.com

Casino Executive Search
Ridgewood Plaza
Suite 205
Northfield, NJ 08225
Phone: (732) 583-0597
Fax: (732) 583-4411
http://www.casinoexecutivesearch.
   com

Robert W. Dingman Co., Inc.
650 Hampshire Road
Westlake Village, CA 91361
Phone: (805) 778-1777
Fax: (805) 778-9288
http://www.dingman.com

Ferree & Associates, Inc.
P.O. Box 677
Gig Harbor, WA 98335
Phone: (253) 851-7300

Fax: (253) 851-6818
http://www.FerreeAssociates.com

Charles Foster Staffing
7301 Rivers Avenue
North Charleston, SC 29406
Phone: (843) 572-8100
Fax: (843) 576-0000
http://www.charlesfoster.net

Gecko Hospitality
718 Ogden Avenue
Downers Grove, IL 60615
Phone: (630) 390-1000
Fax: (630) 598-0753
http://www.geckohospitality.com

Horizon Hospitality Associates
14516 Woodson Street
Overland Park, KS 66223
Phone: (913) 897-3100
Fax: (913) 897-3103
http://www.horizonhospitality.com

Hospitality Careers
1507 Springtree Circle
Richardson, TX 75082
Phone: (972) 437-0900
Fax: (972) 437-0959
http://www.hospitalitycareersusa.
   com

Hospitality Career Services
5035 East Barwick Drive
Cave Creek, AZ 85331

Phone: (480) 585-0707
Fax: (480) 585-7377
http://www.hotelheadhunter.com

Hospitality Executive
2222 Michelson Drive
Irvine, CA 92612
Phone: (714) 389-3675
Fax: (714) 389-3681
http://www.hospitalityexecutive.
   com

Hospitality Management Solutions
3 Plummer Road
Bolton, ON, L7E 1V1
Phone: (905) 857-0040
Fax: (905) 857-0043
http://www.hmscareers.com

Lyons Associates
480 Broadway
Saratoga Springs, NY 12866
Phone: (518) 583-0444
Fax: (518) 583-0421

Navagante Group
4335 South Industrial Road
Las Vegas, NV 89013
Phone: (702) 798-1000
http://www.navegantegroup.com

Specialty Search International, Inc.
P.O. Box 984

Oldsmar, FL 34677
Phone: (813) 818-7800
Fax: (813) 818-7400
http://www.ssirecruiting.com

J. E. Wottowa & Associates, Inc.
1108 Olive Street
Suite 100

St. Louis, MO 63101
Phone: (314) 621-4900
Fax: (314) 621-2683
http://www.jewottowa.com

Windsor Executive Search
2541 White Mountain Highway
Unit 74

North Conway, NH 03860
Phone: (800) 383-8211
Fax: (603) 383-4475
http://www.windsorexecutivesearch.
  com

BIBLIOGRAPHY

A. BOOKS

There are thousands of books written on all aspects of casino and casino hotel careers. The books listed below are separated into general categories. The subject matter in many of the books overlaps into other categories.

These books can be found in bookstores and libraries. If your local library does not have the books you want, you might ask your librarian to order them for you through the interlibrary loan system.

The list is meant as a beginning. For other books that might interest you, look in the career section of the bookstores and libraries. You can also check *Books in Print* (found in the reference section or online in libraries) for other books on the subject.

ACCOUNTING AND FINANCIAL MANAGEMENT

Cote, Raymond. *Basic Hotel and Restaurant Accounting.* Lansing, Mich.: Educational Institute of the American Hotel and Motel Association, 2006.

Harris, Peter J. *Accounting and Financial Management: Developments in the International Hospitality Industry.* Burlington, N.J.: Elsevier Science & Technology Books, 2006.

Jagels, Martin G. *Hospitality Management Accounting.* Hoboken, N.J.: John Wiley & Sons, 2006.

Schmidgall, Raymond S. *Hospitality Industry Managerial Accounting.* Lansing, Mich.: Educational Institute of the American Hotel & Lodging Association, 2006.

Weygandt, Jerry J. *Hospitality Financial Accounting.* Hoboken, N.J.: John Wiley and Sons, 2008.

ADVERTISING CAREERS

Field, Shelly. *Career Opportunities in Advertising and Public Relations.* New York: Facts On File, 2005.

BARTENDING

Daugherty, Shaun. *Extra Dry, with a Twist: An Insider's Guide to Bartending.* Bloomington, Ind.: iUniverse, Incorporated, 2007.

Julyan, Brian K. *Sales and Service for the Wine Professional.* London: Cengage Learning, 2008.

Katsigris, Costas. *The Bar and Beverage Book.* Hoboken, N.J.: John Wiley & Sons, 2007.

Marcus, Lori. *Bartending Inside-Out: The Guide to Profession, Profit, and Fun.* Crystal Bay, Nev.: Cadillac Press, 2008.

Miron, Amanda. *The Professional Bar and Beverage Manager's Handbook: How to Open and Operate a Financially Successful Bar, Tavern and Night Club.* Ocala, Fla.: Atlantic Publishing Company, 2006.

Parry, Chris. *Bar and Beverage Operation: Ensuring Success and Maximum Profit.* Ocala, Fla.: Atlantic Publishing Company, 2006.

Plotkin, Robert. *1001 Questions Every Bartender and Lounge Lizard Should Know How to Answer.* Tucson, Ariz.: Bar Media, 2005.

Schmid, Albert W. A. *Hospitality Manager's Guide to Wines, Beers, and Spirits.* Old Tappan, N.J.: Prentice Hall PTR, 2007.

CASINO DESIGN

Geller, Michael D. *Don't Play the Slot Machines (until You've Read This Book).* Darby, Pa.: Diane Publishing Company, 2005.

Henderson, Justin. *Casino Design: Resorts Hotels and Themed Entertainment Spaces.* Cincinnati: F & W Publications, 2003.

CASINO ENTERTAINMENT

Eade, Vincent H. *Introduction to the Casino Entertainment Industry.* East Rutherford, N.J.: Prentice Hall PTR, 1999.

CASINO HOTELS

Cafferata, Patty. *Mapes Hotel and Casino: The History of Reno's Landmark Hotel.* Reno, Nev.: Eastern Slope Publisher, 2005.

CASINO OPERATIONS & MANAGEMENT

Eadington, William R. *The Business of Gaming: Economic and Management Issues.* Reno, Nev.: University of Nevada, 1998.

Hashimoto, Kathryn. *Casino Management: A Strategic Approach*. Old Tappan, N.J.: Prentice Hall PTR, 2007.

Hsu, Cathy H. C. *Casino Industry in Asia Pacific: Development, Operation, and Impact*. New York: Routledge, 2005.

Kilby, Jim. *Casino Operations Management*. Hoboken, N.J.: John Wiley and Sons, 2007.

CASINO MARKETING

McNamee, Michael. *Understanding Casino Marketing*. Ocean City, N.J.: Michael McNamee Publishing, 2002.

Romero, John S. *Casino Marketing*. Parker, Colo.: American Eagle Arts & Letters, 1994.

Romero, John S. *Secrets of Casino Marketing: How Casinos Find Gamblers and Keep Them Coming Back*. Parker, Colo.: American Eagle Arts & Letters, 1998.

CASINO SECURITY & SURVEILLANCE

Hashimoto, Kathryn. *Casino Gaming Methods: An Inside Look at Casino Games, Probabilities, Security and Surveillance*. East Rutherford, N.J.: Prentice Hall PTR, 2007.

Lewis, George L., Jr. *Casino Surveillance: The Eye that Never Blinks*. Las Vegas: G & G Surveillance Specialists, 1996.

Litchko, James. *Know IT Security: Secure IT Systems Casino Style*. Kensington, Md.: Know Book Publishing, 2004.

McDowell, Marcia A. *Techniques of Casino Surveillance*. Las Vegas: Candlelight Publishing, 1995.

Powell, Gary L. *Casino Surveillance and Security: 150 Things You Should Know*. Alexandria, Va.: ASIS International, 2003.

Williams, John, J. *Casino Security*. Albuquerque, N.M.: Consumertronics, 1999.

CONCIERGE

Adams, Melinda. *The Shopping Concierge Las Vegas: Your Personal Guide to Great Shopping on the Las Vegas Strip*. Bloomington, Ind.: iUniverse, 2007.

Dismore, Heather. *Start Your Own Personal Concierge Service: Your Step-by-Step Guide to Success*. Irvine, Calif.: Entrepreneur Press, 2007.

CONFERENCES AND CONVENTIONS

Fenich, George G. *Meetings, Expositions, Events, and Conventions: An Introduction to the Industry*. East Rutherford, N.J.: Prentice Hall PTR, 2007.

Golden-Romero, Pat. *Hotel Convention Sales, Services and Operations*. New York: Elsevier Science & Technology Books, 2007.

CULINARY

Chesser, Jerald W. *The World of Culinary Supervision, Training, and Management*. Boston: Prentice Hall Higher Education, 2008.

CUSTOMER SERVICE

Gallagher, Richard S. *What to Say to a Porcupine: 20 Humorous Tales That Get to the Heart of Great Customer Service*. New York: Amacom, 2008.

Kennedy, Dan. *No B. S. Marketing to the Affluent: The No Holds Barred, Kick Butt, Take No Prisoners Guide to Getting Really Rich*. Irvine, Calif.: Entrepreneur Press, 2008.

Livingston, Bob. *How You Do . . . What You Do: Create Service Excellence that Wins Clients for Life*. New York: McGraw-Hill Companies, 2008.

Martinez, Mario. *Building a Customer Service Culture: The Seven Service Elements of Customer Success*. Charlotte, N.C.: Information Age Publishing, 2008.

Michelli, Joseph. *The New Gold Standard: Five Leadership Principles for Creating a Legendary Customer Experience Courtesy of the Ritz-Carlton Hotel Company*. New York: McGraw-Hill Companies, 2008.

Saporito, Richard. *How to Improve Dining Room Service: Includes a Restaurant Performance Evaluation Guide*. Bloomington, Ind.: AuthorHouse, 2007.

Thyne, Maree. *Hospitality, Tourism, and Lifestyle Concepts: Implications for Quality Management and Customer Satisfaction*. New York: Routledge, 2005.

Tisch, Jonathan M. *Chocolates on the Pillow Aren't Enough: Reinventing the Customer Experience*. Hoboken, N.J.: John Wiley & Sons, 2007.

ECONOMICS OF GAMING

Walker, Douglas M. *The Economics of Casino Gambling*. New York: Springer Press, 2007.

FOOD AND BEVERAGE MANAGEMENT

Alcott, Peter. *Food and Beverage Management*. Burlington, Mass.: Elsevier Science & Technology Books, 2008.

FOOD SERVICE

Chesser, Jerald W. *The World of Culinary Supervision, Training, and Management*. Boston: Prentice Hall Higher Education, 2008.

Dopson, Lea R. *Food and Beverage Cost Control.* Hoboken, N.J.: John Wiley & Sons, 2007.

Edelstein, Sari. *Managing Food and Nutrition Services for Culinary, Hospitality, and Nutrition Professionals.* Sudbury, Mass.: Jones & Barlett Publishers, 2007.

Lynch, Francis T. *The Book of Yields: Accuracy in Food Costing and Purchasing.* Edison, N.J.: John Wiley & Sons, 2007.

Morgan, James L. *Culinary Creation: An Introduction to Foodservice and World Cuisine.* Burlington, Mass.: Elsevier Science & Technology Books, 2006.

Theis, Monica. *Introduction to Foodservice.* Boston: Prentice Hall Higher Education, 2008.

FRONT OFFICE MANAGEMENT

Bardi, James A. *Hotel Front Office Management.* Hoboken, N.J.: John Wiley & Sons, 2006.

Kasavana, Michael L. *Managing Front Office Operations.* 7th ed. Lansing, Mich.: Educational Institute of the American Hotel & Lodging Association, 2005.

GAMBLING & GAMING

Anonymous. *Casino Confidential: A Pit Boss's Guide to Beating the House.* Philadelphia: Quirk Books, 2007.

Apostolico, David. *The Pocket Idiot's Guide to Casino Comps.* New York: Penguin Group, 2007.

Cintron, Hector L. *The Other Side of the Table.* Bloomington, Ind.: AuthorHouse, 2008.

Friedberg, Mark Ira. *Confessions of a Poker Dealer: A Short History of Poker Played in Casino's since the Late 1970's.* Bloomington, Ind.: AuthorHouse, 2007.

Gollehon, John. *Strike the Casino with Winning Strategies.* Grand Rapids, Mich.: Gollehon Press, 2007.

Hoffer, Richard. *Jackpot Nation: Rambling and Gambling across Our Landscape of Luck.* New York: Harper Collins Publishers, 2008.

Mendelson, Paul. *The Mammoth Book of Poker.* Philadelphia: Running Press Book Publishers, 2008.

Sinkow, Barry. *The Count in Monte Carlo: An Insider's Look at Casino Life.* Bloomington, Ind.: AuthorHouse, 2008.

Smith, James W. *Deal by Me: A Golden Opportunity Blown.* Bloomington, Ind.: AuthorHouse, 2008.

Smith, Shane. *Tournament Tips from the Poker Pros.* New York: Cardoza Publishing, 2008.

GAMING INDUSTRY

Bloom, Steve. *Casino City's Global Gaming Almanac.* Newton, Mass.: Casino City Press, 2007.

Meister, Alan. *Casino City's Indian Gaming Industry Report: 2007–2008 Edition.* Newton, Mass.: Casino City Press, 2007.

Nevada Gaming Industry Business Law Handbook. Washington, D.C.: International Business Publications, 2005.

HISTORY OF GAMBLING

Schwartz, David G. *Roll the Bones: The History of Gambling.* Collingdale, Pa.: Diane Publishing, 2008.

HOSPITALITY BUSINESS, MANAGEMENT AND OPERATIONS

Barrows, Clayton W. *Introduction to Management in the Hospitality Industry.* Edison, N.J.: John Wiley & Sons, 2008.

Walker, John R. *Introduction to Hospitality Management.* Upper Saddle River, N.J.: Pearson Education, 2005.

HOSPITALITY MARKETING

Lazer, William. *Hospitality and Tourism Marketing.* Lansing, Mich.: Educational Institute of the American Hotel & Lodging Association, 2006.

HOSPITALITY INDUSTRY HUMAN RESOURCES

Hayes, David K. *Human Resources Management in the Hospitality Industry.* Hoboken, N.J.: John Wiley and Sons, 2008.

Reynolds, Dennis, and Karthikeyan Namasivayam. *Human Resources in the Foodservice Industry: Organizational Behavior Management Approaches.* Boca Raton, Fla.: CRC Press, 2007.

Schilagi, Frank J. *Reality Check for Leaders: A Workable Approach to Maximizing your Results as a Leader in the Hospitality Industry.* N.C.: Directions Incorporated, 2007.

HOSPITALITY INDUSTRY OPERATIONS AND MANAGEMENT

Hayes, David K. *Hotel Operations Management.* Moorpark, Calif.: Academic Internet Publishers, 2006.

Powers, Tom. *Introduction to Management in the Hospitality Industry.* Hoboken, N.J.: John, Wiley & Sons, 2008.

Rutherford, Denney G. *Hotel Management and Operations.* Hoboken, N.J.: John Wiley & Sons, 2006.

Vallen, Gary, and Jerome Vallen. *Check-In Check-Out: Managing Hotel Operations*. Boston: Prentice Hall Higher Education, 2008.

INDIAN GAMING

Kallen, Stuart A. *Indian Gaming*. Farmington Hills, Mich.: Gale, 2005.

Light, Steven Andrew. *Indian Gaming and Tribal Sovereignty: The Casino Compromise*. Lawrence: University Press of Kansas, 2007.

Meister, Alan. *Casino City's Indian Gaming Industry Report*. Newton, Mass.: Casino City Press, 2008.

Rand, Kathryn R. L. *Indian Gaming Law: Cases and Materials*. Durham, N.C.: Carolina Academic Press, 2008.

U.S. Senate Committee on Indian Affairs. *Off-Reservation Gaming: Hearing Before the Committee on Indian Affairs. United States Senate, One Hundred Ninth Congress, Second Session, on Oversight Hearing for the Process of Considering Gaming Applications*. Washington, D.C.: U.S. Government Printing Office, 2006.

Valley, David J. *Jackpot Trail: Indian Gaming in Southern California*. El Cajon, Calif.: Sunbelt Publications, 2003.

West, Patsy. *The Enduring Semioles: From Alligator Wrestling to Casino Gaming*. Gainesville: University Press of Florida, 2008.

LAS VEGAS

Burbank, Jeff. *Las Vegas Babylon: The True Tales of Glitter, Glamour, and Greed*. New York: M. Evans & Company, 2008.

Fenster, Jay, and Avery Cardoza. *Open Road's Best of Las Vegas*. 2nd ed. Cold Spring Harbor, N.Y.: Open Road Publishing, 2008.

Gould, Lark Ellen. *Little Black Book of Las Vegas: The Essential Guide to Sin City*. White Plains, N.Y.: Peter Pauper Press, 2008.

RESTAURANT MANAGEMENT

De Cali, Emery. *Excellence for Restaurant and Hotel Owners Secrets Revealed*. Charleston, S.C.: BookSurge, 2008.

Meyer, Danny. *Setting the Table: The Transforming Power of Hospitality in Business*. New York: HarperCollins Publishers, 2008.

SALES AND MARKETING

Oh, Haemoon. *Handbook of Hospitality Marketing Management*. Burlington, Mass.: Elsevier Science & Technology Books, 2008.

Pike, Steven. *Destination Marketing: An Integrated Marketing Communication Approach*. Burlington, Mass.: Elsevier Science & Technology Books, 2008.

Shoemaker, Stowe. *Marketing Essentials in Hospitality and Tourism: Foundations and Practices*. East Rutherford, N.J.: Prentice Hall PTR, 2007.

Sweeney, Susan. *101 Ways to Promote Your Tourism Web Site*. Gulf Breeze, Fla.: Maximum Press, 2008.

SPECIAL EVENTS AND EVENT MANAGEMENT

Allen, Johnny. *Festival and Special Event Management*. Hoboken, N.J.: John Wiley & Sons, 2008.

Carter, Laurence. *Event Planning*. Bloomington, Ind.: AuthorHouse, 2007.

Mancuso, Jennifer. *Guide to Being an Event Planner: Insider Advice on Turning Your Creative Energy into a Rewarding Career*. Avon, Mass.: Adams, 2007.

Matthews, Doug. *Special Event Production: The Resources*. Burlington, Mass.: Elsevier Science & Technology Books, 2007.

Owens, John. *Opening Night: Creating Successful Events*. Charleston: BookSurge, 2008.

Robertson, Martin. *Events and Festivals: Current Trends and Issues*. New York: Routledge, 2008.

TOURISM

Kozak, Metin, and Ozan Bahan. *Tourism Economics: Concepts and Practices*. Hauppauge, N.Y.: Nova Science Publishers, 2008.

Kozak, Metin. *Progress in Tourism Marketing*. Burlington, Mass.: Elsevier Science & Technology Books, 2006.

WRITING

Konradt, Brian. *Freelance Poker Writing: How to Make Money Writing for the Gaming Industry*. Surfside Beach, S.C.: Writing Career Press, 2007.

B. PERIODICALS

Magazines, newspapers, membership bulletins, and newsletters may be helpful for finding information about a specific job category, finding a job in a specific field, or giving you insight into what certain jobs entail.

As with the books in the previous section, this list should serve as a beginning. The gaming industry, like others, has trade publications as well as consumer publications.

There are many periodicals that are not listed because of space limitations. The subject matter of some periodicals may overlap with others. Periodicals also tend to come and go. Look in your local library or in the newspaper/magazine shop for other periodicals that might interest you.

ADVERTISING

Advertising Age
Crain Communications, Inc.
711 Third Avenue
New York, NY 10017
Phone: 212-210-0280
E-mail: info@crain.com
http://www.crain.com

ATLANTIC CITY

Atlantic City Insider
Casino Journal Publishing Group
8025 Black Horse Pike
Atlantic City, NJ 08232
Phone: (609) 484-8866
Fax: (609) 645-1661
http://www.casinocenter.com

Atlantic City Magazine
South Jersey Publishing Company
1000 West Washington Avenue
Pleasantville, NJ 08232
Phone: (609) 272-7900
Fax: (609) 272-7900

Atlantic City Weekly
1701 Walnut Street
Philadelphia, PA 19103
Phone: (215) 563-7400
E-mail: editorial@whoot.com
http://www.acweekly.com

New Jersey. Casino Control Commission Annual Report
Public Information Assistant
Arcade Building
Tennessee Avenue & The Boardwalk
Atlantic City, NJ 08401
Phone: (609) 441-3749

New Jersey State Bar Association Casino Law Section Newsletter
One Constitution Square
New Brunswick, NJ 08901
Phone: (732) 249-5000
Fax: (732) 828-0034

BINGO

Bingo Bugle
Frontier Publications, Inc.
P.O. Box 527
Vashon, WA 98070
Phone: (206) 463-5656
Fax: (206) 463-5630
http://www.bingobugle.com

Bingo Manager
P.O. Box 14268
St. Paul, MN 55114

CANADIAN CASINOS

Bingo News & Gambling Hi-Lites
806-10135 Saskatchewan Drive Northwest
Edmonton, AB T6E 4R5
Canada
Phone: (780) 433-9740
Fax: (780) 433-9842

The Eastern Door
Kahnawake Mohawk Territory Newspaper
P.O. Box 1170
Kahnawake, QC J0L 1B0
Canada
Phone: (450) 635-3050
Fax: (450) 635-8479
http://www.easterndoor.com

The Gambler
1600 Steeles Avenue West
Concord, ON L4K 4M2
Canada

CASINOS AND GAMING

Caesars Player: The Luxury Lifestyle and Gaming Magazine of Caesars
960 Alton Road
Miami Beach, FL 33139
Phone: (305) 673-0400
Fax: (305) 673-3575
E-mail: info@onboard.com
http://www.onboard.com

Casino Chip and Token News
c/o Belinda Hixon, Secretary
P.O. Box 1195
Colleyville, TX 76034

Casino Chronicle
P.O. Box 740465
Boynton Beach, FL 33474

Casino City's Casino Vendors Guide
Casino City Press
95 Wells Avenue
Newton, MA 02459
Phone: (617) 332-2850
Fax: (617) 964-2280
http://www.casinocitypress.com

Casino City's Gaming Business Directory
Casino City Press
95 Wells Avenue
Newton, MA 02459
Phone: (617) 332-2850
Fax: (617) 964-2280
http://www.casinocitypress.com

Casino City's Gaming Business Review
Casino City Press
95 Wells Avenue
Newton, MA 02459
Phone: (617) 332-2850
Fax: (617) 964-2280
http://www.casinocitypress.com

Casino City's Gaming Revue News
Casino City Press
95 Wells Avenue
Newton, MA 02459
Phone: (617) 332-2850
Fax: (617) 964-2280
http://www.casinocitypress.com

Casino City's Indian Gaming Industry Report
Casino City Press
95 Wells Avenue
Newton, MA 02459
Phone: (617) 332-2850
Fax: (617) 964-2280
http://www.casinocitypress.com

Casino Connection
Global Gaming Business LLC
1600 West Riverside Drive
Atlantic City, NJ 08401
Phone: (609) 344-7561
Fax: (609) 344-6235

Casino Enterprise Management
10544 40th Street North
Moorhead, MN 56560
Phone: (701) 293-7775
Fax: (701) 293-7774

Casino Games Magazine
Compass International, Inc.
1009 Nawkee Drive
North Las Vegas, NV 89031
Phone: (702) 399-3998
Fax: (702) 399-3997

Casino Gaming International
Public Gaming Research Institute
4020 Lake Washington Boulevard
  Northeast
Kirkland, WA 98033

Casino Journal
BNP Media
505 East Capovilla Avenue
#102
Las Vegas, NV 89102
Phone: (702) 794-0718
Fax: (702) 794-0799
http://www.bnpmedia.com

Casino Player
Casino Journal Publishing Group
8025 Black Horse Pike
Atlantic City, NJ 08232
Phone: (609) 641-3200
http://www.casinocenter.com

Casino World
P.O. Box 2003
Madison Square Station
New York, NY 10159
Phone: (212) 228-4769
Gambling Times Magazine
3883 Wes Century Boulevard
#608
Inglewood, CA 90303
Phone: (818) 781-9355
Fax: (818) 781-3125

Gaming Industry Daily Report
Casino Journal Publishing
8025 Black Horse Pike
Atlantic City, NJ 08232
Phone: (609) 484-8866
Fax: (609) 645-1661
E-mail: comments@casinocenter.
  com
http://www.casinocenter.com

Gaming Industry Weekly
Casino Journal Publishing
8025 Black Horse Pike
Atlantic City, NJ 08232
Phone: (609) 484-8866
Fax: (609) 645-1661
E-mail: comments@casinocenter.
  com
http://www.casinocenter.com

Gaming Law Review & Economics
140 Huguenot Street
New Rochelle, NY 10801
Phone: (914) 740-2100

Fax: (914) 740-2101
E-mail: info@liebertpub.com
http://www.liebertpub.com

Gaming Products and Services
P.O. Box 14268
St. Paul, MN 55114

Gaming Systems Source Directory
P.O. Box 97
Sylva, NC 28779

Global Gaming Business
6625 South Valley View Boulevard
Las Vegas, NV 89118

Great Lakes Gaming and Poker Magazine
1318 West Court Street
Flint, MI 48503
Phone: (810) 233-3000
Fax: (810) 239-1797

High Roller
11877 Douglas Road
Alpharetta, GA 30005
Phone: (678) 990-0285
Fax: (678) 990-0285
E-mail: inquiry@highrollerlife.com
http://www.highrollerlife.com

Indiana Gaming Insight
P.O. Box 383
Noblesville, IN 46061
Phone: (317) 817-9997
Fax: (317) 817-9998
E-mail: info@ingrouponline.com
http://www.ingrouponline.com

International Gaming & Wagering Business
505 East Capovilla Avenue
Las Vegas, NV 89119
Phone: (702) 794-0718
Fax: (702) 794-0799
http://www.bnpmedia.com

Midwest Players
17321 Sandy Court Southeast
Big Lake, MN 55309
Phone: (763) 263-5815
Fax: (763) 263-5817

Rolling Good Times Online
205 South Main Street
St. Charles, MO 63301
Phone: (314) 946-0820
E-mail: rgt@rgtonline.com
http://www.rgtonline.com

Public Gaming International
4020 Lake Washington Boulevard
  Northeast
Kirkland, WA 98033

Venetian Style
2290 Corporate Circle
Suite 250
Henderson, NV 89074
Phone: (702) 990-2400
Fax: (702) 990-2590
E-mail: susan.wallace@gmg.com
http://www.greenspunmedia.com

GAMES

Blackjack Forum
2565 Chandler Avenue
Las Vegas, NV 89120
Phone: (510) 465-6452
Fax: (510) 652-4330
E-mail: asnyder@rge21.com
http://www.rge21.com

Card Player
Barry and Jeff Shulman
6940 O'Bannon Drive
Las Vegas, NV 89117

Current Blackjack News
PI Yee Press
4855 West Nevso Drive
Las Vegas, NV 89103
Phone: (702) 579-7711

The Dealer's News
No. 37, 1801 East Tropicana Avenue
Las Vegas, NV 89119
http://www.thedealersnews.com

**Doubledown: Your Guide
  to Casino Action and
  Entertainment**
View and Travel Publishing
332 South Michigan Avenue
Chicago, IL 60604

Poker Digest
5240 South Eastern Avenue
Las Vegas, NV 89119
Phone: (702) 740-2273
Fax: (702) 740-2257
http://www.pokerdigest.com

HOSPITALITY, HOTELS & FOOD SERVICE MANAGEMENT

Chef Magazine
20 West Kinzie Street
Chicago, IL 60610
Phone: (312) 849-2220
Fax: (312) 849-2174
E-mail: talcottpub@talcott.com
http://www.talcott.com

Hospitality Manager
120 Hayward Avenue
Ames, IA 50010
Phone: (515) 296-2400

Hotel and Motel Management
600 Superior Avenue East
Cleveland, OH 44114
Phone: (216) 706-3700
Fax: (216) 706-3711
E-mail: questex@sunbeltfs.com
http://www.questex.com

**Lodging Hospitality: Ideas
  for Hotel Developers &
  Operators**
9800 Metcalf Avenue
Overland Park, KS 66212
E-mail: information@penton.com
http://www.penton.com

Restaurant Hospitality
1300 East 9th Street
Cleveland, OH 44114
Phone: (216) 696-7000
Fax: (216) 696-1752
http://www.penton.com

HOUSEKEEPING

Executive Housekeeping Today
International Executive
  Housekeepers Association, Inc.
1001 Eastwind Drive

Westerville, OH 43081
Phone: (614) 895-7166
E-mail: excel@ieha.org
http://www.ieha.org

INDIAN GAMING

Indian Gaming
14205 Southeast 36th Street
Bellevue, WA 98006
Phone: (425) 519-3710
Fax: (425) 883-7209
E-mail: info@indiangaming.com
http://www.indiangaming.com

Indian Gaming Business
505 East Capovilla Avenue
Las Vegas, NV 89119
Phone: (702) 794-0718
Fax: (702) 794- 0799
http://www.bnpmedia.com

Indian Gaming Insight
P.O. Box 383
Noblesville, IN 46061
Phone: (317) 817-9997
Fax: (317) 817-9998
E-mail: info@ingrouponline.com
http://www.ingrouponline.com

National Indian Gaming Digest
3702 Pender Drive
Fairfax, VA 22030
Phone: (703) 352-2250
Fax: (703) 352-2323
E-mail: information@falmouth
  institute.com
http://www.falmouthinstitute.com

LAS VEGAS

Las Vegas Insider
P.O. Box 29274
Las Vegas, NV 89126
Phone: (520) 636-1649

Las Vegas Today
P.O. Box 370250
Las Vegas, NV 89137
Phone: (702) 221-5056

Showbiz Magazine
2290 Corporate Circle Drive

Henderson, NV 89074
Phone: (702) 383-7185
Fax: (702) 383-1089
E-mail: Showbiz@lasvegassun.
    com
http://www.lasvegassun.com

What's On!: The Las Vegas Guide

4425 South Industrial Road
Las Vegas, NV 89103
Phone: (702) 891-8811
Fax: (702) 891-8804
E-mail: whatson@ilovevegas.com
http://www.whats-on.com

LOTTERY

Lottery & Casino News

P.O. Box 487

Marlton, NJ 08053
Phone: (609) 778-8900
Fax: (609) 273-6350
E-mail: regalpub@lottery-casino-
    news.com
http://www.lottery-casino-news.
    com

Lottery, Parimutuel & Casino Regulation–State Capitals

P.O. Box 7376
Alexandria, VA 22307
Phone: (703) 768-9600
Fax: (703) 768-9690
E-mail: newsletters@statecapitals.
    com
http://www.statecapitals.com

SLOTS

Slot Manager

505 East Capovilla Avenue
Las Vegas, NV 89119
Phone: (702) 794-0718
Fax: (702) 794-0799
http://www.bnpmedia.com

Strictly Slots

Casino Journal Publishing Group
8025 Black Horse Pike
Atlantic City, NJ 08232
Phone: (609) 484-8866
Fax: (609) 645-1661
http://www.casinocenter.com

INDEX

human resources people ix
human resources supervisor 203

I

IAAP. *See* International Association of Administrative Professionals
IACEP. *See* International Association of Corporate Entertainment Producers
IACP. *See* International Association of Culinary Professionals
IATSE. *See* International Alliance of Theatrical Stage Employees
IBEW. *See* International Brotherhood of Electrical Workers
IDEA Health and Fitness Association 213
IEHA. *See* Executive Housekeepers Association
IFEBP. *See* International Foundation of Employee Benefit Plans
IGRA xvii
Indian gaming xvii
intern 83
intern, stage manager 152
International Alliance of Theatrical Stage Employees (IATSE) 153, 155, 157
International Association of Administrative Professionals (IAAP) 225, 227
International Association of Corporate Entertainment Producers (IACEP) 150
International Association of Culinary Professionals (IACP) 166, 168, 170, 174
International Brotherhood of Electrical Workers (IBEW) 157
International Foundation of Employee Benefit Plans (IFEBP) 201, 203
International Professional Association (IProA) 232, 235
International Spa Association (ISA) 212
International Webmasters Association (IWA) 232
IProA (International Professional Association 232
IT professionals ix

IWA (International Webmasters Association) 232

J

jobs in casino operations xviii
jobs on the gaming floor xviii
journalist 83, 99, 233

K

keno runner 54, 55, 56–47
keno supervisor 52–53, 54
keno writer 52, 54–55, 56, 57
keno writer supervisor 56

L

largest casino in North America xv
last US state to make gambling illegal xvii
Las Vegas Spa Association (LVSA) 212
lead operator 144
lighting designer 156, 157
lighting person (lighting man, lighting woman) 156, 157
lighting technician 156–157
lighting technician apprentice 156, 157
Local 54 of the Hotel Employees and Restaurants Employees International Union 182, 187, 189
locations and settings for jobs xix
lotteries xvii
loyalty club representative 78

M

magician 158, 159
maitre d'hotel 177–178, 179, 180, 181, 182
manager, casinos 2
manager, hotel 116
manager of restaurant operations 175, 176
manager of slots 39
managers ix
marketing assistant 76
marketing director 74
marketing manager, website 236
marketing office administrators 77

marketing people ix
Marketing Research Association (MRA) 238
marketing staffer 87
Mashantucket Pequot Tribal Nation xv
media coordinator 85
member of the military 107
minimum age requirements xix
musician 158, 159

N

National Indian Gaming Commission (NIGC) xvii
National Restaurant Association (NRA) 170, 180, 182, 184, 187, 189, 191
National Retail Federation (NRF) 219
National Retail Merchants Association (NRMA) 221
National Safety Council 216
Native American Indian gaming ix
new in the second edition ix–x
NIGC. *See* National Indian Gaming Commission
nightclub manager 183–185
NRA. *See* National Restaurant Association
NRMA. *See* National Retail Merchants Association
nurses ix

O

online director of marketing 236
online marketing director 236
only state allowing gaming xvii
operator 144
organization of material x
overnight shift ix, 11

P

pari-mutuel wagering xvii
pastry chef 169–170, 171
pastry chef apprentice 169, 170
paymaster 66, 67, 68, 69
payroll specialist 206
payroll supervisor 206, 207
PBX attendant 144

ABOUT THE AUTHOR

Shelly Field is a nationally recognized motivational speaker, career expert, and author of more than 20 best-selling books in the business and career fields.

Her books instruct people on how to obtain jobs in a wide array of areas, including the hospitality, music, sports, and communications industries; casinos and casino hotels; advertising; public relations; theater; the performing arts; entertainment; animal rights; health care; writing; and art, as well as how to choose the best career for the new century.

She is a frequent guest on local, regional, and national radio, cable, and television talk, information, and news shows and she also does numerous print interviews and personal appearances.

Field is a featured speaker at casinos, conventions, expos, corporate functions, employee training and development sessions, career fairs, spouse programs, and events nationwide. She speaks on empowerment, motivation, gaming, careers, human resources; attracting, retaining, and motivating employees; customer service;

and stress reduction. Her popular seminar, "STRESS BUSTERS: Beating the Stress in Your Work and Your Life" is a favorite around the country.

Field is a career consultant to businesses, educational institutions, employment agencies, women's groups, and individuals. She is a corporate consultant to casinos throughout the country, appearing at job fairs and providing assistance with human resources issues, such as attracting, retaining, and motivating employees, customer service training, and stress management in the workplace.

President and CEO of The Shelly Field Organization, a public relations and management firm handling national clients, she also does corporate consulting and has represented celebrities in the sports, music, and entertainment industries, as well as authors, businesses, and corporations.

For information about personal appearances or seminars contact The Shelly Field Organization at P.O. Box 711, Monticello, NY 12701 or log on to www.shellyfield.com.